Culture, control, and commitment

To Judith Johansen Kalleberg and Russell and Robbie Lincoln

CULTURE, CONTROL, AND COMMITMENT

A study of work organization and work attitudes in the United States and Japan

James R. Lincoln
University of California at Berkeley

Arne L. Kalleberg
University of North Carolina at Chapel Hill

With the collaboration of Mitsuyo Hanada and Kerry McBride

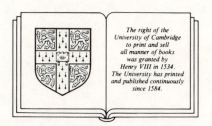

The right of the
University of Cambridge
to print and sell
all manner of books
was granted by
Henry VIII in 1534.
The University has printed
and published continuously
since 1584.

Cambridge University Press

Cambridge
New York   Port Chester
Melbourne   Sydney

Published by the Press Syndicate of the University of Cambridge
The Pitt Building, Trumpington Street, Cambridge CB2 1RF
40 West 20th Street, New York, NY 10011, USA
10 Stamford Road, Oakleigh, Melbourne 3166, Australia

First published 1990

Printed in Great Britain at The Bath Press, Avon

British Library cataloguing in publication data

Lincoln, James R.
Culture, control, and commitment: a study of work organization
and work attitudes in the United States and Japan.
1. Work Psychosocial aspects
1. Title 11. Kalleberg, Arne L.
306′.36

Library of Congress cataloguing in publication data

Lincoln, James R.
Culture, control, and commitment: a study of work organization
and work attitudes in the United States and Japan / James R.
Lincoln, Arne L. Kalleberg: with the collaboration of Mitsuyo
Hanada and Kerry McBride.
        p.   cm.
Bibliography.
ISBN 0 521 36517 1
1. Organizational behavior – United States. 2. Job satisfaction –
United States. 3. Employee attitude surveys – United States.
4. Organizational behavior – Japan. 5. Job satisfaction – Japan.
6. Employee attitude surveys – Japan. 7. Organizational behavior –
Mathematical models. 8. Job satisfaction – Mathematical models.
1. Kalleberg, Arne L. 11. Title.
HD58.7.L55 1989
306′.36–dc19   88-37705 CIP

ISBN 0 521 36517 1

Contents

Figure and tables

Figure

Tables

Preface

This book presents findings from a large and complex survey research investigation to which many people have made valuable contributions. The book's authorship reflects responsibilities for the analysis and writing, not for the research design and data collection tasks, which we shared with many others. The project grew out of a number of converging interests and inquiries. While they were sociology faculty members at Indiana University, Kalleberg, with interests in work structures and attitudes, and Lincoln, with interests in organizations, had for some years discussed plans for a large-scale multilevel study that would link characteristics of employing organizations with the attributes, attitudes, and behaviors of employees. The opportunity to conduct a US–Japan comparative study arose when Kerry McBride, then an Indiana doctoral student in Sociology and East Asian Studies, received a Fulbright scholarship to study patterns of work organization in Japan. Her principal collaborator in Japan was Mitsuyo Hanada (now Professor at Tokyo's SANNO Institute of Business Administration and Director of the Center for Organizational Research and Education), an active organizational researcher and consultant on Japanese management topics. Hanada and Lincoln had previously collaborated on a study of Japanese-owned companies in the Los Angeles area when Hanada was a doctoral student and Lincoln a faculty member at the University of Southern California. Given the nature of the research, the support and participation of the Indiana University School of Business was essential, and Professor Janet Near, with interests and research experience in problems of organization design and job attitudes, joined the Indiana research team. Kalleberg, Lincoln, and Near received funding from the National Science Foundation (grants #SES-82-07854, SES-84-98849, and SES-84-15961), the Japan Foundation, and the Indiana State Department of Commerce to support the Indiana and Kanagawa phases of the study. We are grateful for this funding as well as that received from The Karl Eller Center at the University of Arizona which supported Lincoln during the analysis and writing phase, and from the John Simon Guggenheim Memorial Foundation, which supported Kalleberg. Once the data were collected, separate research interests and orientations led Janet Near to pursue her own agenda of analysis and writing, while Kalleberg, Lincoln, Hanada, and

McBride, in varying combinations, continued to work together. Nevertheless, Janet's contributions to the design and implementation of the project were indeed substantial ones.

The Indiana component of the study was carried out as part of the Indianapolis Area Project, a research practicum for doctoral students at Indiana University. This program provided us with a corps of talented graduate students to help us carry out the research tasks, and gave us access to the facilities and staff of Indiana University's Institute of Social Research. Dr. Suzanne B. Lincoln, IAP Study Director, capably managed project operations and performed admirably in the critical and delicate role of liaison to the participating firms. Four senior doctoral students – Karyn Loscocco, Steve Parker, Michael Wallace, and Robert White – participated in designing the instruments, in interviewing the managers and union leaders, and in supervising the collection of questionnaires from workers. Other Indiana University graduate students, particularly Kevin Leicht, also played major roles in the collection and preparation of the data. We heartily thank them; we could not have asked for a higher level of competence, dedication and responsibility than that which they so cheerfully volunteered.

Likewise in Japan, the project's success was very much an outcome of the efforts and dedication of numerous capable people. Mitsuyo Hanada and Kerry McBride designed the Japanese versions of the survey instruments, arranged access to firms, and planned and executed the data collection in close collaboration with the US team. Hanada provided a base for the study at SANNO Institute and at the Center for Organizational Research and Education in Tokyo, including office space and administrative and clerical support. His considerable expertise and experience in research on Japanese organization was essential to the study. The critically important matter of research access to companies was facilitated by SANNO's consulting and educational ties with local firms, plus the support of the Japanese chambers of commerce.

The Japanese interviews were conducted by a team which included Kerry McBride and at least one Japanese colleague. The latter included: Hanada, Yasuaki Kido (then at Kanazawa College of Economics), Takenori Takase, (then a Sociology graduate student at Tokyo University), as well as several of Hanada's seminar students. The project also benefited substantially from the guidance and suggestions of Professors Ken'ichi Tominaga and Toru Takahashi at Tokyo University, where McBride was a research student, and the members of Tominaga's Organization Study Group.

We are much indebted to all of these people for their effort and commitment that helped to make this large and (at times) unwieldy project succeed. We also thank ISR secretaries Rosalie Harris and Lois Kelly, who provided valuable secretarial and administrative assistance to the project. And, of course, we are deeply grateful to the many people at all levels in the companies we studied for their willingness to open their doors and give generously of their time, energy, and knowledge to make this study a success. Finally, this book has been greatly improved by the thoughtful and helpful criticism provided by Robert Cole, William Form, and Aage Sørensen, all of whom waded through previous drafts of the manuscript.

Introduction

Though long traditions of theory and research in the social sciences address the orientations of employees to their jobs and places of employment, there has been in recent years a convergence of interest, from highly diverse quarters, in the problem of commitment to the work organization. From industrial psychologists to organizational sociologists to Marxist labor process theorists, a focus on the efforts by companies to foster dependence, loyalty and identification in a workforce has superseded older scholarly concerns with industrial attitudes, performance, and conflict. Part of the reason for the renewed attention to the question of commitment is a widening theoretical interest in the role it plays in modern organizational control systems. But the more fundamental reason may be a perception that broad, even global shifts in the internal structures and employment practices of companies are inducing fundamental changes in the ties that bind employees to the workplace. These shifts, in turn, are tied to transformations in worldwide economic and industrial organization.

In the United States, corporations that were once content to tolerate a limited, instrumental attachment on the part of rank-and-file workers have been demanding more. In the concentrated, "core" industries of the American economy, labor–management relations had long been stable and contractual, reflecting a basic consensus on the rights and obligations of both sides in a highly institutionalized collective-bargaining environment. Companies were prosperous, unperturbed by foreign competition, and able to pass on the costs of union wage demands to consumers. American labor, on the other hand, essentially ceded to management the right to organize work and govern the company without extensive worker interference or involvement. Once employees' demands for wages, security, and protection from harsh and arbitrary supervision were met, they asked little more of the firm. The companies, for their part, accepted a fundamentally instrumental, even alienated, blue-collar posture as the normal and acceptable state of affairs so long as militancy was kept under tight controls.

Today, however, this once comfortable arrangement is largely a thing of the past. American firms have lost ground to more efficient foreign producers, the rise of sunbelt and high-tech industry has accelerated the decline of an already stagnant labor movement, and a wave of mergers and acquisitions has diverted investment capital out of manufacturing into service and extractive industries yielding higher short-term profit margins. Faced with these changes and the Scylla and Charybdis of inflation and unemployment, there has been much talk of the need for a *rapprochement* between labor and management and a new level of commitment on the part of industrial workers to the goals and operations of their firms. The public policy issue of worker alienation as a problem for American industry is itself hardly new: it was posed as a serious matter in the early 1970s, when the HEW report, *Work in America*, urged the federal government to take steps to upgrade the quality of American working life. But the decline of American manufacturing has served to hasten a process, already well underway, in which a new pattern of industrial relations is replacing the old system of highly contained and institutionalized labor–management struggle (Snyder, 1975). Through an array of incremental shifts in corporate culture and management practice, along with a proliferation of quick-fix fads and an occasional wholesale reorganization, e.g. GM's Saturn plant, American companies have followed the lead of European and Japanese firms in designing jobs and organizations aimed so as to give greater meaning to work and fostering a sense of participation and membership in the enterprise.

There is wide variation in the labels given by diverse writers to the organizational form which has evolved around an imperative of maximizing workforce commitment, but the pattern they describe is very much the same. For Ronald Dore (1973), it is "welfare corporatism," a set of workplace institutions which has reached its highest level of deployment in Japan but is fast replacing the "market individualism" of early industrialization in the Western countries as well. To William Ouchi (1981) it is "Theory Z," an organizational design and culture which have much in common with Japanese management practice but have also reached a high degree of development in the internal organization of such corporate high-performers as IBM and Hewlett Packard. From Richard Edwards' (1979) Marxist perspective, it is "bureaucratic control," the most advanced and efficient system of securing employee compliance to company demands, and the successor to the personal control of the small business entrepreneur, the hierarchical control of the first-line supervisor, and the technical control of the mechanized factory. Also from a Marxist perspective, Michael Burawoy (1983) terms these developments "hegemonic despotism" and emphasizes their dual capacity for fostering commitment and dependence through the carrots of welfare services and internal labor markets and the sticks of plant closings and production outsourcing. Marxist writers of course reject Ouchi's enthusiastic claims for the benefits to workers and managers alike of "Theory Z" forms, nor are they inclined toward Dore's vision of enterprise evolution, which, if mildly critical of welfare (as contrasted with "democratic") corporatism, is nonetheless generally benign. Instead, the Marxist view holds such changes to be a new escalation of class struggle in the workplace, the aims of capital being total control and intensified exploitation of the labor process (Hill, 1981: chapter 3).

It is no accident that these and other writers look to Japanese enterprise as the world's foremost exemplar of welfare corporatism, to use Dore's term for this general pattern of commitment-maximizing organization. The management styles, organizational structures, and employment systems distinctive of Japanese industry were for years perceived to be exotic Eastern ways which flew in the face of widely accepted Western principles of economic and administrative rationality. Early observers such as Abegglen (1958) considered Japanese practices to be residues of a traditional communalism which would ultimately pose major obstacles to Japan's economic growth. But as the Japanese economy has catapulted to its present status as the world's premier producer of efficiently manufactured high-quality goods, both foreign and domestic critics have done an about face. No longer are Japanese ways perceived to be irrational anachronisms. On the contrary, now Japan is held to be the vanguard of a movement spreading fundamental change throughout the economic institutions of the capitalist industrial world. The earmarks of that movement are: (a) the abolition of destructive Western-style industrial relations and its replacement by a new harmonious order in which labor and unions collaborate with management in advancing the fortunes of firms; (b) the creation of organizational and job structures that increase workers' control over the production process and make work more meaningful and rewarding; (c) the provision of job security, welfare services, and training programs which integrate employees in an inclusive and ongoing enterprise community providing broadly for its members and demanding loyalty and commitment in return.

It is not merely Japan's unparalleled economic growth and the extraordinary efficiency and productivity of Japanese manufacturing that, in combination with the welfare-corporatist organization of Japanese firms, has produced the conviction that herein lies a formula for corporate success in the modern world economy. The critical factor seen to mediate this relationship is the quality of Japanese labor. At least since Abegglen's pioneering study of the Japanese factory, a pervasive theme in studies of Japanese industry has been the extraordinary commitment, identification, and loyalty exhibited by employees toward their firms. Japanese workers are widely thought to be the most diligent and devoted employees in the world. Low strike, absenteeism, and turnover rates combined with high worker productivity and production quality have contributed to a global image of the Japanese as wholly committed to the success of their companies. Their long work weeks, penchant for after-hours socializing with superiors and workmates, and (most incredible to Americans) reluctance to take all their allotted vacation time further reinforce this perception (Cole, 1979:232). Moreover, there is reason to believe that the Japanese work ethic is less a generalized commitment to work *per se* than a motivation to serve one's company loyally and contribute to its success. Drawing from his own research and a review of other surveys of Japanese and Western workers, Cole (1979:231) concluded that: "Japanese employees have unusually strong identification with the company, but not necessarily high job satisfaction or strong commitment to the performance of specific job tasks."

The configuration, then, of strong corporate performance, a workforce devoted to the company, and a set of management and employment practices which seem consciously designed to produce strong worker attachments to a cohesive enterprise community suggests the simple causal chain of: welfare corporatist organization → workforce commitment → company performance. Though by no means the only factor in the changes now going on in American firms, it seems clear that, even as American managers and labor leaders blame the Japanese competitive advantage on trade barriers, unfair government subsidies, price-fixing, and the like, many US firms are either implementing or contemplating programs and reorganizations inspired by the Japanese example.

Yet the critical question is whether the "commitment gap" between US and Japanese workers can be attributed to the greater effectiveness of the corporatist structures of Japanese companies in eliciting the motivation and commitment of employees than the traditional market individualism of Western industry. An alternative explanation, often stressed in anthropological and historical explanations of Japanese institutions and practices, is that the Japanese work ethic has deep roots in Japanese culture and national character. From this perspective, commitment runs high in the Japanese workforce, not because Japanese management styles and organizational structures effectively inspire it, but because hard work and devotion to the corporate group – today the company but in times past the village, family, and, of course, nauion–state – are linked to key Japanese values encouraging the immersion of the individual in the collectivity (Vogel, 1963). These values facilitate the creation of an enterprise community and motivate employees to subordinate their personal or class interests to those of the firm. To suggest that Japanese organizational forms combine with Japanese cultural values in ways which are highly effective in motivating Japanese workers, then, is to deny that those same forms would elicit the commitment of workers in countries, such as the US, with very different cultural traditions.

Few would contest the importance and timeliness of these issues to Western scholars, managers, and policy-makers in the late 1980s. Yet systematic comparative studies of Japanese and US factory organization and the attitudes, behaviors, and values of employees are generally scarce. Moreover, while we in no way disparage the value of the superb case studies of Japanese work life and industrial organization by Cole (1971), Dore (1973), Rohlen (1974), and Clark (1979), it is self-evident that the rich insights they have generated require validation by means of systematic, large-sample, hypothesis-testing research.

This book reports the findings of a major survey investigation of the organizational, job, and individual-level determinants of work attitudes, values, and behaviors among Japanese and US manufacturing employees. This study, conducted between 1981–1983, has produced a rich and multifaceted data set. Through personal interviews with managers, documentary evidence, and direct observation, our research team collected extensive data on the history, operations, market environment, organization and personnel policies of 51 Japanese and 55 American factories in seven manufacturing industries. In addition, we gathered questionnaire data from samples of managers, supervisors, and workers employed by these plants: 4,567 in the US and 3,735 in Japan. To our knowledge, this study represents the largest and most comprehensive survey to date of Japanese and US manufacturing workers and their places of employment.

Explicitly comparative from the start, our investigation made use of similar data collection procedures and measurement instruments in each country (see Cole, 1979:5). This has enabled us to conduct a thoroughgoing statistical inquiry into an array of forces operating at multiple levels of analysis – individual, job, workplace, industry, country – to shape employees' work orientations and reactions. From our analyses of the effects on company commitment and job satisfaction of organizational structures and production technology at a macro level and workers' backgrounds, relations, jobs, and positions at a micro one, we are able to draw inferences about the form and functioning of commitment-maximizing organization.

In the first chapter, we discuss the broad theoretical issues raised by our attempt to link differences in organizational structures to employees' work orientations. We review theories of work organization and the employment relationship and develop the concept of welfare corporatism as a commitment-maximizing organizational form. We then consider the nature of commitment as a social–psychological variable and contrast it with such alternative attitudinal states as job satisfaction and work alienation.

In chapter 2, we provide background information on the study and describe the process of data collection. We discuss the research design; the method of gaining access to plants and workers; sampling and data collection procedures; and an overview of the resulting data set.

Chapter 3 reviews existing evidence on the question of US–Japan differences in employee work attitudes and behaviors. The analysis is kept simple and preliminary, yet the basic findings about country differences are, in general, unperturbed by the more complex analysis which follows.

The next two chapters report detailed analyses of a set of employee- and job-level attributes which we conceive as antecedent to company commitment and job satisfaction. Chapter 4 examines the effects of employee position in the organization (authority position, functional area, quality circle participation, and company tenure), job rewards (both intrinsic and extrinsic), task characteristics such as complexity and autonomy, and the strength of social bonds with supervisors and coworkers. Chapter 5 continues this inquiry in considering the influences of employee work values and background characteristics such as age, gender, marital status, and education. The role of values and expectations is obviously integral to any explanation of work attitudes, but takes on special significance in a comparative study of societies as culturally distinct as the United States and Japan.

In chapters 6 and 7, the focus is shifted to the level of the organization and individual employees are ignored. We examine industry and societal differences in the production technologies of manufacturing plants and organizational structures. This inquiry speaks to the hypothesis of diversity in organizational structures and management styles between Japan and the US, addressing in particular the hypothesis that Japanese firms are closer approximations to the "welfare corporatist" model of commitment-maximizing organization.

Chapter 8, in a sense, pulls it all together, for here we construct our final multilevel models of the process whereby manufacturing employees across societies, factories, and industries vary in their commitment to the firm and satisfaction with the job.

In chapter 9, we summarize the results of the investigation and speculate on their significance for scholars and policy-makers.

1 Work organization, culture, and work attitudes: theoretical issues

Introduction

The introduction laid out the themes of our study: the new concern among scholars, managers, and policy-makers with the commitment of employees to the firm and the belief that emergent forms of work organization have a commitment-maximizing logic. The apparent prevalence of these forms in the Japanese economy, moreover, may provide the explanation for the extraordinary motivation and productivity of Japanese workers. In this chapter, we explore these issues in greater depth. First we undertake a wide-ranging review of theories of corporatist-type employment relationships. Then we consider several variations on the "culturalist" alternative theory, that the US–Japan commitment gap is not so much a matter of management and organization as it is a reflection of deep-rooted cultural strains in both societies. Next we address the nature of organizational commitment and job satisfaction, distinguishing each from the other and from such related concepts as work alienation. Finally, we outline a causal model which will guide our study of the linkages between work organization and employee work attitudes.

Theories of control and commitment in organizations

Recent theories of work organization identify evolutionary shifts in management structure and employment practice that appear aimed at making commitment the centerpiece in modern strategies of workplace control. We first provide an overview of such theories, then present our own derivative model of commitment-maximizing organization.

Dore's welfare corporatism

The concept of welfare corporatism grows out of Ronald Dore's comparative study of British and Japanese electronics plants. It refers to the features of the Japanese employment system toward which he sees Britain and other industrial economies gravitating. These include: "factory and company based trade union and bargaining structures, enterprise welfare and security, greater stability of employment and integration of manual workers as 'full members' of the enterprise, greater bureaucratization and a cooperative or corporate ideology." Other elements of Japanese work organization, particularly those whose roots in Japanese culture run deepest, are less likely to be assimilated by the West. These include: "the proliferation of status hierarchies, the easy acceptance of deference to organizational superiors, ... or the 'devotion' to work which subordinates private life and the claims of the family to the claims of the organization. The resistance to 'corporatism' of this kind in Britain is strong" (Dore, 1973:370).

As this passage testifies, Dore is of two minds in this rich and diverse volume as to the sources of corporate integration and commitment in the Japanese workforce. On the one hand, the Japanese company itself appears designed in numerous ways to forge a powerful bond between the employee and the firm. Moreover, he sees similar designs with similar long-term consequences for employee attitudes and behavior multiplying in British industry. On the other hand, part of the organizational commitment of the Japanese springs from cultural sources. These, of course, are unique to Japan and may with time, Dore thinks, diminish in importance. Given this much acknowledgment of cultural influences, it would be an easy step to argue that the concrete features of the Japanese employment system themselves have cultural roots. But Dore's explanation of the success of corporatist organization in Japanese industry is the fundamentally acultural "late developer" hypothesis. The core of this thesis is that nations embarking upon industrialization in an era when developed economies abound have the opportunity to select from the most advanced available technologies for producing goods and building production organizations. Older industrial societies, e.g., Britain, lack this flexibility, owing to sunk costs in organizational and material technologies which date back to the early days of the industrial revolution.

Welfare corporatist forms are likely to arise where large corporations appear *after:* (a) the establishment of unions as a stable and legitimate feature of labor–management relations; (b) the institutionalization of mass systems of public education; and (c) the existence of advanced methods of production and organizational technology evolved in earlier industrialized countries which present themselves as models to be emulated. Welfare corporatism appears first and spreads fastest in late developers, Dore argues, because it faces fewer encumbrances from the individualistic and market-oriented employment patterns associated with early industrialization. But because it represents a form which is in fact best adapted to a world economy dominated by large, bureaucratic organizations, it becomes the standard toward which other national economies ultimately, if more slowly, evolve.

Marxist perspectives on control systems

Dore's central premise that the Japanese have implemented on a broad scale a pattern of organizing work and authority relations which is appearing with growing regularity among progressive and technologically advanced companies in the older industrial economies of the world, is one which numerous scholars have embraced in recent years. Though not directly addressing the case of Japan, Richard Edwards' (1979) highly influential Marxist analysis of historical evolution in the organizational control systems used by American employers to direct, monitor, and sanction employees is wholly consonant with the thrust of Dore's account of corporatist organization. Edwards describes the drift of American companies from a reliance upon predominantly coercive methods of labor control to "bureaucratic control" systems aimed at the dual goals of dissolving class solidarity while maximizing commitment to and dependence on the firm. Previous strategies of control – personal domination by supervisors, Scientific Management, and machine pacing – had all been tested and abandoned either because of mounting worker resistance or because shifts in the scale of enterprise, the production technology, or the nature of markets had made them obsolete and inefficient. No longer focused on motivating the performance of specific work tasks, modern control systems reward commitment to the organization as a whole. Promotions, pay, security, and other benefits go to employees who are good corporate citizens, who are loyal to the company, share its values, and integrate themselves and their families in the enterprise community. Once committed, so this logic goes, workers can be counted on to perform well, and their attachment to the firm, as opposed to particular jobs or departments within it, facilitates a flexible and efficient allocation of manpower within the firm.

Many of Edwards' themes are echoed in the writings of other recent neo-Marxist students of the labor process (Clawson, 1980; Edwards, Gordon and Reich, 1975; Hill, 1981). Andrew Friedman (1977), for example, identifies two major ways that top managers have sought to exercise authority over the labor force: direct control, where workers are coerced on the basis of their economic self-interest and treated as machines; and "responsible autonomy," the goal of which is to harness the commitment of workers through the enducement of non-economic rewards such as status, autonomy, and responsibility. Responsible autonomy requires an elaborate ideological apparatus for coopting workers as well as employment security to reinforce a model of the firm as a community. Like bureaucratic control, the goal of responsible autonomy is to have workers behave as though they were participating in a process which reflected their own needs, abilities, and wills, rather than one aimed exclusively at accumulation and profits.

Moreover, Michael Burawoy (1983) classifies factory regimes by the degree to which they rely on coercion or consent. He, too, notes that early capitalism is characterized by despotic work organizations, where coercion prevails over consent and is reinforced by the whips of labor market competition, deskilling, work intensification, and automation. The paternalism of the small entrepreneur which, to Edwards, interjects an element of legitimacy in early capitalist employment relations, does not, to Burawoy, diminish the thoroughly coercive character of market despotic regimes. In advanced capitalist societies, however, owing to state-imposed constraints on the prerogatives of management to set wages and impose sanctions, managers must harness workers' ingenuity and cooperation by incorporating them within the firm. Hence, despotic regimes give way to hegemonic factory regimes, whence coercive compliance is replaced by normative control, as management makes concessions (in terms of job guarantees, curbs on supervisory discretion, and quality of work life programs) in order to persuade workers to collaborate in advancing the fortunes of the firm. As with "bureaucratic control" and "responsible autonomy," hegemonic regimes create an internal state: the worker becomes an industrial citizen having contractually defined rights and obligations entering into a social contract with the firm. Moreover, workers as well as managers are subordinated to the impersonal rule of law. In the modern period, marked by the internationalization of capital and the intensification of competition, however, Burawoy sees hegemonic regimes transforming into *hegemonic despotism*, which, under the threat of plant closings and industrial relocation, shifts the burdens of cooperation and concession entirely to labor.

Though the theorists discussed above adopt a Marxist framework for conceptualizing structures and processes of work organization, many of their arguments directly descend from an intellectual tradition tracing back to Weber and Durkheim, sociology's other founding fathers.

Weberian approaches to the employment relationship

To Weber, the rising professionalization and bureaucratization of enterprise, much more than capitalist relations of production themselves, were behind the appropriation of control from direct producers and its concentration in the hands of organizational elites. Writers in the Weberian tradition, like the neo-Marxists, also class relations between employers and employees along a continuum from adversarial (where employees are treated as commodities) to cooperative (where employees are encouraged to see themselves as part of an enterprise community and thus identify with company goals). Weber (1947) argued that coercion is not a viable basis for compliance, and his theory of domination treats bureaucratization as an effective solution to the problem of labor control in advanced societies. The significance of this organizational form lies both in its superiority over older forms in sheer technical efficiency terms *and* its capacity to secure consent to domination through the legitimacy of formal rules, internal careers, and a rational allocation of authority and rewards.

Halaby (1986) has laid out a framework and a set of empirical findings on the nature of worker attachment to the firm which he argues is more faithful to the Weberian (hence sociological) tradition than what he terms the "job satisfaction/organizational commitment" paradigm of industrial psychology or the "capital value" perspective of economics. In attempting to distinguish between the JS/OC perspective (which he attributes to us) and the Weberian "workplace authority" framework which he sets out to champion, Halaby asserts that the former casts the employment relation "as a non-instrumental, emotionally-charged, affective psychological bond linking worker to employer" (1986:634), whereas worker attachment from the "workplace authority" perspective: "depends on neither 'love' nor 'money', but on the perceived *legitimacy* of employer governance regimes." In fact, Halaby's stress on the use of legal–rational mechanisms (formal rules, codes, and procedures laying out rights and responsibilities of corporate citizenship) to legitimate workplace authority relationships is thoroughly consistent with the conception of corporatist organization that frames our inquiries in this volume. Though some writings on employee commitment have indeed concentrated on the internal psychodynamics of the commitment process and ignored the external workplace governance patterns to which it represents an employee-level response, the perception of legitimacy, in our view, is a critical intervening mechanism in the arousal of commitment as a strategy of corporatist control.

Durkheim and corporate organization

The notion of commitment-maximizing organization also owes a considerable intellectual debt to Emile Durkheim, who helped lay the groundwork for the comparative study of corporative organizations. Durkheim's chief concern was with the emergent sources of moral influence and authority as societies changed from mechanical to organic forms of solidarity. In the preface to the second edition of *The Division of Labor in Society* (1933), he located these in the corporation, the heir to the family as the basis for social solidarity. Durkheim acknowledged that the nature of corporative organizations is altered by changes in economic life and other features of societies: at the early stages of industrialization, he equated the "corporation" with occupational groups, especially the established professions; in the modern period, corporations are firms.

Unlike Marx and Weber, Durkheim did not perceive the workplace to be rent by conflicts of interest among its constituent parties, since a presumption that conflict is the normal state of affairs in work organizations would seriously compromise the argument that they represent major sources of moral authority in society. Durkheim assumed that the corporative organization, like the family, is as "continuous as life," with no room for discontinuous interests. However, he recognized that there are still objective differences between managers and workers which, if not checked, might lead to conflict. Hence, it is incumbent upon economic firms to incorporate their employees by establishing rules which govern the duties of employers and workmen. These rules are inspired by the corporative interest, not the narrow self-interests of individuals: "the subordination of particular interests is, indeed, the source of all moral activities" (p. 14). These structures create feelings of solidarity between assistants and the assisted, and produce in firms a certain intellectual and moral homogeneity comparable to that prevailing in professional occupations.

Williamson and transaction cost economics

From a very different intellectual tradition comes another recent and widely influential perspective on organization which, at least implicitly, accords an important role to employee commitment. This paradigm portrays the firm, not as a "contested terrain" on which the power struggles between irreconcilable interests are day-to-day fought out, but as a setting in which the exchanges of self-interested parties may be better monitored and controlled than in free markets where actors enter, consummate, and dissolve associations from one transaction to the next. To Oliver Williamson (1975; 1985), organizations arise as markets fail to keep transactions among economic agents (individuals or firms) freed of opportunistic behavior. When information is limited or impacted, to use Williamson's terminology, agents may be inclined to misrepresent their true skills and capabilities in bargaining with a principal, such as an employer or supplier. Organizations emerge in part because the internalization of transactions in an employment relationship allows for better monitoring and control of the performance of self-interested parties than markets typically do. One such mechanism of control, not labeled such by Williamson, is clearly commitment. Organizations, unlike markets, are systems to which human beings become socioemotionally attached. The aggregation of these tendencies across a workforce brings about an atmosphere of shared expectations and values which, in turn, encourage "consummate" as opposed to "perfunctory" performance and avert the guileful behavior which causes markets to fail. The specific mechanisms of hierarchy or organization that Williamson identifies as conducive to the development of atmosphere include certain key structures of corporatist or bureaucratic control: in particular, internal labor markets. ILMs, as we will argue, require a heavy personal investment on the part of the employee in the firm and its future. Moreover, they involve a formal, legal apparatus laying out criteria and procedures for compensation and promotion. This structure of rules helps foster a positive atmosphere by imbuing with legitimacy and equity the conditions for advancement and reward.

Ouchi (1980) has extended Williamson's view of atmosphere-generating organizations – i.e., where strong shared norms and values prevail – in arguing that it constitutes a third (after markets and hierarchies) mode of organizing transactions: the *clan*. Ouchi's concept of clan, which is largely drawn from Durkheim's theory of mechanical solidarity, evokes an image of the relatively unstructured professional and occupational community where strong social bonds and value consensus form the bases for collective action. In attributing clan-like qualities to Japanese organization, Ouchi joins with a long tradition of scholars who place central stress on the communal and familial elements of Japanese company life. Our conception of welfare corporatism, however, is perhaps better aligned with Edwards' conception of bureaucratic control: a highly structured, formal organization which finds ways of fostering loyalty and consent. The clan concept, much like Burns and Stalker's (1961) notion of organic organization, calls to mind a much more fluid and diffuse pattern of organizing than we believe is justified by the realities of the Japanese case.

Technology theorists

A final stream of theorizing which will play a central role in our work in this volume comes from writers who perceive a technological imperative behind the evolution of workplace organization. Blauner (1964), Woodward (1965) and Touraine (1955) saw the advance of production technology as a force transforming industrial relations and increasing the scope of workers' involvement in the firm, such that the strife and alienation of factory life under older technologies would give way to a new cooperation and community (Gallie, 1978). Like Edwards, who believes the loyalty of workers to be high in the early, entrepreneurial phases of capitalism as well as in the late corporatist phase, technological imperative theorists see a curvilinear response of workplace social structures and worker reactions to the growing complexity of technology. First, there was the small workshop producing goods to order by skilled craftsmen enjoying high flexibility and control in their work and communal relations with their fellows. This gave way to the mechanized mass production factory, bureaucratically organizing legions of workers in the performance of narrow, routine tasks. With this change in production organization came alienation and detachment, the rise of an instrumental orientation to work, and the search for meaning in nonwork leisure-time and family pursuits. But as the evolution of technology pressed on, new production systems and work organizations arose which restored community and commitment to the workplace as the machines completed their takeover of the production process, leaving workers to pursue management and monitoring functions freed of the harsh control structures of the mass production factory.

Dimensions of corporatist organization

As this review implies, we see striking parallels in the visions of a number of diverse writers of an emergent set of labor structures and practices which achieve control, not through coercive or utilitarian means, but through normative and symbolic inducements (Etzioni, 1961). We characterize as "corporatist" this general pattern of organization which substitutes workplace commitment and community for alienation and conflict. This use of the term follows Dore's application of it to Japanese and other work organizations which attempt to transform the employment relationship into an enveloping, communal, and harmonious interface between the company and its workforce. Hence, we label as corporatist those organizational structures and management practices aimed at fostering corporate loyalty, commitment, and dependence on the part of labor, though we acknowledge that this usage, while implied, we believe, in European social and political theories of corporatist society, is an uncommon extension into intraorganizational structures and processes.[1]

The corporatist organizational form is, of course, an ideal type, and represents our attempt to abstract from the observations of a number of theorists, all of whom dealt with the rise of new workplace structures and the reactions they evoke in employees. Extrapolating from several authors, but especially from the writings of Edwards, Dore, and Blauner, we identify the following with corporatist work organization.

Structures facilitating participation

A pervasive theme in theories foreseeing the rise of a new workplace community in the internal organization of modern, progressive firms is that they provide mechanisms for participation in decision-making. These restore to the worker a sense of control over the production process and of partnership in the running of the firm. They include: work reform programs aimed at enriching and enlarging jobs by expanding the range of tasks and level of responsibility assigned an individual; small group programs organizing workers in production teams, quality circles, and zero-defect groups; sociotechnical systems aimed at achieving a more logical and humane interface between job designs and technology; and management information systems designed to integrate workers in plant-wide communication networks. Yet as Cole and Dore make clear of Japanese corporatist organization and Edwards implies of bureaucratically controlled American firms, such forms of shop-floor participation rarely involve elements of real industrial democracy wherein workers and managers share profits, ownership, and high-level governance of firms. Programs such as quality circles, which elicit the collective input of rank-and-file workers in production decisions, are typically designed and controlled by management. They diffuse responsibility and commit workers to organizational decisions, without producing significant alterations in the governance structure of the firm (Hill, 1981:53).

Structures facilitating integration

Since Marx, the large-scale mass production factory has been thought a fertile breeding ground for working-class consciousness and organization, for not only is the work deemed alienating and exploitative, but the concentration of a mass of homogeneous workers in a single work site serves to aggregate grievances and foster class solidarity (Kerr and Siegel, 1954; Lincoln, 1978). Yet corporatist organization, as Blauner argued of continuous process industry, Dore of Japanese firms, and Edwards of American high-tech, introduces numerous divisions into the production workforce which fragment workers as a class while encouraging vertical contacts and dependency relations across class and status barriers. This is achieved through a proliferation of subunits such as departments, sections, and teams and the substitution of continuous, finely graduated job and status hierarchies for the old monolithic divisions of manager and worker (Gordon, 1972:77–8; Littler, 1982). It is also promoted through corporate symbols and rituals that evoke feelings of enterprise community and pride, programs for socializing workers in a strong organizational culture (Deal and Kennedy, 1982), and welfare and recreational programs which foster expressive social relations among coworkers and thus extend the reach of the company into nominally nonwork spheres of life. The symbolism, ritual, and welfarism associated with the Japanese brand of corporatist organization is, of course, well known, but these are also highly conspicuous dimensions of corporate life in such "Theory Z" companies as IBM and Hewlett-Packard.

Structures facilitating individual mobility and careers

Firm internal labor markets (FILMs) are another central feature of corporatist organization, acknowledged by quite diverse writers as instrumental in bringing about employee commitment to and dependence on the organization. Several of the structures that contribute to FILM formation also function to raise employee commitment in other ways. Careful recruitment and lifetime employment, as widely practiced both by Japanese companies and such exemplars of Western welfare corporatism as IBM, function to achieve an optimum fit between the values and expectations of employees and the norms and goals of the company. Highly differentiated job and status hierarchies, which Blauner and Dore see channeling relations and communications in a vertical direction and hence favorable to the firm, imply greater opportunities for career mobility within the boundaries of a single organization. When the primary route to improved social and economic standing is individual advancement within a company, the result, in Albert Hirschman's (1970) terms is loyalty, as against the voice of collective action or exit to opportunities with a different employer. Another facet of firm internal labor-market organization with strong implications for control and commitment is a stress on firm-specific skills and knowledge, which have value to a particular employer but are not readily transferable to jobs with other companies. Organizational designs that stress job rotation and team production, coupled with strong corporate cultures and intensive on-the-job train-ing, represent a formula for the creation of enterprise-specific skills at the expense of easily portable occupation-specific skills.

Structures fostering legitimacy and constitutional order within the firm

In a thoughtful review of evidence on the spread of new forms of labor control in modern work organizations, Hill (1981:53) comments that: "The most far-reaching transformation of conventional employment relationships in modern capitalism can be found in large-scale Japanese corporations, which combine paternalism and bureaucracy in a unique synthesis." The identification of welfare corporatist organization with formal bureaucracy is a consistent thread in writings addressed to these issues, whether the setting is Japan, as in Dore's analysis, or the US, as in Richard Edwards' conceptualiza-tion of bureaucratic control. To observers acquainted with older traditions of theory and research on work attitudes and their organizational antecedents, this association may seem odd, for a cardinal tenet of much humanistic industrial psychology and sociology has been that bureaucratic structures, whatever their capacities for efficiency and productivity, constitute alienating work environments for individuals. How can one reconcile this stance with the now-current assertion that, in welfare corporatism, bureaucracy serves to dissolve competing loyalties based on class, occupation, and union, while substituting strong commitment to the company as a whole? The answer, it appears, is simply that the new breed of Marxist students of the labor process, Japan scholars, and other theorists whose writings converge around a strikingly similar vision of commitment-maximizing organization see the trappings of bureaucracy in a very different light from that illuminating the observations of the old schools of workplace study. Bureaucracy implies complex, differentiated organizational structures, which studies in the tradi-tional mold contended would disintegrate and alienate a workforce. As our discussion thus far suggests, however, corporatist theorists see structures such as tall hierarchies and proliferating departments functioning to separate workers from class and occupational bases of identification, while thrusting them into closer and more enveloping relations with supervisors and managers. Corporatist theory likewise sees highly differentiated job and status structures and the procedural mechanisms governing job bidding and promotion as creating the framework for internal labor markets with their considerable potential for building commitment. Finally, in the view of numerous theorists, corporatist organization substitutes for the arbitrary power of supervisors or the domination of machines, a complex system of formal rules and procedures which simultaneously safeguard employee rights while delineating obligations in an impersonal and legitimate manner. Such formalization confers on each employee the status of corporate citizen of an internal state.

Culture and commitment in Japan and the US

Two propositions that are central to the argument of this book are: (a) that the archetypal welfare corporatist form is best approximated in the structures and practices of the modern Japanese firm; and (b) that it is in fact such structures and practices which are responsible for the extraordinary commitment displayed by Japanese employees toward their companies. As we have noted, however, there is a long-standing competing explanation for the Japanese commitment edge. This is the "culturalist" argument that work-related attitudes and behaviors are reflections of widely shared and deeply rooted cultural values and beliefs. In particular, the organizational commitment of the Japanese workforce is seen to be a manifestation of traditional Japanese values stressing groupism and loyalty. One frequently heard piece of testimony for this view is that the commitment of the young to work and company has fallen from the levels of past generations (Odaka, 1975; Sengoku, 1985). This change is attributed to a gradual erosion of traditional values of duty and submission to the group, owing, among other reasons, to rising incomes, more leisure time, and exposure to Western values. It seems unlikely, though not impossible, that a significant decline in work commitment in younger cohorts of Japanese workers could be attributed to shifts in the management practices of firms.

Another essentially culturalist perspective on the respective roles of organization and culture in determining the work commitment of the Japanese is a variant on the "contingency" models of organizational theory which hold that success at organizing requires adaptive moves toward maximizing "fit" with an organization's environment (Scott, 1987). Early formulations of the contingency view were in a strongly rationalist vein (e.g. Lawrence and Lorsch, 1967). The relevant environments for firms were task environments, narrowly construed as the direct external market, technology, and regulatory pressures with which companies in a capitalist economy were forced to contend. More recently, however, the notion of an "institutional environment" has been put forward to take into account the broader mix of institutional rules, state and community structures, and, of course, cultural values and traditions which likewise constrain the actions and designs of organizations (DiMaggio and Powell, 1983; Meyer and Scott, 1983). A premise of the institutional perspective is that survival and performance require adaptation to an environment but not necessarily the "task" environment of mainstream rationalist theory (Carroll and Huo, 1986). The effectiveness of many organizations may depend less on maximizing the fit between their structures and their technologies or markets – indeed that fit may be unknowable and unachievable. Rather it depends on the compatibility between their structures and the rules and expectations of certain external audiences. Thus the survival and prosperity of the organization may hinge much more directly on its fidelity to traditional norms and customs than its capacity to optimize in an economic or technological sense.

Institutional theory in this sense is particularly receptive, much as rationalist theory has been hostile (see, e.g. Hickson *et al.* 1979), to the idea that organizations in different institutional and cultural settings will pursue unique adaptations to those environments and thereby enhance their viability. Institutional theory would thus suggest that Japanese organizational designs and management practices are fitted to Japanese norms and values in such a way as to elicit favorable motivational and behavioral responses from workers steeped in Japanese culture. This view, which we later label "cultural contingency," has important implications which are quite different from those to be derived from the general theory that Japan is the leader of an international movement toward the redesign of work organizations along corporatist lines. The thrust of the latter, as put forward by Dore, Edwards, Ouchi, and others is universalist: that irrespective of the societal/cultural context, the welfare corporatist mode of organizing breaks down class antagonisms in the workplace and draws the individual employee deep within the bosom of the firm. To suggest that Japanese organizational forms combine with cultural values in ways that are highly effective in motivating Japanese workers is also to deny that those same forms would be of much use to managers in countries characterized by very different values, institutions, and traditions, such as the United States.

There is, of course, a good deal of support for this interpretation of Japanese work patterns. Many observers have seen in Japanese organizational arrangements and the orientations of Japanese workers the same set of antecedent conditions: a cluster of cultural values which stress the subordination of the individual to the group and extol the importance of harmony, duty, and loyalty (Nakane, 1970; Vogel, 1963). These values not only facilitate the design of work organizations which embody the corporatist principle of a total enterprise community, they also motivate employees to subordinate their personal, occupational, and class interests to the purposes of the firm.

A considerable body of evidence suggests that the expectations and values of Japanese workers are congruent with the concrete structural arrangements of Japanese firms. In comparative surveys of Japanese and US workers such as Whitehill and Takezawa's (1968; Takezawa and Whitehill, 1981), the Japanese workers often expressed values – for close supervisor–subordinate ties, for a familial, paternal posture by the company – which seemed to coincide with the management practices of Japanese firms but were scarcely echoed by the Americans, who preferred a more contractual, instrumental connection to the company. Surveys of British workers by Dore (1973) and Goldthorpe, Lockwood, Bechhofer and Platt (1968), moreover, have likewise found an orientation to worklife and company which seems considerably more detached and distant than what the Japanese appear to prefer. And

Crozier's (1964) characterization of the French as a people whose disdain of workplace dependency relations leads them to build inordinately rigid and formal organizations surely implies a set of worklife expectations diametrically opposed to those attributed to the Japanese (Rohlen, 1974). These considerations undercut the entire thrust of the welfare corporatist thesis that Japanese-type organization is a beacon toward which the rest of the industrial world is gravitating. To impose organizational arrangements designed to breed community and dependency on a workforce with strong tastes for a rationalist and individualist calculation of interest is hardly likely to produce the payoff in motivation and commitment which managers desire.

Yet another view of the isomorphism between Japanese work values and Japanese organizational forms is that the former have been heavily conditioned by the latter. Values and expectations associated with work and organizational life, this argument goes, are chiefly a function of the prevailing rules and practices associated with a given management and employment system. Western economic institutions are built on principles of rationalism, individualism, and limited commitment. Westerners have been socialized in these values and find them reinforced daily in their actual encounters with the firm. Japanese styles of organization embody different principles and impart values which buttress those principles. Indeed, one of the distinctive elements of the welfare corporatist program is the attempt to indoctrinate employees thoroughly in the norms and values of an enterprise community through symbols, rituals, ceremony, planned social and recreational activities, and extensive training programs focused more on general socialization than on specific job skills (Rohlen, 1974).

Thus, while there should be little disagreement that workers' values and expectations interact with objective organizational and job structures in determining the effectiveness of a given system of labor control, it is extremely difficult to make strong assertions regarding the direction of the causality here. Cultural norms and values, as institutional theory suggests, will certainly have an impact on structures, but structures may also give rise to values, and both phenomena may be shaped by broader institutional and historical currents within the society as a whole. Corporatist organization is apt to fail if imposed wholesale and without the consent of workers whose expectations for work life and the employment relationship are for nothing of the kind. Indeed, some of the cynicism with which the current corporate quality of worklife programs have been greeted by workers and unions suggests that employee resistance may run deep (Berg, Freedman, and Freeman, 1978). But given time, the lack of viable alternatives, and a broad-based program of socialization and public relations, that resistance, American companies seem to feel, can be overcome and a new set of work values, far more supportive of the enterprise and its goals, will ultimately be set in place.

Convergence and culturalism in work organization

Much of this discussion can be fitted into the broad and long-standing debate over "convergence" theories of industrialization and social change (Cole, 1979; Hickson *et al.*, 1974, 1979; Marsh and Mannari, 1976). The convergence hypothesis essentially holds that the constraints of technology and economic efficiency place narrow limits on the range of industrial and organizational forms that a society can adopt (Kerr, Dunlop, Harbison and Myers, 1960). Though agrarian economies can be organized in a variety of ways and are compatible with a host of different value systems, fewer alternatives are available to countries which aim to industrialize, and even these are unequal when measured by the yardstick of efficiency. Hence, industrial societies facing common sets of technological and organizational imperatives should develop increasingly similar social structures and institutions.

Rationalist contingency theories of organization that seek to explain the structures of individual organizations represent a very similar perspective at a lower level of aggregation. They hold that the forces of scale, production technology, and market constraint determine the internal organization of a firm, regardless of the societal setting in which it is embedded. At both levels – society and organization – the mechanism that constrains the range of organizing options from which the firm can viably select is the imperative of performance/efficiency/survival. Organizations whose structures are ill-suited to the requirements of their markets, technologies, and scale will either be selected out through competition or forced to reorganize to achieve a higher level of adaptation (Hannan and Freeman, 1977). Either way, the effect is the same: basic similarity across cultures and societies in the organization of firms operating in similar task environments.

The convergence model then proceeds to link organizational forms, constrained to similarity by the imperatives of efficiency and competition, to the attitudes, values, and behaviors of individuals (e.g. Inkeles, 1960). Attributes of individual modernity such as rationalism, individualism, and universalism are fostered by the spread of "modern" organizational forms, technologies, and networks throughout a society. Persons who spend their work lives in such settings assimilate the rationalism of the organization as a new value system which they, in turn, pass on to others. Ultimately, then, as societies develop, their organizations and institutions converge, and their citizens become more homogeneous in outlook, habits, values, and beliefs.

Japan and the United States: convergence or culturalism?

Much writing on Japanese organization and industrial relations takes sides on the culture vs. convergence question. For years, Japan was cast as the negative case which disproved the theory of societal convergence through the mechanism of industrialization (Abegglen, 1958; Dore, 1973). As an advanced industrial society which appeared to retain many preindustrial (e.g. paternalism, familism) and economically nonrational (e.g. permanent employment, *nenko* wage system) elements, it was held up as a dramatic example of the validity of the functional alternatives view (Cole, 1972). The Japanese case demonstrated that industrialization and rapid economic growth were possible within an institutional and cultural framework which was at considerable odds with the Western model of rationality and modernity. Some critics argued that the case for Japanese uniqueness had been overstated by area specialists eager to find evidence favoring a culturalist or historicist interpretation. Marsh and Mannari (1976), for example, conclude from their extensive analysis of survey data gathered from Japanese workers in three factories that the conditions which shape attitudes toward work, supervisors, and the company appear appreciably similar in Japan and the US. In their view, such results run counter to the predictions of the lifetime commitment model – the theory of Japanese cultural uniqueness in work organization and behavior first put forward by Abegglen. Similarly, Azumi and his colleagues (Azumi *et al.*, 1981; Tracy and Azumi, 1976) have argued forcefully that universalist contiogency theories of organization appear as valid for Japanese organizations as for Western organizations, for research on the structuring of Japanese firms show them to vary with size and technology in much the way that studies of Western organizations have documented.

The theory that corporatist organization represents a new adaptation to changing world markets, production methods, and the scale and diversification of enterprise has turned on its head the culturalist/convergence debate with respect to Japan. Ronald Dore, as we have noted, argues that Japanese distinctiveness is not so much due to the preservation of cultural traditions in modern Japanese work organization as to Japan's status as a late-developing economy. Dore's revisionist interpretation of Japanese welfare corporatism, then, is that far from an anachronism, it is the wave of the future. The bureaucratization, internal labor markets, welfare services, participatory decision-making, strong culture, job guarantees, need-based compensation, and other components of "Japanese-style" employment are the trappings of a modern corporate form which is becoming dominant among Western companies as well. Dore's theory, then, has the rest of the Western industrial world converging toward the model of Japan.

A strong proponent of the functional alternatives model of societal differences, Robert Cole (1971; 1972; 1979) steers a middle course between culturalist and convergence perspectives. In several thoughtful essays, he has made the case that modern Japanese work institutions have emerged as responses to crises of industrialization which are common to all rapidly developing economies. A significant problem faced by both US and Japanese managers, for example, was the necessity of securing workers who possessed the appropriate skills for working with the unfamiliar technologies introduced with rapidly changing production modes. The strategies undertaken by management in the two countries were different, but equally rational, solutions to the problem of labor supply, each involving its own set of trade-offs. For example, Japanese employers developed corporate paternalism in the late 1920s and early 1930s in order to deal with the problem of labor supply. Their strategy was incorporation, utilizing existing social relationships to maintain ideological control over employees for production purposes. They successfully prevented the build-up of a tradition of industrial craftsmanship and commitment to occupational skills; instead, these became channeled into commitment to the organization. This system was reinforced by the Japanese government's lack of provision of welfare services and other social safety nets, thus increasing the dependence of employees upon firms. Their own brief experiments with welfarism notwithstanding (Brody, 1980), Western capitalism has for more of its history incorporated principles of individualism, the commodity status of labor, and the free play of market forces.

Commitment, satisfaction, and alienation

To this point, we have concerned ourselves with the concept of "welfare corporatist" organization as an emergent form in modern capitalism which is grounded in an imperative of maximizing the commitment of employees to the enterprise. We have also given some consideration to two general propositions regarding the sources of the apparent commitment gap between Japanese and US workers: (a) that it derives from the wider deployment of corporatist management and employment practice in Japanese industry; and (b) that it flows directly from differences between Japan and the US in the cultural values and expectations motivating individual workers' attitudes and behaviors. Now we turn our attention directly to the meaning of commitment to a work organization, its implications for workforce behavior and control, and how it might be distinguished from the closely related and much-studied work phenomena of job satisfaction and work alienation.

Organizational commitment implies identification with an organization and acceptance of its goals and values as one's own (March and Simon, 1958; Salancik, 1977). The company's fortunes matter to the worker. The committed employee's involvement in the organization takes on moral overtones, and his stake extends beyond the satisfaction of a merely personal interest in employment, income, and intrinsically rewarding work. The employee becomes conscious of the needs of the organization and sensitive to how his or her actions contribute to the fulfillment of those needs. To identify with the organization, then, implies that the worker is willing to expend effort for the sake of the company, and the firm's performance is experienced as a personal success or failure as well. Moreover, committed employees are loyal to the organization, feel personally defensive when it is threatened, and desire to maintain the employment relationship even when presented with attractive alternatives.

Organizational commitment also involves a corresponding sacrifice of allegiance to subgroups and strata within the firm. Such alternative objects of attachment compete for the individual's loyalty and thereby detract from commitment to the organization as a whole. Commitment to an occupation or profession, to a class or status group such as management or labor, to a department or division such as marketing or production, and even to peer groups formed on the basis of age, gender, and ethnicity introduce divisiveness in the workplace by fostering conflicting loyalties and identities. In this respect, the homogeneity of the Japanese population, as contrasted with the extreme heterogeneity of the US, is often seen as a force for harmony and consensus in the Japanese company.[2] But the welfare corporatist design of Japanese organization itself functions to minimize the formation of divisive subgroups through, for example, eliminating or muting visible disparities in privilege, rewards, and lifestyle. As labor control theorists such as Edwards (1979) emphasize, though, the creation of structures aimed at dissolving class and occupation-based loyalties in favor of an attachment to the company as a whole is in no way unique to Japan but is everywhere characteristic of corporatist-type organization.

Commitment to an employing organization is also distinct from commitment to work *per se* (see chapter 3). People who are heavily involved in their work roles, who place great importance on the work component of their lives may well behave in ways that coincide with the interests of the firm and its management. But there is a difference between the worker who is highly motivated because of interest in and commitment to the work itself and one whose efforts are expended primarily out of devotion to the organization. The work-committed employee may be oriented to an occupational specialty and less inclined to accept alternative tasks for the good of the organization or for the sake of maintaining an employment relationship with it. Furthermore, absorption in a work role may lead to a neglect of activities such as administrative tasks and housekeeping chores which are clearly in the organization's interests but take time away from one's primary set of occupational or professional concerns. This conflict in commitments is commonplace in university settings where research-oriented faculty resist committee assignments, program development, and even teaching duties so as to conserve time for scholarly tasks. The goal of the organization is not merely to motivate hard and careful work, but to motivate it on the organization's behalf.

When an organization finds the means to elicit the commitment of its members, it has at its disposal a very powerful mechanism of control. Indeed, the new interest in organizational commitment as an employee work orientation appears to stem from the realization that the problem of control in organizations is in large measure solved when the commitment of its members is high. Committed workers are self-directed and motivated actors whose inducement to participation and compliance is their moral bond to the organization, not the coercive or utilitarian incentives which elicit the effort to secure the reward or avert the sanction but fail to produce and may even diminish a broad commitment to the organization (Clark and Wilson, 1961; Edwards, 1979; Etzioni, 1961).

It is important to maintain a distinction between commitments which reflect group pressures and prevailing norms and those which represent the subjective feeling states of individuals. Loyalty, for example, might be associated with strong feelings of attachment to and identification with the organization or it might be a direct behavioral reflection of workplace norms and institutionalized constraints that discourage job-changing. Discussions of the commitment of Japanese workers commonly point to low turnover and absenteeism, high overtime, and a disinclination on the part of workers to take advantage of all the vacation and leave time allotted them. Frequent socializing with coworkers after work hours in bars and at parties likewise suggests an extraordinary commitment to work. This may be true, but it is also probable that these behaviors stem not solely from individual preferences but from strong group pressures to conform to well-established behavioral norms governing Japanese worklife (Nakane, 1970). Hence, behavioral commitment may simply reflect individual adaptations to external structures and thus an absence of choice.

Though dominant norms and the social attitudes of a majority of the population are perhaps by definition aligned, there are always sizable minorities who conform to commonly prescribed ways of doing things, not out of personal preference or inclination, but because of the external pressure produced by others' expectations. Moreover, in a time of social change, institutionalized patterns may be out of sync with the attitudes of individuals. In Japan, as we noted above, it is widely believed that the preferences of the young are for more leisure time, a higher standard of living, and other personal pursuits. They are, nonetheless, parties to a system which has traditionally valued the submission of individuals' goals and interests to those of the corporate group. As Odaka (1975) has suggested, then, young Japanese workers may remain committed in the sense of conforming to prevailing cultural rules demanding subordination of individual to corporate interests, but such commitment is born of external constraints and not internal psychological leanings. In Odaka's view, the traditional pressures in Japanese society for organizational commitment and loyalty have come into conflict with young workers' acquired tastes for leisure and consumption activities, producing a decline in satisfaction with work.[3]

Job satisfaction

Job satisfaction is a generalized affective work orientation toward one's present job and employer. It is less a zero-sum concept than organizational commitment, since one can be satisfied with a great many or relatively few facets of the employment relation. As a summary indicator of the perceived quality of one's work experience, it is perhaps the most widely studied and discussed work attitude. Responses to a set of job satisfaction questions are an obvious and direct way to measure an important question of broad interest to social scientists, policy-makers, and practitioners: do people like their work and are they generally getting what they wanted from their jobs? Yet the results from job satisfaction surveys in the US have provoked much discussion of what workers really mean when they express satisfaction with their jobs (US Department of HEW, 1972). The percentages of the workforce reporting general satisfaction have tended to be so high (around 80 percent), that many observers, struck by the considerable behavioral evidence to the contrary (e.g. high rates of absenteeism, turnover, militancy) have been skeptical of the validity of such findings (e.g. Blauner, 1960).

Much of the interest in job satisfaction on the part of organizational psychologists stems from the presumed link between positive work attitudes and performance behavior (Hackman and Oldham, 1980). Yet, as a number of reviews of the research literature testify, the evidence that satisfied workers will invest more effort and care in their job tasks is thin to nil (see, e.g. Perrow, 1979). There is somewhat stronger evidence that job satisfaction is associated with a reduced incidence of turnover, absenteeism, and other negative work-related acts (Mowday, Porter, and Steers, 1982; Porter and Lawler, 1965). This pattern makes obvious intuitive sense, and, in fact, forms the core of Herzberg's famous two-factor theory of work motivation (e.g. Herzberg, Mausner, and Snyderman, 1959). Employees who are basically content with their jobs and their workplace associations are not likely to quit or fail to show up on a regular basis. But neither is there any particular reason to suppose they will be inclined to expend a significant effort in carrying out their tasks. Indeed, what is satisfying about the job may be precisely that it makes few stringent demands on the employee and allows him or her to set a leisurely pace, take frequent breaks, and thus avoid arduous or distasteful activity. This, of course, evokes the idea that job satisfaction depends as much on work values and expectations as on the objective circumstances of the work itself (Kalleberg, 1977). Herein may lie an explanation for the extraordinarily high reported levels of job satisfaction in the US labor force. If workers have low expectations for job rewards – if, as Goldthorpe *et al.* (1968) suggest of affluent British workers, their orientation to work is chiefly instrumental – then the very possession of a tolerable but well-paying job may be sufficient to produce a state of satisfaction no matter how few intrinsic rewards can be derived from the work itself.

Thus, the net effect of commitment on satisfaction may be negative: strong commitment generates high expectations which, in turn, raise threshold levels of satisfaction for a given level of job reward (Vroom, 1964). Moreover, if one is committed to the ideals of work and service to a company, he/she may have an expressive (as opposed to instrumental) work orientation, hence high expectations for work life rewards. This reasoning may account for the strikingly consistent finding of Japanese labor force surveys that reported levels of job satisfaction run much lower than in Western industrialized countries. Cole's (1979) explanation is that high job satisfaction (particularly in a passive, complacent sense of the word) should not be expected from such a highly committed and motivated workforce. Because there is so much employee involvement and identification with the Japanese company, this argument goes, expectations for fulfillment through work are high as well, and this, in turn, evokes discontent.

It seems patently clear that commitment looms larger than satisfaction as an attitudinal cause of employee performance and productivity. The very definition of commitment involves a motivation to invest effort in seeing organizational goals achieved. This recognition of the significance of commitment for work behavior is, of course, behind the equation of commitment with control. There is as yet little research directly documenting the association between commitment and worker productivity, although a sizable empirical literature finds commitment negatively correlated with turnover and absenteeism (Mowday *et al.*, 1982). Even so, it is hard to discount the prima-facie case for commitment over satisfaction as the primary antecedent of care and effort on the job.

Alienation from work

In contrast to the fairly recent scholarly preoccupation with organizational commitment, its ostensible antithesis – alienation – has a long and broad tradition in worklife theory and research. Though Marx saw the alienation of labor under industrial capitalism as an objective, *structural* condition – the separation of the worker from ownership of the means and fruits of production – most contemporary social scientists view it as a *subjective* condition, though the subjective experience is typically assumed to reflect an objective reality. Following Durkheim, they have elaborated the notion of a general form of psychological detachment and distress with roots in the bureaucratized, mechanized, and urbanized character of modern society.

The lack of consensus on the meaning of alienation no doubt stems largely from its multidimensional nature; virtually all attempts to define the condition see it as comprising a variety of distinct facets. Blauner (1964), building on Seeman's (1959) pioneering discussion, identifies four components of alienation from work: powerlessness, or lack of control over the pace, content, and methods of work; meaninglessness, or inability to understand how one's work is linked to others and to the production process as a whole; social isolation, or the lack of a sense of participation and integration in a work community; and self-estrangement, the tendency for work to be viewed instrumentally, as only a means to the fulfillment of nonwork needs.

It will be evident in later chapters that many of our concerns with job characteristics, workplace relationships, authority and decision-making structures, and so on, deal directly with the phenomenon that Seeman, Blauner and others have termed work alienation. However, we avoid this term for several reasons. First, the concept of alienation was formulated within a historical period and set of intellectual and social concerns that were quite distinct from those prevailing now. It was an idea whose heyday in American social thought was the 1950s and early 1960s, when full employment, low inflation, rising wages, and general optimism challenged social scientists to seek out the dark side of the affluent society. Today, faced with an eroding industrial base, weak productivity, and strong competition from abroad, work alienation in this earlier sense has lost much of its intellectual and political urgency. Alienation in the peak decades of American prosperity referred to an almost metaphysical *malaise*; an inability to find meaning, purpose, and self-fulfillment in work, despite rising material well-being. As a social issue, there is scant evidence that it was of much concern to the owners and managers of industrial enterprises themselves (see US Department of HEW, 1972). This situation contrasts with the broad interest in commitment and motivation that today pervades management as well as academic circles. The difference – and this is a key theme of our investigation – is that corporations and their leaders have come to see commitment as an orientation on the part of employees which, if properly manipulated by the firm, will provide the solutions to fundamental problems of labor control and productivity.

A second reason for distancing ourselves from the idea of alienation is that its conceptual status with respect to other attitudinal orientations to worklife has rarely been made clear. Motivated perhaps by a desire to ground their research problems in important theoretical concerns, researchers not uncommonly announce their interest in alienation, then measure it with indicators of organizational commitment or job satisfaction (e.g. Aiken and Hage, 1966; Blauner, 1964). Given our sense that commitment and satisfaction have very different implications for the motivation and behavior of Japanese and US employees, we address specifically the perceptual and experiential worklife variables of which the concept of alienation is composed.

Welfare corporatism and culturalism as alternative hypotheses

Our inquiry is broadly concerned with the proposition that new patterns of work organization, formed around a logic of maximizing employee commitment, have been rapidly gaining ground in industrial enterprise worldwide. We specifically address the hypothesis that such organizational forms and employment practices are more prevalent in Japanese work organizations than in US plants and companies, and that such prevalence accounts for the presumed higher commitment of the Japanese workforce. Yet we also take up

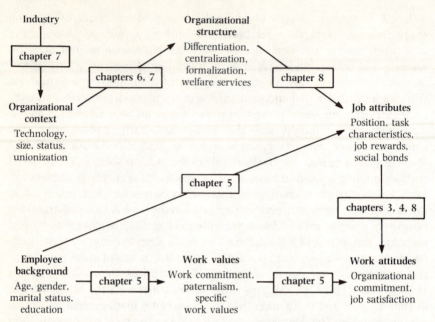

Figure 1   A multilevel model of work organization and work attitudes

the convergence hypothesis of Dore, Ouchi, and others that, wherever the elements of corporatist organization materialize, their impact on the workforce is the same, i.e. levels of commitment rise. Should these hypotheses be confirmed, we will have gone a long way toward validating the core of the welfare corporatist thesis, as advanced, in particular, by Dore: that the dedication and commitment of Japanese workers derive from Japan's leading edge status as an adopter and implementer of a new and highly successful technology of organization control.

Yet these hypotheses are by no means easily tested, and discriminating between them and a compelling alternative model is a major challenge to our research. That alternative model is the culturalist one: that the commitment of Japanese workers is not to a significant degree a function of the organization of Japanese firms, but is a direct reflection instead of the values and beliefs embedded in Japanese culture and internalized through the socialization process by individual Japanese. A thoroughgoing test of the culturalist alternative would demand the gathering and analysis of extensive data on the values and belief systems of Japanese and US workers. While we do in fact pursue a limited inquiry of this sort, we make no claim that this is an exhaustive study of the impact of Japanese and US cultural dispositions on work attitudes and behaviours.

Figure 1 diagrams the general multilevel causal model which guides our empirical inquiries in this book. Although not shown in the figure, Japan/US differences are presumed to materialize in both the *levels* of all variables and the *causal relations* among them. The ultimate outcomes which the model seeks to explain are the employee work attitudes of commitment to the organization and satisfaction with the job. Immediately antecedent to these are attributes of the job held by the employee and the work values that persons bring to the employment relationship. Our general position is that work values (e.g. the extent to which work is a central life interest) are molded through upbringing and socialization and, unlike attitudes, are less likely to be shaped by facets of the job or organization. (We do, however, subject parts of this assumption to empirical test). Job attributes, on the other hand, including management position, task complexity and skill, job rewards and social relations, are the end result of a causal sequence which originates with the industry (and therefore the product mix) of the firm. Industry-level forces shape economies of scale and production technologies. The latter, as a large empirical literature demonstrates, engender variations in internal organization and employment practice, including those structures which we associate with "corporatist" organization. A key question for our inquiry is whether variations in plant production technology, as opposed to societal differences (US vs. Japan), play the greater role in shaping the organization of the plants in our sample. Organization, in turn, is experienced by individual employees chiefly (though probably not exclusively) through the nature of the jobs they hold.

As the figure suggests, the subject matter of our inquiry consists in explorations of the various multilevel links in this complex causal chain. Research on the nature of work organization and work attitudes has long been plagued by a failure to explicate the chains of causal relations that link individuals to more macroscopic structures. On one hand, "the weakness of the psychological emphasis on micro levels is the present lack of knowledge regarding how characteristics of organizational levels above the immediate workgroup influence behavior and attitudes" (James and Jones, 1976:75). On the other hand, while sociologists have examined such macro-level determinants of work attitudes as organizational size and industrial sector, the linkages between such structures and individuals' reactions are not well specified in prior research (e.g. Blauner, 1964). Though some significant exceptions exist (e.g. Rousseau, 1978), the specification and estimation of effects on work attitudes of multilevel work structures remains problematic and an important topic for future research (see House, 1977).

2 Research design, data collection, and the samples

In order to investigate our research questions – in particular the hypothesis of welfare corporatism as a set of organizational arrangements that engender employee commitment – our data should meet several criteria. It is necessary to collect comparable information on plants and employees in the US and Japan. The samples of employing organizations should be large enough to represent a range of diverse industries. Moreover, the samples of employees should be representative of the primary management levels and occupational groupings commonly found in manufacturing establishments. To our knowledge, no cross-national research investigations to date have met these criteria. This, we believe, is a key reason why many important theoretical propositions relating work organization structures to employee-level outcomes have eluded rigorous test. Our purpose in mounting this study was to overcome the limitations of past research in gathering a data set that would allow us to examine with considerable precision the consequences of organizational structures and management practices for employee work attitudes and behaviors in the US and Japan.

In this chapter, we describe our research design and the various stages of our study: sampling; negotiating access; and methods of data collection. We then provide an overview of the US and Japanese samples. Finally, we consider some general issues pertaining to cross-cultural measurement and research. This will set the stage for our discussion of empirical results in subsequent chapters. We begin by outlining some of the alternative strategies widely used in previous research on work behavior and work organization.

Types of research designs

Household sample surveys

This is by far the most common method of gathering data on workforce characteristics. It is a favorite methodology among social scientists and the vehicle for the collection of many key social and economic indicators (such as those obtained in the dicennial US Censuses of Population and in the Current Population Surveys). The specific techniques involved in area sampling, instrument design, and interviewing that are associated with household sample surveys have achieved a high level of sophistication and complexity. The core of the design is the selection of a sample of households (preferably according to rigorous probability sampling techniques), and interviewing employed persons within the household regarding their demographic attributes, work histories and experiences, job characteristics, and their attitudes toward work and their employer (see, for example, Cole, 1979; Kohn and Schooler, 1973). This survey methodology has certain clear advantages: it is relatively easy to obtain a sampling frame of households in specified geographical areas; respondents' work time and duties are not interrupted when interviews are conducted in their homes; and it is typically not necessary to obtain permission from someone other than the respondent to conduct the research. When employees are surveyed in the workplace – as in the present study (see below) – it is necessary to obtain the permission of management and, where one exists, the union. These obstacles reduce the access rate, and, in order to bypass them, it is often necessary to make compromises in research strategy. By contrast, a well-executed household survey normally yields satisfactory response rates without pressure to invest significant resources in negotiating access. Moreover, as Kohn and Schooler (1973:99) point out: "the method is useful ... for studying the immediate conditions of a man's own job."

However, the validity of the household survey as a research design is seriously undermined if the objective is to study precisely how the overall organization of the workplace, and the various departments and strata within it, condition individual employees' attitudes and experiences. Rank-and-file employees typically cannot be counted on to make reliable and valid reports concerning aspects of workplace organization or management practice that are to some degree removed from their day-to-day job experiences and perceptions. This is true even with respect to such seemingly simple variables as firm or establishment size, and the amount of reporting inaccuracy escalates rapidly when questions of structure (e.g. the degree of centralization or bureaucratization) are at stake. Even worse, response errors in employees' perceptions of organizational structures are not likely to be random, but tend to be correlated with many of the employee-level attitudes and behaviors that the investigator is trying to explain (see Lincoln and Zeitz, 1980). Alienated workers, for example, are apt to perceive management practices as centralized and authoritarian while committed and motivated employees tend, not surprisingly, to take a different point of view. Hence, as Kohn and Schooler (1973:99) note: "the method is not well adapted for studying the industrial and technological context in which the job is embedded." A valid design for addressing these questions, it would seem, must obtain reports on organizational structure and functioning from sources independent of and better informed than workers themselves.

A variant of the household sample survey seeks to overcome these limitations by collecting data on places of employment independently of the employee survey. With this approach, the researcher obtains from respondents the names and addresses of their employers, then directly gathers data on these companies. This can be done either from various documentary sources (see, for example, Hodson, 1983); or from interviews with key informants in the employing establishments (such as personnel managers – see Villemez and Bridges, 1986). Such two-stage research designs circumvent the problems of systematic response bias that arise when rank-and-file employees serve as informants regarding organization and management variables. Indeed, they are potentially very powerful designs, as they provide a representative sample, not only of the labor force of a specified area, but of their places of employment as well.

However, this type of two-stage approach has several important limitations for studying the relationship between organizational structures and individual outcomes. Documentary sources (such as Moody's *Industrial Manual* or Dun and Bradstreet's Market Identifier files) will never list all the employers that turn up in a household sample survey; in particular, data on small firms and establishments are likely to be omitted. The alternative strategy of gathering data from informants in the employing establishments identified by survey respondents faces formidable barriers as well. With the possible exception of communities dominated by one or two very large employers, a household-based survey can easily yield nearly as many establishments as individual respondents. Hodson (1983), for example, reports that the 6,602 persons in his sample of Wisconsin high school graduates were employed by 4,200 different companies. Within each of these, then, an informant must be identified and interviewed or sent a questionnaire in order to generate matching organizational data for the person sampled in the household survey. The resource constraints on this process all but guarantee that no more than a single informant per workplace will be contacted, thus seriously compromising the reliability of the organizational data. A growing methodological literature has demonstrated the importance of using multiple informants in surveys aimed at measuring organizational properties (Phillips, 1981; Lincoln and Zeitz, 1980). Even if the investigation settles for a single informant per establishment, the problem of research access to so many employers is surely a formidable one, and significant problems with missing data seem unavoidable.

Moreover, since household-based samples rarely include more than one or two people that work in the same firm, this design does not generally permit the researcher to investigate important and pervasive within-plant variations in work attitudes, job attributes and rewards, and other variables. Kohn and Schooler (1973:99) comment that: "a sample of men scattered across many occupations and many work places does not contain enough people in any occupation or any work place to trace out ... belief systems [or other plant-specific phenomena]." Indeed, there is considerable potential for erroneous causal inferences, for nearly every observed difference between jobs, departments, or supervisors will also be generally assumed to represent a difference in work organization.

Case studies

The primary alternative to the household- or individual-based sample design is the employee survey conducted within a single plant or handful of purposively selected plants. The validity of the case study methodology stands or falls on the representativeness or theoretical significance of the work sites chosen. In research of this sort, the investigator gains access to one or more organizations for the purpose of studying work arrangements and workers. S/he then attempts to draw a (sometimes representative) sample of the plant's workforce, often stratifying it according to key internal divisions such as authority position, department, and occupation. This research design enables the investigator to observe work behavior and worker interaction directly and intensively and to conduct open-ended interviews with key organizational informants such as managers and shop stewards. It also facilitates the collection of documentary information on the organization, past and present. Several important comparative studies of Japanese work life have followed this approach. Dore's (1973) classic study used a design which involved worker surveys, informant interviewing, archival analysis, and direct observation in two Hitachi plants and two English Electric plants. Marsh and Mannari (1976) used a similar methodology in their research on three Japanese factories in three quite different industries. Both studies combine rich, detailed description of the factories studied with a statistical analysis of employee questionnaire data. Whitehill and Takezawa (1968; see also Takezawa and Whitehill, 1981) surveyed over 2,000 workers in two Ohio plants and a comparable number in two Japanese plants. Unlike the Dore and Marsh and Mannari studies, their analysis sticks closely to the survey data, and we learn little of the firms themselves.

The greatest strength of the case study methodology corresponds to the major weakness of the household-based survey technique: elaborate investigation and in-depth understanding of *intra*workplace structures and processes complement and enliven the survey inquiry. However, because the case study approach requires that the researcher obtain management (and often union) permission to gain entry, and because of the considerable time involved in intensive field work, these studies rarely consider more than a small number of establishments. Consequently, while qualitative comparisons can sometimes be made between individual plants (in Dore's study, both within and between countries), it is generally not possible to measure specific plant-level properties and to use statistical techniques such as regression analysis to link them to employee-level variables. This points up a critical shortcoming of this research design: one can only guess at precisely what it is about the plant studied that produces the particular structural arrangements and patterns of behavior within it. Whether the organization's structure is representative of its industry or national economy cannot readily be ascertained. In a cross-cultural study such as Dore's, where only one company (though two plants) in Japan and one in Britain were studied, the danger, of course, is that any and all differences between companies (hence between countries) become fair game for explanations couched in cultural or societal terms. Were a large number of diverse plants in each country sampled, real differences between countries could much more reliably be sorted out.

Organization-based, two-stage designs

Neither the household sample survey nor the plant case-study approach, then, puts the investigator in a strong position to make causal inferences as to the impact of employing organizations on individual-level work processes and outcomes. In order carefully to assess variations in work attitudes among and within organizational settings, a third type of research design is necessary. This strategy involves two steps. First, a large sample of companies is selected from a well-defined population of organizations that is representative of a range of industries. Information is then collected on the structures and management practices of these organizations from interviews with key informants within each company and from documentary sources. Secondly, a representative sample of employees is drawn within each of these organizations who are then surveyed about their jobs, employment situations and work attitudes. Such a two-stage research design permits the collection of data on a representative sample of plants *and* on the employees who staff those plants.

The key advantages of this approach over the household-followed-by-employer survey method are that: (a) data can be collected from a number of firms large enough to permit multivariate analysis but small enough to enable fairly detailed data to be collected from each; and (b) there will be considerable variation in employee and job attributes *within* as well as *between* plants. In contrast to the household survey design, the two-stage plant-employee methodology yields a less representative sample of the labor force residing in a particular region: it tends to under-represent the labor force employed in small establishments, especially when the sample of plants is stratified (as in our research) by employment size. This can be a major disadvantage if the main objective of the study is to generalize to the labor force as a whole. On the other hand, this organization-based, two-stage approach is an optimal research design for addressing questions about the relationship between plant-level organizational systems and employee attitudes and behaviors. It is, therefore, the method of the present study.

The regions

The first step in our research methodology was to identify a population of employing organizations. Ideally, of course, our purposes would be nicely served by a representative sample of the universe of business firms in the United States and Japan. Needless to say, resource limitations constrained our sampling in various ways. The first pertained to area: our data collection was limited to one urban region within each country. Although any comparative study not based on national samples is vulnerable to the charge that the regions surveyed may not be representative of their respective nations nor comparable to each other, the regions selected – South Central Indiana (chiefly the Indianapolis metropolitan area) and the Atsugi region of Kanagawa prefecture in Japan – are, in fact, quite similar with respect to level of urbanization, proximity to major metropolitan centers (e.g. Chicago and Tokyo), and industry mix. Both have diversified economies, with no one industry dominating. Moreover, both contain a mix of establishments, including those operated by large, national corporations as well as small, locally owned concerns. This was an important consideration in our research, for a common criticism of past studies of the Japanese employment system is that they emphasize the practices of large, national corporations – the core of the Japanese economy – while ignoring the quite different patterns of employment that characterize the small firm periphery. Consequently, a priority for our sampling strategy was to include a range of plant and firm sizes that would allow us to assess differences between sectors of the Japanese and US dual economies. Last, but by no means least in importance, the Atsugi and Indianapolis areas were regions to which our research teams had relatively easy access for reasons of geographic proximity and a history of relations with our universities. We briefly describe these two regions.

Indianapolis metropolitan area

The Indianapolis metropolitan region includes eight counties with a total land area of over 3,000 square miles. The SMSA had a population of over 1,200,000 in 1980, with over 60 percent of its population located in the city of Indianapolis and about 2/3 in Marion county. Its labor force of over 550,000 is also primarily concentrated in Marion county, the main site of our survey. Despite its relatively high level of unionization, this region is attractive to the business community. Geographically, the Indianapolis metropolitan area occupies a central location in the United States, with more than 65 percent of the total population of the US living within 700 miles of Indianapolis and 22 percent within 300 miles. It is also the most centrally located city in the US to the top 100 markets, and it is at the crossroads of the national interstate highway system: more national highways converge in Indianapolis than in any other US city.

We have noted that an important feature of the Indianapolis metropolitan area for our purposes is that it has a diverse distribution of industries that closely parallels the economy of the United States as a whole. Approximately 25 percent of its labor force in 1980 was employed in manufacturing industries, as compared to about 22 percent of the US labor force. Within the manufacturing sector, there is also a wide range of industries represented, with the largest proportions of the manufacturing labor force found in transportation equipment (25 percent), electrical machinery (15 percent), non-electrical machinery (13 percent), fabricated metals (8 percent) and chemicals (8 percent). Of these manufacturing industries, the highest earnings in 1979 were obtained by production workers in transportation equipment, about $22,000.

Atsugi region

The Atsugi region of Kanagawa prefecture is approximately 50 miles from Tokyo and 30 miles from Yokohama. Given Japan's extreme dependence on raw material imports and exports of finished products, access to a port (Yokohama) makes the region highly attractive to Japanese manufacturers. Proximity to Tokyo, and to major highway and train routes are other factors which have contributed to the area becoming one of the key industrial regions in Japan.

Much like central Indiana, Atsugi retains many elements of rural life. Farming and forestry, dominant industries until the 1960s, remain important today. The city of Isehara, where our project was headquartered, emerged from the consolidation in 1954 of several smaller towns and villages. The suburban character of the area is also evident in the large number of cars, shopping centers, road-side restaurants, and freeways. In contrast with Tokyo, where public conveyance is the rule, people in Atsugi generally drive to work.

In 1980, Kanagawa prefecture had a population of 5,216,000, approximately half of which was outside Yokohama. The plants included in our sample were located in the cities of Atsugi, Isehara, Hiratsuka, Ebina, and Odawara.

The industrial composition of Kanagawa is generally similar to that of central Indiana. Of the labor force, 30 percent is employed in manufacturing. Of the manufacturing workforce, 18 percent is in transportation equipment, 28 percent in electrical machinery, 13 percent in non-electrical machinery, 9 percent in fabricated metals, and 5 percent in chemicals.

The industries

A fully representative sample of firms or establishments in either the Japanese or US economies would require extensive sampling within as well as across the range of industrial sectors: the primary sector of agriculture, mining, and forestry; the secondary industries of manufacturing and construction; and tertiary industries such as wholesale and retail trade, services, and so on. The considerable diversity of economic and sociotechnical processes involved in producing goods and services from one industry to the next makes it difficult to devise measures of industrial structure that are comparable across major industry groupings. For example, the concept of production technology, which plays a central role in much of the workplace theory that concerns us in this volume, does not convert readily into terms and operations that are equivalent between manufacturing and service industries. Similar comparability problems are presented by the very different occupational composition of manufacturing establishments (which are chiefly blue collar at the rank-and-file level) as contrasted with service industries (with their heavy concentrations of white-collar workers).

In view of these considerations, we felt it necessary to limit our study to manufacturing industries. We targeted our sampling at the following seven: transportation equipment; electronics and electronic equipment; chemicals; prefabricated metals; non-electrical machinery; printing and publishing; and food processing. Restricting our analysis to manufacturing industries is consistent with the focus of most of the existing theory, research, and media commentary on work organization in Japan and the West that inform our study. Indeed, though Japanese financial services firms and trading companies have become formidable competitors in world markets, it is primarily with respect to manufacturing that the Japanese have made the greatest gains in labor productivity. During the period 1974–1984, for example, the average Japanese manufacturing worker's output increased by 104 percent, as compared with a US gain of 27 percent. According to the Japan Productivity Center (see Keizai Koho Center, 1983), very large gains in productivity in Japan relative to the US occurred in the automobile, electronics, chemicals, and food industries.

The diversity of the seven manufacturing industries we study enables us to control to some extent for a possible "recession effect" in the US sample. The period in which our data were collected (1981–1983) encompassed the 1981 recession in which the unemployment rate in the US rose to 9.5 percent, as compared with an average of 2.4 percent for the same period in Japan. Manufacturing workers in midwestern regions such as central Indiana were particularly hard hit, and many young workers were laid off. Unemployment rates are normally higher in the US than in Japan, but the recessionary climate and attendant workforce reductions posed a potentially serious comparability problem for our research. It is reflected, for instance, in the surprisingly small difference we find in the average company tenure of US and Japanese employees in our samples: the mean number of years the US workers were employed in their firms is nearly equal that of the Japanese employees (11.3 vs. 12.0), though other studies report a considerably greater pattern of job stability among the Japanese (Cole, 1979; Koike, 1983). The industrial diversity of our sample helps to circumvent this problem somewhat, for certain of these industries (e.g. printing and food processing), were scarcely touched by the recession and experienced few layoffs, while others (e.g. transportation equipment), were greatly affected.

Sampling

Sampling organizations

There was considerable variation in our samples as to the corporate status of each establishment studied. This is a dimension which has important implications for the structuring of activities and authority in work organizations, and it has drawn considerable attention in past research (Child, 1972; Lincoln, Olson, Hanada, 1978). Moreover, like employment size, whether the plant is a locally owned, single-site operation or the branch installation of a national, multisite corporation is an important indicator of position in a country's dual economy, and, as such, plays a key role in our attempts to test various predictions from welfare corporatist theory. Although we made no attempt to use corporate status as a criterion for selecting plants, the composition of the two samples in this regard is quite similar: 62 percent of the Japanese establishments are branch plants vs. 55 percent of those in the US sample; 10 percent are subsidiaries in Japan vs. 15 percent in the US; and 28 percent of the Japanese sample comprises independent companies as compared with 30 percent of the US sample. Moreover, the distribution of plants by corporate status across industry categories is similar in the two countries and intuitively correct. For example, independent firms (or principal units) are uncommon in transportation equipment, food processing, and chemicals; they are more prevalent in printing, nonelectrical machinery, and fabricated metals.

We stratified plants within each industry into three size categories: large (2,000 employees and above); medium (100–1,999); and small (less than 100). We then attempted to determine the population of manufacturing plants in each industry-size category by gathering lists from knowledgeable sources. We compiled the lists of Indiana plants from several sources, including the Indiana and Indianapolis Chambers of Commerce directories and Dun and Bradstreet's list of Indianapolis plants. Sampling lists for the Japanese plants were compiled mainly from directories published by the Japanese Chamber of Commerce.

We then systematically selected samples of plants from the lists compiled for each industry-size category.[1] We took considerable care to ensure that the Japanese and American samples were similar with respect to both industry and size composition. Moreover, we sought to obtain a sample of plants that reflected the size distribution of plants in that industry. Our principal method of selecting plants within groups was a combination of random sampling and elimination of unsuitable candidates.[2] We initially chose plants on the basis of random numbers assigned to each plant in a given industry-size list. We aimed at selecting roughly seven plants in each industry, weighting the number chosen for a particular size category by the overall size distribution of plants in that industry. If the management of a targeted plant refused to participate in the study, we systematically chose additional plants in that industry-size category. Our use of random sampling was largely limited to small and medium-sized plants: the number of large plants (2,000+) was sufficiently small that we made contact with nearly all of them.

Sampling employees

The second stage of our sampling procedure was to select a representative set of full-time, nontemporary employees within each plant. First, we stratified employees by location in the management hierarchy: (1) workers, or employees with no supervisory or managerial responsibility; (2) first- and second-line supervisors or foremen who directly oversee production work; and (3) managers, which we defined as all those above the level of foreman. Since many of our substantive interests were related to the organization of production work, we attempted to sample primarily employees involved in direct production activities and those in immediate support groups or departments. These departments included employees involved in: production scheduling; fabrication; manufacturing, plant and product engineering; quality control; and (on-site) warehousing. However, since we also wished to obtain a cross-section of the plant's workforce, we sampled two major groups of nonproduction employees as well. The first included technical people whose jobs were closely linked to the production workflow, such as those in: engineering; maintenance; machine and electrical shop; and materials and scheduling control departments. These employees are both salaried (e.g. college-educated engineers), and hourly. The other category of nonproduction employees includes clerical workers, accounting and purchasing personnel, sales and marketing employees, and personnel department staff.

Our initial objective was to obtain employee lists in major departments that would serve as frames from which we could draw random samples. The difficulty with this procedure was that, in production departments with highly interdependent work processes, the absence of even a small number of workers for the time it took to complete the questionnaire meant that the entire operation had to be shut down. Consequently, it was often necessary to select whole departments wherein questionnaires were administered to all employees. This was often done at a shift change, when operations would be halted anyway, and we sometimes had the opportunity to survey in direct succession workers leaving a shift as well as the new shift arriving to take their places.

Similarly, in the Kanagawa survey, our procedure, without exception, was to sample whole departments and administer questionnaires to all employees in those departments. The reason here, however, was a bit different from that in the US. Management's objection in Japan to the practice of sampling individual employees within departments was that it was unfair to discriminate among workers in the same production group by asking some to participate in the study while excluding others. This in itself constitutes an interesting cultural contrast between the United States and Japan and highlights the priority placed on group identity and cohesion in Japanese companies and in Japanese society more broadly. Rather than let management sample employees, we selected, based on discussions in each plant, certain units to be included in the study (for example, particular product lines or departments). Every employee in these chosen units was then asked to fill out questionnaires.

We aimed to make the sizes of the employee samples roughly proportional to the size of the plant, such that a sample of 100–300 respondents would be taken in plants with over 1,000 members, while in small organizations (c. 100 employees) all production workers and line managers would be surveyed. The size and composition of these samples were often a matter of considerable negotiation, however, and exceptions to these guidelines were unavoidable.

Gaining access to plants and employees

A critical task on which the success of the entire project would depend was to persuade organizational leaders to allow us to enter their companies for purposes of data collection. Fortunately, our research team was a diverse one, composed of faculty and students from Sociology as well as Business School departments at Indiana University and the SANNO Institute of Business Administration. We were thus able to rely in part on the ties with business leaders in the Indianapolis and Atsugi areas that the Indiana University and SANNO Business Schools already had in place. In our negotiations with union representatives, on the other hand, it was often convenient to trot out the sociology professors among us while downplaying our business school connections. In the US, we obtained early support for the study from the labor, government and business communities in Indianapolis. Utilizing a snowball procedure, whereby initial contacts led to others, we developed an overall picture of the public and private structures serving the business and labor communities. We met with leaders of these organizations (for example, the Indiana and Indianapolis Chambers of Commerce; the local chapter of the National Association of Manufacturers) and requested their support. Our activities resulted in considerable pre-study publicity in local newspapers and organization newsletters, and by the time leaders of sampled firms were approached, we had already established a substantial degree of legitimacy.

Likewise, in Japan, we obtained letters of introduction and endorsement from the Chambers of Commerce in each of the towns studied. Members of our Japanese research team also showed prospective participants letters of endorsement, news clippings, etc. from the Indianapolis part of the study.

In negotiating access to the sampled companies, we made initial contact with the plant manager. This procedure was more complicated in the case of establishments that were branch plants or subsidiaries of larger firms; in these cases, the approval of managers in corporate headquarters was sometimes required in order to secure the cooperation of managers in a sampled plant. In addition, particularly in the US where union suspicion of management ran high, we sought the cooperation of union representatives so as not to be viewed by workers as agents of, or consultants to, management. Moreover, managers of unionized plants, anxious to avoid disturbing often delicate labor–management relations, almost always stipulated that their cooperation would be contingent on union approval.

All in all, we obtained access to a relatively large and diverse group of manufacturing plants. In each country, our samples include plants of famous multinational companies as well as private, locally owned concerns. In the Indiana survey, we contacted 138 plants, conducted interviews in 55, and obtained both questionniare and interview data from 52.[3] In Japan, we contacted 90 plants, completed interviews in 51, and collected both questionnaire and interview data from 46. In view of the relatively heavy demands we made of these organizations, both in terms of conducting interviews with managers and distributing questionnaires to their employees, these access rates (38 percent in the US; 51 percent in Japan) compare well with previous surveys of manufacturing plants, which typically ask far less of participants (see, e.g., Blau, Falbe, McKinley, and Tracy, 1976). Moreover, some of the plants classified as nonparticipants include those that we rejected as inappropriate for the research.

Nevertheless, these access rates are lower than we would have liked, particularly in the US, and the question arises as to whether the companies that participated in the survey are different on certain dimensions from those who declined. Although one can never be certain, we discerned few systematic characteristics that distinguished the refusing plants. The reasons given by management were usually fairly idiosyncratic: another survey had recently been done; a major reorganization was underway. One factor that did appear to be important was the viability of the company. For example, some of the US plants refused to let us collect data from their workers on company time (which we made a prerequisite for participation after a certain point in the study – see below) because they could not afford to disrupt production, because of tight schedules, and so on. Hence, it is possible that the participating plants were economically healthier and that the work attitudes of their employees were more favorable than those of the employees of companies that refused to participate. Of course, such potential biases plague all of the research designs discussed at the beginning of this chapter; they are simply more visible in our approach.

Data collection

Interviewing key informants

In both countries, the first stage of data collection consisted of an interview with a key informant. This person was generally the plant manager, production manager, head of the general affairs department, or had some combination of these titles. These interviews yielded information on the structure of the plant (for example, its degree of formalization, specialization, centralization, span of control, and so on), its technology, its management practices, basic contextual information such as its size, whether it was an independent company or a branch of a larger corporation, and so on.

The procedures for interviewing key informants differed slightly in the two countries. In the US, once a plant agreed to participate, we set up an appointment to interview the person who was in charge of the plant. In some cases, this was the same individual who had given us permission to conduct the study in the plant. In other cases, we negotiated access to an organization with managers at the division or corporate level, who gave us the name of the appropriate person to interview within a particular plant. In addition, we conducted an interview with the personnel director in each US plant, except in cases where no full-time personnel manager was present. This was desirable, since a single manager is often unable to know what is going on in all parts of the organization. These interviews focused on the plant's personnel policies, such as its training and promotion systems, the types of fringe benefits it provides, and so on. In unionized plants, we also interviewed the union leader regarding the activities of the union.

In Japan, constraints on resources meant that we were able to conduct only a single interview, although persons in addition to the plant manager (e.g. personnel manager, general affairs manager) were generally present and informants who were more knowledgeable than the interviewee were often called in to answer particular sections of the interview schedule. The procedure in Japan was to make an initial visit to the plant to explain the study and to request its cooperation. The interview schedule was then left behind to be filled out by the informant, and members of the Japanese research team returned to the plant a week or two later. During this visit, researchers reviewed managers' responses, and helped them to complete problematic sections.

Whenever possible, we supplemented the interviews with additional information collected in various ways. For example, in the US, key informants also filled out questionnaires that asked them to provide further information on the structure of the plant, and department heads completed questionnaires that elicited data on the structure of their departments. Moreover, in both countries, we were able to arrange plant tours in many of the companies we studied; these tours often provided opportunities for us to ask specific questions regarding operations, technology, employment systems, and other plant structures. We also collected a variety of documents from the plants, such as organization charts, employee handbooks, union contracts, job descriptions and fringe-benefit brochures.

Collecting questionnaire data from employees

We collected information on employees' work attitudes, job situations, and backgrounds from self-administered questionnaires. These were distributed to the employees we sampled in each of the plants. Each questionnaire took approximately one hour to complete and was designed to elicit similar information from respondents in each country.

Our preferred method of questionnaire administration, which we were generally able to follow in the US but not in Japan, was to have workers complete them on company time. (However, in the US as in Japan, supervisors and managers filled out questionnaires on their own time). In the vast majority of cases in the US, we administered questionnaires to workers in a room set aside by the company for our use. At least one or two members of our research team were present at these sessions. The researchers explained to the workers the purpose of the study, assured them that their responses would be kept confidential, and answered any questions they had during the session. Our presence helped to reassure the workers that the study was not conducted by and for management and that their individual responses would be kept confidential. Indeed, one of the most common remarks made by workers during the questionnaire administration sessions was that they hoped that management would not be able to see their answers.

This method of questionnaire collection in the US yielded relatively high response rates (65 percent, overall) at very low cost. We were able to administer questionnaires in this manner in all but eight of our Indianapolis plants. In the plants in which we were not allowed to have workers fill out questionnaires on company time, we resorted to alternative strategies, such as placing a box in the plant where workers returned the questionnaires (in seven cases), or distributing questionnaires at the union hall (one case). In these cases, the response rates were much lower, about 18 percent (219 of 1,233). Once we determined that such alternative methods of data collection resulted in low return rates, we made a plant's participation in the American phase of the study contingent on management allowing us to distribute questionnaires on company time. Of course, this raised the number of refusals and is in part responsible for the lower access rate in the US.

In Japan, on the other hand, questionnaires were administered by management, based on our instructions. We discussed the procedures with a manager (usually the person we interviewed) and gave him the agreed number of questionnaires. He then gave them to first-line supervisors, who distributed and collected them in sealed envelopes that we provided for each respondent. Supervisors then gave them to managers who returned them to us. Employees completed the questionnaires during breaks, slack periods at work, or at home. Because this was a task typically done on the employee's own time, Japanese managers were especially anxious that we not single out some individuals within a work group to complete this extra chore. Despite the unsupervised conditions under which employees filled out questionnaires, the overall response rate from our Japanese sample is excellent (78 percent). Again we encounter a difference between the countries in reaction to our research procedures which itself constitutes an interesting and significant cultural and organizational contrast between the US and Japan.

We have little reason to suspect that the differences in data collection procedures between the US and Japan – necessitated by the exigencies of doing research in business organizations in these two very different societies and by differences in the resources we were able to allocate to each phase of the study – are largely responsible for the country differences we discuss in this book. Similar information on plant structures in the US and Japan was obtained from key informants, despite the differences in the number of interviews conducted in each country. Moreover, it is likely that any bias introduced by the small group settings in which the majority of the US workers filled out their questionnaires is paralleled in Japan by our sampling of existing work groups.

Overview of the sample

In general, the Japanese and US samples of plants and employees are quite diverse in composition within each country yet quite comparable to each other. In this section, we provide a brief overview of the two samples in order to help the reader to better evaluate the nature of the organizations and individuals discussed in subsequent chapters. We summarize: the types of products produced by the plants in our samples; the distribution of respondents by industry, plant size, authority position, and department; and some background characteristics of the plants and employees.

Products

As might be expected from our use of broad, two-digit industry codes to define the populations of organizations, the plants within each of the seven industrial categories manufactured a wide range of products.

In the *transportation equipment* industry, a number of the Japanese plants produced auto parts and several produced parts for buses (seats) and trucks (bodies). In the US, most plants in this industry produced either truck engines, truck brakes or ventilation equipment for trucks. The US sample contained the only final assembly plant in this industry, a truck manufacturer.

In the *electronics and electric equipment* industry, the products manufactured by the Japanese plants included: computers, small appliances, switches, motors, lights, wires, turbines, and copy machines. In the US, plants in this industry produced: color television sets, videodiscs, cable television components, industrial magnets, medical testing equipment, auto speakers, compressors, and telephones.

In Japan, plants in the *chemical* industry produced: pharmaceuticals, cosmetics, linoleum, soap, toothpaste, silicon rings, and film. In the US, plants in this industry produced: rubber tires, maintenance and cleaning materials, noise control plastics, paints, and industrial coatings.

In the *pre-fabricated metals* industry, the Japanese plants produced: bottle tops, screens, pens and mechanical pencils, blinds, aluminum doors, industrial parts, and heat processing equipment. In the US, goods produced by plants in this industry included: iron molds, belt buckles, screens and awnings, auto springs, ventilation equipment, and jeep bodies.

Japanese plants in the *non-electrical machinery* industry produced: die castings, parts for computers, air filtering equipment, gears, valves and other auto parts, and large machines. In the US, plants in this industry produced: fans for farm use, oil drilling equipment, cutting machines, balance machines, elevators, automatic machinery, and industrial pumps.

In the *food processing* industry, Japanese plants produced: sweets, barbecue sauces, breads, noodles, and dairy products. In the US, goods produced by plants in this industry included: frozen foods, milk and ice cream, processed grains such as soybeans, baked foods, delicatessan foods, and flavorings.

Finally, the two Japanese plants in the *printing and publishing* industry produced advertisements for newspapers. The US sample in this industry included newspaper publishers, a book publisher, and a manufacturer of printed packages.

Distribution of plants and respondents by size and industry

Table 2.1 shows the distribution of participating plants and employees within each of the seven industry categories. Within each sample, the largest plants are found in the electronics industry. Moreover, the average size of the US plants (571) is slightly greater than that of the Japanese plants (461). This is representative of the two economies overall, since the percentage of the labor force employed in small- to medium-sized manufacturing enterprises is much higher in Japan than in the US (see Caves and Uekusa, 1976). Because our samples include plants in a range of size categories, we are able to draw fairly general conclusions about the antecedents of work attitudes in different organizational and industrial settings. In contrast, most of the literature on

Table 2.1 *Distribution of plants (respondents) by employment size and industry*

Plant size	Industry							
	Electrical	Chemicals	Metals	Food	Machinery	Transport	Printing	Total
	US							
<100	2	4	4	2	0	0	1	13
	(148)	(75)	(91)	(89)			(24)	(427)
100–999	3	4	2	7	7	4	6	33
	(342)	(433)	(60)	(529)	(581)	(848)	(420)	(3,213)
1,000–1,999	2	0	0	0	0	1	0	3
	(270)					(35)		(305)
2,000+	2	0	0	0	0	1	0	3
	(376)					(244)		(620)
Total	9	8	6	9	7	6	7	52
	(1,136)	(508)	(153)	(618)	(581)	(1,127)	(444)	(4,567)
	Japan							
<100	0	1	1	1	0	0	0	3
		(70)	(40)	(62)				(172)
100–999	4	5	6	5	7	5	2	36
	(339)	(420)	(577)	(297)	(527)	(294)	(102)	(2,556)
1,000–1,999	2	0	0	0	1	1		5
	(265)				(148)			(413)
2,000+	2	0	0	0	0	0	0	2
	(311)							(311)
Total	9	6	8	7	8	6	2	46
	(888)	(490)	(706)	(455)	(651)	(442)	(102)	(3,735)

Note: Columns and rows may not sum to totals due to missing data

Japanese work organizations deals primarily with very large companies, which are most likely to abide by the permanent employment norm and other well-known Japanese employment practices.

The distributions of plants and employees among size and industry categories are fairly comparable in the two samples. The two industries in which marked discrepancies occur are: (a) the number of plants and respondents in printing and publishing, a relatively under-represented industry in the Atsugi area; and (b) the number of respondents in prefabricated metals, an industry in which the US plants were quite small.

Distribution of respondents by authority level and functional area

Table 2.2 indicates that the distributions of respondents by functional classification and authority level are also reasonably comparable in the two countries. With respect to authority level, a key difference is that more than

Table 2.2 *Distribution of respondents by management position and functional area*

	Management position			
Functional area	Manager	Supervisor	Worker	Total
US				
Production	64	278	2,788	3,130
Technical support	69	127	761	1,000
Office	72	29	111	209
Total	234	472	3,861	4,567
Japan				
Production	86	519	1,875	2,499
Technical support	52	169	337	630
Office	83	128	339	498
Total	253	835	2,602	3,735

Note: Columns and rows may not sum to totals due to missing data

twice as many Japanese as American employees are supervisors. This, however, is consistent, we believe, with the status distributions of Japanese and US plants more generally. The higher proportion in supervisory positions may reflect the taller hierarchies of Japanese plants (see chapter 7) and the operation of the *nenko* system which, in step with age and seniority, regularly moves employees into higher-ranking positions.

Our functional classification divides the labor force into direct production, technical support, and office staff areas within the plant. These are the key departmental and (broadly conceived) occupational divisions that characterize manufacturing plants. Production employees are hourly workers and line managers and supervisors engaged in the performance or supervision of direct production work. Technical support departments include those employed in maintenance, machine shop, materials control, production engineering, and similar functions involved with the maintenance and support of production. Most truly skilled blue-collar jobs in manufacturing fall into this group. Finally, office employees include those in staff departments such as accounting, marketing, and personnel.

Consistent with our earlier discussion of sampling criteria, table 2.2 indicates that the proportion of employees in direct production departments is by far the largest in each country, followed by technical and office employees. The proportions of each sample in production are very similar: 69 percent in

Japan and 73 percent in the US. However, the division of the remainder into technical and office jobs is somewhat different: 22 percent of the US employees are in the former and 5 percent are in the latter category. In Japan, the respective proportions are 17 percent and 14 percent.

Background characteristics of plants and employees

There are other respects in which our samples of plants and employees are quite comparable. The workforce samples in both countries are heavily unionized, with 71 percent of the Americans and 78 percent of the Japanese employed in plants where labor–management contracts were in effect. On the other hand, more of the Japanese *plants* (71 percent) are unionized than the US plants (56 percent). The higher proportion of unionized Japanese plants reflects the higher rates of union membership in Japan generally: in 1982, about 31 percent of Japan's labor force was unionized, compared to about 20 percent of the US labor force. Moreover, less than 30 percent of the plants in each sample are independent companies, with the US sample slightly more likely to be branch plants or subsidiaries. We also note that the plants in each country have remarkably similar technologies, whether measured by the Woodward indicators of production technology or by our indicators of automation (see chapter 7).

The differences between the employee samples are generally consistent with our knowledge of the composition of the labor force in Japan and the US (see table 5.1). The lower labor force participation of Japanese women shows up in the lower proportion of women than in the US sample (16 percent vs. 27 percent). This reflects primarily differences in the proportion of women supervisors (.11 in US; .02 in Japan) and workers (.30 in US; .22 in Japan); the proportion of women managers is very low in both countries (.06 in US; .04 in Japan). The inclusion of a sizeable number of women in our samples overcomes a major limitation of previous studies of US–Japanese differences in work attitudes, which have been generally restricted to men (e.g. Cole, 1979).

The employees in our US sample are about 3.5 years older on the average than those in the Japanese sample. The average age of managers is the same in both countries (43), though American workers (38 vs. 33) and supervisors (43 vs. 39) are older than the Japanese. As noted earlier, we attribute these age differences between the samples primarily to the higher unemployment rates in the US at the time of the survey and the fact that layoffs (usually of workers with low seniority) had taken place at a number of our US plants. This difference in average age, moreover, helps explain the unexpectedly small difference we find between the samples in tenure with the employer. Another noteworthy finding is that the levels of schooling of the Japanese and US employees in our samples are almost identical, the average respondent having completed "some high school." Finally, the US employees are slightly more likely to be married.

Problems in cross-cultural measurement

Cross-cultural studies are beset by comparability problems in the measurement of concepts, and some discussion of those problems is mandatory here. As Form (1979:3) has aptly noted, "[p]robably no field has generated more methodological advice on a smaller data base with fewer results than has comparative sociology." It is indeed true that while comparative research itself remains an altogether far too scarce commodity, there has been no shortage of articles and chapters that: "enumerate the pitfalls of comparative analysis and suggest elaborate strategies to avoid them. Most investigators, however, have found this advice too general, abstract, and demanding to be useful." A dysfunctional consequence of the plethora of published criticism of comparative methodology is that it may have deterred capable investigators from giving it a try. This is an outcome, to our way of thinking, for which the state of social science is much the worse. While the obstacles to careful comparative research are severe, they are hardly unique. In numerous ways, such problems also manifest themselves in studies limited to a single country, though they tend not to attract the attention and concern evoked in the context of comparative work.

One obvious problem in cross-national research that is less likely to arise in studies limited to one country is that posed by language differences. As discussed in a number of useful accounts (Elder, 1976; Form, 1979; Przeworski and Teune, 1970; Straus, 1969), the necessity to translate measurement instruments from one language into another poses a significant threat to the validity of comparative research designs, as substantive differences between countries become confounded with measurement incongruencies. The translation problem has two dimensions. *Literal exactness*, to use Elder's (1976) term, refers to the mere existence of literally equivalent words in different languages. The larger problem, however, is *conceptual equivalence*. Terms such as job satisfaction or organizational commitment may have literal equivalents but evoke such divergent images and understandings that the result is a substantial degree of cross-cultural noncomparability. Literal exactness provides no guarantee of conceptual equivalence.

The problem of linguistic equivalence probably looms largest in the circumstance of a (typically Western) investigator attempting to implement a set of measurement operations normed and tested in his or her home country in another linguistic and cultural setting wherein such measurements and the concepts they tap are wholly foreign. In that regard, the path to a valid Japan–US comparison of survey findings is strewn with fewer hazards than it might at first appear. Despite the dramatically different linguistic structures of Japanese and English, a study of the sort we conducted is greatly facilitated by the Japanese people's long experience with attitude surveys, many of which address the same themes of work motivation and commitment which lie at the heart of our own concerns (Office of the Prime Minister, 1973; 1984).

Most of the attitude and value items used in our study have been translated back and forth between English and Japanese on numerous occasions, and it is likely that most significant problems of conceptual nonequivalence have by now been ironed out.[4]

Moreover, our data analysis itself can provide substantial clues as to whether measurement items couched in Japanese and English are in fact tapping equivalent concepts. As Przeworksi and Teune (1970) discuss, the similarity or dissimilarity of a *pattern* of relationships among variables can provide strong signals as to the equivalence and validity of measures across cultural settings. If a set of survey items designed to tap the same underlying concepts (e.g. commitment and satisfaction) in two countries: (a) displays the same pattern of intercorrelations in each; and (b) that pattern supports the researcher's hypothesis of underlying concepts; then, (c) we are on fairly solid ground in concluding that the items are equivalent and valid. To foreshadow our work in the next chapter, this is the procedure we follow in deriving operational definitions of organizational commitment and job satisfaction in our Japanese and US samples. We estimate a confirmatory factor model specifying that these two latent concepts operate similarly to explain the variation in a set of items in the US and Japan. This makes the strong assumption that the factor loadings are identical across the two samples. To the extent that our data are consistent with this assumption, we will have satisfied ourselves that, language problems notwithstanding, we have achieved comparable measurement in the US and Japan.

Apart from the issue of measurement equivalance, there is the possibility that cultural differences may produce societally-specific response biases which again thwart valid comparison. These include biases wherein individuals systematically adjust their responses to conform to generalized notions of social desirability or perceptions of an investigator's expectations (Elder, 1976). Such biases are often correlated with the variables a researcher seeks to measure. For example, it seems quite likely that commitment to an employer might evoke a tendency to bias report of organizational properties so as to cast the firm in a favorable light. The possibility of such biases underscores the importance of collecting data on organizational structures independently of information on employees' reactions to them, procedures we have followed in this study.

In constructing our questionnaire attitude items, we took precautions to offset one kind of potentially troublesome response bias in contrasting the US and Japan. An apparent manifestation of Japanese collectivism and Western individualism is a tendency for Japanese respondents to give average or noncommital answers, while Anglo–American respondents are somewhat more prone to take strong, even extreme stands on issues (Dore, 1973:232). Many of our attitude items use the standard Likert-scale response codes of "strongly agree, agree, undecided, disagree, strongly disagree." We were seriously concerned that the Japanese in our sample would concentrate their responses in the neutral range of the scale: undecided and the weaker degrees of agreement and disagreement. To offset this tendency, we expanded the number of response codes in the Likert-scaled items on the Japanese question-naire from five to seven by including "slightly agree" and "slightly disagree."

There is finally the epistemologically troublesome question of whether cultural factors shaping work attitudes constitute biases in the sense that individuals over- or underreport their true feelings, or whether there can be in fact genuine societal differences in feeling states. Dore (1973:218) seems to take the latter view:

> There is also involved, perhaps, a difference in culture or average personality, a difference on a dimension which has cheerfulness and good-humored complacency at one pole and a worried earnestness and anxious questing for self-improvement at the other. That such national differences do exist seems clear from a comparison of the results of various surveys of professed 'job satisfaction' carried out in a number of countries. At all occupational levels from professional to unskilled workers, Germans are less likely to say that they were satisfied with their work than Americans or Norwegians.

The "dispositional" perspective on job attitudes is a social psychological framework which allows for the possibility of genuine cultural differences in feeling states toward work and employment. Staw, Bell, and Clausen (1986) argue that many of the findings from job attitude research testify that individuals' job satisfaction is surprisingly invariant across a range of specific task and employment situations. This suggests that persons bring to the job a particular configuration of expectations and feeling states which color their subjective work experiences as much or perhaps more than the objective features of the job itself. Although fundamental personality differences having genetic roots may be one source of these psychological dispositions, clearly another is the socialization process which instills in individuals the values, beliefs, and predilections of a culture and society. In chapter 5, we explore in some detail the effects of cultural values and personal background character-istics (e.g. age, gender, marital status) as "dispositional" sources of individual differences in work attitudes.

The alternative interpretation, of course, is that dispositional factors such as culture and personality do not shape underlying attitudes so much as they affect how individuals report them. Blauner (1960), for example, has argued that the tendency of US workers to rate their job satisfaction high is in fact a form of response bias; i.e. cultural pressures in the US induce individuals to color positively their reports of job experiences. The distinction between cultural differences in underlying feeling states, on the one hand, and how they are publicly portrayed, on the other, can become a very fine one. It is much like the distinction we drew earlier between commitment as a deep-felt experience of individuals and as a normative orientation of groups. When dominant cultural values define a behavior or state as one that should be regarded positively, many persons will come to see it that way.

Summary

The obstacles to high-quality comparative survey research are numerous and formidable. They are made more so in the present research, since our paramount concern is to link the job attitudes and experiences of individual employees to the organizational and technical structures of the workplace. A variety of research designs offer particular advantages and disadvantages for studying work life and job experiences, whether comparative in focus or not. These include: the household survey methodology in which individuals in a region are interviewed as to their work histories and job attitudes and, upon occasion, the management and structure of the firm that employs them; and case studies of the kind conducted by Dore (1973) and Marsh and Mannari (1976) that focus on particular Japanese workplaces and the social structures and behavior patterns of the employees who inhabit them.

We use a third research design in this study: a representative sampling of employing organizations in each of two countries, followed by a survey of a sample of employees *within* each establishment. This organization-based, two-stage research design is uniquely tailored to an inquiry into the relations between the organizational structures and employment systems of manufacturing plants and their employees' work attitudes and behaviors. Our large samples of plants and employees and our independent measurement of the characteristics of each mean that we can effectively address a variety of research topics pertaining to the interplay between work organizations and individual workers at varying levels of analysis. First and foremost, we are well positioned to examine how industrial and organizational attributes condition employees' work attitudes. In addition, we can investigate how work structures such as authority positions, departments and features of the work situation generate variations internal to plants. Moreover, we can study how organizational structures are related to each other in the US as well as Japan. We will report the results of our analyses of these multi-level issues in subsequent chapters. In the next chapter, we provide an overview of Japanese–American differences in commitment and satisfaction, the main dependent variables with which we are concerned in this book.

3 Commitment and job satisfaction in the US and Japan

As we have noted on several occasions thus far, Japanese employees are widely perceived to be extraordinarily committed to their work roles and their employing organizations. Most Americans have heard that labor militancy, absenteeism, and turnover are unusually low in Japan. Japanese workers put in considerable overtime without extra pay, they spend time socializing with coworkers away from their families long after work hours, and they tend not to take advantage of all the vacation and leave time to which they are rightfully entitled (Cole, 1971:231). We also know of the worldwide reputation of Japanese goods for high-quality workmanship, and have seen numerous articles on small group activities in Japanese industry wherein workers volunteer to participate in group meetings on their own time for the purpose of upgrading quality and productivity. The picture of the Japanese worker that emerges from these reports is that of someone totally committed to the workplace and who derives major life satisfaction from work activities and work associations. Surely the Japanese worker finds fulfillment through work involvement to a degree rarely matched in the West.

At the same time, the once strong belief that the work ethic is central to American culture and that motivation and commitment to work account for the dominance of the United States as an industrial power have eroded over the years (Cole, 1979:227). Mass media accounts and scholarly writings alike have argued that the inability of individuals to find meaning and satisfaction through work and workplace associations is a source of considerable strain and malaise in modern American society (US Department of HEW, 1972). These writings emphasize a variety of consequences of this shift: declines in product quality and the competitiveness of American goods in world markets; high levels of absenteeism, turnover, and conflict on the job; reports of drug use and alcoholism; and the mid-life disillusionment and high stress lives of executives. Social scientists have focused in particular on the alienating and demeaning character of many American jobs, and the resultant preoccupation with consumerism and leisure. Though there are counter themes as well – entrepreneurism (particularly in high-tech industries) is presumed alive and flourishing and workaholism is accepted as the price of a yuppie lifestyle – fulfillment through and dedication to work and work organizations are themes that seem to be ebbing from American culture.

An obvious reason for the considerable interest in the question of organizational commitment and loyalty among Japanese manufacturing employees is the presumption that it plays a part in the extraordinarily high levels of labor productivity which the Japanese economy has attained. Many of the efforts by journalists and scholars to explain Japan's phenomenal postwar economic success emphasize the diligence and devotion of the Japanese workforce. The rise of this view complements the growing conviction that the work ethic has declined in the US and that a lack of labor-management cooperation has become a serious impediment to US economic growth and worldwide competitiveness.

Are Japanese employees more committed to their work roles and their employing organizations than their American counterparts? Are American workers less satisfied with their jobs and work lives than the Japanese? We address these questions in this chapter. First, we review the existing research evidence on employee work attitudes and behaviors in Japan and the US. We then explore what our own data have to say on the question of whether Japanese employees are more committed to work and organization than US workers and whether significant country differences exist in other subjective orientations to work. We will see that the answers to these questions are less clear than we might have hoped, and depend on our assumptions about the nature of biases in our measures of these concepts and on the patterns of causation among them.

Accounting for Japan's productivity edge

Structural explanations

In order to understand the role of workforce commitment in accounting for societal differences in economic productivity, we need to recognize that the complex and multifaceted antecedents of labor productivity cannot be reduced to monocausal explanations such as how hard people work. Indeed, few of the explanations of the Japanese productivity advantage stress, at least directly, differences between Japan and the United States in the attitudes and motivations of workers. Instead, many of them focus on structural differences in the economies of the two countries, on the role of government, and on the profitability and growth strategies of high-level management. These accounts, which for years now have filled the pages of the business press, are wide ranging. Some, like the "Japan, Inc." perspective, look to the cooperative relations between government agencies such as MITI and major corporations in Japan, contrasting them with the conflict that often seems to characterize relations between US firms and government regulatory agencies (Johnson, 1982; Thurow, 1985). Other explanations at the level of macro political economy likewise stress Japan's high savings rates, its less volatile stock markets, and the close ties between commercial banks and manufacturers (Wallich and Wallich, 1976). All of these create a large pool of investment capital at low interest rates that is available to major Japanese firms for financing corporate investments. The higher rate of Japan's capital investment, in turn, has been argued to account for the Japanese advantage in manufacturing productivity (Norsworthy and Malmquist, 1983).

Another currently popular explanation stresses the long-term growth orientation of Japanese managers who are willing to forego short-run profits in exchange for a greater share of the market and greater investment in plant and equipment. American managers' obsession with short-term profitability, it is argued, has led to underinvestment in plant and equipment and a diversion of capital out of manufacturing and into service and financial industries. The relative absence of merger and acquisition activity in Japan and the greater tendency of Japanese manufacturing firms to remain specialized in manufacturing have meant greater commitment on the part of their managers to seeing those industries succeed (Abegglen and Stalk, 1985; Clark, 1979). Part of this explanation stresses the differences in the training and background of American and Japanese managers of manufacturing firms: high-level American executives are often specialists in staff functions such as finance and marketing, and thus have little direct experience in the actual production of goods; while top Japanese executives are more often drawn from the ranks of engineering and operations management (Thurow, 1985).

At a less macro level, the shop-floor organization of the Japanese factory and its high level of coordination with suppliers have provided Japanese plants with a substantial efficiency advantage over American plants (Abegglen and Stalk, 1985; Hayes and Wheelwright, 1984; Schonberger, 1982). Small, tightly controlled inventories are achieved by requiring suppliers to make deliveries at the moment they are needed. "Just-in-time" production systems regulate the flow of parts and materials from supplier to manufacturer and from inventory to work stations on the shop floor, so as to minimize waste and inefficiency and thus achieve significant cost reductions. The efficiency and precision of Japanese manufacturing have provided a sharp counterpoint to US production practices which, until recently at least, had been characterized by large inventories, slack scheduling, high scrap and defect rates, and other serious deficiencies.

A "commitment gap"?

These structural explanations suggest that the growth and productivity of the Japanese economy rest on patterns of savings and investment, industrial organization, and production management which have no direct link to worker motivation and commitment. The alternative explanation for Japan's industrial growth and productivity – and the only one our research can directly assess – is that a "commitment gap" separates the workforce of Japan from that of the United States. From this perspective, the secret to Japanese productivity lies in the quality and discipline of Japanese labor which, in turn, derives from a deep commitment to work tasks and employing organizations.

It is extremely difficult to quantify the contribution that labor discipline makes to industrial productivity. Yet the conclusion that worker discipline and motivation play a role in productivity seems inescapable. It is impossible to separate fully the technical, financial, and political forces discussed above from the roles of social and psychological factors such as motivation, commitment, and cohesion. As Cole (1979:225) has suggested, Japan's high savings rate may, in part, be a function of the Japanese work ethic which weighs diligence and frugality above leisure and consumption. Japanese managers' apparent preference for long-term corporate growth over short-term financial performance may well have roots in strong career commitments to a single firm. An obsession with short-term results figures importantly in American managers' strategy of career advancement through a succession of upward moves across divisions or corporations (Ouchi, 1981). Moreover, the impressive control of scheduling, inventories, and workflow processes evidenced in the Japanese plant reflects a Japanese talent for orchestrating organizational functions and responsibilities in a highly harmonious and finely-tuned fashion (Schonberger, 1982). On the other hand, a convincing case can be made that many of the problems of American manufacturing are traceable to certain individualistic and divisive tendencies endemic to Western culture.

Yet unless it can be demonstrated that a commitment gap in favor of the Japanese does indeed exist, the question of whether the productivity of the Japanese economy stems in part from the attitudes and values of Japanese workers is moot. Two kinds of evidence might be brought to bear on the commitment gap hypothesis: (1) behavioral indicators of absenteeism, turnover, time worked, strike rates, and the like; (2) work attitude surveys in Japan and other countries which query employees about their values and motives for working. We suggest that the widespread impression of a strong Japanese work ethic and high commitment to the company rests mostly on the former, behavioral, evidence. On that basis, the case for a commitment gap seems formidable. Japanese workers put in more time on the job per week than American workers (43 vs. 37 hours – in 1982; Keizai Koho Center, 1987); unexcused absenteeism is generally so low as to seem nonexistent (Sengoku, 1985); strike activity is lower in Japan than in the US (though not so low as in other countries such as Germany, for example: Koike, 1978); and unions cooperate with management in achieving corporate goals and in carrying out company programs (Hanami, 1979). Moreover, separation rates are far lower in Japan than the United States, as are job shifts that involve employer changes (Cole, 1979; Mincer and Higuchi, 1987).

Such data offer strong testimony that the behavior of Japanese workers differs in significant ways from that of American workers. However, they do not explain that behavior. In our discussion of the dimensions of commitment in chapter 1, we distinguished between normative/institutional and attitudinal/individual forms of commitment. The low strike rates, long hours spent on the job, low turnover, and similar behavior patterns may simply reflect institutional and normative arrangements which leave individuals little choice but to comply (see Kamata, 1983). Individual Japanese workers with a taste for leisure and the flexibility to change employers face far more imposing barriers to the realization of these values than Americans typically do. It is not at all clear that these behaviors are simple reflections of individuals' positive sentiments toward work and workplace.

Large-scale labor force surveys, on the other hand, can provide evidence on employees' feelings, preferences, and values as distinct from the institutional and social arrangements that constrain individuals' choices. Of course, surveys pose their own considerable problems of interpretation, as we have discussed (chapter 2). One can never know for certain whether a worker's response to a questionnaire or interview item reflects his or her "true" feelings; what the worker really means. In cross-national research, differences in self-expression become even more problematic, since cultural biases may distort our conclusions about the beliefs and sentiments prevalent in a population. The Japanese, for example, are uncomfortable with overt expressions of credit or praise, and appear humble and modest when called upon to characterize themselves and their accomplishments. In contrast, as the cheerleader enthusiasm of the Reagan administration recently underscores, Americans are given to ebullience and optimism, eager to cast themselves as the best and the brightest, and often petulant when foreigners view them as peers. Such cross-national differences in proclivities for under- or over-statement can greatly complicate the task of discovering genuine differences in work orientations and may be impossible to control completely.

Despite their limitations, surveys may be the best way to obtain data on work attitudes and other individual-level outcomes for a large and diverse group of employees. They are particularly useful in comparisons of the US and Japan, for the populations of both countries are frequently polled regarding their attitudes, opinions, and values on a wide range of social, political, and economic issues (Office of the Prime Minister, 1973; 1984). Unfortunately, relatively few surveys have been specifically designed to make explicit comparisons between Japanese and Western workers and, without data on similarly formed questions presented to similarly selected samples, comparisons between the countries are difficult to make. We first examine results from available survey data to see what they tell us about the work attitudes of Japanese and Western workers.

Japanese–American differences in work attitudes: past research

Commitment to work and the organization

We have argued in earlier chapters for a distinction between commitment to work itself and commitment to an employing organization. Work commitment pertains to the importance of work in one's life – the extent to which it constitutes a central life interest (see chapter 5). It is a general value orientation, prioritizing work in relation to other life activities and identities, among them: family time, religious devotion, and recreation (see Dubin, 1956; Loscocco, 1985). Organizational commitment, in contrast, refers to the degree to which one participates in and identifies with a particular employing organization and is consequently motivated to act on its behalf (Halaby, 1986)

We have asserted that the Japanese are clearly more committed both to work tasks and their employing organizations as attested by behavioral indicators such as absenteeism, hours worked, strike activity, and turnover. A number of work attitude surveys suggest the same. Cole (1979:230), for example, notes that diligence is the national character trait the Japanese most often ascribe to themselves in national sample surveys. Another study surveyed 300 Westerners living in Tokyo in 1978 (see Foreign Press Center, 1980). Asked to rate the Japanese on scales of eagerness in work and loyalty to the company, nearly 84 percent of the respondents viewed them as "very" or "somewhat" hard working, while 83 percent saw the Japanese as loyal to their companies.

Several questionnaire items in Takezawa and Whitehill's (1981) survey of workers in two large plants in Japan and the US produced responses that suggested both greater commitment to work and identification with the company in Japan. A far higher percentage of the Japanese (73 percent) than the Americans (21 percent) rated their company lives as equal to or greater in importance than their personal lives. A second question asked what the worker would do if the company experienced a prolonged decline in business and they had the opportunity to take a job with a more prosperous company. While 36 percent of the Americans said they would quit and take the new job, only 5 percent of the Japanese gave this response. Another question blended the issues of work-group cohesion, work motivation, and job specialization: 49 percent of the Japanese vs. 16 percent of the Americans felt it was desirable for their coworkers to "work at maximum capacity, without endangering their health, helping others when their own tasks are completed." While this finding is suggestive, it is hard to interpret given the mix of issues to which the worker was asked to respond. Are the differences due to: (a) the greater work motivation of the Japanese?; (b) their greater willingness to work cooperatively in groups?; or (c) their greater willingness to take on work outside their job areas?

Yet other evidence raises questions about the work commitment of

Japanese *vis-à-vis* US employees. In his survey of Detroit and Yokohama residents, Cole (1979:234) asked three questions pertaining to worker diligence and motivation: (1) how often do you work harder than your employer or supervisor requires?; (2) how often do you get so wrapped up in your work that you lose track of time?; and (3) how often do you spend some time thinking of ways you can do your job better? Summing the three items to produce a composite index, he found the mean of the index to be significantly *lower* in Yokohama than in Detroit, indicating that the Japanese workers were less committed to work than their Detroit counterparts.

The studies of Japanese workers by Odaka (1975:146) and Marsh and Mannari (1976:113) also cast doubt on the presumption that work absorption and commitment are extraordinarily high among the Japanese. In the five Japanese companies he studied, Odaka found that the percentage of employees answering "work" to the question "what makes life worth living?" ranged from 6–14 percent. In contrast, 25–47 percent answered "leisure" and 36–56 percent reported "home." Similarly, Marsh and Mannari's survey of 1,591 workers in two Japanese factories found that only 27 percent of their respondents agreed with the statement that "work is my whole life, more important than anything else."

Finally, a recent comparative survey of Japanese, US, and British manufacturing workers found more Japanese (24 percent) than US workers (14 percent) reporting that they would prefer idleness to work if they were "rich enough to live a comfortable life" (Sengoku, 1985:116).

A possible interpretation of these findings is that the evident behavioral commitment of Japanese employees stems, not from their devotion to work itself, but rather to the organization as a whole (Cole, 1979:241). Yet some of the existing evidence is at odds with this view as well: Dore (1973:216) found only 39 percent of his sample of Hitachi employees willing to characterize their firm as a "good employer," as compared to 71 percent and 89 percent of workers in two British plants. In response to Takezawa and Whitehill's (1981:200) questionnaire item: "I believe workers are willing to work hard on their jobs because...", 34 percent of the Japanese vs. 17 percent of the Americans answered that "they want to live up to the expectations of their family, friends, and society." More than half of the Americans (53 percent) and 46 percent of the Japanese gave the response suggesting greater organizational commitment: "they feel it is their responsibility to the company and to coworkers to do whatever work is assigned them." Finally, a comparison of a survey of employed Japanese men with a national survey of Americans also produced evidence contrary to the hypothesis of greater organizational commitment in Japan. On an interview item measuring the employee's pride in the firm, the US respondents averaged slightly higher (i.e. more proud) scores than the Japanese (Naoi and Schooler, 1985:55).

In sum, the available evidence from work attitude surveys hardly offers clear and consistent support for the picture painted by "hard," behavioral, indicators (absenteeism, turnover, and strike rates) of a Japanese workforce which values work over other life pursuits, is motivated to work hard at all times, and works in order to advance the goals and interests of the company. While some studies produce evidence of high levels of diligence and commitment among the Japanese, others suggest that work is not the only thing on Japanese workers' minds (Leung, 1986). Likewise, past research suggests that their reasons for working are not always loyalty to, and identification with, the company, but may arise from more general familial and community concerns.

Job satisfaction

From the abundant behavioral evidence of high discipline and low alienation (in the sense of low militancy, turnover, and shirking) in the Japanese labor force, it is a short leap to the conclusion that job satisfaction and worker morale must be higher in Japan than in the United States. Yet a striking finding which has appeared with remarkable consistency in comparative survey research on industrial attitudes is that the levels of job satisfaction reported by the Japanese are lower than in the Western industrialized countries. Whether the workers studied are blue collar or white collar, whether employed in manufacturing or service industries, the Japanese respond to questionnaires and interviews that they are less content with their jobs and work lives than Americans and Europeans. For example, a Japanese government-sponsored survey of youth in England, West Germany, France, the United States, Switzerland, Sweden, Yugoslavia, India, and the Philippines found job satisfaction to be lowest in Japan: 60 percent as compared to 82 percent in the United States (Office of the Prime Minister, 1973). Other national surveys of the Japanese have likewise shown the percentage of workers who say they are satisfied with their jobs running at 50–60 percent, as compared with consistent findings of over 80 percent satisfied in the US. In a study of 3000 manufacturing workers in two Japanese plants, Odaka (1975) found that 45 percent were satisfied with their jobs. Azumi and McMillan's (1975) survey of Japanese, British, and Swedish workers in 12 plants in each country found only 39 percent of the Japanese to be satisfied with their jobs as contrasted with 70 percent of the British and 83 percent of the Swedish workers (see also, Azumi and McMillan, 1976). Additional comparisons of Japanese and American workers by Pascale and Maguire (1980) and Naoi and Schooler (1985) also show the Japanese to be significantly less satisfied with their jobs.

Many of these studies apparently used a direct question, such as "are you satisfied with your job?", to assess country differences in job satisfaction. One might suspect that subtle differences in the Japanese and English meanings of "job" and "satisfaction" contribute to the differences in reported levels of satisfaction. Indeed, the Japanese word for satisfaction (*manzoku*) may connote fulfillment or completion to a greater degree than the English word does. However, Cole's (1979) survey of probability samples of Detroit and Yokohama workers posed the question of whether the respondent would take the same job again, a commonly used measure of job satisfaction that tends to elicit lower levels of satisfaction than the direct measure (see Kalleberg, 1974, for a discussion). Cole found that 54 percent of the Detroit respondents would do the same work again vs. 33 percent of the Yokohama residents. Another indirect question yielded similar results: 71 percent of those in Detroit would have recommended the job to a friend as compared to no more than 44 percent of the Yokohama respondents.

Cole (1979:238) argues that the lower satisfaction of the Japanese is to be expected given the high value they tend to place on work activities. Noting that psychological theories of work attitudes have long held that satisfaction falls as expectations for work fulfillment rise, he suggests that it is precisely because the Japanese subscribe to a strong work ethic that they are less likely to feel that their expectations have been met. German workers, too, have been found to report relatively low job satisfaction, and Germany, like Japan, is a country where the workforce is commonly perceived to be highly disciplined, dedicated, and diligent (Inkeles, 1960). This explanation suggests that low satisfaction should be coupled with high commitment: high motivation and a willingness to invest heavily in the fortunes of a work organization are attributes of employees who want more from their work lives and the employment relationship than they presently believe they are getting. Evidence on such unmet expectations is provided by a survey conducted by the Youth Research Institute of the Japanese Prime Minister's Office (Office of the Prime Minister, 1973) specifically comparing Japanese, US, and English workers: while 78 percent of the American workers and 73 percent of the British indicated that the expectations they had when they started working had been generally fulfilled, only 51 percent of the Japanese said so. Evidence to the contrary, however, appears in Haire, Ghiselli, and Porter's (1966) finding that the Japanese scored no lower than managers from other industrial countries on a series of explicit indicators of work life need satisfaction. Such measures were designed to tap the congruence between an employee's work aspirations and the degree to which these were perceived to be fulfilled.

We find it hard to avoid the suspicion that problems of cross-cultural measurement are implicated in this research. It seems doubtful that job satisfaction is truly as low in the Japanese workforce as the attitude surveys suggest. Rather, as we discussed in the last chapter, there would appear to be cultural biases operating to generate overly positive assessments of work life on the part of American employees and understatements by the Japanese (e.g. Blauner, 1960; Dore, 1973:218). A study by Lincoln, Hanada, and Olson (1981) found a clear pattern in a sample of employees from the same 28 US-based Japanese-owned firms: Japanese nationals expressed lowest job satisfaction; Americans highest; and Japanese–Americans (a prominent group in Japanese-owned companies in the US) fell in between. Since these nationality groups were employed in the same organizations, hence were exposed to similar organizational structures and operations technologies, the conclusion seems inescapable that cultural dispositions produced the observed group differences in job satisfaction (see also Kelley and Reeser, 1973). Indeed, the middle position of the Japanese–American respondents strongly suggests that something about Japanese culture – in which they presumably were immersed to a degree intermediate between the Japanese nationals and the other US employees – prompted lower satisfaction ratings.

In sum, the available evidence from work attitude surveys does not provide clear and consistent support for the picture painted by the behavioral evidence on Japanese and US work patterns. With these results from past research in mind, we turn to an examination of our own data.

Commitment and satisfaction: initial comparisons

Work commitment

We first consider the question of work commitment, or the extent to which an individual values work over other life activities. The concept of work commitment, unlike those of organizational commitment and job satisfaction, does not evoke an image of a *specific* job or employer, and we conceptualize it as a *value orientation*. Consistent with our multilevel model of the determinants of work attitudes (see figure 1), then, we view work commitment as causally antecedent to organizational commitment and job satisfaction in the subsequent analysis of chapter 5.

Table 3.1 presents the distributions of responses to the three work commitment items for the US and Japanese samples.[1]

On the first item, the Japanese seem to be less committed to work than the Americans: they are more likely to agree that they have other activities that are more important than work. On the remaining two items, however, the pattern reverses. The Americans are more likely to agree that work represents but a small part of "who they are",[2] and far more likely to rate their family lives as more important than their work lives. The lower work commitment expressed by the Japanese to the "other activities" item may reflect the fact that many of their off-the-job activities involve interactions with coworkers and participation in company-sponsored functions. These may be defined as nonwork pursuits, even though they involve work life associations that are instrumental to getting work done.

The item comparing work to family life elicits the largest difference between employees in the two countries. There has been much discussion of changing values in Japan in which home and family concerns are believed to be replacing work and company activities as a central life interest, with dangerous negative implications for Japan's productivity and competitive posture in the world (Vogel, 1963). As Dore amusingly (1973:212) puts it:

> *(M)ai-homu-shugi* or "my-home-ism"... refers to the "privatized" concerns of the man of small ambition – chiefly concerned to get a pretty little house and a pretty little wife and two model children, to have a colour TV and a cooler and to join the ranks of *maikaa-zoku*, the "my car tribe." ... there are many Japanese, too, for whom my-homeism is an object of contempt ... It is a renunciation of masculine ambition, a lapse into reprehensible hedonism, a menace to that capacity for vigorous dedication to causes greater than one's family which in the past made Mitsubishi great and in consequence made Japan great.

"My-homeism" does not yet appear to pose a serious threat to the Japanese work ethic, as only 35 percent of our Japanese sample (vs. 70 percent of the Americans) rate family life as more important than work responsibilities. Another question in our survey likewise demonstrates the lower priority assigned to family life in Japan. To the statement, "when I work late or on holidays, my family complains," 61 percent of the Japanese disagreed as compared to 47 percent of the Americans. These results are in line with what most observers have found concerning the work and family roles of Japanese men. Expected to support their families and to set an example of responsibility and diligence, the actual amount of time they spend with family members and in family pursuits remains quite small. Americans, however, rate family and home life as top priorities and invest much effort and time in family activities. Hence, while less than a third of the Americans say that "other activities" outweigh work in importance, fully 70 percent regard family life as more important than work. It would seem that family time is less likely to occur to American respondents as an "other activity" taking precedence over work responsibilities.[3]

The tendency for Japanese employees to value work over family to a greater extent than employees in the US is consistent with the hypothesis that work commitment runs deeper in Japan. But it may seem at odds with the Japanese firm's fabled responsiveness to family needs and values, as in: marriage and family size adjustments to wages; welfare services available to family members; and, in the attention the company pays to family crises and joyous events such as death and childbirth. Yet the apparent inconsistency has its logic. To quote Dore (1973:210) again:

> The (Japanese) firm's recognition of the fact that their workers are not just individual sellers of labour, but also family men, is two-edged. The British system sharply separates the man's role as employee from his role as husband and father, and the firm disclaims responsibility for, or jurisdiction over, the latter. The Japanese firm, by contrast, admits a concern for both, but where there is a possibility of conflict requires – to some degree at least – the subordination of the family role. The fact that a man had planned to take his children for an outing would be seen as a rather "selfish" reason for trying to avoid overtime work on a Sunday if an order had to be finished.

Table 3.1 *Japanese–US percentage differences on items measuring work commitment, organizational commitment, and job satisfaction*

	US			Japan		
	Percentage agree	Percentage undecided	Percentage disagree	Percentage agree	Percentage undecided	Percentage disagree
Work commitment						
"I have other activities more important than my work"	30.8	24.9	44.2	43.6	26.2	30.2
"To me, my work is only a small part of who I am"	54.1	17.4	28.5	46.0	16.0	38.0
"The most important things that happen to me involve my family rather than my work"	70.0	20.3	9.7	35.4	39.9	24.7
Organizational commitment						
"I am willing to work harder than I have to in order to help this company succeed"	74.3	19.1	6.6	54.3	29.4	16.3
"I feel very little loyalty to this company"	22.2	20.2	57.7	19.0	31.3	49.8
"I would take any job in order to continue working for this company"	41.2	26.9	31.9	39.7	29.8	30.5
"My values and the values of this company are quite similar"	41.5	31.8	26.6	19.3	39.3	41.4
"I am proud to work for this company"	63.8	27.5	8.7	57.9	26.2	16.0

	US			Japan		
	Percentage positive	Percentage undecided	Percentage negative	Percentage positive	Percentage undecided	Percentage negative[a]
"I would turn down another job for more pay in order to stay with this company"	26.3	28.8	44.8	20.4	38.8	40.8
Job satisfaction						
"All in all, how satisfied would you say you are with your job?"	34.0	61.4	4.5	17.8	66.4	15.9
"If a good friend of yours told you that he or she was interested in working at a job like yours at this company, what would you say?"	63.4	25.3	11.3	18.5	53.9	27.6
"Knowing what you know now, if you had to decide all over again whether to take the job you now have, what would you decide?"	69.1	22.9	8.0	23.3	37.1	39.6
"How much does your job measure up to the kind of job you wanted when you first took it?"	33.6	52.3	14.0	5.2	32.3	62.5

Notes: [a] See note 6, chapter 3

This passage strongly underscores the labor control objectives of welfare corporatism, for it identifies a strategy of cooptation underlying the Japanese firm's efforts to integrate the employee's family in the affairs of the firm. By incorporating the family within the firm, the possibility is foreclosed that family life will present serious competition to work activities for the hearts and minds of workers.

Overall, the differences between our samples on these three questions suggest that the Japanese employees are slightly more committed to work than are US workers: on the work commitment scale created from these three items (see table 5.1), the mean score for the Japanese is 2.84, as compared to 2.62 for the Americans. Given the sharp reversals we have witnessed in the responses to these specific items, however, we should be cautious in attaching importance to the composite scores.

Organizational commitment

In selecting questionnaire items to measure the concept of organizational commitment, we drew from a well-tested scale: the Porter Organizational Commitment Scale (see, for example, Porter, Steers, Mowday, and Boulian, 1974; Mowday, Steers, and Porter, 1979). The original Porter scale consists of 15 items designed to measure various facets of commitment to the work organization such as loyalty, identification, and willingness to expend effort in support of company goals (see also Mowday *et al.*, 1982). The Porter items constitute the most commonly utilized survey instrument in studies of organizational commitment. Yet they are not without their critics. O'Reilly and Chatman (1986:497) have recently faulted the Porter approach for failure to differentiate between such subdimensions as identification with organizational goals, motivation to exert effort on the organization's behalf, and intention to maintain the employment relationship. We agree that careful analytic attention to the kinds of commitments tapped by the Porter scale do indicate such multidimensionality. We were particularly concerned to exclude those items which bore no direct relation to the concept of commitment as a social psychological state; e.g. those addressing simple intention to stay with the company. Variation between the US and Japan in employee responses to this item would likely reflect well-known structural differences in the labor markets of the two countries and thus say little about commitment as a form of psychological bonding to a firm. Yet some of the other conceptual distinctions that concern O'Reilly and Chatman are less troublesome to us. One might indeed see motivation to work hard for a company as a *consequence* of identification with the company's goals, but both constitute satisfactory indicators of psychological commitment, broadly construed, and well represent the forms of attachments to the organization on which differences between Japanese and US employees are widely presumed to exist.

Besides the items excluded as too likely to reflect structural constraints, we omitted additional items which appeared either redundant or to have lower face validity as indicators of the kind of commitment that Japanese employees are believed to display. The items selected for our analysis are presented in table 3.1, along with the percentages of American and Japanese employees agreeing, undecided, and disagreeing with each.[4]

As we noted in the previous chapter, an important difference exists between the Japanese and US surveys in the response coding of our Likert-style questionnaire items. Consistent with our and other researchers' (e.g. Dore, 1973:232) sense that the Japanese tend to eschew extreme opinions and characterizations, we added the response categories "slightly agree" and "slightly disagree" to the Japanese version of the Likert items, but not to the US version. Thus, the Japanese items were originally scored on a seven-point ordinal scale, while the American items used a five-point scale. Our intent here was to counter an anticipated predilection on the part of the Japanese to opt for the "undecided" category by permitting them to select a weaker form of agree/disagree (Dore, 1973). Even with the addition of two milder agreement codes on the Japanese instruments, table 3.1 reveals a tendency for the Japanese to give the "undecided" response more frequently. Our procedure may disturb some readers who feel that identical measurement procedures should have been followed in the two countries. Yet herein lies the central dilemma of cross-cultural research. Had we used the same five-item Likert scale in both surveys, we would have had surface measurement equivalence, but failed to correct for a known response bias. In any event, we note that our conclusions about differences between Japan and the US in average scores on our Likert-type items are affected only slightly by alternative ways of collapsing the seven-point Japanese scale into a five-point index.[5]

Our first measure of organizational commitment taps the employee's willingness to expend effort on behalf of the company. It is similar to Cole's question, "how often do you work harder than your employer or supervisor requires," with the important exception that our item stipulates the purpose of work to be the company's success. Yet we find, as did Cole (1979:234), that the Americans are more likely to agree with this statement than the Japanese. Are US employees, then, more motivated to work for the sake of their companies than the Japanese? This seems an unlikely finding, given prevailing impressions of the behaviors of manufacturing workers in the two countries. One possible, though certainly *ad hoc*, explanation is that the Japanese are already working longer and harder than American workers, hence are understandably reluctant to put out even more. Another possible interpretation is that because of high levels of unemployment in the US at the time of our surveys, American workers may have been especially motivated to help their companies survive and thus to preserve their jobs.

More insight into the meaning of this finding is provided by the responses to another questionnaire item measuring one's willingness to work hard for the company in more behavioral terms. This question, not a Porter item, asked workers to indicate their agreement with the statement: "employees shouldn't take time off when things are busy, even though they have a right to take the time off"; 49 percent of the Japanese agreed with this item as compared to 28 percent of the Americans (see also chapter 5). It could be that we have here an instance of attitudes correlating poorly with behavior. The American workers say they are willing to "work harder than they have to," but when directly presented with a specific cost of extra effort (e.g. sacrificing leisure time), they have a change of heart. On the other hand, we cannot overlook the fact that breaks during the workday, vacation and sick leave, and other rights to time off from work have become highly institutionalized in the US employment system: many such guarantees were hard-won by American unions in labor–management struggles (Jacoby, 1985). Time off from work, as we have pointed out before, is less institutionalized in Japan. Moreover, we doubt that Japanese workers take less of their legally allotted leave time simply because of their passion for spending time in the company. More likely it is in response to strong, if informal, workgroup and supervisor pressures and a general community opprobrium directed against persons who are not seen as fulfilling their work responsibilities (see Kamata, 1983). Here again we confront the importance of societal and workplace norms for understanding the work attitudes of individuals. Just as numerous American studies in industrial sociology have shown that piece rates often fail as incentive systems because of the work-group norms that emerge to keep production down (Roy, 1952), dominant work norms in Japan may function to keep workers on the job more than they are legally required or would be had they followed their personal inclinations.

The next Porter item taps feelings of loyalty to the company. On this reverse-scored item, a "disagree" response indicates loyalty, and it is made by slightly more US employees than Japanese. However, the percentages agreeing in each sample are virtually the same. Allowing for the penchant of the Japanese to opt for "undecided," we cannot confirm the existence of a difference in reported loyalty.

Furthermore, the distributions of US and Japanese respondents are also nearly identical with respect to willingness to change jobs in order to stay with the company. On the assumption that Americans tend to be more occupation-conscious than the Japanese (Cole and Tominaga, 1976), we expect the Japanese to give the responses indicative of greater organizational commitment. We should remember, however, that the hourly workers in our sample are primarily in line production departments and for the most part unskilled and semiskilled. These kinds of employees are less likely than others to identify with the job or occupation *per se*. Moreover, in light of the high unemployment rates prevailing at the time of the survey, employees in the US were perhaps less likely than usual to quibble over job assignments.

On the other hand, there is a clear tendency for the Americans to give more committed responses to the item measuring the employee's acceptance of corporate values: twice as many US as Japanese employees agreed with this statement. However, another question, not a Porter item, dealing with worker acceptance of company norms and practices reveals no country difference. Roughly one-fifth of the workers in both countries give the committed response to the question: "I often disagree with this company on matters relating to its employees"; whereas approximately half indicate that they take issue with the company's treatment of its employees. The contrast among the Americans between their responses to this item and the Porter question about values is interesting: they are considerably more likely to agree with the nonspecific statement of sharing the company's values than they are to endorse the company's particular policies with respect to its treatment of workers.

Another small difference between the Japanese and US workers materializes with respect to: "I am proud to work for this company": the Americans are slightly more likely to agree, and less likely to disagree, than the Japanese. The patterns of responses in each sample, however, are quite similar: most employees agree; about a quarter are undecided; and relatively small percentages disagree. It is noteworthy that so little difference between countries appears on this item, since it is close to being a measure of satisfaction with the employer. Indeed, of all the commitment items, this one exhibits the highest correlation with job satisfaction. This suggests an interpretation which we will develop in more depth as the analysis proceeds: though the Japanese, as measured by these items, are certainly no more proud of their companies than the US respondents, the Japanese level of pride is much higher *relative* to their level of job satisfaction. Thus, the rather negative reports that the Japanese employees on the average give concerning their jobs (see below) do not carry over to their feelings about their companies.

The final Porter item is a key indicator of commitment: whether the employee would turn down another job for more pay in order to remain with the company. Because a considerably higher percentage of the Japanese are undecided and higher percentages of the Americans both agree and disagree with this statement, we find no meaningful country difference. No more than one quarter in either sample are so devoted to their employers that they would pass up a better paying job elsewhere. In light of the evidence that actual job shifts between companies are less frequent in Japan, this finding might suggest that lack of opportunity is what keeps the Japanese from moving. Presented with the chance to make more money with another company, the employees in our Japanese sample seem as inclined as Americans to change employers.

Given these comparisons, we are hardly in a position to conclude that the Japanese are more committed to their work organizations than are US employees. With respect to most of the Porter items, little difference appears.

On the two items on which relatively large country differences exist – willingness to work hard for the company and acceptance of the company's values – we find the *Americans* seeming more committed than the Japanese. We speculate further on the meaning and implications of these results for organizational commitment after considering the case of job satisfaction.

Job satisfaction

The distributions of responses to the items measuring job satisfaction are also presented in table 3.1. Our results for the direct indicator, the most commonly used measure of job satisfaction ("all in all, how satisfied are you with your job?"), are consistent with the findings of past surveys of Japanese and Western workers: morale, it would seem, is lower in Japan. Given our coding scheme,[6] we should not be surprised that the majority of employees in both samples fall in the middle response category: about 66 percent of the Japanese and 61 percent of the Americans. However, there is an appreciable difference between the countries in the percentages falling in the remaining two categories, with twice as great a proportion of the Americans expressing satisfaction, and nearly four times as many of the Japanese expressing dissatisfaction.

In a sense, the direct indicator is the weakest question on which to base strong conclusions about societal contrasts in job satisfaction, since the concepts of job and satisfaction may not translate exactly. A number of students of Japanese work patterns have commented on the difficulty of conveying Western notions of "job" to Japanese workers; and, as we suggested earlier, the Japanese word for satisfaction (*manzoku*), may convey a stronger sense of fulfillment or completion than the English word. Country differences in workers' responses to this question must therefore be interpreted with caution. Since our other items tapping this concept do not use the word satisfaction, however, they do not suffer from the translation problems afflicting this one.

Yet the pattern observed on the other, more behavioral, measures of job satisfaction is strong and consistent and tells an identical story. For example, when asked: "if a good friend of yours told you that he or she was interested in working in a job like yours at this company, what would you say?", a much larger proportion of the Japanese would "advise against this job" or "have some doubts," while over three times as many of the Americans would "recommend this job without hesitation." Another indirect indicator of job satisfaction asked the respondent: "knowing what you know now, if you had to decide all over again whether to take the job you now have, what would you decide?" In previous surveys of US workers, this item reveals far less satisfaction than the simple direct question of "are you satisfied with your job?" (see Kalleberg, 1974). For this reason, it is held by some to be a superior and more valid measure of overall job satisfaction. We find that almost 70 percent of our sample of American employees would take the same job again, about a quarter would have second thoughts, and less than 10 percent would opt for a different job. The picture is markedly different for the Japanese. Less than a quarter would opt for the same job, more than a third would have doubts, and fully 40 percent would seek a different job. Responses to the final item show the same pattern: a far higher percentage of the Japanese than the Americans report that their present job is "not at all what I wanted when I first took it." This result is very similar to that obtained for a nearly identical item in Cole's (1979) survey of Detroit and Yokohama workers.

The finding of lower job satisfaction in Japan than in the US is a very frequent and stable one, as our earlier review of past research pointed out. In subsequent chapters, we evaluate a number of hypotheses, derived from theories of job satisfaction, for this observed satisfaction gap. These include explanations based on differences in job rewards (e.g. earnings, challenge and other inducements) and in the degree to which work values (e.g. for pay or promotion) are fulfilled. However, in the previous chapter we raised the possibility that there may also be country differences in the very meaning of satisfaction or in the propensities of Japanese and US employees to under- or over-report their true feeling states. We here briefly discuss several potential country differences that may help account for a gap in satisfaction between the US and Japan.

First, we have noted that the Japanese may have very high expectations for what constitutes a satisfying job: to them it may mean fulfillment of a rather lofty ideal of work. On the other hand, Americans may be more likely to say that they are satisfied if they are *not dissatisfied*, if they secure a minimal level of contentment from the job (US Department of HEW, 1972). This is sufficient to keep them from leaving, but hardly fulfills all their work aspirations.

The issue of job security should be considered in weighing the meanings that Americans and Japanese attach to job satisfaction. We noted in the last chapter that unemployment was considerably higher in the US than in Japan during the period in which our surveys were conducted. American manufacturing workers are more likely to be exposed to the ever-present possibility that a dip in business activity will cause them to lose their jobs, at least temporarily. Many of the plants in our sample had laid off workers, and some were dangerously close to going out of business. Indeed, three American plants have closed since our data collection was completed. In this economic climate, many manufacturing workers were undoubtedly glad that they were employed at all, particularly in well-paid hourly manufacturing jobs. Hence, when the alternative to one's present job is unemployment, the job in hand may well afford satisfaction. On the other hand, the prospect of unemployment is considerably more remote to Japanese than to American employees. If the alternative to the present job is some abstract ideal of employment, no doubt the real-world job pales in comparison.

Similarly, job shifts involving a change in employers are considerably less common in Japan than in the US (see Cole, 1979). Not only does the norm of permanent employment reduce the likelihood that employers will terminate workers either for poor performance or bad business conditions, but a complementary norm discourages voluntary leaving. Though the rate of voluntary job changing seems to be increasing in Japan, bringing with it a reduction in the stigma attached to mid-career changes, it is still not the common and widely accepted practice that it is in the US.

Another effect of Japan's job stability norms is to make the decision to accept a given job a potentially lifetime commitment to an employer and a line of work (Marsh and Mannari, 1976). Having made the choice to take a job, the worker is not likely to be fired, nor is voluntary leaving an easy option to pursue. Thus, the question "would you take this job again" may weigh much more heavily on the minds of Japanese than US workers. Similarly, the questions, "would you recommend the job to a friend?" and "does the job measure up to your expectations?" may likewise be taken much more seriously by the Japanese who understand a job choice to be a critical life decision, rather than the American's interpretation of it as one (potentially reversible) career decision among many.

Is there a commitment gap?

Two general conclusions from this overview of findings seem warranted. First, the pattern of differences in organizational commitment and job satisfaction between Japanese and US employees runs strongly counter to the behavioral evidence of a highly committed Japanese labor force. The organizational commitment of the Japanese is either equal to or slightly lower, and their job satisfaction is far lower, than that of our American sample. Only with regard to work commitment do our survey results seem to square with expectations: on two out of three items, work appears more important to the Japanese.

Secondly, the evidence from our survey is in general highly consistent with the available evidence from other studies. Although an occasional survey item, as in Takezawa and Whitehill's study, suggests a strong tendency toward greater commitment in Japan, most indicate either no substantial difference or even the opposite pattern of commitment appearing to be greater among Western workers. Moreover, our data converge with all the other survey evidence of which we are aware in demonstrating markedly lower job satisfaction among the Japanese.

One interpretation of these findings is that the indisputable discipline and compliance of the Japanese workforce are rooted, not in individual workers' feelings of commitment to and identification with firms, but rather in management, work-group, and community pressures. This is the normative/institutional interpretation of commitment to which we have earlier referred. It holds that commitment is essentially a property of social aggregates –

groups, organizations, communities – which keep their members in line through a variety of social constraints. Given the tight-knit structure and strong cultures of Japanese groups and organizations, this theory has much to recommend it. Another often suggested possibility is that the attribution of extraordinary commitment to individual Japanese employees is meaningful for no more than a small segment of the economy – such as male workers in large companies – and is not an accurate characterization of the Japanese labor force in general.

These are plausible explanations for the lack of clear evidence of greater attitudinal commitment to employing organizations in Japan. Nonetheless, we are hesitant to accept these preliminary findings of societal differences in commitment at face value. As the methodological literature on comparative social research has often stressed (Przeworski and Teune, 1970), cross-national comparisons of means on perceptual measures are most perilous, as they are far more sensitive to cultural response biases than are measures of effect or association. We present two kinds of cross-national comparisons in this volume: (a) those pertaining to average *levels* (means and proportions) of our Japanese and US samples on single variables (e.g. commitment, satisfaction); and (b) those pertaining to the *relationships* among variables (e.g. between age and commitment). We are in general on firmer ground in comparing regression slopes and other estimates of causal relations than when we compare means or proportions. This is because the main kinds of measurement biases that are likely to be operative are the constant tendencies to overreport (in the US case) or underreport (the Japanese case) underlying attitudes and values. Such constant errors bias the means, and therefore the intercepts of least-squares regression equations, but do not affect the variances or covariances on which estimates of effect parameters (e.g. slopes) are based.

We can speculate on how under- and over-reporting biases in the measurement of work attitudes might produce the pattern of findings observed in our Japanese and US surveys. Sharply contrary to our expectations, we have found Japanese workforce members to be no more committed to their employing organizations than US workers and far less satisfied with their jobs. Consider a hypothetical state of the world, more consistent with our initial expectations, in which levels of job satisfaction are essentially similar between US and Japanese industrial employees, while commitment to the company runs far deeper in Japan. Assuming that the cultural response bias components in our measures of commitment and satisfaction are equal, we would infer that the "true" commitment of the Japanese exceeds that of the US respondents by an amount equal to the difference in the satisfaction scores.

This scenario, which assumes that Japanese and US workers are comparably satisfied with their jobs, clearly stacks the deck in favor of finding greater commitment in Japan. Despite the pervasive evidence of minimal behavioral alienation among Japanese industrial workers, there may well be grounds for presuming their level of job satisfaction to be truly lower than that of US employees. As organizational psychologists have argued (Vroom, 1964), high satisfaction may imply low motivation to perform on the job, whereas commitment strongly connotes willingness to expend effort for the sake of the organization. As we have noted, job satisfaction and organizational commitment are reciprocally related constructs: highly committed workers, such as the Germans and the Japanese, may genuinely feel less satisfaction because of higher expectations and stronger motivation for goal achievement on the job (see Cole, 1979).

We can statistically model these scenarios with our data, and thus obtain empirical estimates that illuminate the commitment–satisfaction relation. As in all such modeling exercises, the results necessarily depend on certain simplifying assumptions, so that certainty that we have the right scenario/model will forever elude us. Yet to take the unadjusted means on the attitude items as unambiguous evidence of the actual levels of these variables requires a leap of faith which is scarcely less breathtaking than some of the alternatives we entertain below.

Our modeling exercise necessitates that we first combine our indicators of commitment and satisfaction into composite scales (see table 3.2). Moreover, nearly all our analyses from this point on will require us to use multiple-item indices of these work attitudes. Aggregating items into scales is made considerably more complex by the comparative focus of our inquiry; a recurrent and foreboding obstacle to cross-cultural survey research is that items which are valid and reliable indicators of particular concepts in one country may fail to be so in another (Miller, Slomczynski, and Schoenberg, 1981). In statistical terms, the factor structure of a set of items may differ between the populations compared. For example, a measurement model in which our satisfaction items correlate highly with one factor and the commitment items with another may fit the US data well. But these same items, because of translation and other measurement errors as well as deep-rooted differences in the meanings of concepts, may produce an altogether different factor structure in Japan. Such an outcome would constitute a strong signal that our survey items measure different things in different countries. This would of course largely invalidate our analysis of the organization-, job-, and individual-level determinants of organizational commitment and job satisfaction in Japan and the US. Some researchers circumvent the risky process of testing whether a single measurement model fits different populations by simply adding together items having face validity into scales and evaluating the resulting indices for internal consistency reliability (e.g. with coefficient *alpha*, see Cronbach, 1951). Given the size and complexity of our data analysis, we follow this procedure ourselves in constructing multiple-item indices of variables seen as causally prior to organizational commitment and job satisfaction. For these two ultimate outcomes, however,

Table 3.2 *Descriptive statistics for measures of organizational commitment and job satisfaction*

	US Mean (SD)	Japan Mean (SD)
Organizational commitment scale (alpha = .75, US; .79, Japan) "I am willing to work harder than I have to in order to help this company succeed" (1 = strongly disagree, 5 = strongly agree)	2.13 (.469)	2.04 (.503)*
Lambda = .520.[a] "I would take any job in order to continue working for this company" (same codes)	3.91 (.895)	3.44 (.983)*
Lambda = .565 "My values and the values of this company are quite similar"	3.12 (1.14)	3.07 (1.13)
(same codes) Lambda = .742 "I am proud to work for this company" (same codes)	3.15 (1.06)	2.68 (.949)*
Lambda = .834 "I would turn down another job for more pay in order to stay with this company" (same codes)	3.70 (.943)	3.51 (1.02)*
Lambda = .632 "I feel very little loyalty to this company" (1 = strongly agree, 5 = strongly disagree)	2.71 (1.17)	2.68 (1.08)
Lambda = .520	3.45 (1.13)	3.40 (1.03)
Job satisfaction scale (alpha = .78, US; .65, Japan) "All in all, how satisfied would you say you are with your job?" (0 = not at all, 4 = very)	1.54 (.449)	.962 (.350)*
Lambda = .850 "If a good friend of yours told you that he or she was interested in working at a job like yours at this company, what would you say?" (0 = would advise against it, 1 = would have second thoughts, 2 = would recommend it) Lambda = .454	2.95 (1.12)	2.12 (1.06)*
"Knowing what you know now, if you had to decide all over again whether to take the job you now have, what would you	1.52 (.690)	.909 (.673)*

Table 3.2 *(cont.)*

	US Mean (SD)	Japan Mean (SD)
decide?" (0 = would not take job again, 1 = would have some second thoughts, 2 = would take job again) Lambda = .412	1.61 (.630)	.837 (.776)*
"How much does your job measure up to the kind of job you wanted when you first took it?" (0 = not what I wanted, 1 = somewhat, 2 = what I wanted) Lambda = .378	1.20 (.662)	.427 (.591)*

Notes: [a] Lambdas were obtained from a confirmatory factor (LISREL) analysis of organizational commitment and job satisfaction items – see Lincoln and Kalleberg, 1985
* difference in means between countries significant at p < .001

we use a more rigorous approach: first, we specify a model that assumes equivalent measurement structures in the US and Japan; and, second, we assess the fit of that model to our data.

Our measurement model assumes that only two latent constructs ("factors") – organizational commitment and job satisfaction – are needed to account for the interrelations among the ten items we used to measure these concepts (see table 3.2). It further assumes that the measures are *congeneric*: the satisfaction items depend ("load") exclusively on one factor and the commitment items on the other. We finally assume that the loadings (the *lambda* parameters whose estimates are given in table 3.2) are identical in Japan and the US, although the model does allow for country-specific patterns of correlation among the errors in individual items (Miller *et al.*, 1981).[7] The results obtained from estimating this model are consistent with the hypothesis that the factorial structures for commitment and satisfaction are identical in Japan and the US.[8] It appears, then, that our assumption that these items provide equivalent measurement of commitment and satisfaction in these two samples does not do serious violence to reality.

We can now use these measures of commitment and satisfaction to examine their reciprocal causation and how they differ between Japan and the US. We note initially that the correlations between the scales are very high in each sample (US: $r = .81$; Japan: $r = .73$), yet the satisfaction gap between countries is large while the commitment difference is small to nonexistent. We believe that the strong association between commitment and satisfaction stems primarily from the latter's influence on the former rather than vice versa: good feelings about one's job and employer breed

Table 3.3 *Standardized LISREL estimates of nonrecursive models of commitment and satisfaction for the pooled sample*

	Endogenous variables					
Predetermined Variables	Commitment	Satisfaction	Commitment	Satisfaction	Commitment	Satisfaction
	(1)		(2)		(3)	
Satisfaction	.809[b]		.797		.843	
Commitment		−.135		−.112		.323
US (=1)	−.211	.514	−.258	.458	−.233	.405
Tenure	.140	.134				
Earnings			.142	.136		
Promotion chances					.089	
Job complexity						.200
Psi(1,2)[c]						−.237
Adj. R^2	.081	.471	.112	.470	.540	.455

Notes: [a] Models (1) and (2) were identified by constraining the metric coefficients estimated for tenure and earnings to equality and the correlation between the disturbances to zero

[b] All coefficients are significantly different between countries beyond the .001 level

[c] Correlation between equation disturbances

company identification and loyalty; while commitment, by increasing expectations, may produce a net reduction in satisfaction. If these assumptions are correct, and if differences in job satisfaction between the US and Japan are exaggerated due to cultural and other differences, then the inflated satisfaction gap may be masking real differences in organizational commitment.

We estimated three simple exploratory models designed to get at the reciprocal relationship between commitment and satisfaction in Japan and the US. In table 3.3, we present LISREL estimates of these simultaneous equation models. The models differ in their identifying constraints. Model (1) assumes that the metric effects of employee tenure on satisfaction and commitment are identical and the equation disturbances are uncorrelated. The same constraints are used to identify model (2), though in this case we use earnings rather than tenure as the instrumental variable (an exogenous variable required for model identification). The changes in specification between these two models produce very little difference in the pattern of findings; this is generally the case with other instrumental variables not reported here. Satisfaction, it appears, makes a large positive contribution to commitment, but the reverse effect, while decidedly small, is negative. Moreover, commitment, when adjusted for the influence of satisfaction, is greater in the Japanese sample than in the US sample.[9] These results are consistent with Cole's (1979) argument that the Japanese are more committed to their employing organizations and less satisfied with their jobs because commitment, by raising motivation and expectations, makes satisfaction more difficult to achieve.

Models 1 and 2 incorporate the strong assumption that error terms are uncorrelated. This implies the clearly unrealistic state of affairs that any exogenous variables jointly influencing commitment and satisfaction have been included in the model. That cannot be the case, as these are highly abbreviated, exploratory models from which many causal variables that we will later consider are excluded (see chapter 8). Consequently, in model 3, we relax the assumption of uncorrelated disturbances by estimating that correlation as a free parameter. This requires us to find another identifying constraint: we assume that promotion expectations affect commitment but not satisfaction, while job complexity affects satisfaction but not commitment. These, too, are rather implausible assumptions (see chapter 4), though the results are still suggestive. The basic pattern of lower satisfaction and higher commitment in Japan than in the US is unchanged, and satisfaction still makes a very large contribution to commitment. However, the negative effect of commitment on satisfaction has been replaced by a moderately sized positive coefficient, and we now have a negative correlation in the equation disturbance terms.

Taken as a whole, these models provide fairly solid evidence that once we adjust for the causal reciprocity between work attitude dimensions, commitment is higher in the Japanese workforce, and satisfaction is lower.[10] The combination of high commitment and low satisfaction does indeed evoke an image of a highly motivated workforce, and is squarely consistent with mainstream theories of work motivation which view this attitudinal state as a response to unmet goals or needs (see, e.g. Herzberg *et al.*, 1959; Maslow, 1954; Vroom, 1964).

These "gaps" between the work attitudes of Japanese and US manufacturing employees are what our study ultimately seeks to explain. The remainder of this book asks whether the variation in organizational commitment and job satisfaction between and within our Japanese and US samples can be shown to stem from the job-, individual-, and plant-level factors measured in our survey. Do attitudes warrant so much attention? Isn't the real issue for productivity and competitiveness how employees behave? We do note in passing that our data reveal employee attitudes to be substantially predictive of at least one important kind of workplace behavior: quits. The correlation between the factory quit rate (as compiled by the plant's personnel department) and the plant mean of our organizational commitment scale is $-.265$ in the US and $-.491$ in Japan. The corresponding correlations with satisfaction are $-.154$ and $-.249$. Quit rates are not our primary concern here; work attitudes are. But these correlations should allay to some degree the anticipated skepticism that self-reported employee attitudes bear any appreciable or important relationship to workforce discipline.

4 Job attributes and work attitudes: an employee-level analysis

Introduction

The last chapter addressed in some detail the pattern of similarities and differences in employee work attitudes between Japan and the US. Our task now and throughout the remainder of this volume is to discover the sources of variation in work attitudes which lie within and as well as between these countries. Our general approach to this problem follows a well-established methodology in the social sciences for explaining a difference between groups. That is, we seek the reasons for the Japan/US contrasts in commitment and satisfaction in differences in a set of other, presumably causal, variables. Indeed, our overarching hypothesis is that the edge in worker commitment enjoyed by Japanese industry is a function of differences in the organization of Japanese and US firms, and in the capacity of Japanese management practices to foster in a workforce task involvement, career opportunities, and strong social bonds.

The job-related variables we consider in this chapter are grouped into the following sets: (1) the structural position of the individual within the organization, indexed by management rank, functional area, quality circle membership, and tenure with the company; (2) characteristics of the task or work role as perceived by the employee, such as skill, complexity, and control. Such job properties have been widely studied by students of organizational behavior for their effects on employee motivation and morale (e.g. Hackman and Lawler, 1971; Mowday *et al.*, 1982); (3) the rewards the job provides its incumbent, both intrinsic (in the sense of stimulating and self-actualizing work) and extrinsic (i.e. earnings and career opportunities); and (4) the extent to which it integrates the employee in the organization through the development of strong social bonds with coworkers and supervisors. Like task complexity and intrinsic rewards, informal ties and group cohesion are objects of much theory and research, from the motivation studies of business school psychologists (e.g. Vroom, 1964) to the radical critiques advanced by labor process sociologists and economists (Burawoy, 1983; Edwards, 1979; Gordon, 1972).

Our vision of welfare corporatism as a commitment-maximizing organizational form is thus very much in the mainstream in positing that these facets of work roles are the mechanisms whereby companies secure the loyalty and devotion of workers. Decentralized and participatory decision-making, flexible division of labor, internal labor markets, along with welfare, training, and social programs translate at the individual employee level into more interesting and challenging jobs, greater freedom and flexibility, and warmer, broader, relations with workmates and managers.

Moreover, consistent with our assumption that commitment-maximizing organization is more prevalent in Japanese than US industry, we anticipate finding that Japanese manufacturing employees experience their jobs as more complex and varied, involving more autonomy and control, providing more intrinsic rewards, and enmeshing them in dense networks of strong ties with coworkers. This general picture of the jobs and work-life orientations of the Japanese, while not directly demonstrated in previous survey research, is strongly suggested in the qualitative case study literature on Japanese organization and industrial relations (Cole, 1979; Dore, 1973; Rohlen, 1974). It is, furthermore, thought to explain the powerful hold that Japanese companies appear to have on their employees.

Our analysis follows the causal model outlined in figure 1. We examine a series of measures, derived from our survey questionnaire, of the four sets of job attributes given above. As in chapter 3, we search for differences between our Japanese and US samples that might play a role in explaining the commitment and satisfaction gaps. However, we also search for contrasts between the countries in the *processes* leading to perceived job complexity, social integration, and job rewards. A particularly important question in a Japan–US comparison is whether the implications of authority structures and job designs for perceived job quality and rewards differ between Japan and the US. Much past work on Japanese forms of organization would have us believe that they do.

Position in the organization

The workforce of a manufacturing plant is structurally differentiated in several key ways. Such axes of workforce segmentation have important consequences for employee work attitudes, behaviors and relations. We consider four dimensions defining an employee's position in the organization (1) authority level (whether a manager, supervisor or worker); (2) functional area (direct production, technical support, and office personnel); (3) quality circle membership and (4) length of tenure with the company.

Authority position

It is well known that "low-placed members tend to have less commitment and emotional attachment to the organization than higher-placed members" (Goffman, 1961:201). Indeed, the proposition that motivation, commitment, and morale rise rapidly with shifts from low to high in the management hierarchy is one of the most replicated findings in organizational social psychology (Porter and Lawler, 1965; Tannenbaum, Kavcic, Rosner, Vianello, and Wieser, 1974). We expect the same pattern in our samples of Japanese and US manufacturing employees.

This is not to say, however, that we anticipate no differences between countries in the association of rank with work attitudes and perceptions. On the contrary, the structuring of status hierarchies is often cited as a highly distinctive feature of Japanese companies and is compatible with a logic of minimizing internal division and maximizing commitment. As we discuss in more detail in chapter 7, their tall, finely-graded character implies job ladders for upward mobility and higher rates of interaction between superiors and subordinates (Clark, 1979; Dore, 1973). There is considerable evidence, moreover, that Japanese hierarchies are characterized by less overall inequality than is typical of American or British firms. The income gap between managers and workers is smaller, and many of the symbolic trappings of status, such as separate eating areas and parking lots for management and production personnel, are eliminated (Abegglen and Stalk, 1985).

These considerations suggest that highly differentiated hierarchies should have, at the level of the firm, a positive impact on the commitment of its workforce. We take up this hypothesis in chapter 8. For the present, we concern ourselves with the corollary hypothesis that, within firms, Japanese-styled (more generally, corporatist) stratification systems should produce less divergence (i.e. more consensus) in the attitudes and behaviors of managers, supervisors, and workers. Moreover, a common perception is that there is less class consciousness and conflict separating managers and workers in Japan than in the US, with consciousness of common organizational interests being correspondingly higher. These considerations suggest that in a comparison with the US there will be smaller differences in organizational commitment and job satisfaction across the management levels of Japanese firms.

Functional area

A second key axis differentiating a company's workforce is the general functional area or department in which they work. We classify the employees in our samples into the three primary functions found in factory organization: direct production; technical support; and office personnel.

As we noted earlier, the composition of the Japanese and US samples is generally similar (see table 2.2). In both countries, roughly 70 percent of employees are in production. A higher proportion of the Japanese are in office functions and a slightly higher proportion of the Americans are in technical support. Moreover, authority and function are associated classifications. People of management rank are more likely to be found in office departments (e.g. representing the staff functions of marketing, personnel, accounting, and planning). We discuss the reasons for this and other staffing patterns in chapter 7, which deals explicitly with contrasts in the structuring of Japanese and US plants.

Quality circle membership

No contemporary discussion of the Japanese workplace, nor, indeed, modern forms of work structuring and control, can ignore the implications of quality circles for the reactions of employees to job and employer. These are programs in which groups of workers meet to discuss quality and productivity improvements in the production process, then propose and carry out changes (Thomas and Shimada, 1983; Cole, 1979; 1980). A Japanese innovation, they were heavily influenced by the principles of statistical quality control devised by W. E. Deming and other American experts. Already near-universal in Japanese industry and rapidly expanding in the US, QC has come to symbolize participatory work reform, and strong claims have been made for its effectiveness in motivating commitment and cooperation on the part of managers and workers (Ouchi, 1981).

Cole (1979) estimates that one out of every eight employees in the Japanese workforce was a member of such groups in 1978. In our Japanese sample, 81 percent of the plants reported that they have QC programs, and 76 percent of their employees claim to be members, for a 94 percent participation rate. Of the plants in our American sample 62 percent had QC programs. However, only 27 percent of the US employees report that they are members of quality circle-type groups, for a 44 percent participation rate. Our measure of QC participation is coded "1" if the employee is a member of such groups and "0" if he or she is not.

There is, of course, likely to be considerable variation among plants in the form and content of quality circle programs. None of the US plants we studied had anything resembling the rigorous program at Toyota Auto Body which Cole (1979) has described in considerable detail. In particular, we did not hear of serious attempts to train American workers in statistical quality control techniques, although some initial training was typical. Moreover, quality circles met on regular company time in the US plants, not after official work hours as is commonly the case in Japan. Cole (1979:161) notes that workers at Toyota Auto Body were paid half their normal hourly wage for after-hours QC meetings. In addition, while some of the American programs were quite structured, involved frequent meetings, provided training in QC techniques, and granted circles the authority to truly experiment with production innovations, others appeared to be little more than group suggestion-making mechanisms in which members met irregularly for informal discussions. Suggestions coming out of these meetings were reviewed by management who made the determination as to whether or not they would be implemented.

While one might well expect QC programs in the US to be generally weak gestures at shop-floor participation, a number of observers find the Japanese programs failing, particularly as their novelty wears off, to hold the interest of workers. Cole (1980) notes that workers have come to perceive QC participation as yet another chore demanded by management. A personnel manager in a showcase automobile plant informed us in a personal interview that attendance at circle meetings had fallen to roughly 50 percent, and the state of the program was a matter of serious concern to the company. Odaka (1982:232) quotes Japanese workers' complaints that management is often lax in providing the training, time, and facilities necessary for QC operations. Tokunaga (1983:323) argues that the participation of Japanese workers in QC and Zero Defect groups is semicompulsory and is often considered in personnel evaluations. He cites a 1970 survey of union members showing that only 7–10 percent of the workers responding felt a "sense of active involvement in the work," as opposed to feeling burdened by it.

While the primary function of shop-floor small group programs is the enhancement of quality and productivity, a secondary function of equal importance is the fostering of a sense of participation in and influence over workflow decisions among workers. Indeed, quality circles are perhaps the most widely implemented expression of the movement to upgrade the quality of work life through enriched jobs and increased teamwork (Berg *et al.*, 1978). Our interviews with American managers regarding their hopes and motivations for QC programs revealed that their expectations were in many cases pinned more on the potential payoffs in workforce morale and motivation than on tangible improvements in product quality *per se.*

Tenure with the company

The length of time the employee has been with a company is also an important indicator of position in the organization. With greater seniority, one accumulates skill and familiarity with the ways of the organization, broader access to its social networks, and, partly for these reasons, greater resources and power. Moreover, variations in firms' propensity to retain employees is, as we have noted before, symptomatic of differences in internal labor market organization, a kind of structuring which is central to our understanding of welfare corporatism as a commitment-engendering organizational form (Doeringer and Piore, 1971).

Employee tenure, furthermore, is an aspect of the employment relationship that takes on special significance in a comparative study of the United States and Japan. Although the extent and uniqueness of "permanent employment" in Japan may have been exaggerated (Galenson, 1976; Koike, 1978), there is abundant evidence that turnover and interfirm mobility – especially among blue-collar workers – is lower and average tenure higher in Japanese than American labor markets. Part of this difference, however, stems from the fact that, among industrial countries, the US ranks high in both voluntary labor mobility and managerial reliance on layoffs as a means of controlling workforce size (Cole, 1979; Hashimoto and Raisian, 1985).

The average tenure of the Japanese employees in our study (12 years) is only slightly higher than that of the American sample (11.3 years), although the variance is smaller in the Japanese sample and they average 3.5 years younger. One reason why the difference in average tenure is not larger may be that our sample includes a considerable number of small firms. The practice of "permanent employment" in Japan is to a considerable extent a large firm phenomenon. Another consideration, noted earlier, is the weak business conditions prevailing in the US at the time of our survey which meant a high rate of layoffs among younger employees with low levels of seniority.

Task characteristics

We reduce the broad category of task characteristics to four fundamental dimensions: (1) the job's complexity or skill content; (2) the extent to which the job involves cooperation and teamwork; (3) the intensity of supervision; and (4) the autonomy or discretionary content associated with the job. Expanding on the general model outlined in chapter 1, we see these forming a simple causal chain. The complexity of tasks is shaped by position in the organization (management rank, functional area, QC membership, and tenure) in addition to such background and human capital variables as age, marital status, gender, and education. The degree to which the job calls for teamwork comes next in this sequence, followed by patterns of supervision, and, finally, the amount of discretion or autonomy which the employee is able to exercise over the task.

Job complexity

Our approach to measuring task characteristics relies on employees' self-reports, a common method in labor force surveys (e.g. Kohn and Schooler, 1983). This mode of data collection is, of course, vulnerable to the charge that individuals' subjective assessments of the nature of their jobs are distorted due to selective perception or lack of information. In a large questionnaire survey involving many work establishments, the option of gathering independent measures was simply not available. Nevertheless, there is good reason to believe that self-reports of job conditions, while imperfect, provide generally valid information. Some research shows considerable convergence between subjective and objective measures of job attributes (see, for example, Quinn, 1977; Hackman and Lawler, 1971). Finally, individuals' perceptions of skill-related attributes such as complexity and autonomy are theoretically important since we assume that skills inhere in *both* people and jobs. Some jobs are more complex and difficult than others and make more stringent demands of the people who perform them. However, jobs derive social meaning from people who differ in their abilities; hence, individuals in similar "jobs" commonly exercise different skills.

Our measures of job complexity are listed in table 4.1. Four items tapped complexity. These asked for employees' subjective assessments of: the amount of training required to perform their jobs; the general skill level of their jobs; their opportunity to learn new things on their jobs; and the level of task variety.

There is reason to expect Japanese manufacturing employees to experience their tasks as more complex than US workers do. US manufacturing jobs are widely acknowledged to be fragmented and narrowly defined, with both unions and management concerned with setting rigid rules and standards for the performance of tasks and the qualifications of the worker (Berg *et al.*, 1978; Cole, 1979; Piore and Sabel, 1984). In contrast, detailed job classifications and rigid job definitions have generally been the exception in Japanese industry (Cole and Tominaga, 1976). Moreover, at both management and production worker levels, rotation of employees between jobs and departments is a common practice in Japan. Such rotation demands considerable cross-training, another practice for which Japanese firms are well-known (Aoki, 1984). Given this set of conditions, then, it seems likely that Japanese employees perceive their jobs as less routine, more varied and complex than what US workers experience.

A comparison of the means on the job complexity scale, however, finds the American employees reporting more complexity than the Japanese (table 4.1). On only one item do we find the reverse: although American managers and supervisors believe their jobs require lengthier training than do their Japanese counterparts, the Japanese *workers* see their jobs requiring more training than do the American workers. This pattern is corroborated by a recent Japan–US comparative survey conducted by Naoi and Schooler (1985) who also found a lower level of variety in the tasks perceived by Japanese employees than in a comparable sample of Americans.

Teamwork

Much commentary and research on the Japanese workplace suggest that Japanese jobs involve high levels of teamwork and cooperation (Dore, 1973:231). The work group organization of much Japanese production, and the wide use of small-group methods of worker participation, elicit a degree of cooperation and involvement in shop-floor decision-making that has traditionally been scarce, but appears to be increasing, in American industry. The group is the unit to which the Japanese firm assigns responsibility for a work function, and within it there is considerable rotation of tasks among the members (Aoki, 1984). Decision-making and problem-solving are also taken

Table 4.1 *Descriptive statistics for job attributes variables*

	US Mean (SD)		Japan Mean (SD)	
Position in the organization				
Employee a manager (= 1)	.051	(.221)	.068	(.251)*
Employee a supervisor (= 1)	.103	(.304)	.224	(.417)*
Employee in technical support department (= 1)	.167	(.373)	.174	(.379)
Employee in line production department (= 1)	.728	(.445)	.689	(.463)*
Years employed at plant (tenure)	11.3	(9.57)	12.0	(8.14) *
Quality circle member (= 1)	.268	(.443)	.763	(.426)*
Task Characteristics				
Job complexity scale (alpha = .75, US; .64, Japan)	3.30	(1.01)	3.08	(.873)*
"How long would it take to train someone to do your work?" (0 = a few hours, 6 = five years or more)	2.39	(1.74)	2.54	(1.56)*
"My job requires a high level of skill" (1 = strong. disag., 5 = strong. agree)	3.54	(1.14)	3.30	(1.07)*
"My job keeps me learning new things" (same codes)	3.55	(1.21)	3.52	(1.13)
"There is a lot of variety in the kinds of things that I do in my job" (same codes)	3.69	(1.16)	2.96	(1.20)*
OJT: "How important a source of skill was on-the-job training?" (0 = never had; 4 = very important)	3.33	(.929)	2.36	(1.38)*
Teamwork: "I have to work closely with others to do my job well" (1 = strongly disagree, 5 = strongly agree)	3.22	(1.21)	3.80	(1.01)*
Supervisor contact: "Your supervisor lets you alone unless you ask for help" (1 = strongly agree, 5 = strongly disagree)	2.13	(.915)	3.20	(1.05)*
Supervisor control: (0 = I decide what I do and how I do it; 1 = my supervisor decides what I do, but I decide how to do it; 2 = my supervisor decides what I do and how I do it)	1.07	(.624)	1.08	(.657)
Autonomy scale (alpha = .52, US; .53, Japan)	3.59	(.895)	3.24	(.821)*
"My job gives me freedom as to how I do my work" (1 = strongly disagree, 5 = strongly agree)	3.56	(1.04)	3.05	(1.16)*

"My job lets me decide the speed
that I work" (same codes)   3.29 (1.16)   3.28 (1.22)

The degree to which "my judgment"
was cited (1 = least effect, 5 = most
effect) in response to: "What has the
most effect on what you actually do
on your job?"   3.91 (1.44)   3.38 (1.01)*

Job Rewards

Intrinsic rewards scale   3.52 (.761)   3.49 (.635)
(alpha = .65, US; .49, Japan)

"My job does not let me use my skills
and knowledge (1 = strongly agree,
5 = strongly disagree)   3.22 (1.23)   3.58 (1.06)*

"The problems I solve in my job are
not very challenging" (same codes)   3.18 (1.16)   2.91 (1.02)*

"The work I do on my job is
meaningful to me" (1 = strongly
disagree, 5 = strongly agree)   3.79 (1.00)   3.55 (.965)*

"My job lets me see the results
of my work" (same codes)   3.88 (.946)   3.92 (.992)

Earnings: employee's report of
annual earnings. Yen converted to
US dollars at exchange rate of
250 yen = 1$ 19,110 (9,603)   12,699 (5,785)*

Promotion chances:
Employee expects to be promoted
(1 = yes, 0 = no)   .264 (.441)   .256 (.436)

Social bonds
Quality of vertical ties:
relations with supervisors
scale (alpha = .70, US; .66, Japan)   2.48 (.792)   2.61 (.681)*

"Your supervisor encourages teamwork"
(1 = strongly disagree, 5 = strongly
agree)   3.52 (1.07)   3.59 (1.01)

"Your supervisor is someone [the employee]
confides in about [employee's]
personal life (same codes)   2.27 (1.09)   2.80 (1.13)*

"How satisfied are you with your
supervisor?" (1 = not at all
satisfied, 3 = very satisfied)   2.84 (1.25)   1.95 (1.11)*

"How often do you talk with your
supervisor about your work?"
(0 = seldom or never, 3 = daily)   2.16 (1.18)   2.57 (.867)*

"How often do you talk with your
supervisor about things other than
work?" (same codes)   1.63 (1.29)   2.15 (1.11)*

Table 4.1 *(cont.)*

	US Mean (SD)		Japan Mean (SD)	
Quality of ties with co-workers				
scale (alpha = .74, US; .69, Japan)	3.95	(.711)	3.54	(.689)*
"People in my work unit are friendly and helpful" (1 = strongly disagree, 5 = strongly agree)	3.91	(.781)	3.38	(1.04)*
"I feel that I am really a part of my work group" (same codes)	3.79	(.795)	3.71	(.814)*
"I have confidence and trust in the people in my work group" (same codes)	3.65	(.861)	3.70	(.873)*
"How satisfied are you with your co-workers?" (0 = not at all satisfied, 3 = very satisfied)	4.21	(.841)	3.45	(.917)*
Outside socializing scale				
(alpha = .51, US; .81, Japan)	.409	(.555)	1.60	(.895)*
"How often do you get together with your coworkers outside of work?" (0 = seldom or never, 3 = once a week or more)	.801	(1.09)	2.14	(.946)*
"How often do you get together with your supervisor outside of work?" (same codes)	.203	(.547)	1.37	(1.10)*
"How often do you get together outside of work with managers other than your supervisor?" (same codes)	.225	(.593)	1.31	(1.10)*
Coworker friends: "About how many of your close friends work in this company?" (0 = almost none, 4 = almost all)	.923	(.911)	2.03	(1.24)*

Notes: * Difference between means is significant at p < .001 (2-tail test)

over by groups in Japanese companies, as witnessed by the prolific literature on the *ringi* system of consensus-seeking decision-making (Vogel, 1975; Yoshino, 1968), and the widespread use of quality circles as a means of eliciting worker input to production workflow decisions. Yet some of the emphasis on group-centered production and decision-making in Japan is no doubt overdrawn. As accounts of Japanese auto assembly-lines make clear (Osako, 1977; Kamata, 1983), the constraints of mass production technology sharply limit the amount of coworker interaction and the degree to which groups are able to take over the production process. Workers on the Japanese assembly line, like their American counterparts, often perform narrow tasks tied to fixed work stations which allow for little direct contact or consultation with others.

Our question bearing on the issue of teamwork asked the employee whether s/he "has to work closely with others in order to do the job well." This measure reflects the extent to which production is organized in work teams and other structures that require considerable coordination. We find the Japanese employees to be much more likely than the US employees to report that their jobs entail working with others (table 4.1). Given so many indications of greater workgroup organization in Japanese companies, the validity of our measurement would have been placed in serious question had the results proven otherwise.

Table 4.2, presenting the results of a regression analysis, suggests that an important predictor of working with others is job complexity.[1] This, of course, accords with past theory and research on job design: complex, nonroutine tasks involve greater problem-solving "search," hence, more communication and cooperation with others (March and Simon, 1958). But were the differences in reported teamwork mostly attributable to differences in perceived job complexity, we should expect to find more group activity in the US!

Closeness of supervision

In addition to teamwork being more pervasive in Japanese organization, a very common observation is that styles of supervision are highly distinctive, with strong personal bonds developing between superior and subordinate. Japanese foremen have a wide mandate to involve themselves broadly in their subordinates' lives both on and off the job (Cole, 1972:169; Dore, 1973:219). The paternalism and discretion associated with the foreman's role in Japanese factories appears at first similar to the arbitrary power and favoritism exercised by American foremen under the "drive" system of labor control in the early decades of the 20th Century (Gordon, Edwards, and Reich, 1982). As Jacoby's (1985) careful historical analysis documents, supervisory paternalism in US factories to a large extent collapsed under pressures from trade unionists, professional personnel managers, and middle-class reformers to democratize and rationalize the workplace. Such pressures have been less evident historically in Japan. Unions, in particular, have generally shunned the US precedent of demanding stringent work rules governing internal labor practices.

Yet it is misleading to draw too close an analogy between Japanese supervisory paternalism and the arbitrary rule of US foremen under the drive system. First, indications abound that such vertical dependency bonds have strong roots in Japanese culture (Nakane, 1970). Indeed, numerous surveys, including our own (see chapter 5), testify that this kind of broad, paternalistic leadership appears to be preferred by a very large segment of the Japanese workforce. Finally, while arbitrariness and favoritism are no doubt integral to Japanese foremen's supervisory style, there is also much evidence that the stress on consultation and consensus in Japanese decision-making tends to

Table 4.2 *Standardized regressions of task characteristics on employee background and position*

Independent variable	Job complexity		Teamwork		Dependent variables Supervisor contact		Supervisor control		Autonomy	
	US	Japan	US	Japan	US	Japan	US	Japan	US	Japan
Background										
Age	(.156**)	(-.049+)	[.024]	.092**)	[-.090**	-.204**]	(.092**	.073*)	.076**	.069*
Gender	(-.144**)	(-.204**)	[-.006]	-.033**]	-.062**	-.041+	[.131**	.077**]	-.039+	-.032+
Education	.031+	.010	[.032+	-.027]	-.024	.003	-.081**	-.063**	-.022	.027
Marital	.074**	.086*	.025	.013	[.002]	.055+]	-.011	-.039	.008	-.002
Position										
Manager	(.185**	.089)	(.139**	.046**)	[.040+	.004]	[-.164**	-.113**]	[.045+	.005]
Supervisor	(.183**	.129**)	(.205*	.060**)	.069**	.068**	-.144**	-.159**	(-.032	-.015)
Technical	-.032	.144**	[-.014	-.067**]	[.045+	-.009]	.003	.025	.014	-.005
Production	-.116**	-.112**	-.022	-.030	.037	.012	[.044+	.094**]	-.069**	-.071**
QC member	.030+	.028	.068**	.058**	(-.001	.059**)	-.014	-.030+	[.041+	.018]
Tenure	(-.054*	.060*)	[.023]	-.033]	[-.008]	.060**]	(-.052*	-.192**)	[-.012	.065+]
Task characteristics										
Job complexity			.107**	.197**	(-.107**	.016	-.134**	-.119**	.184**	.181**
Teamwork					.034+	.042+	.036+	-.001	(-.035*	.100**)
Spvr contact							(.184**	.035+)	(-.184**	-.039*)
Spvr control									-.274**	-.275**
Mean	(3.297)	3.079)	(3.216)	3.801)	(2.125)	3.204)	1.069	1.075	[3.591]	3.236]
Adj. Mean	(3.337)	2.996)	(3.281)	3.794)	(2.162)	2.941)	1.060	1.105	[3.501]	3.252]
Adj. R²	.183	.191	.110	.074	.027	.036	.181	.178	.225	.262

Notes: +p < .05
* p < .01
** p < .001
[ ] Difference in estimates is significant at the .05 level
( ) Difference in estimates is significant at the .01 level

avert the one-sided domination attributed to US foremen, particularly in times past.

Much of our analysis speaks directly or indirectly to the issue of supervisory style, and our findings do testify that the character of vertical relations is strikingly divergent in US and Japanese work settings. First, consider an item which is in a sense analogous to the "teamwork" question but pertains to supervisor contact: whether one's "supervisor leaves the worker alone unless s/he asks for help." Table 4.1 shows the Japanese are much more prone to disagree; to indicate, in other words, that their supervisors tend to initiate unsolicited contact more frequently than in the US.

What determines whether a supervisor tends to "let a worker alone" as opposed to staying in close contact? First, it would seem that where teamwork is the norm, greater communication between managers and workers should result. Table 4.2 hints that this is true in both countries, although the statistical relationships between teamwork and supervisor contact are extremely weak.

The direct effect of job complexity differs with the country. In Japan, there is none. Yet in the US we find a clear tendency for increments in job complexity to diminish the rate of supervisor contact. Thus, skilled US workers appear to distance themselves from supervisors in a way that is foreign to the Japanese workplace.

One explanation to consider is the US tradition of autonomy of the skilled trades and craft union control (Blauner, 1964; Form, 1980; Lipset, Trow, and Coleman, 1956). A common view is that complex jobs requiring high levels of training cannot be managed by supervisors hovering over the worker, giving directions and monitoring action. The skilled worker is entrusted to perform the task without such direct "behavior" control (Ouchi and Johnson, 1978), and, indeed, the nature of complex tasks would render this kind of supervisory domination highly ineffective in any case. On the other hand, the narrow spans of control associated with nonroutine tasks and highly skilled labor have suggested to some researchers that dense communications across ranks may accompany such work but without the connotation of direct, asymmetric control (Blau, 1968; Galbraith, 1977).

An item which gets much more directly at the style, as opposed to the frequency, of supervision is our measure of supervisory control, which taps the control and discretion of the employee *vis-à-vis* the supervisor in determining how the task should be performed: "to what extent does your supervisor or yourself determine what you do and how you do it?" There is no significant difference between the Japanese and US samples on this item (see table 4.1 and 4.2) – the average score of each corresponds to the category of "supervisor deciding what is to be done, employee deciding how to do it." There is, however, a considerable difference in the part that supervisor contact plays with respect to style of supervision. In the US workplace, it is clear that more such contact spells sharply increased control by supervisors, diminished control by workers. In the Japanese sample, we find a trivially significant tendency in the same direction, but it is so weak as to be substantively meaningless. There seems to be little question that supervisor involvement in subordinates' tasks does not have the same connotation of external control and domination that it conveys in the US factory.[2]

Autonomy

Autonomy refers to the amount of discretion an employee is able to exercise on the job. Our index is composed of three items (see table 4.1): how much freedom employees have in carrying out their job tasks; how much control they have over the speed of their work; and the degree to which their judgment affects what they actually do on their jobs.[3] We find the Americans reporting more freedom in how they do their work and more frequent use of their own judgment. There is no difference between the samples as to the amount of control employees exercise over the speed of work. Yet Dore's (1973:231) survey found a far higher percentage (78 percent) of British than Japanese (25 percent) employees reporting that they controlled the pace at which they worked. Coupled with our earlier findings regarding job complexity, a genuine pattern is apparent here of Japanese employees perceiving less complexity and autonomy in their jobs.

Once again, the more interesting findings concern the similarities and dissimilarities between countries in the processes giving rise to job autonomy. First, the strongest predictor is supervisor control, which has virtually identical effects in the two countries. Job complexity behaves likewise: whether Japanese or American, employees doing nonroutine, complex jobs enjoy more control and freedom. However, the implications of teamwork and supervisor contact are quite different between the countries. As with the previous measures of worker autonomy vs. supervisor control, American workers show a marked increase in the autonomy index when their supervisors "let them alone." Among the Japanese, this association, while in the same direction and marginally significant, is far weaker. A similar contrast is evident in the effects of teamwork. In the US, "working with others" has a small negative impact on autonomy. The relationship reverses in Japan: teamwork actually *increases* employees' feelings of freedom and control.

Thus far, we have encountered little evidence in support of the expectation that Japanese manufacturing employees perceive their jobs as more complex and allowing of more control and autonomy than the jobs of Americans. To speculate a bit beyond the data, this suggests to us the following, somewhat paradoxical, portrait of the situation faced by Japanese workers. There *are* structural arrangements in Japanese factories – e.g. cohesive work teams, nondirective supervision – that elicit workers' input on job decisions. Nonetheless, the picture of Japanese work life conveyed in ethnographic studies such as Cole's (1971), Dore's (1973), and Rohlen's (1974) hardly suggests that *individuals* enjoy a high degree of autonomy and discretion in the execution of their work roles. Workplace discipline is unquestionably high in Japanese industry – as amply evidenced by the behavioral indications of low absenteeism and militancy and high productivity – and pressures for conformity are great. Strong testimony can be found in Kamata's (1983) dramatic account of his days as an assembly worker in a Toyota truck manufacturing plant. The considerable degree of regimentation and control of production tasks in Japanese factories that he reports seems high even by the reportedly grim standards of American auto assembly lines (Chinoy, 1955; Walker and Guest, 1952). But as Dore stresses in a revealing introduction to Kamata's book, the discipline of Japanese labor described by Kamata emanates from all sides. It reflects the pressures of membership in a total community, which bends the individual to a monolithic collective will. It seems a rather different phenomenon from the heavily downward control directed at American or British workers which they experience as *external* coercion and thus collectively resist.

Effects of employee position on task characteristics

To this point, we have scrutinized US/Japan differences in the task characteristics of complexity, teamwork, supervision, and autonomy. Our attention now turns to how such aspects of the task depend on the positional variables of management rank, functional area, quality circle membership, and tenure in the firm.

Effects of management position   As indicated at the outset of this chapter, our broadest expectation for the impact of the management status hierarchy on all the job attributes and work orientations considered in this study is that the contrasts between levels are greater in US industry. Japanese companies appear to favor greater equality and homogeneity in a surprisingly broad array of areas: not just pay and benefits, but also responsibility, skill, control, and work conditions. This generalization is supported with remarkable consistency by the empirical findings we review in this section.

First, though managers and supervisors in both countries (expectedly) report their jobs to be more complex than those of workers, the differences are larger in the US (table 4.2). The contrast is even greater with respect to the amount of teamwork: American managers and supervisors are much more likely to work closely with others than is true of workers. In Japan, the variation across levels in teamwork is almost too small to be taken seriously. No doubt this contrast between the countries testifies to the prevalence in Japanese industry of truly shop-floor work teams and other small group activities such as QC and zero-defect. Presumably, management everywhere involves a high level of communication and cooperation with others. In US manufacturing, by contrast, production workers' jobs imply a degree of isolation from others that is clearly absent in Japan.

We also find that managers in both countries are subject to less supervisory control and enjoy more autonomy than workers, though the gaps are again larger in the US. The effects of status are similar in the US and Japan with respect to supervisory contacts: supervisors are less likely than either managers or workers to report that their own superiors leave them alone unless they ask for help. The intensity of supervision, then, is highest for the employees "in the middle," those who oversee the work of others but are themselves subject to the authority of higher-ups.

Functional area   Given the diversity in size and industry of the factories we surveyed and the significant obstacles to establishing comparable job categories across organizations *and* countries, the closest we come in this study to evaluating occupational differences in employee work orientations is a consideration of broad functional areas – production, technical support, and office.[4] Still, function, along with management level, are the key divisions in a manufacturing workforce in terms of skill and training, nature of task, and what, for want of a better label, might be termed occupational or industrial "culture." Production jobs generally involve semi-skilled manual labor, and, as long traditions of industrial sociology and psychology document, routine, repetitive tasks subject to extensive supervisory or machine control. Technical support jobs such as maintenance and the skilled trades (electricians, machinists) are the high-skill, blue-collar factory occupations. As laid out in such classic accounts of factory life as Crozier (1964), technical workers enjoy considerably more variety, control, and flexibility than production workers. In factory office jobs, the variance in skill may be considerable – from highly trained programmers and accountants to low-paid clerical staff – but they have in common non-manual, information-oriented tasks, a middle-class culture, and typically less-rigid work routines and patterns of supervision.

Consistent with these impressions of tasks in manufacturing production departments, our results in table 4.2 indicate, even with management rank held constant, that employees in production areas in both countries perceive their jobs to be less complex and involve more supervisory control and less autonomy than do technical and office employees. Only in the Japanese sample do technical workers clearly perceive greater complexity in their jobs than do office workers. One likely reason is the Japanese practice, which we have noted before, of employing large numbers of unskilled female clerical workers to perform routine, often personal service functions.

QC membership   We expect QC involvement to raise the perceived complexity of an employee's job. In their ideal form, as described, say, by Cole (1979), QC members undergo intensive training which upgrades their skills and knowledge of the production process. Moreover, the act of pooling information with others and jointly analyzing problems not only augments skill but also expands and deepens the work role. One likely reason for the rapid spread of QC activity in Japan is that the practice of frequent retraining and cross-training of workers to equip them for shifts in job responsibility was already institutionalized, and the training and pooling of tasks required by QC was not a significant break with established procedure. In the US, where job specialization is more common and rotation less so, serious QC activity involves more drastic change in traditional manpower and job design practices. This fuels the suspicion that American QC programs are more often token gestures at work reform. Table 4.2 indicates that QC in fact bears no more than a trivial relation to job complexity in either country.

Whether or not QC augments the skill content and task variety of manufacturing jobs, it is clearly aimed at increasing the worker's sense of participation in shop-floor decisions and control over operations, and, through these mechanisms, commitment and morale. QC, moreover, is designed to alter the relationship between supervisor and subordinate by reducing domination and control, while increasing communication and cooperation. Indeed, some evidence on the plant-level distribution of QC programs presented in chapter 7 suggests the interpretation that QC may reduce the power of lower-ranking supervisors. Table 4.2 indicates that QC participation fosters teamwork in both countries, and increases contacts with supervisors in Japan. Moreover, QC members in each country report slightly higher levels of discretion: in the US, as measured by the autonomy scale; in Japan, as indicated by freedom from supervisor control.

Tenure   A central theme in discussions of Japanese labor markets and employment practices concerns the *nenko* practice wherein seniority is made a key criterion for compensation and promotion. The roots of *nenko* lie in Japanese unions' postwar efforts to require companies to defray the reproduction costs of labor by ensuring, that with increasing age and responsibility (including family needs), the worker could count on income gains and career advancement. We discuss below the impact of seniority on the specific labor market outcomes of promotion chances and earnings. For now, our prediction is that the *nenko* mechanism implies a strong association between the employee's seniority and the quality of the job in terms of complexity and control. An alternative prediction, however, rests on the observation that status and reward in Japanese companies are only loosely tied to job responsibilities. Thus, an employee can advance in pay and status without undergoing significant shifts in task or authority (Clark, 1979; Pucik, 1984). This decoupling of responsibility and status allows the organization to reward seniority (loyalty), while nonetheless allocating tasks on the basis of competence.

Our data support the first hypothesis: that job complexity and control are more closely pegged to seniority in Japan than in the United States. Japanese

Table 4.3. *Standardized regressions of job reward variables on employee background, position, and task characteristics*

	Dependent Variables					
	Intrinsic rewards		Earnings		Promotion chances	
Independent variable	US	Japan	US	Japan	US	Japan
Background						
Age	.032+	.058+	.069**	.136**	−.177**	−.139**
Gender	.035*	−.023	−.228**	−.251**	−.047**	−.144**
Education	−.073**	−.011	.149**	.075**	.120**	.212**
Marital	[.006]	.043+]	.074**	.173**	−.012	.059*
Position						
Manager	.100**	.013	.143**	.088*	.112**	.038+
Supervisor	.083**	.026	−.107**	.097**	.120**	.045*
Technical	−.034+	.048+	.076**	−.009	.005	.031
Production	[−.036+]	.016	.024	−.005	.021	.005
QC member	.051**	.065**			[.043**]	[.000]
Tenure	−.015	−.036	.250**	.333**	−.055*	−.021
Task characteristics						
Job complexity	.567**	.373**	[.100**]	.040*	.135**	.117**
Teamwork	.009	.104**				
Spvr contact	−.061**	.125**				
Spvr control	−.011	−.043*				
Autonomy	.096**	.128**			(.008)	.065**

			OJT			
			(.001)	.078**)		
Mean	3.517	3.486	(20,319.2)	12,699.1)	.264	.256
Adj. Mean	3.463	3.451	(21,181.8)	2,229.93)	[.290]	[.235]
Adj. R²	.442	.272	.298	.618	.214	.235

Notes: +p < .05
* p < .01
** p < .001
[] Difference in estimates is significant at the .05 level
() Difference in estimates is significant at the .01 level

employees with longer tenures have jobs that are more complex, give more autonomy, and involve less direct supervisory control. However, in the US sample, tenure is unrelated to autonomy and negatively related to complexity. One explanation for this pattern is the far greater tendency on the part of American companies to hire experienced employees from the external labor market to perform complex tasks. Such mid-career recruiting, while perhaps on the rise in Japan, is still quite rare, and most companies adhere to the traditional practice of recruiting inexperienced junior employees and preparing them in-house.

Job rewards

Job rewards refer broadly to the benefits and utilities that individuals obtain from work. Such rewards should be especially important determinants of commitment and satisfaction in work organizations such as manufacturing plants, which rely primarily on incentives other than normative ones to elicit compliance from their members. We consider differences in work attitudes produced by two general kinds of job rewards: intrinsic; and extrinsic (earnings and opportunities for promotion).

Intrinsic rewards

I think most of us are looking for a calling, not a job. Most of us, like the assembly line worker, have jobs that are too small for our spirit. Jobs are not big enough for people. (Nora Watson, Editor, from Studs Terkel, *Working*, 1972)

Intrinsic rewards are benefits that employees derive *from* task performance as opposed to those they receive *for* such performance. Such rewards provide symbolic satisfactions (Brown, 1969), and commitment has been shown to be enhanced when people are given opportunities to accomplish, as individuals, things over which they have some degree of control (Angle and Perry, 1983; Aranya and Jacobson, 1975). Deriving instrinsic rewards from work is, moreover, the antithesis of alienation in the self-estrangement sense since people are able to express themselves through meaningful work by using and developing their skills and abilities (Blauner, 1964).

We measure intrinsic rewards by the extent of agreement or disagreement to four questionnaire items that tap the degree of fulfillment the employee derives from work. These include the extent to which he or she finds the job to: (1) be challenging; (2) be meaningful; (3) enable use of skills; and (4) permit the employee to see results (see table 4.1 for the wording and coding of these items.) Intrinisc rewards differ from the task characteristics we discussed in the last section in that they are highly subjective assessments, and in no way logically imply specific objective features of work. Quite diverse kinds of tasks may be regarded as "meaningful" or "challenging," depending on the person. In contrast, variables such as job complexity, autonomy, and close supervision represent perceptions of objective job characteristics.

A cardinal theme in the social–psychological literature on job attributes and motivation holds that jobs that are complex, require high skills, and permit high discretion are much more intrinsically rewarding (Herzberg *et al.*, 1959; Maslow, 1954). Some authors, however, have argued that these relations may be contingent on the worker's expectations and values (Blood and Hulin, 1967; Turner and Lawrence, 1965). We find very similar effects of job complexity and autonomy on the intrinsic rewards scale in Japan and the US; with one, by now familiar, exception. US employees whose supervisors "leave them alone" (supervisor contact) see their jobs as more rewarding. Among the Japanese, we find the opposite relationship: unsolicited supervisory intervention is a source of greater intrinsic job rewards. This pattern of findings concerning supervisory intervention, especially when coupled with other researchers' observations on Japanese superior–subordinates ties, identifies a striking and significant contrast in the vertical organization of the Japanese and American workplace with obvious implications for cooperative industrial relations and organizational loyalty.

Our results in tables 4.1 and 4.3 indicate that American and Japanese employees obtain similar overall levels of intrinsic reward from their jobs. However, we find some country differences on specific items: the Americans are more likely to see their jobs as meaningful and challenging; while the Japanese believe their jobs make better use of their skills (see table 4.1). A speculative interpretation of this last finding is that it reflects the greater penchant of Japanese plants for rotating employees among a variety of tasks. On the other hand, Japanese and US employees are equally likely to feel that their jobs let them see the results of their work.

Within countries, levels of intrinsic reward differ by position in the organization. In the US, but not in Japan, managers and supervisors find their work to be more rewarding than workers typically do. This appears to testify again to the success of Japanese companies in smoothing the distribution of rewards across management levels. US employees in direct production and technical departments report slightly lower intrinsic rewards than office people. In Japan, however, members of technical support departments enjoy greater intrinsic rewards. Moreover, quality circle members receive higher intrinsic rewards. Finally, tenure is unrelated to intrinsic rewards in either country.

Extrinsic rewards: earnings and promotions

Our focus thus far in this chapter has been on aspects of jobs and the employment relationship which affect commitment and morale through the positive or negative contributions they make to employees' sense of meaningful, interesting work and attachment to a cohesive and supportive work community. Organizations that seek control through commitment, we have argued, use sophisticated means to make the work experience an intrinsically rewarding one in an effort to forestall the alienation and detachment so often associated with factory life. Yet in all this, we can hardly forget that people take jobs in large measure to earn incomes and advance careers, and such extrinsic inducements obviously play a fundamental role in motivating the decision to join, stay with, and work for a firm (see Goldthorpe *et al.*, 1968). Even so, there is a strong tendency, particularly in the humanistic wings of organizational psychology and sociology, to view extrinsic or utilitarian inducements as insufficient to ensure a high level of participation. They are seen as unreliable guarantors of employee performance, for while they may evoke the specific behavior to which the inducement is geared, they contribute little to the development of strong and lasting commitment to the organization (Clark and Wilson, 1961; Edwards, 1979; Etzioni, 1961).

The extent to which earnings predominate among the repertoire of inducements which firms offer to secure the participation and commitment of their employees undoubtedly varies cross-nationally and culturally. While no serious observer would downplay the importance of earnings as a reason for working among the Japanese (Odaka, 1975), there is a widespread perception that strong cultural values extolling the virtues of work and membership in a large corporation are more powerful inducements (Vogel, 1963). Indeed, as contrasted with the instrumentally oriented affluent workers Goldthorpe *et al.* (1968) studied, neglecting work pursuits for the sake of home and family has been denigrated by staunch defenders of traditional Japanese virtues as "my-homeism." Recall that our own results, described in chapter 3, revealed that the Japanese rate family relative to work life considerably below the rankings made by the Americans in our sample. On the other hand, commentators on Japanese work trends have suggested that dissatisfaction with pay, particularly among younger workers, is a major source of work discontent (Odaka, 1975; Takezawa, 1976; Woronoff, 1981). Levels of starting pay are indeed quite low in Japanese industry, although, under the *nenko* system, opportunities for regular increases with advancing seniority and family responsibilities are typically better than those Western workers enjoy (Koike, 1983).

Direct comparisons between the earnings of Japanese and American employees are made notoriously difficult by shifting exchange rates, cost of living differences, and the tendency for Japanese employees to receive a greater proportion of their compensation in the form of non-wage benefits. Most analyses have shown the wages of Japanese employees to be less than the average earnings of American employees, although Vogel (1979) has claimed that pay levels in Japan are at least on a par with those in the United States. His estimates, however, are based on an exchange rate of 180 yen to the dollar. This was less than the exchange rate at the time we conducted our surveys, and the one we use in our analyses – 250 yen to the dollar – though it is more than the current (1988) rate of approximately 130. Using Vogel's exchange rate, we find that Japanese employees in our sample earn $17,638 on the average, trailing by less than $2,000 the Americans who on average earn $19,110. Using the 250 yen exchange rate, the Japanese figure shrinks to $12,699.

It is, in any case, difficult to ascertain how the purchasing power and standard of living of Japanese manufacturing employees compare to that of US workers. Fewer import restrictions, abundant land, and cheap credit have put many goods and services within reach of American workers. Yet company subsidized housing, education, family allowances, and other welfare services extend the paychecks of many Japanese. A more important question than that of country differences in levels of earnings is the extent to which the *processes* of wage determination differ between Japan and the US. Here is an area in which numerous observers have identified sharp differences between Japanese and US practice. Our treatment is an abbreviated version of a more detailed statistical inquiry which is reported in Kalleberg and Lincoln (1988).[5]

The Nenko *system* Nenko is the label given to a bundle of Japanese practices which place a heavy stress on seniority, age, and family responsibilities as criteria for pay and promotion, and a corresponding deemphasis on job-based and merit criteria. It is a central element in the Japanese wage system, which, as described in a number of useful accounts, has several distinctive features and a clearly delineated history since World War II (Cole, 1971; Koike, 1983; Umemura, 1980). For our purposes, a particularly interesting aspect of that history is the debate that has transpired in Japan over the use of job or occupation-based skill and merit criteria, as opposed to seniority and life cycle need criteria, for the allocation of wages. In the immediate postwar period of high inflation and serious shortages of essentials such as food and housing, Japanese unions demanded that companies take responsibility for the reproduction costs of labor – the amount required to sustain an adequate standard of living for the worker and his family. Thus, the livelihood wage became the first and basic component of the employee wage package, and its magnitude was tied to life cycle circumstances associated with age, seniority, marital status, and childbearing.

As the economy grew, the argument for a minimum standard of living became less compelling, and firms, under the growing influence of American personnel practices, moved to rationalize the wage system by tying pay to job content, workers' skills and productivity. Moreover, rapid technological changes, by rendering the skills of older workers obsolete, began to erode the relationship between seniority and skill. However, while some Japanese management circles in the postwar era have continuously pushed for a larger role for job classification and evaluation in wage determination, there has been strong resistance to these moves. Many companies fear the rigidity of tight job classifications and the constraints they imply on management discretion in allocating labor within the firm. In addition, Japanese unions have consistently opposed occupational wage systems, even to the point of defensively arguing for merit-based compensation tied not to job characteristics but to the qualifications of employees (Dore, 1973:98; Ono, 1980:157). As Daito (1984:124) puts it:

> These days, therefore, many firms prefer the 'payment by ability' scheme to the 'payment by job' scheme. Under the payment by ability scheme, workers are paid according to their ability to perform a job even if they are not performing it at the time the evaluation is made. This ... serves to maintain the flexibility of manpower utilization and job assignments.

Koike (1983:50) likewise argues that the seniority (*nenko*) system: "means that each wage rate is determined primarily by length of service, but partially by merit-rating, although the basic rates are negotiated by the local union". On the other hand, there are "no significant differentials in basic wages according to ... occupation."

One clear case of successful union opposition to occupation-based wage differentials was the movement to abolish status discrimination between blue- and white-collar workers in the years immediately following World War II (Daito, 1984:127; Shirai, 1983:130). There is considerable evidence that wage and benefit differentials between these groups are markedly smaller than in other industrialized countries (Dore, 1973; Koike, 1983:37; Shirai, 1983:131). Koike (1983:38) sees these efforts as resulting in a white-collarization of the Japanese blue-collar workforce: Japanese blue-collar workers appear similar to white-collar employees in Japan and other industrial countries as regards employment stability, level of fringe benefits, and the shape of the seniority wage curve (See Kalleberg and Berg, 1987, for a discussion of the growing homogeneity between white- and blue-collar occupations in the US).

Similarly, the fundamental division between managers and workers does not appear to be as crucial for earnings determination in Japan as in the US and other Western countries. As we have noted, Japanese authority hierarchies are more finely graded in the sense that vertical differentiation is greater but total inequality is less (Dore, 1973:257). Moreover, many of the symbols of management status (white collars, separate parking lots and dining rooms, salaried pay schedules) are missing or muted in Japanese firms, suggesting a general corporate strategy of fostering integration by keeping inequality down.

What explanations exist for the rise and institutionalization of the seniority wage system in Japanese industry? One view is that because of Japan's late industrialization, unskilled rural migrants until recently constituted the chief source of industrial labor supply. This state of affairs required companies to make a heavy investment in training employees in job skills, plant operations, and modern factory organization. The most readily available sources of expertise in these areas were older and more experienced workers, who took on the responsibility for on-the-job training of new recruits. Thus, this system implied a strong association between workers' age and seniority, on the one hand, and their skill and experience, on the other. It also guaranteed that the skills transferred were highly specific to the particular enterprise in which the veteran and novice workers were employed. One can also see in these arrangements the groundwork for the oft-noted Japanese practice of recruiting generalists and subjecting them to intensive in-house training and socialization.

An alternative though not competing explanation for the *nenko* wage system sees it as an integral part of the control logic of the firm internal labor market. Careful screening of prospective employees, high job security, frequent job rotation, intensive internal training, internal career mobility and seniority-based pay and promotion constitute a set of practices that foster high employee dependence on the firm and strong commitment to the pursuit of company goals. Burawoy (1983), Edwards (1979), and others view firm internal labor markets as highly effective mechanisms of control, for they motivate productive effort on the firm's behalf without the costs associated with more specific and instrumental rewards and sanctions. Moreover, Lazear (1979) has argued that, under lifetime employment, a seniority wage system that pays workers less than the value of their marginal product in their early career and at a rate exceeding that later in life, results in greater productivity at no increased cost to the worker or the firm. The reason is that such a system averts the "agency" problem of workers' "shirking" by raising their stake in the future of the firm (Mincer and Higuchi, 1987). However, a seniority wage system demands mandatory retirement in order to ensure that wages paid to older workers do not exceed the lifetime value of their marginal product. The low (age 55–60) mandatory retirement age which is the norm in Japanese industry is, of course, wholly in line with this theory.

We have clear and consistent evidence in table 4.3 that individuals' jobs and positions play a greater role in the determination of earnings in the US than in the Japanese sample of manufacturing employees. Job complexity has a larger impact in the US. Moreover, there are earnings inequalities among functional divisions in US plants which are absent in Japan; specifically, technical employees receive higher net earnings than production or office people.

Furthermore, consistent with the common observation that top-to-bottom earnings inequality is greater in US than in Japanese companies (Abegglen and Stalk, 1985; Dore, 1973), we find that management position has less direct impact on wage determination in Japan. Using the exchange rate at the time of the study of 250 yen to the dollar, the Japanese workers in our sample earn $10,673, the Americans $18,062; the Japanese supervisors average $16,222, the Americans $19,589; and the Japanese managers earn $20,541, while the American managers earn $35,542. In *absolute* terms, the earnings advantage of managers over workers is much larger in the US sample, but as a *percent* of workers' earnings the gaps are about the same. The earnings regression given in table 4.3, however, shows that the manager–worker gap contributes a larger proportion of the earnings variance in the US than in Japan. It appears that a substantial part of the earnings inequality among Japanese managers, supervisors, and workers can be attributed to the background, position, and task variables held constant in the regression. In Japan, the net earnings gap between managers and workers is $5,028, or half the gross difference. The US managers' net advantage is $12,311, or more than 71 percent of the gross difference. The smaller capacity of the background and job variables to explain the earnings advantage enjoyed by US managers reinforces the suspicion that a more fundamental "class" barrier separates managers and workers in US as compared with Japanese factories.

The other interesting societal contrast in these data concerns the compensation of supervisors. In the Japanese sample, supervisors' earnings fall roughly midway between managers' and workers' earnings. Among the Americans, however, supervisors on average earn only about $1,500 more than workers, and when their advantages in terms of human capital and job quality are controlled (table 4.3), their net earnings actually drops *below* that of workers. Thus, the distribution of earnings has a rather different shape in US and Japanese manufacturing. Not only is there less overall inequality between top management and direct labor in Japan, but the distribution is less skewed and discontinuous, owing, perhaps to the *nenko* practice of awarding incremental increases with rising age, seniority, and status. In the US, there tends to be a large earnings gap between the college-educated managers who run the enterprise and the first-line supervisors and hourly workers who oversee and do the actual work of production.

If job characteristics and management position play smaller roles in Japanese processes of earnings determination, the other side of the *nenko* system is the greater importance attached to the internal labor market mechanisms of seniority and internal training and the ascriptive personal attributes of age and family responsibility. Both these expectations are supported by our data. Tenure proves to be important in both countries but significantly less so in the US. Our internal training measure, moreover, is related to earnings only in the Japan case. Years of schooling, on the other hand, play a somewhat larger role in setting US earnings. This is consistent with our general sense that external qualifications and certification are less consequential for internal rewards and opportunities in the Japanese workplace.

Age and marital status, our only measures of personal background characteristics, behave as the *nenko* model would have us expect: while both have significant and positive influences on earnings, these effects are larger in the Japanese sample. One might wonder about the mechanism linking marriage and earnings for male workers in the US, where family maintenance needs rarely trigger the allocation of economic rewards. We speculate that in the US, a large portion of this effect is the tangible cost of divorce (coded as "unmarried" in our data), a component which, given the far lower divorce rates, is surely negligible in Japan.

Opportunities for promotion

More than earnings, we think, opportunity for promotion is a key weapon in the corporatist arsenal for winning the compliance and commitment of employees: workers who perceive that they have a career with the company are more likely to be committed to its goals and fortunes over a long period of time. Our measure of the employee's promotion prospects is a dichotomous variable tapping whether ($=1$) or not ($=0$) the employee expects to be promoted. This perceptual measure is an evaluation by the employee of his or her chances of promotion, and thus reflects both objective promotion opportunities and the worker's subjective evaluation of them.

As a number of analysts have observed, characteristic features of Japanese companies such as permanent employment, selective recruitment, internal training and intrafirm career mobility are expressions of the general structure of a firm internal labor market. From the premise that Japanese plants are more likely than American companies to be organized in this fashion, we expect there to be greater opportunities for upward mobility in Japan. Japanese companies are thought to start workers at low wages but to provide steady increments in earnings and other job rewards through regular advancements. In contrast, while entry-level positions may provide relatively high earnings in US manufacturing plants, they are often seen as dead-end jobs for production workers, as the prospects for upward movement into skilled trades or management positions are small.

Despite the additional complexity posed by the subjective nature of our promotion probability indicator, our framework for understanding this form of extrinsic reward is similar to the case of earnings. The hypothesis is that *nenko* and other internal labor market factors play greater roles in shaping Japanese organizational careers, whereas occupational/positional considerations are more operative in the US. Indeed, from the premise that Japanese firms are more likely to be organized as internal labor markets, we expect, following Cole (1979), greater overall promotion rates. Such internal movements are viewed as complementing the lower rates of interfirm job-changing that are well-documented in the Japanese economy. Despite our lack of data on actual moves, this proposition translates into higher perceived odds of promotion for the Japanese.

However, tables 4.1 and 4.3 indicate that there is no overall difference between US and Japanese employees in perceived likelihood of promotion: just over a quarter of the employees in each sample anticipate one. Moreover, when we control for differences in sample composition in job characteristics and demographics, it appears that promotion expectations are slightly higher in the US (see the adjusted means in table 4.3).

How can we account for the finding that perceived promotion opportunities are no higher than the US and perhaps lower in Japanese organizations? First note that this result parallels Cole's (1979) finding of lower actual intrafirm mobility in the Yokohama than in the Detroit labor market. Cole's explanation was that jobs are not well defined in Japanese companies, hence the regular increments in pay and status that characterize Japanese careers may not be seen as promotions involving a real change in job function and responsibility. Consequently, a variety of moves not perceived or even measurable as job changes could in fact be taking place.

It is also possible that American employees are simply more optimistic, overrating their actual promotion chances, while the fatalistic Japanese underrate them. We suggested earlier that cultural differences in modes of self-expression might produce biases in reports of expectations and attitudes. Yet perceived promotion opportunities are less subjective than feelings of job satisfaction and are less likely to be colored by biases of this sort.

Our prediction of higher promotion rates in Japanese plants derived from the assumption that the latter are more apt to be organized as internal labor markets. Not only has that prediction proved wrong, but the evidence from our regression analyses of the antecedents of promotion expectation likewise gives mixed support at best for the ILM interpretation.[6] In support of it, however, training increases promotion expectations only among the Japanese.

On the other hand, some of the patterns we observe seem more consistent with the operation of the *nenko* principle. In both countries, age is strongly and negatively related to promotion expectations. No surprise in this, as older employees are closer to the ends of their careers and, in any case, have adjusted their expectations to the realities of workplace opportunity structures. The effects of tenure and age are similar in the US: promotion expectations decline with time spent in the organization. Among the Japanese, however, the impact of tenure, while similarly signed, is miniscule and nonsignificant. This suggests that our initial impression of overall equal promotion expectations in Japan and the US may be somewhat misleading. The fact that perceived promotion probabilities stay constant over the Japanese employee's involvement with the firm suggests that real opportunities are not foreclosed as early in the career. Some observers have argued that promotion tends to be slow in Japanese organizations, since, unless the firm is growing rapidly, permanent employment means that vacancies become available chiefly through retirement, and *nenko* requires that members of each cohort move upward in a fixed sequence (Pucik and Hatvany, 1983:113). Fast-tracking is a rare phenomenon in Japanese companies. It may be, then, that while the odds of internal promotion over the course of the employee's career *are* higher in Japanese labor markets, promotion chances in the short run are no better, and perhaps worse for particularly able employees than is typical of the US.

Another pattern consistent with the *nenko*, though not necessarily the FILM, interpretation is that, in Japan, location in the management hierarchy is less fateful for the distribution of opportunities and rewards. While the percentage of workers anticipating promotion is roughly 20 percent in each country, American managers and supervisors perceive their promotion chances to be better than their Japanese counterparts: 43 percent of the US vs. 36 percent of the Japanese supervisors expect promotion, and 56 percent vs. 46 percent of managers. A final piece of evidence that the *nenko* process has a hand in the structuring of opportunities in the Japanese workplace concerns the effect of marital status. It makes a small positive contribution to the promotion expectations of the Japanese; none at all in the case of the Americans.

Otherwise, there is little notable evidence that promotion processes vary between Japan and the US. Functional area makes no difference in either country. Women of both nationalities are disadvantaged, although their handicap is greater in Japan. Educational attainments enhance promotion expectations in both countries, though more so among the Japanese. Finally, job complexity raises promotion expectations in both the US and Japan.

Social bonds

We have discussed several measures of the degree to which the employee is involved in work groups or in other kinds of relationships with supervisors and coworkers. Now we extend our analysis of social relations to the web of informal bonds that evolves within the workplace society. The difference between the relational variables we examine here and those we termed task characteristics (teamwork, supervisor contact and control) turns on the latter being instrumental or work-related ties required by the job, while the former reflect informal, nonprescribed associations.

The topic of social bonds has long been central to theory and research on the workplace. Radicals from Marx onward have bemoaned the disintegrating features of capitalist employment relations that atomize the working class and inhibit the formation of solidary labor associations (Gordon, Edwards, and Reich, 1982). Mainstream theories of work alienation also stress the socially isolating qualities of large scale, bureaucratic, and mass production factories (Blauner, 1964). Moreover, much organizational social psychology assumes that social relations and informal group processes play key roles in determining worker motivation and productivity and sees them as manipulable to management's advantage through careful organizational design and leadership practice.

The issue of workplace social integration also takes on special significance in a comparative study of work life in Japan and the US. A central theme in accounts of Japanese work life and organization is the high degree of work-group cohesion, the close and personal relations with work mates and supervisors, and the overall solidarity and familial character of the firm. Coworkers spend considerable time together in off-the-job socializing, drinking, and participating in sports and recreational activities. Friendships and leisure-time visiting tend to involve other employees to a degree that is remarkable by American standards (see Cole, 1971; Rohlen, 1974). Relations between supervisors and subordinates as some of our analyses thus far have suggested, are often diffuse, warm, and paternalistic – terms not often used to describe the same relations in the US.

These social structural qualities of Japanese work organizations are widely seen as instrumental in binding workers to, and fostering strong identification with, the firm. Indeed, as such relations are deliberately nurtured and manipulated by the firm through group-based production and decision-making and company-sponsored social and recreational programs, they appear to be an ingredient in the general corporatist control objectives of limiting turnover and fostering compliance and dependence. However, as in so many questions concerning the roots of Japanese employment practice, it is no easy matter to ascertain whether the social integration of Japanese employees flows from corporate efforts to engender it, or whether those efforts are simply reflections of a culturally grounded Japanese impulse to seek solitary group attachments in diverse spheres of life.

Measuring social integration and cohesion

We have argued for two main ways of classifying social relations in the workplace: "vertical," superior-subordinate, ties; and "horizontal" ties among coworkers of equal rank. We constructed composite scales that tap the quality of each of these kinds of relations (see table 4.1 for details on these measures). The *quality of vertical ties* scale is the average of the responses to five questions dealing with the frequency and nature of relations with supervisors, the degree of satisfaction with supervisors, and the extent to which supervisors encourage teamwork. The *quality of coworker ties* scale is the average of the responses to four questions tapping the employee's satisfaction with his or her coworkers, whether coworkers are friendly and helpful, the extent of trust and confidence placed in coworkers, and the degree to which the employee feels a part of the work group. The correlations between the horizontal and vertical social relations scales are .24 (in the US) and .36 (in Japan).

Given our findings to this point and our general sense for the distinctive qualities of superior–subordinate ties in Japanese organizations, we expect the Japanese to score higher on the quality of vertical relations scale. The difference between the unadjusted means (see tables 4.1 and 4.4) is in this direction and is highly significant. However, when adjusted for the covariates in table 4.4, the difference reverses, indicating better vertical ties in US plants.

Focusing only on the composite indices masks some important differences in the specific items that comprise them. Of the five items in the vertical ties scale, the Japanese means are clearly higher on the three which deal directly with the strength and frequency of super/subordinate relations (see table 4.1). They are: (a) the employee's willingness to confide in his supervisor concerning personal matters; (b) the frequency with which the employee talks with the superior about work; and (c) frequency of talking to the superior about matters other than work. An item on which there is no difference is the extent to which the supervisor encourages teamwork. The only item in the quality of vertical ties scale on which the Japanese score markedly below the Americans is the measure of satisfaction with supervisors. By now we have seen that almost any kind of satisfaction question tends to elicit low assessments from the Japanese.

Both adjusted and unadjusted means of the quality-of-coworker-ties scale are higher for the American employees: they saw their workmates as more helpful; were more satisfied with their coworkers; and were slightly more inclined to say that they were really a part of their work groups. One should consider, however, that US workers' expectations for work-group helpfulness are probably lower, since the Japanese are involved in teamwork to a considerably greater extent. The same holds for feelings of being a part of the group. Again, satisfaction with coworkers is probably colored by response bias. Further, the Japanese report greater confidence and trust in the members of their work groups.

Another composite scale measuring informal social bonds deals directly with the extent to which employees engage in outside, after-hours *socializing* with one another. The index is based on three items derived from the responses to the question: "how often [seldom or never = 0, to once a week or more = 3] do you get together outside of work with: your coworkers; your supervisor; and other managers?" Again we have a criterion for evaluating the validity of our survey methodology: off-the-job contacts, for both work and leisure purposes, have been observed and reported so often in qualitative and journalistic studies of Japanese work life that our failure to document them would seriously jeopardize the credibility of our inquiry. Fortunately, the Japanese in our sample report far more outside contacts with coworkers and (especially) supervisors than do the Americans.

These three items are only moderately correlated in the US sample (.26 to .28), but are quite strongly associated in the Japanese data (.52 to .74). This points to a substantively interesting societal difference. In the US, relations with coworkers and supervisors are distinct phenomena. While the Americans only get together with coworkers on an average of several times a year, they "seldom" or "never" socialize with their supervisors. In contrast, off-the-job interactions in Japan are not only more common than in the US, but they also reflect a single underlying dimension. This pattern is consistent with what many observers have previously noted regarding Japanese work relations: strong social bonds extend both horizontally and vertically.

The final item tapping the strength of social bonds in the workplace is simply the direct question: "how many of your close friends [from $0 =$ almost none, to $4 =$ almost all] work in this company?" Again, there is no contest: the Japanese report an average of two close friends in the company as compared to less than one for the Americans. Another interesting aspect of this question concerns its correlations with the off-the-job socializing items. In the US sample, employees who have more close friends at the workplace are also more likely to go out with coworkers off-the-job (.28), though they are only marginally more likely to socialize with supervisors/managers (.09/.10). However, in the Japanese sample, the number of close friends is correlated no higher than .15 with any of the three off-the-job interaction items. These findings are consistent with the interpretation that much of the after-hours socializing that Japanese employees pursue with coworkers and superiors is really not leisure at all but rather an extension of the workday in a more relaxed and informal mode. Business is done and work problems are solved at these sessions; they are not purely social events pursued by people who work together and happen to like each others' company.[7]

Job position, task characteristics and social bonds

How are workplace social networks shaped by an employee's job attributes, and do these processes differ in Japanese and US industry?

Task characteristics   First, we find impressive evidence in both countries for the effectiveness of quality circles as agents of social integration and cohesion (see table 4.4). The effects of QC membership are significant and positive with respect to all four social bond indices. The effectiveness of QC in stimulating both vertical and horizontal integration in the two countries is particularly impressive, given our sense for important differences, not only in the design and goals of QC programs in Japan and the US, but also in the patterning of superior/subordinate relations.

We certainly expect informal ties and after-hours socializing with workmates to vary with the extent to which the job requires close working relations with others, and the data show this to be the case. The *teamwork* item is positively associated with the social bond indicators (table 4.4). Surprisingly, these effects of teamwork on informal ties are generally not stronger in the Japanese sample; indeed, they are nonsignificant in the case of friendships. Since informal bonding is so much weaker in US plants, an *ad hoc* interpretation is that it primarily occurs where workers' jobs require much close cooperation.

By promoting teamwork, job complexity indirectly enhances social integration. It also appears to have positive direct effects in both countries on every social bond dimension but friendships.

Supervisor contact has been shown to have a very different significance to our Japanese and US respondents. In the US, for example, there was clearly a connotation of domineering supervision which was absent in Japan. We find an even stronger contrast in the impact of this factor on informal relations. In Japan, a supervisor "who leaves the worker alone" diminishes the employee's integration on all four social bond dimensions – quality of supervisor and coworker relations, outside socializing, and close friends. In the US sample, the picture is dramatically different. We find strong tendencies for American employees to assign higher ratings to the quality of their superior and coworker ties as supervisor contact declines. It has no effect, however, on friendships and outside get-togethers.

Once again, our results point to significant differences between US and Japanese factories in the role of the supervisor and in the supervisory expectations of subordinates. As we observed earlier, a pervasive theme in the study of Japanese work organization is that the Japanese supervisor is less an overseer giving orders than a group leader and facilitator, more concerned with maintaining work-group cohesion and *esprit de corps* than controling the actions of employees. Our findings concerning the divergent implications of supervisor contact in Japan and the US are wholly consistent with the following passage from Cole (1979:245):

> the Japanese supervisor is expected to check a subordinate's work during the course of the work. If he doesn't the subordinate will feel that the supervisor is not concerned about him. There is the need to constantly depend upon supervisors. By contrast ... British workers are content to have their work evaluated after it is done. To be constantly checked while doing the work would be interpreted by subordinates as negative behavior.

The American factory worker's feelings about supervision are summed up by Mike Lefevre, a steelworker interviewed by Studs Terkel in *Working:*

> Working is bad enough, don't bug me. I would rather work my ass off for eight hours a day with nobody watching me than five minutes with a guy watching me.

Finally, we note that employees who perceive greater job autonomy have higher quality social relations in the workplace. Autonomy thus appears to have little in common with isolation, and workers who enjoy more control and discretion are probably more at ease about developing strong ties with superiors and other workers. Moreover, it is likely that the causality between autonomy and social integration is reciprocal: access to social networks is a resource in workplace society which increases the employee's perception of power and freedom in the work role.

Authority and function We find the familiar pattern of larger differences among management levels in the US than in Japan. American supervisors

Table 4.4 Standardized regressions of social bond measures on employee background, position, and task characteristics

| | Dependent variables | | | | | | | |
| | Socializing | | Friends | | Quality of vertical ties | | Quality of coworker ties | |
Independent variable	US	Japan	US	Japan	US	Japan	US	Japan
Background								
Age	(−.246**)	(−.060+)	−.168**	−.134**	.032	.051+	[.100**]	.062+
Gender (1=F)	(−.071**)	(.024)	−.009	.014	.023	−.009	.018	.031
Education	[−.003]	[−.050*]	−.056**	(−.100**)	−.057**	(.026)	−.018	.006
Married (=1)	[−.094**]	[−.035]	−.014	.062*)	−.011	.055*)	.030	−.001
Position								
Manager	(.144**)	(.033)	[−.041+]	.011]	.026	.002	.001	−.013
Supervisor	.043*	.021	(−.048*)	.015)	(.093**)	(−.008)	.006	−.025
Technical	[−.056*]	[−.003]	.042	.072**	−.009	−.023	.001	−.011
Production	[−.045+]	[.014]	.044+	.025	−.022	−.038	.037	−.010
QC Member	.082**	.058**	.079**	.069**	.091**	.102**	[.029+]	.056**
Tenure	.003	.027	(.271**)	.258**)	−.021	.003	−.025	−.037
Task characteristics								
Job complexity	.092**	.095**	.026	.022	(.145**)	.048*)	[.087**]	.040+
Teamwork	.071**	.059**	[.077**]	.031	.077**	.044*	[.101**]	.157**
Spvr contact	(−.009)	.060**	.001	.070**)	(−.177**)	.147**)	[−.102*]	.036+
Spvr control	(−.026)	(−.082**)	−.020	−.022	−.008	−.026	(.044*)	−.016)
Autonomy	.030	.027	.053**	.000	.117**	.106**	.109**	.089**

Social bonds

	(1)	(2)	(3)	(4)	(5)	(6)	(7)	(8)
Socializing					.139**	.314	[.061**]	[.130**]
Friends					.070**	−.004	.139**	.089**
Mean	(.409)	1.604	(.923)	2.033	(2.483)	2.612	[3.950]	[3.540]
Adj. Mean	(.471)	1.525	(.975)	1.866	(2.574)	2.373	(3.998)	(3.403)
Adj. R²	.132	.043	.064	.091	.181	.208	.052	.088

Notes: +p < .05
*p < .01
**p < .001
[] Difference in estimates is significant at the .05 level
() Difference in estimates is significant at the .01 level

have a much more positive view of *their* superiors than do American workers. Such differences do not appear in the Japanese sample. With respect to after-hours get togethers, the sharpest American contrast is between the managers on the one hand – whose level of socializing approaches the Japanese average – and supervisors and workers, on the other.

There is little variation across functional areas in feelings toward co-workers or, in Japan at least, outside socializing. In the US, office employees are more prone to after-work encounters than either production or technical workers, yet friendships are most common among production workers in the US and among technical workers in Japan.

Finally, we expect informal integration to rise with time spent in the organization. Indeed, the strong social bonds and sense of community that our research and others' finds in the Japanese company (and other corporatist organizations such as IBM) are wholly consistent with the practice of long-term, secure employment (see Edwards, 1979; Ouchi, 1981). Yet tenure appears to increase friendships only. Close friendships are, of course, the strongest form of personal tie, and no doubt take more time to develop. Still, we anticipated finding stronger indications of social integration rising with tenure in the firm.

In general, then, the findings of this section support the expectation that Japanese employees enjoy stronger social bonds. They appear to have better and more frequent relations with their supervisors, both on and off the job. They are more likely to develop close friendships with their workmates and to see them after work. They are more likely to perceive their jobs as requiring interaction and coordination with others, and they are much more likely to participate in shop-floor small group activities such as quality circles. Only with regard to quality of coworker ties did the US employees exhibit greater social cohesion.

Effects of job attributes on organizational commitment and job satisfaction

Although country differences in task characteristics, job rewards, and workplace relations are of considerable interest in their own right, our purpose in examining them is ultimately to explore their role in accounting for workforce differences in organizational commitment and job satisfaction. We now consider this issue in examining the relationships between commitment and satisfaction, on the one hand, and position, task characteristics, job rewards, and social bonds on the other. Table 4.5 presents the results of our analysis.

Determining how specific variables within these four broad sets affect commitment and morale is a complex task, since we know them to be causally intertwined in intricate ways. We will see, for example, that the impact of job complexity on commitment is mainly indirect through its

Table 4.5 *Standardized regressions of organizational commitment and job satisfaction on job attributes*[a]

	Dependent variables											
	Commitment						Satisfaction					
	(1)		(2)		(3)		(1)		(2)		(3)	
Independent variable	US	Japan	US	Japan	US	Japan	US	Japan	US	Japan	US	Japan
Position												
Manager	(.164**	.111**)	.119**	.088**	.050**	.076**	.135**	.103**]	.075**	.072**	.021	.078*]
Supervisor	(.146**	.078**)	(.111**	.039+)	.069**	.030	.074**	.070**	.025	.021	−.019	.022
Technical	.002	−.042*]	−.008	−.060*]	.027	−.071**	.025	.028	.009	.001	.009	−.015
Production	[−.011	−.075**]	.030	−.040	.082**	−.029	−.033	−.114**]	.020	−.069*)	.019	−.058+)
QC member	(.152**	.075**)	(.133**	.065**)	−.045*	.026	(.114**	.044+)	(.091**	.033)	.039*	−.009
Tenure	−.052+	.007	−.059**	−.012			−.090**	−.097**	−.099**	−.126**	−.087	−.077**
Task characteristics												
Job complexity			.188**	.141*	−.031	.035+			(.282**	.198**)	.037*	.076**)
Teamwork			[.037*	.079**]	−.001	.016			.015	.042*	−.026	−.034+
Supervisor contact			(−.123**	−.059**)	−.060**	−.010			(−.114**	.062*)	[−.041**	−.012]
Supervisor control			−.011	−.020	−.021	−.046**			.003	.006	.005	.032+
Autonomy			.151**	.116**	.082**	.047+			[.171**	.147**]	.091**	.071**
Social bonds												
Outside socializing					−.019	.008					(−.034+	.014)
Coworker friends					.022	.033+					.023	.020
Vertical tie quality					(.186**	.227**)					.024**	.218**
Coworker tie quality					[.132**	.160**]					.175**	.200**
Job rewards												
Intrinsic rewards					(.284**	.171**)					(.345**	.229**)
Promotion chances					.109**	.094**					.046*	.075**
Earnings					[.082**	−.006					(.036+	−.078**)
Adj. Mean	2.164	2.014	2.111	2.013	2.243	2.294	1.558	.959	1.500	.972	1.650	1.161
Adj. R²	.172	.210	.259	.251	.390	.399	.119	.145	.253	.213	.420	.388

Notes: [a] Equations control for employee background and organization-level variables

+ p < .05
* p < .01
** p < .001
[ ] Difference in estimates is significant at the .05 level
( ) Difference in estimates is significant at the .01 level

influence on intrinsic rewards, promotion chances, and social integration.[8] Our interpretation of how job attributes affect commitment and satisfaction, then, relies considerably on the findings already reported in this chapter. We start by discussing the most proximate causes of commitment and satisfaction (i.e. social bonds, job rewards); then summarize the results for task characteristics and job position.

Effects of social relations on commitment and satisfaction

We have argued that highly cohesive social networks characterize the Japanese workplace, as well as corporatist organization more generally, and are a central mechanism in building commitment to the firm. Our results in table 4.5 provide some support for this expectation: in both countries, the indices of quality of relations with coworkers and supervisors are positively related to commitment and satisfaction.[9] From the premise that strong vertical ties are a particularly important mode of binding employees to Japanese organizations, we might have anticipated the evidence that this variable is a slightly better predictor of commitment in Japan than in the US.

On the other hand, the effects of friendships on commitment and satisfaction are small to nonexistent. Moreover, given our observations about the contrasting roles played by outside socializing with coworkers among Japanese and US workers, we might have expected such socializing to enhance commitment only among the Japanese. The hypothesis in the US case is confirmed – outside get-togethers contribute nothing to organizational commitment and may even diminish job satisfaction. The surprise is that socializing is also unrelated to either outcome in Japan. Could it thus be that the oft-noted drinking and dining outings pursued by Japanese employees really play no role in fostering attachment to the firm? In fact, they do, but only indirectly through the mechanisms of higher-quality supervisory and coworker relations: with the quality-of-tie scales removed from the regressions, the effects of socializing on commitment and satisfaction are highly positive and significant in the Japanese sample (not shown). In the comparable US model, the socializing index displays a marginally significant positive link to commitment, but none to satisfaction. As our earlier discussion suggested, the reason outside get-togethers play a greater commitment-raising role in Japan is not that the effect of such relations materializes only where Japanese cultural values prevail, but rather that the *form* they take is rather different in the two countries. Among the Japanese, they are orchestrated by and require the participation of supervisors, and thus involve the blessing if not the sponsorship of the firm. Similar kinds of outings in the US tend to be confined to managers, while the social contacts among rank-and-file workers are spontaneous, unlikely to involve supervisors, and rarely for the purpose of transacting business. Japanese companies have, in a sense, absorbed or coopted informal relations, making them a vehicle of organizational control.

Effects of job rewards on commitment and satisfaction

We have argued that the logic of corporatist control strategies in organizations rests heavily on the use of intrinsic inducements such as challenging and meaningful tasks and the satisfactions associated with friendly workmates and a cohesive employee community. Heavy reliance on extrinsic rewards such as earnings risks engendering the kinds of employment relationships exemplified by Goldthorpe *et al.*'s British workers: loyal to the company in the sense that high wages foreclose changing jobs, but otherwise preoccupied with their home lives and unconcerned with company affairs.

Table 4.5 reveals very strong positive associations in each country between the perception of intrinsic rewards and work attitudes. It should be acknowledged that part of this association probably stems from correlated errors of measurement – given the highly subjective nature of both intrinsic rewards and commitment/satisfaction – as well as reciprocal causation. Unaffected by such biases, however, are the indications that intrinsic rewards play a greater role in shaping work attitudes in the US than in Japan, and in both countries have more to do with satisfaction than commitment. Part of the reason for the first pattern, as we explore further below, is that the main factor driving variation in intrinsic rewards is job complexity. This may well be more salient to work attitudes in the US than in Japan because of higher occupational consciousness and greater odds of staying with the same job specialty over a long span of time (Cole and Tominaga, 1976).

Intrinsic rewards enhance satisfaction more than commitment, we suspect, because they represent an *immediate* return to participation in the workplace. As chapter 1 discussed, most theories of commitment see it as a consequence, less of direct returns to organizational participation than of past investments and anticipated future rewards (Kanter, 1968; Salancik, 1977). The promise of promotion and the chance to build a career within the organization are, from this perspective, likely to be particularly effective inducements to commitment, and, indeed, internal labor market structures are widely identified as integral to corporatist-type strategies of control. This reasoning anticipates our finding in both countries of larger positive effects of promotion expectations on commitment than on satisfaction.

This argument for the greater power of future as opposed to present rewards in building commitment over satisfaction also has implications for the role of earnings in Japanese and US incentive plans. Starting wages, even for skilled, professional employees are low in Japanese companies, but, as our own analysis demonstrated, show steeper increase with age and seniority than typically occurs in the US. In the eyes of numerous writers (Hashimoto and Raisian, 1985; Koike, 1983; Lazear, 1979), this is a compensation regime that seems designed to build commitment, even if it likely spells low satisfaction on the part of many workers with their present levels of pay. Our only measure of earnings, unfortunately, is earnings at the time of the survey, not the future or anticipated wage stream. Present earnings should produce an increment in job satisfaction, but, if the above logic holds, have little bearing on commitment.

However, table 4.5 reveals the opposite to be the case. In both countries, earnings has a greater positive impact on commitment than satisfaction. Indeed, the net effect of earnings on satisfaction in the Japanese sample is a highly significant *negative* value. This outcome is so at odds with our expectations and most other motivational theory that we are at a loss to explain it. Though it suits the argument, taken up in the next chapter, that the Japanese have historically attached a lower value to pay than Western workers and that the present wage matters less than the lifetime value of the earnings stream, we find implausible the possibility that more pay truly depresses job satisfaction in Japan. We should note that much of the variance in wages lies between plants and these models control for the plant-level variables examined in chapter 8. When organization-level variables are excluded (not shown), the effect of earnings on satisfaction in the Japanese sample goes to zero and we find the same positive effect on commitment that is apparent in the US data.

Effects of task characteristics on commitment and satisfaction

Task characteristics make important contributions to organizational commitment and job satisfaction at least indirectly through their impact on job rewards and social bonds. We have shown in earlier sections that complexity, closeness of supervision, and autonomy have strong influences on intrinsic rewards, social integration, and pay and promotion; job rewards and social bonds, in turn, condition work attitudes. The complexity of the job appears to affect commitment and satisfaction almost entirely through its effect on job rewards, particularly the intrinsic sort. With the reward variables omitted from the regression (column 2), complexity has strong positive effects that are larger with respect to satisfaction than commitment; larger in the US than in Japan. Recall that this is the same pattern of country differences we observed for intrinsic rewards (see table 4.3). With the reward variables in the equation, the complexity effects are sharply reduced. It seems clear that intrinsic rewards – perceptions of meaning, challenge, and fulfill-ment – are the mechanism whereby jobs requiring high training and skill foster favorable work attitudes. Involvement in such jobs produces satisfac-tion and probably identification with one's own work role, but not strong commitment to the firm. Indeed, the potential for occupations characterized by skill, variety, and control to themselves become objects of loyalty and commitment has been recognized by various theorists as a possible threat to organizational control strategies which aim at building commitment (Blauner, 1964; Edwards, 1979). From this perspective, job proliferation in the US workplace (Baron and Bielby, 1986; Gordon *et al.*, 1982) and job rotation in Japan are designs aimed at eliminating the occupation as an anchor for worker loyalty and identification which may compete with the company itself.

We have found that informal ties with coworkers and supervisors are denser and stronger in Japanese than US plants, and that participation in such relations enhances commitment. This is the kind of pattern that contributes to an explanation of the US Japan commitment gap: Japanese workers are more committed to their companies because of greater social integration. We find a similar pattern with regard to teamwork. Our data, plus the evidence of numerous other studies, indicate that the Japanese workplace is organized to a greater extent in terms of cohesive work groups. Since teamwork leads to better relations with supervisors and coworkers, it thus indirectly builds commitment to the firm. Table 4.5, in fact, shows that the impact of teamwork on commitment is *only* indirect; when the measures of job rewards and social bonds are included in the equation, the teamwork coefficient goes to zero.

One of the most interesting outcomes from our earlier analysis of supervisory styles was the very different patterns in the US and Japan displayed by supervisor contact. In general, to be left alone by supervisors meant lower social integration and fewer intrinsic rewards for Japanese employees. In the US, we generally found the opposite. This pattern has implications for commitment and satisfaction. With the job reward and social bond variables excluded from the regression, supervisor contact improves work attitudes among the Japanese, worsens them among the Americans. Adding the intervening job reward and social bond variables to the equations reveals that these effects are wholly mediated in the Japanese case; only partly so in the US sample.

Finally, consider the task characteristics of autonomy and control. We find autonomy enhancing both commitment and satisfaction in each country. As with complexity, some of this is due to the greater intrinsic rewards associated with more autonomous tasks (see table 4.3). But such rewards do not totally explain the influence of autonomy on work attitudes, as indicated by positive and significant direct effects in the third columns of table 4.5. On the other hand, the measure of supervisor (vs. worker) control appears from equations 1 and 2 to have nothing to do with work attitudes in either country. We know from table 4.2, of course, that in both countries supervisor control produces large reductions in perceived autonomy which, in turn, are strongly linked to commitment and satisfaction. Yet when autonomy and the other job-level variables are excluded from the analysis (not shown), we find significant positive effects in the Japanese sample. It thus appears, that, net of its implications for complexity, autonomy, and other task characteristics, supervisory intervention is a positive motivational force among the Japanese.

Effects of job position on commitment and satisfaction

We finally consider the implications for organizational commitment and job satisfaction of position within the organization, defined in terms of management authority, functional area, QC membership, and tenure. We have seen, in the course of this chapter, that these variables have important, wide-ranging influences on task characteristics, job rewards, and social networks, all of which, in turn, help to explain the variation in commitment and satisfaction. Thus, we know position makes a difference; the question is how large a difference and how much of it is mediated by these intervening processes.

Authority position A sweepingly consistent finding in our inquiry to this point is that inequalities in work experiences, perceptions, and rewards are far greater across the authority levels of US factories. We observe the same pattern with respect to work attitudes. While the basic ordering of commitment and satisfaction levels among management ranks (managers the highest, then supervisors, workers the lowest) holds in both countries, the differences are greater in the US. The preponderance of this positional variance in work attitudes can be attributed to differences in task characteristics, job rewards, and social relations among authority levels reported throughout this chapter: with these held constant, the effects of rank on satisfaction disappear entirely in the US sample, and the differences in commitment are sharply reduced (see column 3). In the full model estimated on the Japanese sample (column 3), the attitude gap between supervisors and workers has closed, although the net commitment and satisfaction of managers remain slightly higher.

Functional area The traditional picture of alienated manufacturing workers portrays production tasks as arduous, routine, and machine-driven (Blauner, 1964; Chinoy, 1955; Walker and Guest, 1952). Other factory occupations – in particular, the skilled trades and office work – are of a very different sort. Workers experience more control and variety in their tasks, are subject to less close supervision, and are more likely to operate in teams. Only in Japan, however, do we find significantly less commitment and satisfaction among production workers, about half of which difference is explained by their disadvantages in task complexity, job rewards, and social bonds. A speculative interpretation is that this finding supports the hypothesis that discipline, regimentation, and control are particularly high in the production departments of Japanese manufacturing plants (Hanada, 1984; Junkerman, 1983; Kamata, 1983)

In the US sample, we find no differences between technical and office workers with respect to either organizational commitment or job satisfaction. In the Japanese sample, on the other hand, the net commitment level of the technical workers appears significantly lower than that of office employees, and the gaps are larger when the intervening task, reward, and integration variables are controlled. In statistical parlance, this pattern represents a "suppressor effect." Technical people enjoy more complex tasks, job rewards, and teamwork than other employees. These attributes, as previously shown, operate to raise their commitment to the organization. But when we statistically adjust for such differences in job quality and benefits, technical staff exhibit less loyalty to the organization. This is the pattern that Blauner identified with printers in his 1964 study and with craft work more generally: though alienation levels are low, so is commitment to and integration in the firm, for such workers participate in an independent occupational community which becomes a competing source of loyalty and identification.

Quality circles These and other kinds of small group activities are designed to draw workers into decision-making and diffuse responsibility for quality and production problems, thus heightening feelings of participation in a workplace community and, in turn, commitment to the firm. As such, QC has considerable prima-facie validity as an indicator of the corporatist strategy of control. Does it, however, perform as advertised? Our data suggest that it does: QC membership raises commitment in both countries. The effect is somewhat larger in the US, suggesting perhaps a greater novelty value of QC in American work settings (Cole, 1980). This interpretation is buttressed by evidence that the task, reward, and integration variables do not fully explain the QC effect in the US, whereas they do in Japan. In both countries, it appears that the greatest share of the QC effect operates through its contribution to good relations with coworkers and supervisors. QC contributes a much smaller increment to job satisfaction.

Can we be sure that the association between QC and work attitudes reflects the impact of the former on the latter rather than vice versa? Perhaps highly motivated employees volunteer for QC or are selected by their supervisors. This explanation is precluded, we think, by the fact that QC membership was very nearly universal in plants where a QC program was in place. The variation in QC participation in our Japanese sample is almost entirely between plants; i.e. if a plant had a program, the vast majority of employees were members. In the US sample, a much smaller percentage of employees of plants with QC programs were participants, but in this case the variation was chiefly among departments within the same plants; i.e. a program would be implemented in a selected work unit, and all workers in that unit would become members. We suspect that individual workers have little leeway to select themselves or be selected in or out of QC activity.

Tenure A core proposition of most theories of organizational commitment is that loyalty and identification grow with time spent in the system. The reasons are numerous, some having to do with the accumulation of adaptations, resources, and rewards (e.g. friends, power), others involving more complex psychological processes such as the need to reduce cognitive dissonance by justifying to oneself the costs of opportunities foregone (see, e.g. Kanter, 1968). Thus, theories stressing the role of commitment in strategies of organizational control emphasize the function internal labor markets perform in creating secure jobs and career opportunities within the firm. This, of course, is a key explanation for the prevalence of high employer tenure ("permanent employment") in the Japanese labor market.

Our results in table 4.5 indicate that tenure has either no or negative effects on the organizational commitment and job satisfaction of US and Japanese employees. These equations, however, control for age, which is highly correlated with tenure (.67 in the US, .68 in Japan). When we remove age from the regressions and re-estimate them (not shown), we find the expected positive effect of tenure on commitment in both samples (see Lincoln and Kalleberg, 1985). Moreover, tenure bears a stronger relation to commitment than satisfaction: in both countries, the impact of tenure on satisfaction vanishes when the age variable is removed. This fits the view that the accumulation of investments in the company – hence the employee's dependence on and commitment to the organization – increases with time in the firm. But tenure does not necessarily translate into higher satisfaction with the current job, for with advancing seniority also comes an accumulation of unrealized values.

Summary

This chapter has focused on four classes of *job attributes* in Japanese and US plants: *position* (authority level, functional area, quality circle membership, and company tenure); *task characteristics* (supervision, complexity, and autonomy); *job rewards* (earnings, intrinsic rewards, promotion chances); and *social bonds* (friendships, outside socializing, quality of vertical and coworker ties). Our analyses have focused on the causal interrelations among these factors as well as their effects on organizational commitment and job satisfaction.

The US manufacturing employees in our sample experience greater job autonomy and complexity while the Japanese report stronger social bonds with workmates and supervisors. Promotion opportunities are perceived to be approximately the same. Consequently, perhaps, we find no difference between the countries in the intrinsic rewards available from the job.

There is strong evidence that inequalities across levels of the management hierarchy in work attitudes and in job quality and rewards are smaller in Japan than in the US, confirming the impressions of numerous observers of Japanese work organization. Regardless of rank, production employees in both countries perceive their jobs to have less complexity and control, and (in Japan at least) technical support employees perceive more. Quality circle membership, while unrelated to perceptions of job complexity, is strongly linked to employees' reports of teamwork and social integration and consequently to commitment. Our analysis of the determinants of such labor market outcomes as earnings and promotion chances produced results that were generally consistent with the expectation that the Japanese *nenko* system continues to govern Japanese internal labor market processes.

Job quality (in terms of complexity and control), job rewards, and integration in workplace social networks are important factors contributing to the organizational commitment and job satisfaction of Japanese and US employees alike.

Taken as a whole, then, the findings of this chapter suggest that organizational designs and management practices which engender "responsible autonomy," to use Friedman's (1977) phrase, as well as participation, integration, careers, and intrinsic rewards foster loyalty and diminish alienation in a workforce. This, of course, is the rationale for welfare corporatist organization. However, job attributes are only part of the story. Work attitudes are also responses to work values and background differences among employees. We investigate these issues in the following chapter.

5 Work values and employee background effects

The degree to which individuals are committed to their companies and content with their jobs depends on the kinds of people they are as well as on the kinds of work they do. This chapter continues our focus on the *micro-level*, within-plant variables that shape the attitudes and behaviors of manufacturing employees. However, our attention now turns to attributes of individuals affecting their organizational commitment and job satisfaction which are either wholly or partially determined by conditions external to the work environment. First, we consider variations in the *values* which orient employees to various aspects of work and organizational life. These include both very general motives and desires as to the role of work and economic activity in one's life (e.g. the Protestant ethic), but also assessments of the importance of specific dimensions of work life such as pay, promotion opportunities, job security, and social relationships.

The second set of factors producing individual differences – to use the term favored by organizational psychologists – in how employees react to job and workplace conditions comprises such personal background attributes as age, gender, family obligations, and schooling. Besides having a direct impact on one's general orientation to a job and an employer, these factors condition how work responsibilities and rewards are assigned and how individuals react to them. Our analysis in the last chapter held such variables constant in assessing relationships among job attributes and perceptions. Now we return to those analyses and ask the reverse question: with job-level causes controlled, how do personal background characteristics bear on the task perceptions, social relations, and job rewards of Japanese and American employees?

Both kinds of "individual differences" warrant careful scrutiny in a comparative study of Japanese and US industrial firms and workers. One of the oldest and, to many, still most persuasive explanations for the apparent contrasts in the discipline and commitment of US and Japanese workers stresses national differences in cultural values regarding work and organization and their interplay with other life experiences. There are also strong grounds for supposing that employee age and gender have contrasting implications for the work attitudes and behaviors of Japanese and US workers. In particular, much has been written about the age-grading of Japanese work organizations and the effects of life-cycle transitions on employees' workplace experiences and rewards (Rohlen, 1974). In addition, though disadvantaged in both countries, the position of women is clearly more subordinate and precarious in the Japanese workplace, for the division of labor between the sexes remains more rigid and traditional in Japan (Cook and Hayashi, 1980).

We first examine how employees in the US and Japan differ in their work values, how these values are linked to job-related characteristics, and how they shape work attitudes in the two countries. We then examine how organizational commitment and job satisfaction vary among employees differentiated on the demographic background dimensions of age, gender, marital status, and education.

Work values

A strong case can be made that if Japanese employees *are* really more inclined than Westerners to devote their hearts and minds to an employing organization, the reasons lie in deep-seated cultural values. Drawing from a range of prior scholarship on the Japanese value system, Vogel (1963:146) concluded that:

> (T)he two general (value) characteristics which strike a Western observer as being of fundamental importance are loyalty and competence ... In its extreme form, loyalty means that the individual can be counted on to place group interests above his own. Group loyalty means not only identification with group goals but a willingness to co-operate with the other members and to respond to group consensus enthusiastically ... Competence is defined partly as talent or genius (*tensai*) but partly as the capacity for hard work (*kinben*) and perseverance (*gamanzuyoi*).

These orientations are evident in a variety of Japanese social settings, from family to local community to nation state. But, Vogel argues, employment by a business corporation charts the clearest course to the realizaticn of such values in modern Japan. In its insistence on full cooperation and loyalty coupled with maximum task performance it invokes the ideals of loyalty and competence in a way that few institutions can. The family, by contrast, is an object of loyalty but does not condition acceptance of its members on strong performance demands; to be self-employed, on the other hand, provides an outlet for hard work and perseverance but not loyalty. Thus, the diligence and selfless devotion shown by Japanese employees – hence the labor discipline and productivity of the Japanese economy – may need no other explanation than that the compliance and performance demands of large companies find a perfect match with the fundamental values of the Japanese people.

This is a hypothesis to be tested, and one that motivates much of our analysis in this book. As we noted in chapter 1, our test is chiefly indirect, by weighing the alternative: that differences in the work attitudes and behaviors of Japanese and American employees stem from organizational designs and employment practices. Should we fail to explain the commitment gap in terms of forces operating at the level of the workplace, for example, then, without being tested directly, the case for a purely culturalist model of Japanese work behavior will receive a significant boost. However, in this chapter, we make a modest attempt at measuring values so as to assess how they differ between Japan and the US and how they impact on work attitudes.

Of course, the distinction between work values and attitudes is subtle, and some might argue that organizational commitment, our ultimate dependent variable, could as easily be cast as a value. Is not commitment to a company precisely the sort of group loyalty to which Vogel referred? We think there is a difference, even though it may not matter greatly to the substance of our inquiry. Yet both our conceptualization and our measurement of the outcome variables on which this study is ultimately focused concern commitment to *a particular company* and satisfaction with *a particular job*. Loyalty and diligence are general value orientations which structure behavior in a *variety* of social roles and settings. Strong feelings of identification with Toyota or General Motors and a commitment to perform diligently on the company's behalf constitute an attitude or orientation toward a particular company which may well be more prevalent among employees socialized in the abstract values of loyalty and diligence. The two remain distinct phenomena nonetheless.

It is this reasoning that has led us to characterize work commitment as a value orientation, and thus as causally antecedent to organizational commitment and job satisfaction. (This is also the causal ordering assumed in past research on work as a central life interest; e.g. Dubin, Champoux, and Porter, 1975). As we noted in chapter 3, work commitment refers to the centrality of work to a person's overall identity and its importance in an individual's life. It is a global work value since it compares one's involvement in the work role to the other social roles the person plays. As such it contrasts with the valuations people place on specific dimensions of work and employment, such as earnings, career opportunities, social relationships, and so on. Both kinds of work values concern us in this chapter.

Commitment to work

Work is an essential part of being alive. Your work is your identity. It tells you who you are. (Kay Stepkin, director of a bakery cooperative interviewed by Studs Terkel in *Working*.)

As our review in chapter 3 indicated, survey evidence on work commitment among the Japanese is spotty. National opinion polls repeatedly turn up diligence and hard work as attributes ranked high in how the Japanese think about themselves. On the other hand, specific work motivation items, including the commitment scale Cole (1979) employed in his Detroit/ Yokohama survey, have failed to put the Japanese consistently ahead of other industrial workers. Recall (from chapter 3) that our own three-item work commitment scale (see table 5.1) gave an uncertain portrait of the work commitment of the Japanese: they were more likely than Americans to give priority to work over family concerns and to disagree that "work is but a small part of who I am"; though they were also more likely to rate "other activities" as more important than work.[1]

Causes of work commitment

Our results in table 5.2 shed additional light on the sources of variation in work commitment among US and Japanese manufacturing employees. This and the other regression models we consider in this chapter take as antecedent to work values the full set of background, positional, task, social bond, and job reward variables we examined at length in chapter 4. An overarching hypothesis is that facets of the work role such as complexity, supervision, or autonomy have relatively little to do with the shaping of values which to a large degree are formed outside the workplace. On the other hand, background demographics, social relations, and job position (manager vs. worker) are indicative of broad integration in external as well as workplace groups and strata; hence they are more likely to have a bearing on value orientations. *Job rewards*, of course, are likely to be important predictors, since many of the value dimensions we consider concern the work life rewards to which employees aspire. We discuss the role of employee background demographics later in the chapter, when we consider in detail their effects on work values and job rewards.

Work commitment, like organizational commitment, is higher, not surprisingly, among managers and supervisors than among workers. Yet, as always, the gap is greater in the US. In contrast, there are no differences in employee work commitment across functional divisions. Tenure in the company is also unrelated to the centrality of work among the Japanese, though more senior American employees are less committed to work. Given the high correlation between tenure and age, caution is required in interpreting the negative association in the US case. Nevertheless, it is consistent with the observation that plateaued careers among senior employees shift attention away from work to other life pursuits (Kanter, 1977). We would expect such disengagement from work to be more prevalent among Americans for two reasons: (a) the greater legitimacy US society attaches to nonwork pursuits; (b) the likelihood, discussed in the last chapter, that promotion opportunities are more likely to diminish over the course of the American worker's career.

In general, employees enjoying greater job rewards – in particular intrinsic

Table 5.1 Descriptive statistics for employee background and work value measures

	US Mean (SD)	Japan Mean (SD)
Employee background		
Employee's age (in years)	38.6 (11.3)	35.0 (10.0)*
Gender (1 = female, 0 = male)	.267 (.442)	.160 (.367)*
Married (1 = married, 0 = other)	.718 (.450)	.666 (.472)*
Education (0 = none, 7 = more than college degree)	3.14 (1.01)	3.04 (.973)*
Work commitment scale (alpha = .59, US; .57, Japan)	2.62 (.826)	2.84 (.843)*
"I have other activities more important than my work" (1 = strongly agree, 5 = strongly disagree)	3.12 (1.16)	2.82 (1.17)*
"The most important things that happen to me involve my family rather than my work" (same codes)	2.11 (.982)	2.84 (.989)*
"To me, my work is only a small part of who I am" (same codes)	2.61 (1.15)	2.89 (1.23)*
Specific work values		
How important to you is:		
"... good pay?" (0 = not at all important, 3 = very important)	2.80 (.462)	2.33 (.807)*
"... having good chances for promotion?" (same codes)	2.36 (.880)	1.58 (.872)*
"... a stable job without fear of layoffs?" (same codes)	2.84 (.453)	2.22 (.809)*
"... getting along with fellow employees?" (same codes)	2.72 (.568)	2.18 (.783)*
"When I have a choice, I try to work in a group instead of by myself" (1 = strongly disagree, 5 = strongly agree)	3.01 (1.09)	3.27 (1.13)*
"Getting along with co-workers is more important to me than getting along with my bosses" (same codes)	3.22 (1.03)	3.53 (.886)*
"Employees at a company should have an advantage over outsiders in competing for job openings" (same codes)	4.50 (.764)	4.08 (.821)*
Paternalism values		
Company familism "A company should take care of its employees, since a company and its employees are like a		

Table 5.1 *(cont.)*

	US Mean (SD)	Japan Mean (SD)
family and its members" (1 = strongly disagree, 5 = strongly agree)	4.37 (.816)	3.00 (1.08)*
Company orientation scale (alpha = .61, US; .57, Japan)	2.84 (.737)	2.67 (.686)*
"Companies must raise productivity even if it means that people lose their jobs" (1 = strongly disagree, 5 = strongly agree)	2.91 (1.16)	2.71 (1.18)*
"If the demand for a company's product goes down, it is OK for a company to lay off employees" (same codes)	3.42 (.974)	3.04 (1.12)*
"It is OK for a company to fire or lay off employees if new machines begin doing their work" (same codes)	2.43 (1.11)	1.95 (1.04)*
"A company should be able to transfer employees even if it causes the employees problems" (same codes)	2.56 (1.02)	2.52 (1.12)
"Employees shouldn't take time off when things are busy, even though they have a right to take the time off (same codes)	2.79 (1.12)	3.22 (1.12)*

Notes: * Difference between means is significant at p< .001 (2-tail test)

rewards and promotion opportunities – are also more committed to work. These tendencies are particularly pronounced among the Americans. In contrast, close friends on the job enhance work commitment only among the Japanese. This accords with an emerging pattern of findings indicating that informal associations in the workplace play a greater role in binding the Japanese employee to the company. On the other hand, our findings regarding earnings are surprising: in Japan, the better paid are much more committed to work; but earnings have little to do with work commitment among the Americans. We hesitate to place much weight on this outcome, however. Earlier findings (table 4.5) indicated that high earnings enhance both commitment and satisfaction among Americans, but depress satisfaction and are unrelated to organizational commitment among the Japanese. Moreover, as we report below, it appears that US employees attach greater importance to pay than do the Japanese.

Table 5.2 Standardized regressions of value measures on employee background and job attributes

	Dependent variables									
	Work commitment		Good pay		Good promotions		Insider's advantage		Stable work	
Independent variable	US	Japan	US	Japan	US	Japan	US	Japan	US	Japan
Background										
Age	(.258**	.116**)	(−.048+	−.192**)	(−.111**	−.229**)	(.015	.117**)	−.057*	−.010
Gender	.022	.021	(.081**	−.019	(.031+	−.119**)	.054**	.043+	.049**]	−.027
Education	(−.141*	−.027)	[−.049*]	.011	.024	.005	.022]	−.042+]	−.065**	−.014
Married	−.070*)	−.071**	[.011	.066*]	−.011	−.009	.054**]	.007]	.016	.083**)
Position										
Manager	[.105**	.041+)	[−.095**]	−.003)	.026	.048*)	−.088**]	−.031	−.126**]	−.059*)
Supervisor	[.096**]	.057*]	[−.041+	.008]	[.065**]	.033]	−.053*	−.017]	−.037+	.003]
Technical	−.015	.006	.004	.002	−.051+	−.027	−.010	−.022	−.003	−.015
Production	−.019	.004	−.014	.012	−.035	.009	.016	.018	.041	−.005
QC Member	.039	−.023	[.007	.045*]	[.058**]	.010]	−.011]	.038+]	.024]	.058**]
Tenure	(−.079**	−.003)	(.004	−.072*)	−.039	.014	.045+]	−.019	.040	−.010
Task characteristics										
Job Complexity	−.073**	−.053*	.006	.013	.033	−.000	.027	−.023	−.034	.005
Teamwork	−.054**	−.006)	(−.010	.063**)	−.014	.039+]	.025	.051*	−.002	.038+
Spvr Contact	.035+	.045*	[−.020	.032]	.015	.002	−.051**]	.005]	−.020	.014
Spvr Control	.034+	−.024	[.036+]	−.015]	−.013	.007	.003	−.037+	.025]	−.033]
Autonomy	[−.002	−.050*]	−.028	−.010	.030	.036	.014]	.055]	−.025	.019
Social bonds										
Socializing	.012	−.020	−.022	−.006	−.005	.059**)	.022	−.021	−.029	.006
Friends	(.014	.073**)	(−.011	.056**)	−.029	.011	−.005	.036+	−.016	.041**)
Q Vertical Ties	.073**	.064**)	−.005	.022]	.005	.026	−.041+]	.029)	−.001	.098**)
Q Coworker Ties	.030+	−.020	[.088**]	.003]	.022	.003	.051**	.057	.069**	.055*

Dependent variables

Independent variable	Group work		Get along with coworkers		Coworkers vs. boss		Company familism		Company orientation	
	US	Japan	US	Japan	US	Japan	US	Japan	US	Japan
Background										
Age	[-.013]	-.060+	(.049+)	-.117**)	-.102**	.104**	-.005	.020	.173**	.140**
Gender	.044*	.050*	[.063**]	.005	[-.092**]	-.046+]	.008	-.067**	[-.033+]	.015
Education	[-.069**]	-.012]	-.057**	-.040+	.004	-.034	-.054*	-.115**	.060**	.069**
Marital	-.021	-.038	.029	.029	.022	.014	.009	-.010	[-.014]	-.060*
Position										
Manager	.010	.025	[-.046*]	-.001	[-.081**]	-.016	(-.155**)	-.023	.186**	.127**
Supervisor	.056**	-.004	-.018	-.032	-.033+	-.019	[-.097**]	-.045+]	.198**	.108**
Technical	[.050+]	-.018]	-.013	.010	.012	.009	-.014	-.006	(-.033)	-.117**
Production	[.063*]	.004]	-.019	-.002	.022	.047+	[.013]	.063*]	-.057*	-.064*
QC member	(.039*)	-.031)	.038*	.064**	.013	-.012	(.052**)	-.019	(.018)	-.039+
Tenure	-.030	-.003	-.029	-.047	[.032]	-.040]	-.052+	-.049	-.003	-.045
Task characteristics										
Job complexity	[-.024]	.061*]	[-.042+]	.023	.060*	.096**	.012	.075*	[.040+]	-.021
Teamwork	(.182**)	.065**)	(.077**)	.105**)	(.187**)	.060**	-.005	.061**	.031+	-.007
Spvr contact	.025	-.010	[.007]	.047+]	.012	-.062**	-.049**	-.012	-.048**	-.092**
Spvr control	(.086**)	.001)	.047*	.029	-.016	-.019	[.070**]	.033]	(-.040*)	.032
Autonomy	-.055*	-.023	-.012	.002	-.001	.025	.008	.045	.046+	.037+
Rewards										
Intrinsic	(.272**)	.126**	.006	.035+	-.024	.086**	-.034+	.104**	(.010)	.080**
Promotion	.057**	.039+	.042*	.038+	[.207**]	.163**	.004	.001	.026	-.012
Earnings	(-.017)	.258**	(.077**)	.001	-.031	.026	.046+	.049+	.011	.019
Mean	(2.618)	2.838	(2.801)	2.327	(2.356)	1.580	(4.497)	4.082	(2.841)	2.221
Adj. Mean	(2.724)	2.999	(2.809)	2.248	(2.401)	1.504	(4.689)	4.195	(2.853)	2.303
Adj R²	.178	.151	.032	.058	.100	.125	.024	.065	.046	.070

Table 5.2 (*cont.*)

| | Dependent variables | | | | | | | | | |
| | Group work | | Get along with coworkers | | Coworkers vs. boss | | Company familism | | Company orientation | |
Independent variable	US	Japan	US	Japan	US	Japan	US	Japan	US	Japan
Social bonds										
Socializing	.037+	.066*	−.009	.038+	[.032+	−.014]	.060**	.062**	.007	.012
Friends	[.045*	.013]	.072**	.039+	[.056**]	.016]	.017	.016	−.034+	−.041+
Q vertical ties	.003	.009	.035+	.011	−.210**	−.179**	[−.049*	−.001]	.090**	.107**
Q coworker ties	.185**	.199**	(.243**	.116**)	[.152**]	.116**]	.065**	.049*	−.011	.027
Rewards										
Intrinsic	−.020	.020	[.061**	.021]	−.111**	−.066**	.039+	.003	.034+	.043+
Promotion	−.026	.007	[.026	−.026]	[−.094**	−.057*]	.015	.014	.042*	.024
Earnings	[−.013]	−.050]	(−.005]	−.116**)	(.044+)	−.091**)	.016	.005	.042*	.020
Mean	(3.006)	3.265	(2.715)	2.176	(3.222)	3.532	(4.372)	3.003)	(2.839)	2.670
Adj. Mean	(3.396)	3.521	(2.892)	2.126	(3.287)	3.552	(4.417)	3.047)	2.866	2.840
Adj. R²	.101	.076	.118	.091	.137	.082	.068	.043	.215	.084

Notes: + p < .05

* p < .01

** p < .001

[ ] Difference in estimates is significant at the .05 level

( ) Difference in estimates is significant at the .01 level

Effects of work commitment on work attitudes

Employees in both countries who are more committed to work are also more committed to their organizations and (to a lesser degree) satisfied with their jobs (table 5.3). Thus, people who value work in the abstract tend to realize that value through greater attachment to a particular work organization. The finding that work commitment also enhances job satisfaction runs contrary to the proposition that strong values diminish satisfaction by raising expectations for job rewards.

Specific work values

Individuals also differ in the importance they place on specific job rewards and facets of their work situations. Some seek short-run financial rewards, and are motivated by pay and job security. Others value getting ahead and career opportunities. Still others seek meaningful relationships with colleagues in an enterprise community. These value orientations condition the reactions of employees to their jobs and companies. The role of such specific work values was perhaps stated most forcefully by Goldthorpe and his associates in the *Affluent Worker* studies. These researchers argued that the technology and organization of the workplace had relatively little to do with workers' overall feelings about their jobs, for such considerations figured insignificantly in their motivations for working in the first place. Even though the hours might be long, tasks arduous and repetitive, and the work environment unpleasant, what mattered most to these British manufacturing employees was that their pay and benefits were good and the work was stable. Earnings and job security were of paramount importance, owing to the breadwinning responsibilities they had to their families and the strong values they attached to family life.

The work values we examine here pertain to: (1) financial rewards; (2) opportunities for career advancement; (3) job security; (4) and relations with coworkers and supervisors. (See table 5.1 for the specific questionnaire items.)

Importance of pay

There is reason to expect the Japanese to attach less importance to pay than Americans typically do. As Vogel has argued (1963:160), a preoccupation with making money has traditionally carried a greater stigma in Japan than in the US. Moreover, the Japanese system of starting workers at low wages and then regularly incrementing their incomes through bonuses, seniority raises, and family allowances may reassure employees that, though their earnings may be low at the onset of their careers, their patience and loyalty to the firm will in the long run be rewarded (Koike, 1983). A possibility to the contrary is that, after decades of scarcity, there is much pent-

Table 5.3 *Standardized regressions of commitment and satisfaction on employee background and work values*[a]

	Dependent variables											
	Commitment						Satisfaction					
	(1)		(2)		(3)		(1)		(2)		(3)	
Independent variable	US	Japan	US	Japan	US	Japan	US	Japan	US	Japan	US	Japan
Employee background												
Age	.216**	.194**	[.155**]	.192**	(.076**)	.165**	.221**	.232**	.129**	.238**	(.066**)	.213(**)
Gender (1 = F)	.080**	.057**	[.119**]	.083[**]	.106**	.079**	[.100**]	.046*	.145**	.111**	.136**	.106**
Education	(−.093**)	−.026( )	[−.095**]	−.056[**]	−.067	−.058**	−.097**	−.055**	−.084**	−.075**	−.057	−.076**
Married (= 1)	.044*	.101[**]	.023	.047+	[.035*]	.065[**]	[.061**]	.098**	.031+	.051*	.041*	.066**
Work commitment					.166**	.145**					.131**	.100**
Specific work values												
Good pay					(.003)	−.065(**)					(.006)	−.073(**)
Good promotions					(−.057**)	.051(*)					(−.082**)	.019
Stable work					.056**	.061**					.051**	.055**
Group work					.037*	.044*					[.027+]	.059[**]
Get along coworkers					(.070**)	.022					(.066**)	.013
Coworkers vs. boss					−.073[**]	−.044*					[−.068**]	−.039[ ]
Insider's advantages					.011	.037*					[−.041**]	.008
Paternalism values												
Company familism					[.040*]	−.004[ ]					.008	.004
Company orientation					.149**	.122**					.074**	.089**
Adj. Mean	2.164	2.014	2.243	2.294	2.179	2.277	1.558	.959	1.650	1.161	1.619	1.144
Adj. R²	.129	.146	.361	.351	.419	.397	.095	.119	.404	.371	.440	.403

Notes: [a] Equation (1) controls for position; Equations (2) and (3) control for position, task characteristics, job rewards, and social bond variables

+ p < .05

* p < .01

** p < .001

[ ] Difference in estimates is significant at the .05 level

( ) Difference in estimates is significant at the .01 level

up demand among Japanese workers for higher incomes and consumer goods (Odaka, 1975), and that dissatisfaction with pay is a significant source of work alienation.

Our data support the first hypothesis (see tables 5.1 and 5.2): the average Japanese rating of the importance of good pay is significantly lower than the Americans'. Moreover, the extent to which Japanese employees value pay is unrelated to their actual earnings. Rather, they are (slightly) more likely to regard pay as important if they receive high intrinsic rewards, expect to be promoted, and are well integrated in the workplace through QC circles, close working relations (teamwork), and friendships with coworkers. This is a puzzling pattern of findings: why should employees who appear to enjoy a variety of *nonmonetary* rewards place particular emphasis on pay? A possible interpretation that we invoke several times in this chapter is what might be termed the "value hierarchy" principle. This is analogous to Maslow's (1954) classic hierarchy of needs theory of motivation: that some needs (values) become activated only after others have been satisfied. This reasoning may be particularly compelling in the Japanese context, where pay, as we have argued, has historically been a less salient work value than career opportunities, good social relations, and intrinsically interesting work. Once these are in some degree attained, the question of pay comes to the fore. In American work culture, on the other hand, a good income at the outset is a compelling motive for working, and we find, in the US sample, that valuing pay is directly related to the amount of pay received. However, there is also evidence from the American data that positive coworker relations and promotion prospects enhance the value placed on wages, thus suggesting that the value hierarchy model may have some validity in the US as well.

By now we are accustomed to the discovery that management rank is a considerably greater source of variance in the work orientations and job perceptions of American than Japanese employees. This pattern turns up again with respect to valuation of earnings, although here it takes an odd twist. There are no differences among Japanese managers, supervisors, and workers in the importance placed on pay. Yet both American supervisors and managers are less inclined than workers to signify that pay is important to them. A variant on the value hierarchy theme comes to mind: one is less likely to value job rewards with which one is already well supplied. Being considerably better paid than rank-and-file workers and tending to take a large salary for granted, US managers are less inclined to identify pay as one of the first criteria by which they judge a job.

Functional area bears no relation to pay valuation in either sample. There is, however, a significant difference between the samples in the effect of tenure: the importance of pay declines with years spent in Japanese companies; no such association in the US data is apparent. The obvious interpretation is that the *nenko* system operates to underpay young workers and overpay senior workers, thus producing highest levels of pay satisfaction in the late career.

Importance of promotion opportunities

One perspective on the *nenko* process as a Japanese incentive system holds that it has considerable potential to motivate commitment. This stems from the provision over the course of the employee's career of a continuous flow of increments in pay and status, so that dead-end jobs and plateaued careers do not put an end to aspiration and ambition (Cole, 1971:103; Lazear, 1979). Starting pay and job status may be considerably lower than what American companies are likely to offer, but opportunities for advancement are greater in the long run (Koike, 1983). Cole (1971:182) argues, for example, that: "The view that it is desirable to make one's entire work career in one company understandably heightens promotional aspirations within the company and increases the incentive to work hard." Yet our data indicate that the Japanese attach lower priority, not only to pay, but also to promotions than the Americans (see tables 5.1 and 5.2). An explanation consistent with the value hierarchy theme is that regular advancement within the firm of the sort *nenko* is presumed to provide reduces uncertainty, hence concern, with promotion prospects.

In both countries, expectation and valuation of promotion are strongly associated. This is not necessarily at odds with the value hierarchy argument, for anticipating a promotion (unlike getting one) likely concentrates a person's interest and attention on the subject, causing other work values, temporarily at least, to subside in importance. On the other hand, an employee who had just been promoted, by this reasoning, might well attach a lower priority to the prospect of future advancement.

For once, there appears to be little real difference between the countries in the impact of authority level. In each, management groups are slightly more likely to value promotions than workers: supervisors in the US managers in Japan.

Perhaps the major contrast between the countries in the processes shaping promotion values concerns the impact of intrinsic rewards: it is positive in Japan, absent in the American sample. It seems reasonable that employees who find their jobs meaningful and interesting should be more concerned with furthering their careers in the company. But why is this true only in Japan? A speculative interpretation is that, for American employees, promotion generally involves major shifts in job responsibilities as well as status and pay. That is often not the case in Japanese industry, where increments in rank and compensation are possible without real changes in tasks and responsibilities (Clark, 1979; Cole, 1971; Pucik, 1984).

The job and social bond variables have little to do with promotion values in either sample, with the exception that QC membership in the US and outside socializing in Japan have positive effects. It is not unlikely that both activities are perceived by employees to play some instrumental role in paving the way for upward movement within the organization.

Importance of an insider's advantage

A key feature of the internal labor market organization of the Japanese firm is the practice of recruiting outside the firm for entry-level positions only, subsequently filling higher positions from below. Should we not then expect the Japanese to place considerable value on giving employees of the company an advantage over outside applicants in competing for job openings? Yet, as in the case of promotions, American employees are somewhat more likely to value this practice than the Japanese, though both samples tend to favor it. Again the value hierarchy principle comes to mind. Japanese employees may not concern themselves with an arrangement which is taken for granted in Japanese organizations. In contrast, an insider's advantage is a practice which most American employees would no doubt much prefer but they are by no means assured of preferential treatment over outsiders in the competition for better jobs within the company.

Turning to some potential antecedent variables, once again we find differences among management levels in the US data which are absent in Japan. American, but not Japanese, managers and supervisors are less likely than workers to favor internal recruitment. This, of course, accords with the presumption that internal promotion is institutionalized in Japanese industry, endorsed by managers and workers alike. In the US, however, it is a point of contention, with managers preferring the flexibility and control permitted by outside hiring and workers wishing to limit the applicant pool to those already employed.[2] Moreover, employees in each country who receive higher earnings tend to feel that insiders should have an advantage, but there is no relationship between valuing internal promotion and an employee's perception of the odds of promotion. Finally, adherence to the general belief that members of the company should be favored when vacancies are to be filled is significantly influenced in Japan by the extent of intrinsic rewards and in both countries by the quality of coworker ties. These effects are plausible: persons with strong attachments to the workplace want the opportunity to fashion a career within it.

Importance of a stable job

Another key work value is the importance the employee attaches to "a stable job without fear of layoffs." Since employment stability is unquestionably greater and a matter of less uncertainty for the Japanese (Mincer and Higuchi, 1987), it is not surprising (from the value hierarchy perspective) that the Americans attach greater weight to it. We might also expect the time an employee has already been with a company to influence his or her valuation of job stability, but in both samples the effect of tenure is nonsignificant. Among the Japanese, good relations in the workplace, teamwork, and intrinsic rewards from the job are linked to a preference for job stability. In the US sample, only the quality of coworker ties raises the value of continued employment. As in many of our findings thus far, this contrast between the countries suggests a broader pattern in Japan of individual embeddedness in workplace social networks.

Importance of group work

A work value that is particularly important in a comparative study of Japanese and US work organization is the extent to which employees prefer working in groups to working alone. As we have had numerous occasions to note, an orientation to groups has long been a central cultural value and social structural pattern in Japan, and is often contrasted with the individualism presumed dominant in Anglo–American culture (e.g. Nakane, 1970). From the premise that integration and identification with groups are culturally transmitted values which the Japanese internalize and by which they are motivated, we would anticipate Japanese employees to place greater importance on this aspect of work. This is indeed what we find in tables 5.1 and 5.2: the Japanese are significantly more likely to value working in groups, though the difference is fairly small.

Within both countries, it is clear that the importance employees place on group or team work depends on the extent and quality of their social relations in the workplace. We find positive influences, in varying magnitude, of teamwork, outside socializing, the quality of coworker relations, and (in the US) QC participation, and friendships. This pattern is an obvious deviation from the hierarchy of values model wherein employees are seen to desire those qualities which are scarce in their jobs. There is no doubt some tendency here for people who value working in groups to be more apt to do so and hence more likely to make friends at work and develop good feelings toward their coworkers. Yet there are severe constraints on these processes in manufacturing plants, for rank-and-file workers in particular have limited control over job assignments. It is also noteworthy that the effects of teamwork and friendships are stronger in the American sample. This may indicate that the Japanese group orientation arises chiefly from cultural values, whereas in the US it reflects to a greater degree the actual conditions of one's present job. Indeed, the only other variables that are related to the importance placed on group work in the Japanese sample are job complexity, age, and gender. In contrast, US supervisors are more likely than workers to favor group activities, and both technical and direct production employees have a greater preference for group work than their colleagues in office departments.

Importance of relations with co-workers

We used two measures to tap the employees' valuation of good relations with coworkers. One item assessed the importance of getting along with fellow employees, and we find the Americans more likely to agree than the Japanese (table 5.2). In view of the evidence already reviewed indicating that social ties with coworkers are more prevalent in Japan, the value hierarchy interpretation comes to mind: Japanese employees may regard good relations in the workplace as less problematic than the Americans, thus taking them for granted and attaching less value to them. Moreover, as our findings regarding the valuing of group work suggest, employees who in fact have stronger and better social ties in the company place greater importance on getting along with coworkers, and again this seems more prevalent in the US.

In the US but not in Japan, intrinsically rewarding work is associated with valuing good relations with coworkers. We take this as further evidence that, among the Japanese, such values are shaped more by cultural, less by workplace, forces. A quite puzzling finding is the negative relationships that appear only in the Japanese sample between earnings and valuing coworker relations. We can only speculate on reasons. Since compensation in Japanese firms normally varies little among members of the same cohort, and, indeed, equality and reward sharing is the established practice (Koike, 1983; Rohlen, 1974), it may be that those individuals who are able to advance their salaries beyond the average for their cohort and department tend to disengage from the normally tight solidarity of the work group, perhaps encouraged by the disgruntlement of colleagues. An alternative view is that the quite low starting pay of often highly trained Japanese employees leads to a search for alternative rewards or justifications for the job; e.g. by developing work orientations that emphasize the value of intrinsically rewarding social relations.

A central and perennial issue in the study of workplace relationships is the question of whether employees are oriented toward vertical versus horizontal ties. To specifically address this juxtaposition, we asked respondents the extent to which they agreed or disagreed with the statement: "getting along with fellow employees is more important [to you] than getting along with [your] boss." The Japanese are more inclined than the Americans to place greater importance on getting along with peers. This fits the value hierarchy paradigm: strong vertical ties, as we demonstrated in the previous chapter, are far more prevalent in Japanese industry, and conflict between ranks, by US standards, is low. Frequent tensions between labor and management, and between middle and top management, may well cause American employees to yearn for better hierarchical relations.

Apart from the difference in the sample means on this item, there are some very interesting patterns in how it relates to other variables. Involvement in teamwork, good coworker relations, and (in the US) close friends lead to valuation of coworker over vertical ties, but, as with the previous item, there are generally more and larger such effects in the US. Not surprisingly, good supervisory relations in both countries, and (in Japan) supervisor contact lead to a preference for getting along with superiors. The effect of job rewards is particularly noteworthy. No one will be surprised that employees expecting promotions are motivated to accommodate to their bosses, and in both countries this proves to be the case. Less anticipated is our finding that the experience of intrinsic rewards is coupled with a taste for vertical ties. The dynamic here may well be that workers who find their jobs dull and routine seek support from likewise disenchanted peers. Persons who derive fulfillment from their jobs, as we know, are more likely to identify with the goals of the organization and hence with its management hierarchy. The effect of earnings among the Japanese conforms to our expectations: the higher paid favor the company of supervisors. In the US sample, there is a very slight tendency for pay to be positively related to a preference for peers. We don't know why, and the difference is too small to justify speculation.

Paternalism

Perhaps no other cluster of culturally related work values has been the object of so much writing and discussion in studies of Japanese work life as "paternalism." This idea is sometimes used to refer to the prevalence of welfare services and employee programs in corporatist-type firms (Littler, 1982). However, paternalism is also an important value pattern that implies the general expectation that companies should provide for the welfare of their employees and their families, and that employees should reciprocate with devotion and loyalty to the firm (Cole, 1971; Lincoln *et al.*, 1981). Hence, paternalism has to do with the presumption that the employment contract should extend beyond a mere market exchange to encompass a broader set of reciprocal rights and obligations between employee and company. We focus on three facets of paternalism: company familism, supervisory paternalism, and company–labor reciprocity.

Company familism

The portrayal of the firm as a corporate family has been central to managerial ideology in Japan since the 19th Century (Dore, 1973; Yoshino, 1968), and represents a significant dimension of the organizational culture of US corporatist-styled firms as well (Edwards, 1979:148; Ouchi, 1981). We measure this value by the degree of agreement or disagreement with the statement: "a company should take care of its employees, since a company and its employees are like a family and its members." Past surveys have shown that most Japanese workers respond positively to questions of this sort. For example, in Marsh and Mannari's (1976) samples of Japanese employees of an electronics plant and a shipbuilding factory, over 60 percent agreed with a statement that read: "management thinks they are like parents to workers; therefore they regard it as better to take care of the personal affairs of workers." On the other hand, the value hierarchy hypothesis would predict that, because corporate welfarism and paternalism are more prevalent in Japanese industry, they might be rated as less important by Japanese than American workers who see these practices as an unfamiliar but possibly quite attractive alternative to their usual treatment by the firm.

Our evidence that the Japanese are more inclined to feel undecided or to disagree with this questionnaire item about paternalism in the company family sense is not necessarily surprising. This has been a much-discussed topic, disparaged by some as "feudalism" while defended by others as a traditional practice fostering company loyalty, productivity, and competitiveness (Cole, 1971; Vogel 1963). The truly striking finding here is the Americans' enthusiastic support of the corporate familism ideal. Once again, we should recall that our survey was conducted in a recessionary US economy, when layoffs were high and companies were successfully extracting wage and benefit concessions from labor. Against this background, it is perhaps to be expected that an overwhelming majority of the American employees would favor a more protective and benevolent posture on the part of their employers.

Additional insights into the differences between Japanese and American employees in their responses to this item are provided by the results presented in table 5.2. Readily evident is the essential consensus across management ranks in the Japanese sample: supervisors are only slightly less likely than workers, and managers equally likely, to endorse familism as a proper company role *vis-à-vis* employees. In contrast, American managers and supervisors are considerably less inclined than workers to subscribe to this point of view, though management does not exactly oppose it: whereas the mean for American workers is 4.6 (on a 5-point scale), the averages for supervisors and managers are 4.1 and 3.8, respectively. Even the American managers, then, appear to be more favorable to the idea of paternalism than Japanese workers, who average 3.1 on the same scale. The lack of significant differences between management and labor in the Japanese sample suggests that there is more to this issue in Japan than simply workers' desire for better treatment by the firm. We suspect that the question of the responsibility of companies to their employees is rooted in broad public debates over the proper mix of traditional values and work orientations, on the one hand, and rising individualism on the other.

We might expect the company family ideal to be more prevalent where there is a high level of workplace community, and, indeed, our indicators of social integration and teamwork are generally positively linked to our measure of this work value. In both countries, however, corporate familism declines with time spent in the company. Though these effects are small, they do raise a question about the effectiveness of permanent employment and internal careers in building a cohesive enterprise community.

Supervisory paternalism

A second dimension of paternalism refers to the scope of superior–subordinate ties: the extent to which they are enfused with personal, paternal content and go beyond purely task-related matters. As discussed in the last chapter, much has been written on the strong and diffuse vertical relations in Japanese organizations. A recurring theme is that the paternalism found in Japanese superior–subordinate *dyads* has roots in such traditional patterns of vertical bonding as *oyabun-kobun* (patron–client) and *sempai-kohai* (senior–junior) relations (Cole, 1971). To Nakane (1970), such vertical ties provide the mechanism which drives the Japanese collectivity-orientation and the solidarity of Japanese groups. Social integration in Japan is not a matter of similarly situated peers joining into common interest groupings, but instead derives from a process of strong bonding between status unequals.

Our own data have added considerably to already strong documentation of extensive informal bonds between superiors and subordinates in Japanese work settings. Our question now is the extent to which such relations are expressly *valued* by Japanese workers. The alternative interpretation is that they are institutionalized practices which are supported by management and which individual employees find difficult to resist (Kamata, 1983). Yet previous surveys have produced strong evidence of preferences for paternalistic supervisory styles among Japanese workers. Takezawa and Whitehill's surveys posed a question of this sort. By a huge margin (71 percent and 75 percent vs. 5 percent and 7 percent), American workers were more likely than the Japanese to respond that a superior should not be involved in such a personal matter as a decision to marry (Takezawa and Whitehill, 1981:119) Likewise, Marsh and Mannari (1976) reported that 80 percent of their sample of Japanese manufacturing workers expressed preference for a supervisor described as: "A man who sometimes demands extra work in spite of rules against it, but on the other hand looks after you personally in matters not connected with the work."

Our survey included a similar item: "I like a supervisor who looks after the workers in their personal matters even though he may sometimes ask for extra work." Unfortunately, this item was added to the American questionnaire late in the study, and we have responses from less than half of the US respondents. While we give the distribution of available responses to this particular question, then, we do not consider it further in our analyses.

Consistent with these previous studies, we find the Japanese more likely to agree with the statement than the Americans: 68 percent vs. 49 percent agree, 20 percent vs. 29 percent are undecided, and 12 percent vs. 22 percent disagree. Although the Americans are clearly more ambivalent about the issue than the Japanese, nearly 50 percent agreement seems surprisingly high, especially when compared with Takezawa and Whitehill's results. Again, we speculate that the reasons lie in the poor economic conditions prevailing in central Indiana at the time of the study and an industrial relations environment in which the position of labor had become weak and dependent.

Company–labor reciprocity vs. company orientation

A feature of paternalism in Japanese industry that often surfaces in writings on the topic is that it involves a reciprocal set of rights and obligations between the company and the employee. Although the threat of international competition and the current industrial relations climate in the US appear to be changing expectations somewhat, traditionally the employment relationship in US industry has been of quite a different sort. Employees have demanded relatively little from companies beyond a reasonable rate of pay for a fair day's work. In turn, their participation in the organization has been highly circumscribed, the prevailing view being that the fortunes of the firm should not exercise a major influence over pay, effort, or hours worked. In contrast, the nurturant, paternal posture assumed by Japanese firms practicing corporatist control is assumed to pay dividends in employee loyalty and hence the willingness of workers to invest extra effort to enable their companies to succeed.

We measure this expectation of reciprocity first with respect to the issue of job security. A key obligation of Japanese firms is to provide steady employment without the fear of layoffs and dismissals that perpetually haunt American manufacturing employees. Our questionnaire included several items pertaining to the employee's perception of the responsibilities of companies in this regard (see table 5.1 for the wording and coding of these questions). Three items deal with the permissibility of layoffs and other labor-force reductions under several conditions: if the demand for a company's product goes down; if new machines begin doing the work formerly done by employees; and if companies need to raise productivity. The Japanese employees were more likely to disagree with all three items: to feel that weak demand, automation, and the need for productivity do not justify labor-force reductions. The difference is striking with respect to the question of whether weak demand justifies layoffs. While a majority (56 percent) of the American employees think layoffs are warranted in a business downturn, only 39 percent of the Japanese think so. This pattern is consistent, of course, with the observation that Japanese firms are less apt to dismiss employees for such reasons, but rather attempt to find ways to readjust the workforce (e.g. by job reassignments, normal attrition, early retirement) without recourse to forced terminations. A related item, "a company should be able to transfer employees even if it causes the employees problems," gets away from the specific issue of workforce reductions and consequently does not discriminate between the samples.

If Japanese companies are thought to owe their workers secure and continuous employment even when the need for their labor diminishes, the opposite side of the coin is that Japanese employees should be willing to donate their time to the organization when the demand for their labor is high. As we noted earlier, one of the most striking examples of the ostensible commitment of the Japanese is their tendency to take less of their allotted vacation and leave time than they are entitled. An item that speaks to this issue is: "employees shouldn't take time off when things are busy, though they have a right to take time off." 50 percent of the Japanese respondents agree with this statement compared to roughly 28 percent of the American employees. While it may be, as Kamata's writing (1983) suggests, that this posture does not so much reflect the natural inclinations of Japanese labor as it does intense and unremitting pressures for conformity to informal but highly binding workplace norms, it nonetheless indicates a very large and concrete difference in the sacrifices that American and Japanese employees as collectivities are prepared to accept in the interests of the firm.

The concept of a set of reciprocal rights and obligations between the employee and the firm puts the issue of organizational commitment in a new light. Presumably a *totally* committed employee – one prepared to sacrifice everything for the company – would endorse *all* these items. All five, in fact, are positively intercorrelated and form a single dimension when factor analyzed with other attitudinal and value items. Summing these five items into an unweighted composite gives us a reasonably reliable scale in both countries which we call "company orientation." As we have seen, however, such total subordination of individual to corporate interests is not the kind of "commitment" that any informed observer would attribute to the Japanese workforce or welfare corporatist organization more generally. (It may, however, be akin to what Burawoy, 1983, intends by "hegemonic despotism.") The reciprocity implicit in Japanese paternalism means that employees' willingness to sacrifice for the firm is conditioned upon it honoring certain employee welfare rights (e.g. to job security). In fact, as with the Porter organizational commitment scale (see table 3.2), we find a small but significant tendency for the US sample to display greater "company orientation."

Not surprisingly, our results in table 5.2 indicate that managers and supervisors in both countries are more likely to be company-oriented; to feel that the company should act in its own interests, even if this creates problems for its employees. As usual, the differences among levels are larger in the US. Moreover, office employees appear to subscribe to this view more than technical (at least in Japan) and production employees. This probably reflects the greater tendency of white-collar, salaried employees to identify with the company and its management. Finally, there are indications that strong social bonds with superiors (perhaps through a kind of reference group socialization process) leads to subordination of employee interests to those of the firm.

Effects of work values on commitment and satisfaction

How work values – qualities which persons identify as abstractly desirable or worthwhile in a job – shape work attitudes – defined as subjective dispositions or orientations to the *specific* job and company in which one is employed – is a complex problem to which we cannot do adequate justice here. Researchers have generally taken two perspectives on the relationship between work values and job attitudes. In the *additive* model, value differences increment the variance in work attitudes beyond that explained by characteristics of the job. A common view is that strong values raise levels of expectancy or motivation, such that higher levels of reward are required to produce a psychological equilibrium or satisfaction (Kalleberg, 1977; March and Simon, 1958; Salancik and Pfeffer, 1977; Vroom 1964). In the alternative model, values *interact* with or moderate the effects of job properties. There is much speculation and some evidence, for example, that the effects of job complexity and autonomy are conditioned on the employee's work values and aspirations (Blood and Hulin, 1967; Turner and Lawrence, 1965). Persons for whom work is a central life interest may indeed find challenge and meaning, hence, commitment and fulfillment in demanding, complex tasks. Persons attaching greater priority to leisure and family time, however, may react more positively to undemanding, routine jobs that supply income without requiring a heavy motivational investment.

Both kinds of value effects figure importantly in a comparative study of Japanese and US work patterns. First, there is the essentially culturalist argument that Japanese work motivation is a direct manifestation of the strong cultural values of, say, diligence and loyalty. This is the theory Cole (1979) invokes to account for the low levels of job satisfaction consistently reported in Japanese workforce surveys. Satisfaction is low because values, hence expectancy, are strong, and the individual is in a highly motivated state (Vroom, 1964). American workers, by contrast, are culturally inclined toward values (e.g. individualism, personal freedom, consumerism) which elevate the importance of nonwork pursuits, consequently lowering expectations for intrinsic job rewards.

Similarly, the "values as moderators" theory applies to the case of Japan in important ways. In chapter 1, we discussed the possibility that the success of corporatist forms of organization in eliciting commitment from workers may depend on the presence of certain values and expectations in a workforce. A quite convincing case can be made that the commitment and performance of Japanese labor is neither due simply to cultural norms and values nor to organizational arrangements but rather to a distinctively Japanese combination of the two. Japanese forms of welfare corporatism, so this argument runs, evolved in ways that were isomorphic with the cultural and institutional environment of Japan, largely so as to cloak innovative management and economic practices with the legitimacy of tradition. These work structures are thus fitted to the expectations and aspirations of the Japanese, and their effectiveness is limited to employee populations who share such values. From this perspective, Japanese management and organization are not likely to be exportable, for workers steeped in different work values and traditions cannot be expected to respond as have the Japanese (Lincoln *et al.*, 1981).

Our hypothesis is that, with job attributes held constant, the additive effects of values on job satisfaction should be negative. No such simple across-the-board prediction is available in the case of organizational commitment, since the relationship between commitment and work values no doubt depends to a very large degree on the type of value in question. One semi-general prediction that seems consistent with theories of organizational control and commitment, however, is that values stressing the intrinsic rewards of work and organizational life should foster commitment, whereas valuation of extrinsic inducements should diminish it.

There is some support for this hypothesis in table 5.3. Valuation of pay – the most extrinsic of rewards – is negatively related to commitment among the Japanese, though not in the US. This may testify to more constraints on opportunities to maximize individual income in Japanese employment settings. We might also speculate that pay *per se* tends to be viewed as a more legitimate motivator in US than Japanese corporate culture. The effect on commitment of valuing promotion is interesting: it is positive in Japan, negative in the US. Again to speculate: promotion valuation in the US may well mean an employee is more career- than organization-oriented, for career advancement frequently means a change in employers. Under the Japanese employment system, however, to value promotion is tantamount to wishing to advance one's career within the same organization, a posture which seems likely to induce commitment. Another intriguing finding that may be linked to the issue of career advancement is the negative relationships between commitment in both countries and valuing ties with coworkers over those with superiors. This may suggest an orientation to advancing one's fortunes through cultivating the proper higher-level connections, even if it comes at the expense of bonds with colleagues (see Kanter, 1977).

Valuation of job stability and group work enhances commitment in both countries. The "company familism" value item, surprisingly, has a small positive effect in the US but none in Japan. The main predictors of organizational commitment among the set of value indicators are work commitment and the company orientation index. These come as close as our data permit to representing Vogel's concepts of diligence and loyalty and, indeed, as we have noted, the content domains they tap are similar to that of organizational commitment itself.

Contrary to our prediction, the effects of values on job satisfaction do not differ markedly from those we observed for commitment. The influences of work commitment and company orientation are somewhat smaller, and the negative effects of valuing pay (Japan) and promotion (US) are slightly larger. Moreover, valuing internal recruitment has a slight negative impact on the satisfaction of the US employees, though not on their commitment. In addition, valuing a stable job and close working relations with others lead to greater job satisfaction as well as commitment among American and Japanese employees alike.

Values as moderators

Finally, what about the hypothesis that values condition or moderate the effects of job attributes on an employee's commitment to the company and satisfaction with the job? Overall, we find little evidence that this occurs. Table 5.4 presents the regression coefficients on interaction terms representing theoretically meaningful combinations of values and job attributes. In the Japanese sample, none of the interaction effects on commitment is significant, and, in the equation for satisfaction, only three are. Not unexpectedly, the (positive) impact of teamwork on job satisfaction is intensified among employees who value close working relations with coworkers. Moreover, as an adjunct to an earlier result, we find that good relations with supervisors produce a decrement in satisfaction to the degree the employee values the company of superiors over that of workers. Surprisingly, those who place greater importance on promotions, yet expect to be promoted, are less satisfied.

In the US data, we find two very strong value/job interactions. Valuing vertical relations considerably enhances what we earlier observed to be the negative effect of supervisor contact in US plants. Moreover, analogous to our finding the Japanese data concerning teamwork, the quality of relations with coworkers is more strongly associated with commitment and satisfaction to the extent that the employee values such relations. What we find no evidence for in either sample is the proposition that the effects of job complexity and autonomy are conditioned on work values. Taking work commitment as our indicator of valuation of work tasks *per se*, the only significant interaction this produces with job complexity and autonomy is a marginal and implausible one in the US: complex jobs produce *lower* organizational commitment and job satisfaction among employees with strong work values. Despite its intuitive appeal, then, there is little empirical support here for the proposition that the impact of task characteristics on work attitudes varies with the individual's work values (see Kalleberg, 1977). In these Japanese and US

Table 5.4 *Metric slope coefficients for interactions (product terms) between values and job attributes*[a]

	Dependent variables			
	Commitment		Satisfaction	
Interaction term	US	Japan	US	Japan
Work commitment X job complexity	−.01711[+]	−.00177	−.01877[+]	−.00171
Work commitment X autonomy	−.00303	−.01848	.00047	−.00989
Good pay X earnings	.000001	−.00000	−.00001	.00003
Good promotions X promotion chances	.00436	−.03435	.02227	−.03934[+]
Stable work X tenure	.00034	−.00194	.00084	−.00167
Group work X teamwork	−.00382	.01180	−.00514	.01244[+]
Get along with coworkers X friends	−.00359	−.00069	−.00382	−.00088
Get along with coworkers X quality coworker ties	.02065[**]	.00418	.01904[**]	.00106
Coworkers vs. boss X quality vertical ties	.00647	−.00783	.00269	−.02188[*]
Get along with supervisor X supervisor contact	−.01095[**]	.0004	−.00853[**]	.00025
Insider's advantage X expected promotion	.02285	.00934	.00503	.02285

Notes: [a] Estimates obtained upon adding these product terms to the equations in Table 5.2
[+] $p < .05$
[**] $p < .01$
[**] $p < .001$

samples, perceptions of task complexity and autonomy generally render work more intrinsically rewarding, thus more satisfying and commitment-evoking, regardless of the employee's particular value orientations.

Employees' demographic backgrounds

We are concerned in this chapter with sources of variation in work attitudes which arise, at least in part, outside the employing organization. Work values represent one such set of forces, although, as we have seen, workplace variables do appear to have some determining influence on them. A second set comprises demographic background attributes such as age, gender, marital status, and education. These are much less likely than work values to be changed by processes internal to the organization. Moreover, much of their influence on work attitudes and behaviors is mediated by the impact they have on an individual's job position, rewards, and tasks. We now consider how an employee's background works through such job characteristics as well as work values to shape his or her commitment to the organization and satisfaction with the job.

Age

A basic finding of much research on work attitudes is that older workers are, in general, more committed to their employing organizations and more satisfied with their jobs (for commitment, see Angle and Perry, 1983; Hrebiniak and Alutto, 1972; Sheldon, 1971; for satisfaction, see Kalleberg and Loscocco, 1983; Wright and Hamilton, 1978). Table 5.3 shows that these positive relationships between age and work attitudes are found as well in our samples of manufacturing employees: in each country, older people are both more committed and more satisfied than younger employees.

Age differences in job attributes

It is, of course, very difficult to attach a causal interpretation to statistical associations between an individual's age and workplace positions, experiences and perceptions. So many processes affecting work life are embedded in time that age becomes a proxy for a host of unmeasured and often unknown phenomena. Moreover, as we acknowledged before, there are some problems in interpreting the *net* effects of age and tenure, given that (as long as the employment relationship lasts) a year of one is an exact function of a year of the other. However, we would in general expect that age itself plays a greater direct role in the determination of Japanese than American organizational careers. Employee age, along with tenure, have, via the *nenko* process, traditionally been more explicit criteria for advancement in Japanese firms (Koike, 1983). Indeed, status differences in Japanese work settings have so closely corresponded to age differences that the workplace hierarchy mirrors the pervasive age-grading of Japanese society overall (Nakane, 1970). Surely age as such carries greater significance for the Japanese employee's overall situation in the company.

Yet, with several notable exceptions, we find the relationships between age and job attributes to be rather similar in our Japanese and US samples (see tables 4.2–4.4). In general, older employees experience greater autonomy and intrinsic rewards. Paradoxically, they also see their supervisors having more influence over job decisions (though the effect of tenure in this case is in the opposite direction). Promotion expectations, as we previously reported, decline with age. Moreover, some social disengagement seems to set in: with age, workers have fewer close friends and are less likely (even in

Japan but by a smaller margin) to engage in off-the-job socializing with colleagues. However, they do not see the quality of their relations with coworkers and supervisors declining. The major contrast between the countries concerns the influence of age on job complexity: in the US, age is strongly and positively related to complexity, but in Japan this relationship is weak and negative. As we have suggested before, the Japanese practice of separating functional tasks from status may have something to do with this pattern (Yoshino, 1968). US manufacturing workers move from less to more complex jobs largely through a process of promotion. Because of less job specialization and more rotation, Japanese workers are likely to obtain experience in a greater range of manufacturing jobs without going through promotion and the time lags that this entails.

Age differences in work values

We expect age differences in work values to be particularly large in Japan, which has undergone considerably greater social transformation than the US over the lifetimes of the older employees in our samples. Postwar cohorts have been brought up in a very different society from that constituting prewar Japan, and the pace of change and modernization in the postwar decades has continued to be rapid. A common observation is that the younger Japanese do not adhere to traditional values of sacrifice, hard work, and company loyalty, but seek more personal goals of leisure time, family life, and material consumption (Cole, 1979; Odaka, 1975). While a similar transition is presumed to have occurred in the United States, its origins lie farther back in time and few would argue that it is a marked source of differentiation among current generations of Americans. The United States has been an affluent, leisure-time, and consumption-oriented society since the early years of the postwar period, whereas only very recently are these values becoming widespread in Japan.

Consistent with these arguments, our results suggest that there are greater age differences in work values among the Japanese. For example, economic rewards are considerably more important to young Japanese employees than is the case in the US. Moreover, while older employees in both countries place less value on promotions, the age differences are larger in Japan. Further, older Japanese employees feel more strongly than their younger counterparts that insiders should have an advantage in the competition for job openings within the company, but age is not related to this value among the Americans. On the other hand, our findings for age differences in work commitment run counter to the hypothesis that there is a greater generation gap in Japan: while older employees in each country are more committed to work, the difference between young and old is larger in the US.

A sharp contrast between the countries can be seen in the age differences in the importance attached to social relationships in the company. In Japan, younger employees place greater value on getting along with coworkers in general, but, at the same time, they feel that it is more important to have smooth relations with their superiors. Anticipating a communal spirit and close working relations, young Japanese employees appear to approach the organization with a positive expectation of getting along and fitting in. But, since their advancement is heavily contingent on the approval of superiors, they place a higher priority initially on vertical ties. In contrast, younger American manufacturing employees appear to want to keep their distance from coworkers and when asked about getting along with other employees in general, they attach relatively low importance to such ties. However, they also do not want to be accused by their fellows of "sucking up to the boss," a tendency reflected in their responses to the item rating the importance of coworker relations *vis-à-vis* relations with superiors. When the question is stated as getting along with peers as opposed to bosses, younger Americans are more likely to favor relations with coworkers than are older employees.

We expected to find rather large age differences among the Japanese on the paternalism value items. While we do find marked age effects on the composite "company orientation" measure, these are equally large in the US and Japan. In both countries, older employees express much greater willingness to accept layoffs, transfers, and reduced leisure time for the sake of the firm. Of course, older employees who have more seniority are unlikely to bear the brunt of labor-force reductions and hence may interpret these questions in less personal terms. However, while we might have anticipated that younger Japanese employees would be less likely to subscribe to the "corporate familism" value than older generations, there is no age difference on this dimension in either sample.

Explaining age differences in work attitudes

To what extent do age differences in job characteristics and work values explain our finding of greater commitment and satisfaction among older employees? Table 5.3 shows that there continue to be age differences in both attitude outcomes even when we control for job characteristics and work values. Moreover, these adjusted age differences are larger in Japan than in the US. A comparison of the total effects of age (column 1) with the direct effects (column 3) suggests a reason: much more of the total age effect is mediated by the job and value measures in the US than in Japan. In the US sample, about 60–70 percent of the age differences in commitment and satisfaction are indirect via the measures of job characteristics and work values. This suggests that the reason why older American employees have more positive work attitudes is because they have better jobs and work situations that are more likely to fit their values toward work. In contrast, very little of the age difference in commitment and satisfaction in Japan is explained by the intervening job and value measures: regardless of the specific properties of their jobs and work situations, and the importance they place on them, younger Japanese employees are less committed to their employing organizations and less satisfied with their jobs than their older counterparts.

What accounts, then, for the residual age effect on work attitudes in the Japanese sample? We believe that it provides further evidence for the hypotheses of a fundamental generation gap in Japanese work attitudes. As we suggested, one reason to expect such a gap is that Japanese society has experienced much greater social change than has the US over the postwar period. In large part, such change involved a shift from the scarcity and production mentality of an earlier stage of industrialization, where organizational loyalty was high and people were satisfied with less, to the leisure and consumption orientation of late industrial development, with its wider opportunities for finding commitment and fulfillment outside the workplace.

Gender

The issue of gender inequalities in workplace experiences and job rewards has held center stage in American public policy debates over equal opportunity throughout much of the 70s and 80s. Considerable legislation and numerous legal battles over hiring discrimination, comparable worth, and sexual harassment have produced some significant changes in the hiring and treatment of women by US employers, although numerous barriers to full equality remain. Changes have been occurring in Japan as well – female labor-force participation has been rising and more women appear to be obtaining the job security guarantees that go with regular employee status (Holden, 1983). The 1985 Equal Employment Opportunity law in Japan forbade gender discrimination with respect to job training, retirement, and benefits (though it mandated few sanctions against employers and explicitly stressed the responsibilities of Japanese women to their homes and families). Yet such shifts are on a far smaller scale than in the US, and Japan continues to have a very traditional sexual division of labor (Cook and Hayashi, 1980).

A number of recent studies have documented that women, at least in the US, are more committed to their organizations than men (e.g. Angle and Perry, 1983; Hrebiniak and Alutto, 1972), though studies have generally found little difference between males and females in their levels of job satisfaction (see, for example, Quinn, Staines, and McCullough, 1974). Our results in table 5.3 indicate that the women in both our US and Japanese samples are more committed to their employing organizations than men, as well as more satisfied with their jobs. In order to account for these gender differences in work attitudes, we first examine differences between male and female employees in their job attributes and work values.

Gender differences in job attributes

The tendency for female employees to report greater job satisfaction is particularly striking when one considers that their work situations are palpably inferior in many respects to those of men (see tables 4.2–4.4). In both samples, women's tasks are subject to more supervisory control, though their actual contact with supervisors appears to be less than that of men. Moreover, in each country, but especially in Japan, women: have less complex jobs; are less likely to be involved in QC; receive lower earnings; and have fewer opportunities for promotion. In the US, women are less apt to socialize after hours with other employees; this probably reflects the greater burden of home responsibilities they typically assume. Interestingly, Japanese women employees seem as likely to engage in off-the-job socializing as their male counterparts. One reason, perhaps, is that fewer Japanese women attempt to combine work and family responsibilities. By far the dominant pattern is for women to leave the labor force on the occasion of marriage and childbearing (Holden, 1983).

Gender differences in work values

An explanation frequently given for the surprisingly low levels of work alienation among women despite a considerably lower quality of working life is that women tend to place less importance on work and its rewards. Our results in table 5.2, however, do not appear to bear out this prediction. There is no difference in either country in the work commitment of male and female employees. Moreover, with respect to a number of specific work values, the women in our sample seem to register stronger preferences than their male colleagues. American women place greater importance on pay, promotions, job stability, and on getting along with coworkers than US men; these differences are not observed in the Japanese sample. Japanese women, in fact, attach notably less importance to promotion than do Japanese men, which may well reflect the exclusion of women from the pattern of regular seniority-based advancement in Japan (Cook and Hayashi, 1980). In both countries, women are more likely than men to value working in groups, on giving present employees the edge in competing for job openings, and on getting along with superiors rather than coworkers. This last result may reflect the more dependent posture of women in the organization.

Explaining gender differences in work attitudes

These patterns of gender differences in job characteristics and work values do not appear to explain why women in either country have more positive work attitudes than men. This sense is reinforced by the results in table 5.3, which indicate that, even with job attributes held constant, women continue to be more satisfied with their jobs than men, and are also more committed to their organizations. Indeed, we find in both countries that the gender gap in work attitudes is *greater* once we control for gender differences in job characteristics and work values.

One explanation for the greater commitment of women to their organizations is that they have more to lose by changing companies: women tend to have fewer opportunities to obtain comparable jobs elsewhere. This is especially the case in Japan, where the opportunities of women are more severely constrained than in the US (Cook and Hayashi, 1980). Another plausible explanation for the commitment of women employees is that they have generally had to overcome more barriers to attain their positions in the company. They may place greater value on their organizational attachments than do men (see, e.g. Mowday *et al.*, 1982). The fewer employment alternatives available to women in both countries also help to explain their greater job satisfaction. With fewer jobs to choose from, they have lower expectations as to what constitutes a good job, and thus are satisfied with less.

Marital status

Employees' reactions to work are influenced by their experiences in other social roles, such as the family, an institution of critical importance for understanding work-related attitudes. Marriage places constraints on what one can seek from the work role and shapes the values that individuals bring to the workplace. Our measure of one's involvement in familial roles is a dichotomous variable coded "1" if the person is married and "0" if he or she is not (for whatever reason). Table 5.3 suggests that married employees are more committed to their organizations, and more satisfied with their jobs, especially in Japan. In order to explain these differences, we again consider first the implications of marital status for variations in job attributes and work values.

Marital status and job attributes

In US work organizations, one would not normally expect the employee's marital status to have an appreciable influence on his or her job rewards, for such purely personal characteristics are believed to be beyond the purview of organizational interest and control. In contrast, Japanese companies more often base workplace decisions such as promotions and pay raises on the employee's family situation and other life-course factors. As we reported in detail in chapter 4, our results provide support for the proposition that personal background variables play a greater role in Japanese firms' promotion decisions: married employees in Japan are more likely than the non-married to expect promotion; but marital status is unrelated to promotion expectations in the US. However, married employees in both countries receive higher earnings, though the gap is greater in Japan. In both countries, moreover, unmarried workers have less complex jobs.

We would also expect that married employees, having competing social obligations at home, would be less integrated in life at the workplace. Consistent with our knowledge that Americans place a higher priority on family concerns, we find this to be the case in the US, but not in Japan. Married US employees are less likely to get together with coworkers or superiors outside the workplace. Married Japanese employees report more close friends in the company and better relations with superiors.

Marital status differences in work values

Table 5.2 shows that commitment to work is lower among married employees. The familial obligations associated with marriage obviously compete with the work role for an individual's time and attention. This is the case in the US as well as in Japan, despite the greater weight the Japanese attach to work over family matters as a central life interest.

As for the specific work values, we find that married employees in Japan place more importance on pay and job stability. This no doubt reflects the increased financial responsibilities that marriage entails. We do not, however, observe this same tendency in the US sample. Similarly, married Japanese (but not American) employees score lower on the company orientation scale, owing probably to the fact that layoffs, dismissals, and transfers are perceived as more costly by married employees. On the other hand, married American employees are more likely to value giving insiders an advantage in competing for job openings.

Explaining the marital status effect on work attitudes

In table 5.3, a comparison of the total (column 1) and direct (column 3) effects of marital status on work attitudes indicates that job characteristics and work values account for about a fifth (US) and a third (Japan) of the commitment gap between married and nonmarried employees. They further account for about a third of the difference in satisfaction in both countries. The pattern of indirect effects is both positive and negative: married employees generally have better jobs, which in turn contribute to more positive work attitudes. But married people are also less committed to work, and (in Japan) place greater value on pay, which tends to lower their organizational commitment and job satisfaction relative to non-married employees.

What explains the remaining variation in commitment and satisfaction between married and non-married employees? The higher organizational commitment of married employees is probably largely due to greater family obligations, which constrain opportunities to change employers. Such moves often involve geographical mobility that results in considerable disruption for members of the household, and single workers can more easily contemplate such changes. This appears to be especially true in Japan (see table 5.3). A similar interpretation may account in part for the greater satisfaction of married employees: they are more apt to be satisfied because they have fewer opportunities for alternative employment. It is also possible that married employees tend to view their jobs more positively because they are generally better adjusted and more satisfied with their non-work lives, but we do not have the data to explore this possibility.

Education

In advanced industrial societies such as the United States and Japan, education is a key indicator of social position as well as a major source of variation in status and economic rewards. Consistent with much previous research on education and work attitudes, equation 1 in table 5.3 suggests that better-educated Americans are less committed to their companies (see also Angle and Perry, 1981; Mowday *et al.*, 1982) and less satisfied with their jobs (see also Kalleberg, 1977). In Japan, employees with more schooling are also less satisfied (though this difference is not as pronounced as in the US), but education is unrelated to organizational commitment among the Japanese. We again seek to explain these differences by first examining how education is related to job attributes and work values.

Education and job characteristics

Table 4.3 testified that more educated employees in each country are better paid, though the income returns to education are larger in the US. Those with more schooling are also more likely to expect to be promoted, but schooling is more strongly tied to expectations for advancement in Japan. However, table 4.2 suggested that the relationship of education to task characteristics is remarkably similar and surprisingly weak in the two countries. The only substantial effect of increased education is a decrease in supervisor control. In the US only, there are some very slight positive associations with job complexity and teamwork, but in neither country does schooling have anything to do with supervisor contact or autonomy. Better-educated Americans also report fewer intrinsic job rewards. This parallels the broader finding of lower organizational commitment and job satisfaction among workers with more schooling, and may reflect higher work life expectations.

There are also indications in both countries that employees with more schooling are less well integrated in workplace social networks. Better-schooled employees view fewer coworkers as close friends. In the US, moreover, the better educated assign lower ratings to the quality of their relations with superiors. In Japan, they are less likely to engage in outside socializing with workmates and superiors.

Education and work values

In the US, but not in Japan, more education spells less commitment to work (see table 5.2). This may reflect greater opportunities, particularly in the US, for the better educated to find fulfillment outside the work role. It may also be due to higher expectations, leading to feelings of frustration and unfulfillment on the job (see the results concerning intrinsic rewards), hence motivation to seek gratification in nonwork pursuits.

An employee's schooling is also related to the importance he or she places on a number of specific aspects of work. In the US sample, education negatively influences valuation of pay. This suggests a greater focus on intrinsic rewards, hence the lower level of fulfillment in this regard we noted earlier. There are indications that better-schooled employees are more secure about their labor-market prospects. In Japan, they value internal promotion less and in the US are less concerned with job stability. Our earlier finding that increased schooling gives rise to weaker social bonds is reflected in the value orientations of better-educated employees: they are less likely to value working in groups (in the US) and getting along with coworkers (both countries). A likely explanation is that better-educated employees may be less likely to regard workmates as their reference group, but are cosmopolitans, who are less oriented to workplace associations. Furthermore, in both countries, the more educated reject company familism. The reason that again comes to mind is confidence in their ability to provide for themselves and find rewarding employment elsewhere. The idea of dependence on a benevolent, paternalistic employer thus threatens their autonomy and holds small appeal. The same explanation may account for what at first seems the paradoxical finding that persons with more schooling are more likely to accept the company's rights to reduce the labor force and to demand extra time from workers. The better educated are, of course, less threatened by the prospect of labor force reductions: they see themselves as more valuable and therefore less likely to be fired; and/or perceive their chances of finding another job to be good.

Explaining the education effect on work attitudes

Our results in table 5.3 indicate that once we control for the full set of job characteristics and work values, better-educated employees in each country continue to be less satisfied with their jobs. Moreover, now we find that, like Americans, more schooling gives rise to less organizational commitment among the Japanese.

There is little surprising in the finding that schooling diminishes commitment to an employing organization. With education, expectations for career achievement are likely to grow. Moreover, as the better educated have more employment alternatives, the opportunity costs of loyalty to one firm are raised. Finally, the well educated are also more likely to be members of skilled craft or professional occupations, which compete with the firm for the employee's loyalty.

Summary

Work values and background attributes constitute a set of influences on work attitudes and behaviors which are largely, though by no means exclusively, exogenous to the employment relation and the job. Their effects on commitment and satisfaction can thus be seen as an "intrusion" into the workplace of external social and cultural forces. The extent to which cultural values determine work attitudes is, of course, central to our investigation. We do find a variety of significant differences in the values held by Japanese and US manufacturing employees, though many of these are not easily interpreted within a simple theory of the Japanese as culturally predisposed to collectivism, paternalism, and diligence. A surprising finding was that more Americans than Japanese found the "firm as a family" to be an attractive idea. Consistent with past impressions of Japanese work culture, however, was our evidence that the Japanese favor close, diffuse relations with supervisors and reciprocal obligations linking the employee and the company.

Work values, not surprisingly, do contribute substantially to variation in work attitudes, though perhaps not to the degree that a strongly culturalist theory would predict. In both samples, employees who regarded work as a central life interest were more committed to the firm and satisfied with their jobs. Similarly, those valuing stable work and good relations with supervisors had work attitudes that were more favorable to the company. On the other hand, we found evidence of unfulfilled values with respect to promotion in the US and pay in Japan; i.e. the greater the value, the lower the commitment and satisfaction. The important proposition that work values condition or moderate the effects of job variables on work attitudes found next to no support in our data.

The widespread belief that work values and attitudes are changing rapidly in Japan and that younger cohorts are less work- and company-oriented was supported in our study by the consistently larger effects of age in the Japanese sample, which could not be explained in terms of age variance in job attributes and specific work values. Japan's more traditional sexual division of labor also came across clearly in our data. Though women employees in both countries are disadvantaged in terms of the complexity, control, and rewards of their job, the gender gap proved larger in Japan. Yet both Japanese and US women exhibit more organizational commitment and job satisfaction than men; a pattern which we believe can only be explained in terms of lower expectations for fulfillment at work. In both countries, length of schooling, controlling for job rewards and status, reduces organizational commitment, morale, and integration. Finally, married employees in both countries are more committed and satisfied, but only in the US are they less engaged in work-related social networks.

6 Technology, society, and organization

Introduction

This chapter marks an important transition in our inquiry.[1] To this point, we have not directly considered the organizational settings in which industrial work is embedded. We have not wholly ignored organizational effects – our employee-level models of commitment and satisfaction controlled for a variety of plant differences – but neither have we interpreted them. The influences of variables defined at the level of the organization have remained a black box, substantively unintelligible yet persistently reminding us that an entire domain of important causal forces is still to be explored.

Now we begin the process of investigating the black box of organization-level factors impinging on the workplace attitudes and behaviors of manufacturing employees. In this chapter and the next, we focus exclusively on characteristics of the employing organization. Following the causal framework laid out in chapter 1, we distinguish between two kinds of organizational variables. The first includes what the famed Aston group of organizational researchers termed the *context* of organizing (Pugh, Hickson, Hinings, and Turner, 1969). This includes attributes of firms and establishments such as employment and asset size, industry, age, operations technology, unionization, and dependence on environmental agents such as a parent company or major customers and suppliers. The second set comprises organizational structures, management practices, and employment systems which are in part determined by the "context" of the plant. Our discussion in these chapters will set the stage for our analysis in chapter 8 of how organization context and structure together mold the reactions of employees; i.e. the extent to which they engender commitment and compliance as opposed to alienation and resistance. As our conceptual model (see figure 1) as well as much sociological theory and research suggest, context phenomena such as plant size and production technology affect workers mainly indirectly, via their impact on shaping the jobs and structures of the workplace within which individuals are embedded and carry out their tasks.

Several theoretical concerns guide our forays into the domain of organization-level forces which surround manufacturing employees and to which their work attitudes and behaviors are reactions. At the most general level there is our conception of corporatist organization as a complex of commitment-maximizing organizational structures and employment practices. The corporatist imagery guides our selection of organizational factors which we believe enhance organizational commitment and job satisfaction, much as it guided our interpretation in previous chapters of the intraorganizational processes whereby job attributes, social bonds, and job rewards influenced work attitudes. As we noted in chapter 1, the term originates with Dore (1973), though our conception of welfare corporatism as an emergent organizational form is pieced together from the writings of a diverse set of theorists, all of whom were concerned with explaining the attachments of individuals to employing organizations in modern capitalist economies.[2]

Given the patchwork origins of this concept, not to mention the occasional opaqueness of some theorists' contributions, the corporatist perspective is hardly an infallible guide. Still, it remains valuable as a sensitizing framework, for it reminds us that organizational structures that shape employee social relations and activities are manifestations of a holistic strategy of workplace control.

Explaining work organization: technology vs. society

Operations technology is perhaps the most theoretically interesting of the elements of organizational context thought to have a bearing on organizational form and employee response. Indeed, as our introductory discussion in chapter 1 indicated, one of the converging intellectual streams from which we formed the corporatist mosaic is the technological imperative model of workplace organization put forward by Joan Woodward (1965), Robert Blauner (1964), and Alain Touraine (1955). The core of their thinking is that the complexity and automation of production technology ultimately determine the division of labor and authority structure of the factory which, in turn, account for the extent of workforce integration or alienation.

Moreover, these theorists see technology not merely sufficing to explain the structural variations in a local manufacturing economy at a given point in time. They also see it as the engine behind the historical evolution of workplace organization. As we noted earlier, the technology theorists, like Marxist writers such as Edwards (1979), see a U-shaped evolution of the implications of work organization for labor commitment and integration vs. alienation and resistance. Craft technologies and the simple forms of organization associated with them keep alienation low. Militancy and conflict reached their historical zenith with the large-scale, mechanized mass production factory, which made the worker an appendage to a machine. But highly automated, process technologies remove the worker from the direct production process and in so doing foster cooperation and harmony in the plant. An important difference between the Marxist and technological determinist accounts of this industrial evolution, however, is that the latter see significant commitment to an employing organization as a late development, coupled with the rise of process technology, but absent under craft forms of organization with their basis in loyalty to a trade or occupation and independence from an employer (Blauner, 1964). To Edwards, the distinctive feature of early industrial capitalism is not the prevalence of craft technologies and skills (which most observers agree were experienced by very small numbers of workers), but rather the small size of workshops which divided workers as a class while placing them under the direct and personal control of a founding entrepreneur. This pattern of organization, like the bureaucratic paternalism of welfare corporatism, breeds worker loyalty and dependence.

As chapter 1 discussed, there are strong parallels between organizational theories of technology as a critical contingency and convergence theories of economic development which stress the role of technological advance in fostering similar organizational and institutional forms in societies with very different cultural and historical traditions (Kerr *et al.*, 1960). The basic causal mechanism – the determining role of technology – is essentially the same in both cases, the difference being the level of analysis at which the inquiry is pitched. The forces fostering isomorphism within an economy among work organizations using a common technological mode are also thought to engender institutional convergence between countries as, through processes of diffusion, the same machinery and work methods are implemented across diverse regions of the world.

At the core of societal convergence theory is an assumption that the impact of technological development on social organization is everywhere the same (Gallie, 1978). This assumption likewise underpins rationalist theories of organizing that assume technology to be a critical contingency in the structuring of manufacturing concerns (Brossard and Maurice, 1976). Yet those theories evolved from Western traditions of rational design and from research on organizational populations in mostly Anglo–American settings. In contrast, much writing on Japanese industrial organization and relations suggest that the "institutional" environment – a society's distinctive set of highly established and culturally sanctioned action patterns and expectations – may exert a particularly strong hold on that country's organizational forms (Carroll and Huo, 1986; Meyer and Rowan, 1977). Our reasoning here, like that of numerous writers impressed with the distinctiveness of Japanese culture and history, stresses the country's past isolation, continuing homogeneity, and geographic concentration. Moreover, many of Japan's modern institutions bear the stamp of World War II and its aftermath: Japanese enterprise unionism, employment practices such as the *nenko* seniority wage system, and permanent employment for blue-collar workers all stem from a historically unique mixture of reforms imposed by the US occupation, traditional practices, and *ad hoc* solutions to pressing economic problems (Cole, 1979; Ono, 1980).

Clearly, a strong case can be made that the adaptations of Japanese companies to technological and market environments at home and abroad have been heavily conditioned by an unusually strong set of institutional forces. Such pressures are arguably weaker or at least less uniform in the US, where extreme cultural heterogeneity, political decentralization, and geographic dispersion fragment the institutional environment to which US organizations are constrained to adapt. Considerations such as these have long fueled arguments for Japanese uniqueness. While not *a priori* favoring that point of view, we are compelled by the proposition that cultural/institutional forces may shape the structuring of Japanese organizations to a degree not common in the US. If this is so, it could mean a correspondingly smaller role for technology and other task-related contingency variables.

Indeed, perhaps *the* central question in the comparative, cross-national study of organizational structures is whether societal differences are confined to levels of structural properties or whether they extend to the *causal processes* linking task environments to organizational forms (Przeworski and Teune, 1970). It is one thing to observe, as had Crozier (1964), that French organization is characterized by greater than average centralization and formalization, and quite another to assert, as did Gallie (1978), that highly automated, process technology leads to very different organization structures and industrial relations systems in Britain and France. To David Hickson and his colleagues (1979:29), cross-national variations in structure *per se* are "interesting." They facilitate an understanding of how cultural and historical tendencies complement task environments in explaining the variety of structural adaptations pursued by organizations around the world. But should the task contingencies that mold organizational forms in one country or world region be dramatically different from those operating in the next, the implications would be "terrifying." Their concern, clearly, is that strong evidence of society-specific effects of factors such as scale, technology, and market dependence would severely undermine the body of theory that sees rational adaptation to task environments as the universal imperative behind organizational survival and success. One would then be faced with the daunting prospect of building separate theories to explain the structuring of organizations in France, Britain, Japan, and other countries of the world.

Technology and organization structure

Technology is the complex of machinery and workflow processes which transforms raw materials, or assembles fabricated pieces, into finished goods. Since the nature of the product in large measure dictates the type of technology used to produce it, major variations in production technology correspond to differences among industries, which are groups of firms or plants producing similar goods and services.

Many analysts view the degree of *standardization* of the product as the key dimension along which technologies vary (see, e.g. Piore and Sabel, 1984). Products in which each unit is unique and made on order to a customer's specifications are the least standardized, whereas "dimensional" products, to use Woodward's term, have no unit character but are totally homogeneous substances such as liquids, powders, or sheets (Averitt, 1968). Although the quantity sold of the latter may vary with a customer's order, its qualitative nature is always the same. "Job-shop" is the trade name for companies producing nonstandard products to order. Each order requires a distinct set of operations, work tasks, raw materials, parts, testing procedures, and production scheduling. At the opposite extreme, the production of a homogeneous good involves such uniform operations that it can often be highly automated. Chemical refining food processing, and the manufacture of building materials such as masonite or container materials (e.g. cardboard) allow for long runs of repetitive operations in which the material worked on moves in a continuous flow or sheet form.

Joan Woodward's "Industrial organization"

Between the extremes of job-shop and continuous-process production are technologies associated with intermediate degrees of product standardization and customer-order specificity. In her classic study of English manufacturing firms, Woodward (1965) identified broad technological types on a continuum of production complexity. This continuum, she notes, is one of chronological development, since process production relies upon more recent, highly automated techniques, and unit production is as old as the history of manufacture. Woodward made further subdivisions within each broad class to allow for variations in product size. She thus derived composite types such as standardized fabrication with custom assembly or continuous processing combined with mass production-type packaging.

Woodward's interest lay chiefly with how organizational forms varied among the East Essex firms in her sample. Her data showed that a number of structural characteristics changed linearly with technological complexity: the number of hierarchical levels; the chief executive's span of control; and the ratio of administrative to production workers. However, middle-management spans of control grew smaller with technological advance. This, combined with the tendency for hierarchical depth to increase as well, meant that unit production plants had short broad hierarchies, continuous process plants had tall narrow ones, with large batch and mass production falling in between. Also increasing monotonically with position on the technology scale was the number of staff specialists in such areas as personnel and human relations and the amount spent on employee welfare and service programs. Labor costs as a percentage of total costs, on the other hand, declined with technological complexity. Finally, the ratio of managers and supervisors to nonsupervisory employees also rose as a direct function of technological advance.

Particularly interesting were Woodward's findings that the extreme types – unit/small batch production and continuous-process – had more in common organizationally than either had with the middle type: large batch/ mass production. Spans of control of first-line supervisors were smaller at the ends of the continuum than in the middle. Though she had no direct evidence, Woodward took this to be indicative of the organization of work into small teams in unit/small batch and continuous-process industry. Moreover, the ratio of skilled to semi-skilled workers was lower in the large batch/mass production group. Woodward argues (p. 62) that the techniques of standardized production used in these industries: "had taken the perceptual and conceptual elements of skill out of the main production task, although much of the work still required a fair degree of motor skill and manual dexterity." Touching upon a theme which later became the core of Harry Braverman's *Labor and Monopoly Capital* (1974), she argued that planning, execution, and control are divorced in large batch/mass production technology, so that patterns of work do not permit workers to conceptualize and complete tasks that bear a logical relationship to production goals. The skilled workers in this system are not direct production workers but rather indirect labor performing maintenance and engineering functions. In unit production, on the other hand, the production work revolves around the efforts of the skilled production workers, with semi-skilled and unskilled workers assisting and carrying out peripheral and mechanical tasks. Process technology resembles mass production in that skilled workers are indirect labor in maintenance and engineering departments. The key difference has to do with the greater importance of the maintenance function in continuous process industry, where most of the actual production work is automated, and servicing and controlling the equipment are the chief responsibilities of workers.

Another important difference in the organization of the large batch/mass production plants as contrasted with both the unit/small batch and process plants was the predominance of mechanistic management systems among the former, and the prevalence of organic forms among the latter (see Burns and Stalker, 1961). That is, large batch and mass production plants had more rigid and centralized organization with more formalized definition of duties and responsibilities. The process and unit plants were less highly structured (for example, were less likely to have organization charts), delegated more authority, encouraged wider participation in decision-making, and had a higher rate of lateral communications.

Woodward's general theory of the technology/organization link may be summarized as follows. The unstandardized production in unit and small batch firms and the uncertainty associated with dependence upon customers' orders means that little formal structure can be imposed on work activities and relations. Functions cannot be segregated, machines must be general purpose, workers must be skilled and able to conceptualize and execute all facets of a job from start to finish, communications must be open, and the responsibility for decisions must lie with the people doing the work. In contrast, standardized production means that conception can be separated from execution. This implies that the workforce will be differentiated into unskilled and semi-skilled direct labor jobs and a large corps of managers, supervisors, clerical workers, staff specialists, and indirect production workers. Moreover, jobs can be designed, classified, and routinized by industrial engineering departments and fitted to the machinery and the workflow in a fashion consistent with an overall plan. Greater automation and the use of specialized machinery mean reduced flexibility in the tasks performed by workers.

In both unit/small batch production and large batch/mass production, Woodward sees technology as determining the structure of the work organization. In process production, however, she suggests that the actual production and coordination functions are wholly vested in the machinery, so that the organization forms that arise reflect the needs and interests of the human workforce and not the imperatives of technology. Moreover, the relatively low labor costs in process industry mean that higher wages, more benefits, and more welfare programs and services can be provided without markedly increasing the company's total costs.

Robert Blauner's "alienation and freedom"

Blauner's (1964) specific propositions linking modes of technology to organizational and job structures, and thereby to work attitudes and behaviors, are somewhat harder to sort out. Despite his claim that technology is "...the most important single factor that gives an industry a distinctive character," (p. 6) his focus on comparisons among industries makes it difficult to distinguish the effects of technology *per se* from other organizational and environmental characteristics of the industry. Indeed, his own interpretations of the varying levels of worker alienation among the printing, textile, auto assembly, and chemical industries often stress nontechnological factors; for example, the community setting of textiles, the labor relations history of autos, and so on. Moreover, while much of his argument assumes that organization plays an intervening role, Blauner is less precise than Woodward in demonstrating how technology shapes organization which in turn modifies the tasks, styles of supervision, and pattern of coworker relations experienced by individual employees.

It is mainly with respect to mass production and continuous process technologies that the arguments of Blauner and Woodward converge. Both argued that the effects of mass production and continuous process technology on workers' alienation or integration are largely mediated by the organizational structure of the plant. Much as Woodward contended, Blauner perceived mass production assembly-line work as giving rise to an extreme form of mechanistic bureaucracy, whose characteristics are: large plants; a detailed division of labor; centralized structure of authority; impersonal relations based on specialized work roles; standardization of procedures; and extensive formal rules and regulations. In addition, spans of control are wide – reflecting the substitution of machine pacing and control for the personal domination of the supervisor – and relatively few departmental and hierarchical boundaries divide the workforce. According to Blauner, this lack of internal work-group differentiation in a large plant creates a sense of anonymity and depersonalization. Moreover, the relatively low degree of hierarchical differentiation keeps promotion opportunities low. Workers are thus juxtaposed to management as an undifferentiated, monolithic class. These organizational arrangements, combined with the repetitive, fractionated nature of the work itself, Blauner believed, make auto workers the most alienated members of the blue-collar labor force.

But just as Woodward felt the transition to continuous process industry was leading to the evolution of a work organization which met the needs of workers and fostered integration in the firm, Blauner likewise saw the organization of chemical plants as restoring much of the meaning and value or work to blue-collar employees (see also Averitt, 1968). Smaller in scale, chemical plants are nonetheless more differentiated along departmental and occupational lines, and there is little task fragmentation since work roles involve considerable responsibility and variety. Production under this form of technology is conducted in small workteams. Moreover, a tall hierarchy of status and authority creates career movement and breaks down the labor–management class barrier.

Blauner departs from Woodward in arguing that supervisory spans of control are wide in the chemical industry because workers are not closely supervised. This probably has more to do with the style of interaction between supervisors and subordinates than the ratio of supervisors to subordinates, however, which is likely to be high in an organization with a tall management hierarchy. This is borne out by his later observation that frequent, personal consultations between workers and management are commonplace in the continuous process firm.

Subsequent research on Woodward's and Blauner's hypotheses

Despite rather different research designs and conceptual frameworks, then, Woodward and Blauner presented strikingly similar views of the impact of technological advance on manufacturing organization and the reactions of workers. Both studies substantially influenced the thinking of subsequent scholars about organizational structure and workplace relations. In particular, Woodward's work spawned a long series of empirical studies and spin-off theories in organizational sociology (see, e.g. Child, 1972; Khandwalla, 1974; Pugh, Hickson, Hinings, and Turner, 1969). For a time, technology was the long-sought answer to the question, "why do organizational structures vary?" Indeed, Woodward herself wrote as though a breakthrough on this order had been achieved.

Yet much of the subsequent empirical research on technology and organization has proved disappointing. The statistical associations between measures of technology and structural variables were often weak or varied from study to study. Still, few such investigations arguably constitute genuine replications. Many defined technology in ways that had little to do with Woodward's concept (for example, as task routinization in service organizations). Most made use of purely *linear* models of technology effects, ignoring the nonlinear relations, which were her central and most interesting findings. Still others downplayed the importance of technology effects upon discovering that they were weaker than those of organizational size, although other analysts have shown that organizational variables are often definitionally confounded with size (Mayhew, Levinger, McPherson, and James, 1972).

A few studies (e.g. Blau *et al.*, 1976; Zwerman, 1970) attempted to match Woodward's sample and measurement closely, and these were able to replicate her findings to a substantial degree. These replications concentrated on Woodward's hypotheses regarding technology and formal structure, ignoring her further arguments concerning their effects on modes of employee adjustment, morale, and integration. Similarly, Blauner's work, which dealt more directly and emphatically with the question of worker reactions, has spawned but a few attempts to systematically research his ideas (see Fullan, 1970; Hull, Friedman and Rogers, 1982; Shepard, 1971). This is particularly unfortunate, for Blauner's own study was an impressionistic one, based on evidence gleaned from a few case studies and early workforce surveys. Of course, many of Blauner's specific propositions regarding the effects of task and job properties on work attitudes and behavior have been researched extensively by others. But his claims regarding the organization-level influences of technology and structure have remained largely untested.

Other models of production technology: dual economy

The separation of production modes into unit/small batch, large batch/ mass production, and continuous process has in recent years figured importantly in certain theoretical perspectives on economic organization which, while initially aligned with the Woodward-Blauner framework, go well beyond it in interesting ways. Robert Averitt (1968), in his pioneering work on *The Dual Economy*, argues that the distinctions among these production types correspond to the division between "core" firms and their dependent satellites in the "periphery" sector. Averitt sees unit/small batch producers operating small firms and establishments with higher skilled craft-styled labor and flexible, decentralized management systems. Large batch/mass tech-

nology is associated with high-volume production based on highly structured, repetitive routines. Process production, finally, involves an increase in
average skill level, greater responsibility and participation of labor in management, and, consequently, heightened workforce morale. These observations
are consistent with previous theory. But Averitt draws a critical distinction
between unit/small batch production, which typifies manufacturing firms in
the periphery of the dual economy, and large batch/mass and process
production, which is prevalent in the core. Unit/small batch firms are small in
size, large in number, intensely competitive, and unable to exercise control
over pricing and demand. Large batch/mass production and continuous
process firms are large (in assets if not employment), oligopolistic in behavior,
and capable (through heavy investments in marketing) of fixing prices and
manipulating demand. Moreover, core firms and industries, as many writers
on these topics have argued, are associated with management systems and
employment structures which differ markedly from those found in the
periphery (see Hodson and Kaufman, 1982). In a word, corporatist organization is a core sector phenomenon, for only these firms have the resources,
stability, and scale which are prerequisite to the development of internal labor
markets, elaborate bureaucracy, and abundant welfare services (Edwards,
1979; Jacoby, 1985). A careful statistical investigation of the dimensions of
dualism in the American economy by Baron and Bielby (1984) finds strong
empirical support for Averitt's characterization of unit/small batch production as an indicator of peripheral status.

What is intriguing about Averitt's association of unit/small batch production with the economic periphery and large batch/mass and process production with the core is that, like our model of corporatist organization as a
commitment-maximizing form, it generates predictions as to employee reactions which are sharply different from those advanced by technology theorists
in the Blauner-Woodward-Touraine tradition. If corporatist forms diminish
alienation and engender workforce commitment and high morale we should
expect to find commitment low in unit/small batch industries and high in
more automated production modes.

Societal contrasts in the technology-organization relation

Part of the reason for the widespread interest in the Blauner and
Woodward studies was the idea of historical evolution, driven by technology,
in working-class attitudes and values, in the degree of conflict and cooperation in the workplace, and in the nature and quality of blue-collar work.
Because the technological modes of craft or unit, mass, and continuous
process production correspond to stages in the historical advancement of
technology from less to more complex and from a minor to a major role in the
production process, technologically-linked differences in organization and
workers' attitudes and behaviors suggested potentially sweeping changes in

the labor process and the nature of capitalist class relations. Would the class struggle, which had intensified with the transition from craft to mass production, diminish again as automation took over the production process completely, freeing workers from the oppressive routines and authority relations of mechanized mass production? Theorists such as Bell (1973), Mallet (1975), and Touraine (1955) have explored in depth the society-wide ramifications of the historical trend of technological advance and the substitution of machine for human labor (Sabel, 1982).

The answer to this question is bound up with the relative importance of technological, scale, and market forces as determinants of work organization and industrial relations as contrasted with a host of society-specific historical, cultural, and institutional forces. If attitudes and values toward work and authority/class relations in the workplace are strongly influenced by broad cultural and social structural forces, then changes in technology are not likely to bring about major realignments in the class structure, even though they may produce shifts in the specific occupational composition of the working class.

The implicit universalism of technological imperative theories has in recent years come under sharp attack. Such astute students of comparative organization as Child (1981), Gallie (1978), and Maurice (Brossard and Maurice, 1976; Maurice, Sorge, and Warner, 1980) dispute the claim that similarities across societies in production technology inexorably give rise to the same patterns of organization and industrial relations. Societal, cultural, and institutional factors, in their view, play a greater role than technology and may even condition the impact of technology on organizational structuring. These critiques are buttressed by the findings of empirical cross-national research. Gallie's (1978) rich qualitative investigation of British and French oil refineries produced pervasive evidence of societal contrasts in organizational arrangements and industrial relations despite common use of a production technology which Blauner and Woodward believed would engender participative organization and workforce integration. As other students of French organization had documented, (Crozier, 1964; Suleiman, 1974), Gallie found factory governance in France to be characterized by greater centralization of authority and formalization in law and company regulations than in Britain. Moreover, the amount of real power wielded by French workers was low. British management attempted to obtain the consent of workers to workplace practices, while the French management retained a high degree of discretionary and arbitrary power. These contrasts in structure were further reflected in the attitudes of workers to the firm and in their images of management. Gallie reports that the British workers' complaints to management centered on problems of technical efficiency; such specialized concerns underscored the fundamental consensus they shared with management on factory goals and objectives. In contrast, the French workers' alienation concerned their relations with management whom they saw as distant, exploitative, and capricious.

A quantitative study by Maurice, Sorge, and Warner (1980) likewise examined the contributions of production technology and society to variation in the organizing styles of French, German, and British plants. While they found the technology effects predicted by Woodward, they also observed a far higher percentage of managerial and supervisory staff in France and a more formal, "mechanistic" structure than in the other two countries.

Other researchers have replicated the British Aston studies in a variety of national settings and produced additional evidence of societal effects: US and Canadian organizations appear to be more formalized than British concerns (McMillan, Hickson, Hinings, and Schneck, 1973). In keeping with the usual cultural images, decision-making is less centralized in British than in German firms (Child and Kieser, 1979). Additional investigations, such as Tannenbaum *et al.*'s (1974) four-nation comparison and Hofstede's (1980) mammoth 40-country survey of employees of a single multi-national firm, focus on the implications of organizational hierarchies for perceptions of influence and power in firms. Numerous additional studies examine cross-cultural variations in motivation and managerial values and beliefs (Granick, 1972; Haire *et al.*, 1966). This work adds significantly to the evidence of societal diversity in work organization and in the attitudes and behaviors of workers.

Yet a cautionary note is required. Much such research is based on case studies, haphazardly selected samples, and impressionistic observation which, though yielding often rich and stimulating accounts, give little assurance that societal differences are independent of variations in the task environment dimensions of organization size, technology, market constraint, and the like. Even the quantitative studies which apply standard instruments to the collection of data on organizations that are sampled in like fashion in national settings can be faulted for failing to control for many potentially confounding causes (see, e.g. Lammers and Hickson, 1979). Inferring societal influences is made extremely tricky by the fact that residual differences between countries in work structures and behaviors can be attributed to a grab-bag of unexamined forces, many of which have little to do with a well-reasoned conception of societal effects.

Organizational structures in Japanese and US manufacturing

Our interest in societal differences in work organization and employee reaction is, of course, centered on the case of the United States and Japan. We have noted that Japan, today the second largest economy in the world, has long confounded the convergence doctrine that societies lose their distinctive cultural and institutional features as they become more technologically and industrially advanced. We now focus on specific elements of organizational structure and employment practice which past theory and research lead us to anticipate will differ significantly between the US and Japan. This discussion sets the stage for our empirical inquiry in the next chapter into the relative roles of production technology and country in shaping the internal organization of factories.

Due in no small measure to the competitive threat posed by Japanese firms in an ever-expanding number of markets, there has been a fascination for some years in the US with the topic of Japanese management and organization. However, few of the writings addressed to these issues provide useful guidelines or testable hypotheses for systematic research. Many such accounts are quite impressionistic, positing an often mystical "Japanese management style" which is chiefly distinguished by the sensitivity and concern with which Japanese managers treat their employees. These elements of workplace climate and leadership style may be quite real and indeed may have something to do with the motivation of Japanese employees and the competitive successes of Japanese firms. But they are extremely difficult to measure, and their effects on employee attitudes and behavior are even harder to assess. We concentrate on relatively concrete aspects of organization structure and staffing for which there are strong reasons to anticipate US/Japan differences and which lend themselves to more or less precise measurement.

Division of labor

A long-standing theme in treatments of Japanese work organization is that individuals' work roles lack the specificity and definition typical of Western organizations (Abegglen, 1958; Cole, 1979). Employees are expected to be generalists and to perform a range of job functions over the course of their employment relationship with the firm (Itami, 1985:69). In Western – especially American – organizations, job titles proliferate and individuals generally pursue careers within occupational specialties (Ouchi, 1981). One oft-noted reason for the proliferation of job titles in the US is American labor unions' efforts to preserve control over task assignments and labor supply by insisting on detailed job classifications and work rules (Cole, 1979; Piore and Sabel, 1984). More generally, a case could be made that occupational consciousness and organization play an unusually central role in American culture and social structure, owing to a variety of institutional processes, such as the strength of the professions, the vocational emphasis of American education, and relatively weak attachments to employing organizations and local communities (Cole and Tominaga, 1976). Japanese organizations, as we have argued, tend not to use detailed job and occupational classifications, and in both blue- and white-collar strata, promote job rotation and generalist careers. A common characterization is that Americans pursue careers within occupations that cut across firms, while the opposite pattern holds in Japan.

If the individual incumbents of occupational positions are not the primary functional units in Japanese organizations, what are? The obvious answer is the work group. The cohesion, loyalty, and cooperation associated with work groups in Japanese companies are often cited in qualitative studies (Cole, 1971; Dore, 1983; Pucik and Hatvany, 1983; Osako, 1977; Rohlen, 1974), and our own quantitative results reported in previous chapters point to the importance of the work group in Japan. Although group leaders may make symbolic gestures at accepting responsibility for failures (Clark, 1979), real responsibility is diffused among and borne by the members of the group (Nakane, 1970). It is this collective sharing of responsibility and account-ability that motivates and complements the absence of functional and authority role assignments to individuals and their positions. Several ob-servers (Abegglen, 1958:79; Yoshino, 1968:206) argue that, in accord with this system of allocating responsibilities to collective units, organizational subunits proliferate in Japanese companies. The proliferation of highly cohesive subunits does invite the risk of rivalry among them and disinte-gration for the organization as a whole. In particular, these tendencies have been associated with the informal cliques (*habatsu*) which arise from common cohort membership and school ties (Yoshino, 1968:208). Moreover, it is commonly observed that organization charts in Japan rarely specify indivi-dual employees' positions and roles; they are rather networks of collective units such as departments, sections, and work teams (Clark, 1979; Yoshino, 1968). These groups are the elementary functional units of the Japanese organization – not individuals' positions in the classical Weberian sense – and they proliferate at all levels. As Yoshino (1968:206) puts it: "Another noteworthy feature of the organizational structure of the major Japanese corporation is the fact that it is elaborately and minutely divided into separate and quite distinct organizational units." We thus hypothesize that:

1. Functional specialization of employees' work roles is lower in Japanese than in US organizations (Azumi and McMillan, 1981).
2. Differentiation of collective subunits (departments and sections) is higher in Japanese than in US organizations.

Hierarchy

The forms taken by authority and status hierarchies in Japanese firms and bureaus, the social relations between superiors and subordinates, and the distribution and dynamics of decision-making represent a bundle of organiza-tional structures and processes which have struck numerous observers as highly distinctive and likely instrumental in producing the cohesion and commitment of the Japanese workforce. Some observers of Japanese corporate organization hold that, in contrast with the bloated middle-management ranks of US firms, Japanese companies have lean structures and flatter administrative pyramids (Peters and Waterman, 1982; Pucik, 1984). To the degree such differences exist, they may reflect the smaller size and greater specialization of Japanese corporations (Caves and Uekusa, 1976; Clark, 1979), and their lower reliance on high-level staff departments such as planning and finance.

At the plant or establishment level, on the other hand, a number of studies find just the opposite: Japanese hierarchies are on the average taller than the management pyramids of Western organizations (Azumi and McMillan, 1975). Tall hierarchies are a form of organization which is consonant with the structure of internal labor markets: long job ladders that provide opportunities for upward mobility and careers within the organization. Developing an argument earlier made by Blauner (1964) and later by Edwards (1979), Dore (1973:257) contends that the tall and finely graded hierarchies of Japanese organizations work to avert the class consciousness and alienation typical of British plants with their short, squat authority pyramids. Instead of monolithic classes facing off across a chasm of privilege and reward inequities, Japanese employees are linked to one another in long chains of super-subordinate relations. In such a structure, status equals are scarce and the bulk of interpersonal transactions involve a status difference. Nakane (1970) has broadened this view into a general theory of the Japanese collectivity-orientation. For her, the vertical structure of Japanese society is the mechanism that motivates the strong bonds enmeshing individuals in groups.

Like the pattern of dividing tasks among groups rather than individuals, the tall, finely graded status hierarchies of Japanese firms are viewed, on the one hand, as a structural reflection of the permanent employment and *nenko* promotion systems, and, on the other, an expression of deep-seated, cultural values (Hatvany and Pucik, 1981). An elaborate set of ranks means opportunities for regular advancement over a lifetime career with the same firm (Cole, 1979; Clark, 1979). The "cultural values" argument posits a Japanese propensity to assume a superior or subordinate role in almost any social encounter. Nakane's (1970) treatment portrays vertical differentiation and relations as the foundation for the Japanese collectivity-orientation, which contrasts, in her view, with a typical Western orientation to occupational and other individual positions in a horizontal division of labor.

3. Japanese organizations have more vertical authority/status levels than US organizations.

Another feature of Japanese authority/status hierarchies, as described by Clark (1979), is their high degree of institutionalization in a set of standard ranks. The hierarchical structure and the labels given to different levels show remarkable similarity across Japanese organizations of many different types. The titles (*hancho, bucho, kakaricho,* etc.) have considerable status significance not only in the company but in the wider society and are used in everyday discourse outside the workplace (Clark, 1979:106). Like civil service and military ranks, they designate status more than function, such that positions denoting leadership of a unit may in fact entail little real responsibility (Dore, 1973; Hatvany and Pucik, 1981). To Clark (1979:107), the standard ranks have a unifying influence on the Japanese company, for all employees occupy them – hence climb the same ladder – and they provide a common frame of reference across functionally disparate departments. Thus, the institutionalized quality of Japanese rank systems, along with their finely-graded structure, may be expressions of Nakane's vertical principle motivating groupism in Japanese firms.

Spans of control

Tall hierarchies imply narrow spans of control, and a number of accounts put Japanese spans at smaller numbers of subordinates than typically prevails in Western companies (Dore, 1973; Pascale, 1978b; Yoshino, 1968). Small spans low in the management hierarchy are also thought to be consistent with the work-group organization of the Japanese workplace and the highly distinctive leadership styles of Japanese supervisors. Spans of control are broader at higher levels in the hierarchy, reflecting the tendency for higher-level Japanese managers to have a number of non-line assistants reporting to them (Pucik, 1984:89). Whether structural spans do in fact differ between Japanese and US organizations, there are abundant indications from our research and others' that relations between supervisors and subordinates in Japan have a different quality from that commonly found in, say, the American or British workplace. Observation studies document the strong bonds, on and off the job, between Japanese employees and their supervisors (Cole, 1971; Dore, 1973; Rohlen, 1974). Labor force surveys, including our own (see chapter 4), also provide considerable evidence of paternalistic attitudes and preferences held by Japanese workers toward their superiors (Lincoln, Hanada, Olson, 1981; Marsh and Mannari, 1976; Whitehill and Takezawa, 1968).

One expects that any organization with a large number of vertical levels will have a higher proportion of managers and smaller average spans of control (Child, 1984). The belief that Japanese companies have a higher percentage of employment above the rank of direct worker also follows from the *nenko* system which guarantees promotions in exchange for steady service and organizational loyalty. Several observers report that small spans are indeed characteristic of Japanese companies (Cole, 1971:106; Dore 1973:262; Pascale 1978b:161; Yoshino 1968:206). Apart from the general expectation that Japanese authority pyramids are tall and narrow, small spans in Japanese work settings reflect the high subdivision of work into discrete and specialized collective units, the role of supervisors as coworking team leaders, and the close, personal relations that develop between supervisors and their subordinates (Hatvany and Pucik, 1981; Woronoff, 1981; Yoshino, 1968).

4. Spans of control are smaller in Japanese than in US organizations.
5. The percentage of managers is higher in Japanese than in US organizations.

Decision-making

As much as any aspect of organization, Japanese decision-making styles have captured the interest of Westerners and figure prominently in the array of Japanese methods which popular business writers have energetically marketed to Western companies. Japanese decision-making is commonly cast as participatory and consensual, with the initiative coming from lower levels ("bottom-up") and the responsibility for outcomes lying with groups instead of individuals (Sasaki, 1981: chapter 4; Vogel, 1975; Yoshino, 1968). In these respects, it reflects the broader Japanese patterns of assigning role responsibilities to groups and relying on strong vertical bonds to motivate desired actions on the part of subordinates (Clark, 1979; Hatvany and Pucik, 1981). Once again, the fostering of commitment appears to be the underlying rationale.

Participatory, consensus-oriented decision-making operates at both management and direct worker levels in Japanese organizations. For management-level decisions, the specific practices which have drawn the closest scrutiny are *ringi-seido* and its attendant process of *nemawashi* (Uchida, 1985; Vogel, 1975). The *ringi* system concerns the making of decisions through a process initiated by a lower- or middle-echelon manager who drafts a petition (*ringi-sho*), and sees that it wends its way up the hierarchy, acquiring in the process the "chops" of other relevant officials. By requiring that all proposals go to the top, the chief executive bears symbolic responsibility for every decision, and the organization averts a formal delegation of authority to lower management positions (Allston, 1986; Clark, 1979). Several scholars (Dore, 1973; Vogel, 1975; Yoshino, 1968) see Japanese authority structures combining high concentration of formal authority with decentralization of *de facto* participation. However, as Uchida (1985) points out in a thoughtful study of decision-making in the *sogo shosha* (Japanese trading companies), the circulation of a *ringi-sho* is just the formal manifestation of a process of consensus-building through informal networking termed *nemawashi* ("root-binding"). By the time the *ringi-sho* is drafted, the proposal has been communicated to all affected parties, and their general acquiescence is assured (Hatvany and Pucik, 1981).

Although popular writings on Japanese management characterize decision-making as a "bottom-up" process whereby subordinates take the initiative in decision-making and higher-ups merely extend their passive approval, scholars disagree on just how decentralized Japanese organizations really are (Pascale, 1978a). Yoshino (1968:258) argues that Japanese decision-making is indeed a "bottom-up" system:

> top management can only act on matters submitted by lower levels of management – it cannot itself initiate new ideas ... Thus, under the strict *ringi* system, the role of the president is, in effect, that of legitimizing decisions made by group consensus by affixing his seal of approval. Under this system, top management is not expected to exert strong leaderhip.

But other writers dispute the view that high-level management tends not to take an active, forceful role in organizational decision-making. Vogel (1975:xvii) suggests that organizational leaders often make decisions and entrust loyal subordinates with the task of drafting and circulating proposals consistent with them, a practice termed *ato-ringi*. Craig (1975:24) likewise argues that for most *significant* decisions, the purpose of *ringi* is to circulate information about decisions that are already made (see also Pascale, 1978b:154). Clark (1979:132) in general agrees that top Japanese executives frequently use *ringi* to forge a consensus around actions they wish to see taken, but at middle-management levels, he suggests, truly participatory decision-making exists. This derives from the low level of real authority delegated to the middle manager, in contrast with his US counterpart who likely wields broad power over the operations under him. The Japanese middle manager has little recourse but to negotiate extensively with others in order to fulfill the requirements of his job.

In general, there is wide agreement that Japanese decision-making is group and consensus oriented and involves low delegation of formal authority to positions held by individuals. In Yoshino's (1968:256) view, it is a system that involves: "...*de facto* decentralization of task performance to the lower levels without decentralization of *formal authority* in decision-making [his emphases]" (see also Clark, 1979:131 and Dore, 1973:227). Recognizing that several writers see the participatory, decentralized side of Japanese decision-making as more appearance than substance, we hypothesize that:

6. Centralization of formal authority is greater in Japanese than US organizations (there is less delegation).
7. Centralization of *de facto* decision-making is lower in Japanese than US organizations.
8. In Japanese organizations, the practice of *ringi* is associated with centralization of formal authority but decentralization of *de facto* decision-making participation.

Assigning decision-making authority to groups and relying upon processes of group consultation to arrive at a consensus are practices that are not limited to management levels: the much-touted quality circles and other small group programs in Japanese industry illustrate these same tendencies at the direct production level. As with *ringi*, some writers view quality circles less as structures for eliciting participation in decisions than as methods of diffusing responsibility and building consensus (Cole, 1980; Thomas and Shimada, 1983). We have already demonstrated that QC activity is more widespread in Japanese than US manufacturing plants (chapter 4). Our hypothesis is:

9.   QC activity contributes to decentralization of decision-making in Japanese and US organizations alike.

Formalization

The image of the Japanese organization as an enterprise community comprising personalized and diffuse work roles and relations permeated by a strong culture might suggest a low degree of formal structuring as contrasted with the rationalized and bureaucratized character of Western organizations. Yet Japanese firms and bureaus are highly structured, complex, and differentiated systems despite their celebrated elements of communal or familial integration. From his richly detailed case study of British and Japanese electronics firms, Dore (1973:243) concludes that Japanese companies are also more formalized in the sense that procedures are heavily codified in written form, files and record-keeping abound, and written communications proliferate (Craig, 1975; Rohlen, 1974; Yoshino, 1968; but see Pascale, 1978a). It may be, however, that Japanese firms are not so high on this dimension as British firms are low: research by Maurice, Sorge, and Warner (1980) and McMillan *et al.* (1973) found low levels of formalization in British as compared to North American and French plants.

10.   Formalization is higher in Japanese than in US organizations.

Welfare programs and services

A central feature of welfare corporatist organization is the abundant set of welfare programs and other employee services and activities which companies of this genre provide. Moreover, a comparative study of the labor control strategies of Japanese and US firms can hardly fail to consider variations in the pervasiveness of corporate paternalism and its role in eliciting integration, commitment, and motivation of workers. Along with permanent employment, consensus decision-making, and the *nenko* reward system, the profusion of employee benefits, services, and organized activities observed in Japanese firms has astonished Western observers. Company-supplied housing, health care clinics, job training programs; classes for women in flower arranging, cooking, and dance, as well as sex education, and birth control instruction; religious ceremonies at company shrines, and company schools for children and young workers were among the services supplied by the Japanese companies Abegglen (1958) studied. In the electronics firm more recently researched by Marsh and Mannari (1976), the company also sponsored an impressive array of employee activities: clubs in flower arrangement, home economics, art, photography, nature study, tea ceremony, English conversation, chorus, light music, and chess; not to mention athletic programs in tennis, karate, mountain climbing, basketball, cycling, softball, ping-pong, baseball, volleyball, judo, weight lifting, archery, and track. In addition, the company held numerous parties, festivals, outings, and contests. Most employees in Marsh and Mannari's sample, moreover, reported that they usually participated in these company activities. Other welfare services offered by Japanese firms are described by Cole (1979): cafeteria and lunch subsidies, company discount stores, job training and retraining of employees, and savings plans. Rohlen (1974) provides a fascinating account of ceremonies in Japanese firms on such occasions as the recognition of new employees. The ceremony began with a company song, followed by a speech in which the company president promised the parents of the new employees that he will assume *in loco parentis* responsibility for their care, education, and moral upbringing.

Some observers have contended that such services play a role in the labor cost advantages enjoyed by Japanese over US firms in that they foster a perception of overall compensation comparable to that enjoyed by US workers but (because of scale and other economies associated with such "in-kind" transfers) cost the company less than their equivalent in wages. Obviously, corporate welfarism is not now nor has it been historically a stranger to the US economic landscape, and, indeed, its prevalence among large and progressive "core" sector Western firms figures importantly in theories that view welfare corporatist organization as more than a uniquely Japanese phenomenon (Brody, 1980; Edwards, 1979). American firms typically make available significant health and retirement plans to their employees. They encourage education and job training with tuition-rebate programs, and sponsor in-house courses conducted by internal human resource staff as well as outside instructors (Jacoby, 1985). Companies manufacturing or distributing finished consumer goods frequently permit employees to purchase items at a discount. Company-sponsored clubs, parties, and athletic events are commonplace. Many firms have newspapers which report on the family and social lives of workers as well as workplace happenings of general interest.

Even so, few would likely take issue with the observation that company paternalism plays a more conspicuous role in the Japanese than American workplace. As with the numerous other distinctive facets of Japanese work organization, some observers have succumbed to a simplistic culturalism; i.e. that Japanese company welfarism stems from a deep-seated cultural preference for an inclusive, familial, and protective enterprise attachment. Our analysis in chapter 5, however, lent little support to the notion that enterprise familism is deeply valued by the Japanese workforce while rejected by individualistic US workers who favor a highly circumscribed employment contract with the firm. Moreover, economic history shows that managers in both countries experimented with welfarism as a means of taming an undisciplined and increasingly militant workforce (Brody, 1980). These experiments, moreover, were launched in the same period: the early 1900s (Cole, 1979:18–21). That they then failed and, at least for a time, were abandoned by American firms while retained in Japan may well say something about the relative receptivity of the two societies to the principle of a corporate community and paternalistic employer. But the fact remains that in both settings, welfarism was conceived as a tool consciously applied by management to the problem of labor control.

Japanese organization and welfare corporatism

There is, then, a broad consensus that Japanese organizations have highly distinctive internal structures and employment/industrial relations systems. While expressions of this view often overlook the institutional and cultural diversity of the West, it is nonetheless apparent that a particular pattern of organizing evokes the label "Japanese." What we find striking are the parallels between the portrait of Japanese organization and the structures and practices which other streams of organizational theory and research identify with commitment-maximizing corporatist forms of organizational control. Consider the structures that Blauner, Woodward, and other technology theorists associate with automated, process production technology: tall, finely-graded hierarchies; tasks and responsibilities assigned to groups rather than individuals; small spans of control with supervisors functioning as group leaders rather than bosses; a high ratio of clerical and managerial to production workers; and management by committee and participatory decision-making with much free-flowing communication. These are structural patterns which simultaneously describe the automated firms of Woodward and Blauner and the Japanese prototype as well. The similarities between Japanese organization and the forms attributed to advanced technology manufacturing recalls Dore's (1973) thesis that the distinctive features of Japanese organization have less to do with Japanese culture and tradition than with the fact that Japan, being a late developer, was in a position to make effective use of the latest designs in organization-building. Thus, the similarities between the organization of advanced technology firms and Japanese organization stem from both being "modern" forms.

This theme is echoed in the contention of Richard Edwards and other Marxist theorists that bureaucratic control is fast replacing older management strategies of eliciting compliance and conformity from the labor force. Though the Marxists acknowledge inspiration neither from technology theorists nor students of Japan, we have noted frequently the striking parallels between, for example, Edwards' description of the control structures of modern companies such as Polaroid and the forms associated both with Japan and process manufacturing technology: extensive teamwork, high subunit differentiation, finely-graded status hierarchies, participatory decision-making, career progression in job duties, extensive written rules and regulations, and abundant welfare services. Our contention is that the writings of labor process Marxists, technological imperativists, and Japan scholars have converged on the identification of a common organizational mode: welfare corporatism, whose driving logic is that of labor control through the mechanism of high commitment.

Organizational structures and employee work attitudes: two theories

Despite a fairly slender empirical base in large-sample, systematic research, there is no shortage of theorizing on the effects of organizations on the attitudes and behaviors of their members. Scholars of widely varying stripe have written vast numbers of books and articles on the kinds of organizational structures and settings which elicit from a workforce commitment, morale, and integration – as opposed to alienation, detachment, and rebellion.

The results of much of this theorizing – particularly that which has grown up within mainstream traditions of organizational sociology and psychology – can be distilled into a single broad proposition: formal bureaucratic organization, whatever its merits as a device for the efficient accomplishment of large amounts of routine work, creates an oppressive work environment for individuals. Basic human needs for varied, interesting tasks, so this reasoning goes, cannot be met in a context where work, authority, and communication are highly structured, programmed, and routinized. Adverse reactions of members to the bureaucratic structuring of their organizations range from boredom and listlessness to active alienation and resistance and even to personality impairment (Kohn, 1971; Merton, 1968). We refer to this perspective as the "bureaucratic alienation" theory, although it subsumes much of what has been elsewhere termed the "human relations" school of management and organizational design (e.g. Perrow, 1979). The empirical research which bears most directly on this theory proceeds by disaggregating the concept of bureaucracy into specific dimensions such as centralization, formalization, and specialization. These are then measured with standard scales (e.g. the Aston batteries), and correlated with employee-level indicators of work attitudes and motivation (Aiken and Hage, 1966; Lincoln *et al.*, 1981; Oldham and Hackman, 1981; Porter and Lawler, 1965; Rousseau, 1978).

An alternative paradigm, and one that has framed our discussion throughout this book, is that of welfare corporatism as an emergent, multifaceted strategy of control among modern employing organizations. This model of organizing, whose chief superiority over older forms is its capacity to elicit commitment and loyalty from a workforce, converges with mainstream bureaucratic alienation theory at numerous junctures but clashes sharply with it in other respects. Both regard centralized, authoritarian management as likely to evoke negative employee work attitudes and behaviors. Both stress the value to the firm's control objectives of authority structures which facilitate autonomy, participation, and consultation as opposed to asymmetric, domineering supervisory styles. However, corporatist theorists, as we have previously stressed, see such decentralized and participatory authority structures largely as means for motivating and coopting workers; not for producing real alterations in the corporate governance structures of the sort envisioned by advocates of industrial democracy. Dore (1973), for example, explicitly contrasts the hierarchical corporatism typical of Japanese industry with the democratic corporatism toward which he believes European economies are evolving.

There is less convergence between bureaucratic alienation and corporatist theory with respect to structural and functional differentiation within the workplace. They agree that extreme division of labor with its resulting fragmented, deskilled, and repetitive jobs are, contrary to Frederick Taylor, in the long run at odds with effective labor control. Not only do narrow, routine tasks inspire low commitment and motivation, but they elicit an atomized and homogeneous mass of workers whose individual grievances tend to aggregate into a wall of antipathy to the company and its management (Kerr and Siegel, 1954).

But the alternatives to extreme task differentiation envisioned by bureaucratic and corporatist theory are significantly different. For bureaucratic theory it would appear to be a kind of professional or craft community – the organic organization of Burns and Stalker (1961) – wherein high levels of skill and training reside with individuals and tasks are uncrystallized, diffuse in content, and subject to an ongoing process of redefinition by the community. Formal structural divisions separating jobs, levels, and work units are few and permeable; the organization relies upon the consensus of the group and the socialization of its members to structure activities in a fashion suited to current goals. From the standpoint of bureaucratic alienation theory, corporatist organization represents an extreme of bureaucratic structuring: formal boundaries run everywhere; sections, departments, and teams, along with status levels and occupational titles proliferate. Richard Edwards (1979) sees these developments as typical of Polaroid's system of bureaucratic control:

> Polaroid's system of control is built on a finely graded division and stratification for workers. The divisions run both hierarchically (creating higher and lower positions) and laterally. They tend to break up the homogeneity of the firm's workforce, creating many seemingly separate strata, lines of work, and focuses for job identity.

Thus, internal organizational divisions erode employees' identities as workers and managers, and foster instead an attachment to an organizational subunit or functional area within which semiautonomous and internally cohesive groups can form. Tall, finely-graded status hierarchies (which may in fact be divorced from the pyramid of formal authority or occupational roles) are seen in corporatist theory to raise labor commitment and dependence by increasing the proportion of employees with management responsibilities as well as the density of relationships formed around a status difference. Moreover, tall hierarchies, as we have noted, imply job ladders and promotion opportunities which hold out the promise of career advancement to employees who invest heavily in the fortunes of the firm (Kanter, 1984). Further, the pyramiding of status positions leads employees at each level to take as their reference group those at the next level. This anticipatory socialization in corporate norms and values functions to diffuse the goals of the company and its top executives down through the organization.

The proposition that a tall hierarchy can enhance employee integration and commitment is clearly at odds with the bureaucratic alienation view. A recurrent and central theme in this tradition is that long chains of command obstruct the vertical flow of communication, producing "control loss" by top management and a sense of isolation and neglect on the part of rank-and-file workers (Blau and Scott, 1962; Child, 1984; Williamson, 1975; Worthy, 1950). Indeed, one of the largest streams of empirical research on the reactions of individual employees to organizational structures stems from Worthy's hypothesis that tall management pyramids have adverse consequences for employee social integration and morale (Buchanan, 1974). Some corporatist theorists take the position, however, that the implications of vertical differentiation for worker integration and commitment are curvilinear. While viewing the finely graded hierarchies of large, modern firms as an effective control device, Edwards (1979) also sees the face-to-face encounters between owner–managers and workers in small, simply organized firms as conducive to strong personal bonds and high worker commitment.

The suggestion that hierarchical divisions often have chiefly symbolic and status value, and do not correspond to genuinely distinct spheres of competence or responsibility, is a recurrent theme in accounts of the elaborate structural complexity of Japanese organizations (Clark, 1979; Dore, 1973; Yoshino, 1968). In that context, they are often seen as a reflection of the low degree to which real job and authority specialization characterizes Japanese divisions of labor. Moreover, the Japanese permanent employment and seniority-based promotion systems require that there be opportunities for upward mobility, even if these involve only pay and status changes with no significant shift in authority or responsibility.

Gordon, Edwards, and Reich (1982:139) argue that employers' divide-and-conquer strategy of labor control is historically reflected as well in the proliferation of departments and sections and their location in physically separate rooms and buildings. Prior to 1900, they point out, most factories operated in a single open building. These physical conditions created ample opportunity for workers from all over the plant to observe and interact with one another and thereby develop a sense of common interest. Innovations in construction technique allowed for more flexible and decentralized designs, with separate buildings and partitions dividing up workspace and production operations. Such differentiation and decentralization of workshops and departments at a local manufacturing site furthermore encouraged centralization and formalization of personnel administration within the plant. Physical segregation, of course, is not the only means whereby departmentalization introduces divisions in the workforce; separate units under different supervisors may have their own rules and procedures, cultivate their own departmental culture and *esprit de corps*, and (encouraged by group-based incentive schemes) compete with one another in productivity contests.

Tall hierarchies and proliferating subunits imply narrow supervisory spans of control, and herein lies another area in which bureaucratic and corporatist theory clash in their implications for worker control and commitment. Traditional theory takes them to mean close supervision, for a supervisor with few subordinates is better able to monitor and direct the behavior of each (e.g. Child, 1984). As an element of corporatist organization (e.g. as in Woodward's account of continuous process industry or Dore's description of Japanese firms), small spans imply workteams in which supervisors perform as leaders and facilitators, not dominating overseers. Such an interpretation of small spans, however, has also occurred to researchers working within the bureaucracy theory tradition. Blau (1968), for example, interpreted the small supervisory spans he found in a sample of professional organizations as evidence of high levels of teamwork and dense communication links between superiors and subordinates.

Finally, bureaucratic alienation theory almost uniformly (for an early exception, see Gouldner, 1954) regards formalization as a core dimension of bureaucratic structuring which spells rigidity, impersonality, goal displacement, and, ultimately, alienation among workers. However, corporatist theory, as we construe it, sees formal rules and procedures fostering a constitutional order in which workers' rights and obligations are explicitly set down in corporate "law," and affiliation with the company takes the form of citizenship in an internal state (Burawoy, 1983; Edwards, 1979; Halaby, 1986). The impersonal control achieved with formal rules, moreover, is less alienating than the oversight of the foreman or the pacing of machines, and its packaging as a set of legal rights and obligations of corporate citizenship lends a legitimacy to control efforts not easily obtained through other means. Furthermore, much formalization in work organizations, including job classifications, job bidding procedures, and work rules are installed at the behest of workers wishing to circumscribe management discretion and safeguard employee rights (Jacoby, 1985; Thomas and Shimada, 1983).

If corporatist theory – a vision of an emergent strategy on the part of advanced corporations for securing the compliance of employees through normative, symbolic, and associative inducements (Kanter, 1968) – proffers a different view of the same organizational structures seen in bureaucratic theory as having alienating and disintegrating consequences, it also lays heavy stress on the company's bundle of welfare programs and services. As we have noted, company-sponsored benefits and services have figured prominently in various discussions of corporatist-type organization, from Blauner's and Woodward's accounts of continuous process industry, to Dore's treatment of welfare corporatism in the Japanese employment system, to Edwards' bureaucratic control. Training programs, retreats, and outings socialize employees in a company culture. Recreational and social activities also pass on corporate values and build informal networks across status and job barriers. Company newspapers, ceremonies, songs, pep talks, and calisthenics diffuse and reinforce shared interests and values and breed company-wide *esprit de corps*. And tangible benefits like company housing, low interest loans, and discount merchandise increase dependence on the company and cast it in a benevolent *in loco parentis* role. Through such services, programs, and activities, the scope of the employee's participation in the company is enlarged beyond the narrow employment contracting of labor for a wage. They break down the boundary between work and private life, and do so in a manner that is chiefly on the company's terms.

The evidence gleaned from systematic empirical studies of the link between organizational structures and employee reactions is neither large nor particularly deep. Still, serious attempts to research this connection have been made and thus provide some background and guidance to our efforts here. To our knowledge, no such systematic research has been directed at the impact of corporate services on employee commitment, despite a general consensus that company paternalism plays a role in the development of an enterprise community of cooperative, dedicated employees. Along with organizational structure, welfare services and programs comprise an important dimension along which companies vary and one which is pivotal to our general model of welfare corporatism as a commitment-maximizing organizational form.

A cultural contingency model

We have juxtaposed two perspectives on the links between the structure of work organizations and the reactions of employees. The key point of contention between the two turns on the presumed effects of formal and complex – i.e. bureaucratic – structuring. In the corporatist framework, bureaucratic organization functions to integrate the employee and legitimate the employment relationship, the end product being heightened organizational commitment. In the bureaucratic alienation framework, formal and complex structuring introduces distance, impersonality, and rigidity into workplace associations and activities, such that the employee becomes isolated, adrift, and detached from the center of organizational life. We can test these starkly different predictions with our survey data. There is, however, yet another perspective on the reactions of employees to organizations across sociocultural settings, which we labeled in chapter 1 "cultural contingency." Neither the welfare corporatist nor the bureaucratic alienation perspectives allows for differences between cultures and societies in the impact of organizational arrangements on individuals. Indeed, the assumption that corporatist-style organization evokes comparable degrees of commitment from Western and Japanese employees lies at the explanatory core of corporatist theory as we see it: that the Japanese commitment advantage stems from the wider implementation of welfare corporatist forms in Japanese than in US industry. This hypothesis assumes that corporatist organization is as effective at generating commitment outside as inside Japan.

A cultural (or societal) contingency hypothesis, however, is compelling in several respects, and in various versions has been advanced by numerous students of Japanese organization. It is in close harmony with the thrust of the currently influential institutional perspective in organization theory (Meyer and Scott, 1983). Strongly culturalist in flavor, it asserts that patterns of workplace organization are direct reflections of cultural tendencies – e.g. propensities toward groupism vs. individualism or hierarchy vs. egalitarianism. Survival and growth benefits accrue to firms and bureaus that organize themselves in ways according with local populations' values and beliefs. When the question at hand turns to employees' social psychological reactions to modes of organizing, this reasoning predicts that positive feelings result when employees' sociocultural habits, values, and expectations are not perturbed by the routines of organizational life. The implication is that Japanese organizations have evolved toward greater congruence with the cultural predilections of the Japanese, and the same is true of US organizations. But, given different cultures, there is little reason to expect the same style of organizing to evoke equivalent responses in the US and Japan.

Rather convincing evidence for a cultural contingency model as applied to US and Japanese employees is provided in the study by Lincoln *et al.* (1981) of 28 Japanese-owned firms located in the US, each of which employed a culturally heterogeneous workforce. Regression analyses conducted within three groups (Japanese nationals, Japanese–Americans, US employees with no Japanese ancestry) yielded strong indications that culture/nationality conditioned the effects of organizational structures on employee job satisfaction and social integration. Among the Japanese employees, morale and cohesion rose with increases in the vertical differentiation of the firm and fell with increments in horizontal or functional differentiation. This same pattern was evident, though weaker, in the Japanese–American sample. It was wholly absent in the American sample, where neither form of structural differentiation showed an appreciable relation to employee work attitudes and relations. Since high vertical differentiation and low functional specialization constitute a distinctively Japanese configuration of organizational traits (see chapter 7), this set of findings – particularly the intermediate placement of the Japanese–Americans' responses – is strikingly consistent with the cultural contingency theme. This represents one way in which organizations can be seen adapting to an institutional environment: by adopting forms which signal legitimacy in terms of dominant cultural values, organizations secure from employees socialized in those values, a higher degree of commitment and compliance (Cole, 1979).

7 Organizational structures in Japan and the US: a plant-level analysis

In this chapter, we present data analyses addressed to the hypotheses put forward in the last chapter pertaining to variations in the organizational structures of manufacturing plants between Japan and the United States and across diverse production technologies.[1] While we cannot speak to every proposition advanced there, we can address many of them, and certainly we can determine whether significant contrasts in organizational structures exist between Japan and the US that are net of technology, scale, and other causal variables. This question is of substantial interest in its own right, but the answers also have direct implications for our ultimate objective: to ascertain whether variations in organization, management, and employment practice among US and Japanese plants can account for the work attitudes and behaviors of manufacturing employees in these two countries. In chapter 8, we examine explicitly how organization-level variables affect commitment and satisfaction and whether the pattern of these effects is consistent with the general corporatist theme. Now, we consider whether there are societal as well as technological influences on organizational structures, and whether those influences take the form proposed by corporatist theory.

We first evaluate differences among industries and between societies in plants' production technologies and market organization. We then examine technological, societal, and other contextual (ownership patterns, size, age, unionization) influences on the organizational structures of our sampled plants. Our measures of all such plant-level variables are presented in table 7.1.

Industry differences

Economists define industries as groups of similar products that are produced and sold in similar markets: a theoretical industry consists of products which are close substitutes to a common group of buyers (Bain, 1959:110). Industries are thus defined both in terms of product characteristics and the patterns whereby these products are bought and sold in markets. The importance of industries for our purposes derives from the fact that *firms* produce these goods and services. Hence, a theoretical industry is derivatively a group of firms. Companies in the same industry face similar market, technological, and industrial relations environments which shape their internal structures and employment practices. These and other differences among industries have important implications for the issues with which our study is concerned: the organization of the workplace and the work attitudes and behaviors of employees.

Our sense for the potential importance of industry differences led us to select samples of American and Japanese manufacturing plants which were as comparable as possible in industry composition. In this respect, we were fortunate that the two regions in which our research was conducted – central Indiana and Kanagawa prefecture – have generally similar fairly diversified industry distributions. With the exceptions of printing and food products, the distribution is remarkably uniform in the Kanagawa region, as far as we were able to determine from Chamber of Commerce and similar directories. In the Indianapolis region, there is a larger number of plants in the nonelectrical machinery and fabricated metal products groups, and fewer in transportation equipment; the former two industries are generally composed of rather small companies and plants, whereas the latter included a number of very large automotive factories.

Country, industry, and size comparisons of market organization and technology

The size of a plant, its industry, and whether it is Japanese or American are fundamental characteristics of work organizations that shape an array of plant-level properties. In this section, we examine certain structural characteristics of the markets in which the plants in our samples operate, the kinds of production technologies they use, and their organizational structures and employment systems.

Market organization

Table 7.2 presents the results from a series of regression equations relating several measures of the plant's market position to the employment size of the plant, the seven-industry classification, and country (coded 0 = Japan, 1 = US).[2] The unstandardized regression coefficient associated with "US/Japan" represents the deviation of the American mean on the dependent variable from the Japanese mean, both means being adjusted for country differences in average plant size and industry composition. Thus, a positive coefficient for "US/Japan" indicates that the American mean is greater than the Japanese mean; negative coefficient implies the opposite. Similarly, the unstandardized coefficients associated with each industry variable represent the deviation of the industry's mean from an overall average, these deviations also being adjusted for size and country effects. Finally, the coefficient of (log) size

Table 7.1 *Measures of organization variables and descriptive statistics*

Variable	US Mean (SD)	Japan Mean (SD)	t-value of difference
Independent (1 = independent company;	.296	.280	.178
0 = branch plant or subsidiary)	(.461)	(.454)	
Size. Number of employees in plant	571	461	.684
	(1027)	(583)	
Plant age. Years since founding of	44.3	24.9	.678
plant	(33.8)	(17.3)	
Union. Union contract covers pro-	.556	.706	−1.60
duction workers = 1	(.502)	(.460)	
Custom. Plant manager's rating of extent			
of custom production	3.094	3.021	.254
(1 = not at all, 5 = a great deal)	(1.390)	(1.553)	
Small batch. Plant manager's			
rating of extent (same codes)	2.906	3.450	−1.948*
of small batch production	(1.363)	(1.501)	
Large batch. Plant manager's			
rating of extent of large batch	3.132	3.646	−1.750*
production	(2.63)	(3.01)	
Mass. Plant manager's rating	2.868	2.896	−.082
of extent of mass production	(1.630)	(1.859)	
Process. Plant manager's rating of	1.90	1.96	−.200
continuous process technology	(1.43)	(1.55)	
Automation. Sum of scores			
indicating *most automatic* machinery			
in plant and automation level of *bulk*			
of machinery (hand tools and manual	7.92	7.34	−.926
machines = 0; computer control = 5)	(2.60)	(1.81)	
Workflow Rigidity. Aston			
scale. Proportion applicable of eight			
statements characterizing rigidity/	.540	.396	2.95***
interdependence of workflow processes	(.245)	(.252)	
Specialization. Proportion of 20			
specialist functions which are the sole	.757	.320	8.19***
responsibility of at least one individual	(.260)	(.287)	
No. Departments. Number of units	6.08	5.43	.680
one level below plant manager	(2.09)	(6.45)	
No. Sections. Number of units below	12.9	15.5	−.840
department level	(12.3)	(18.6)	
No. Ranks. Number of hierarchical levels			
from lowest direct worker to highest	4.91	5.47	2.14**
manager in plant	(1.00)	(1.58)	
CEO span. Plant manager's span of	5.96	6.66	−.943
control	(2.19)	(4.81)	
1st-line span. Average first-line	13.4	14.2	−.606
supervisor's span of control	(5.48)	(7.70)	
Mgmt. Ratio. Ratio of managers to	.143	.133	.854
total employees	(.087)	(.142)	

Table 7.1 *(cont.)*

Variable	US Mean (SD)	Japan Mean (SD)	t-value of difference
Prod. Ratio. Ratio of production	.601	.580	.624
workers to total employees	(.185)	(.158)	
Clerical ratio. Ratio of clerical	.091	.112	−1.43
workers to total number of employees	(.080)	(.070)	
Formalization. Aston formalization scale.			
Proportion present of a total of	.680	.766	−2.36**
18 written documents	(.213)	(.137)	
Formal centralization. Mean level of			
formal authority to make 37			
decisions (1 = direct worker, 2 = supervisor,			
3 = middle manager, 4 = dept head,	4.66	4.99	−4.01**
5 = plant manager, 6 = higher unit)	(.482)	(.360)	
De facto centralization. Mean level			
at which 37 decisions are	4.36	3.82	4.91***
in practice made	(.568)	(.563)	
Proportion QC. Proportion of	.267	.952	−31.4***
employees in QC circles	(.143)	(.070)	
Ringi. Proportion of a total of 37			
decisions made using the *ringi* process	.792	.267	—
(Japan) or by groups (US)	(.231)	(.226)	
Welfare services. Number present of			
nine company-sponsored employee	5.235	6.740	−4.14***
services/activities	(2.015)	(1.711)	

Notes: *p < .10 by a two-tailed test
**p < .05
***p < .01

represents the amount of change in the dependent variable associated with a unit change in the logarithm of size.[3]

Table 7.2 reveals a number of differences in the market patterns faced by Japanese and US plants and in their dealings with suppliers and customers. First, the number of product lines manufactured by the plant is on the average larger in the Japanese sample. A number of observers have commented on the flexibility of Japanese production processes: the same plant is equipped to manufacture a range of related products, avoiding engineering that demands a high degree of product specialization. Such specialization, as our data suggest, is more prevalent in the United States (Abegglen and Stalk, 1985; Schonberger, 1982).

Hierarchical relationships between suppliers and customers at different

Table 7.2 Regressions of market organization and technology variables on country, size, and industry[a] (N = 106)

Independent variable				Dependent variable						
	No. production lines	Percentage to largest customer	Percentage from largest supplier	Custom	Small batch	Large batch	Mass	Process	Workflow rigidity	Automation
US/Japan	−1.262***	−14.056***	−19.030***	.114	−.505*	−.655**	−.098	−.221	.122***	.289
(ln) size	.312**	3.880	4.079	−.224	−.181	.199	.232	.166	.033	.471***
Electrical machinery	−.530	−10.983	1.238	.059	.379	−.002	.199	.054	−.097*	−.383
Chemicals	.869**	−3.586	5.196	−.499	−.325	.032	−.520	1.026**	.004	−.592
Metals	.152	−3.793	−6.338	.332	.698**	−.012	−.532	−.421	−.020	−.810*
Food	.268	3.496	2.651	−1.081**	−.686**	.562*	.399	1.407***	.130*	.242
Machinery	−.515	7.556	−.740	.768**	.062	−1.222***	−.926***	−.982**	−.175**	−.661
Transportation equipment	−.292	17.208***	15.257***	−.115	−.147	.128	.878**	−.750**	.076	−.339
Printing and publishing	.046	−9.053	−17.156**	.534	.021	.509	.491	−.320	.081	2.586***
Intercept	2.037	19.159	7.252	4.231	4.425	2.660	1.676	1.138	.230	4.949
Adj. R²	.239	.176	.241	.184	.127	.194	.179	.309	.254	.270

Notes: [a] Industry categories are interpretable as (adjusted) deviations from the overall mean

* p < .10 by a two-tailed test

** p < .05

*** p < .01

stages of processing are another feature of the Japanese economy which have attracted considerable attention. Suppliers to original equipment manufacturers are often highly dependent satellite or "child" companies who have no other buyers and are highly controlled by the "parent" firm. Japanese manufacturing systems such as "just-in-time" production scheduling place a heavy burden on suppliers to deliver parts at the moment they are needed, thereby averting costly inventory buildups and delays in processing. Such precision in the delivery of materials and parts is feasible because of the considerable control that parent firms exercise over satellite suppliers (Gerlach, 1989). We asked plant managers what percentage of their sales went to their largest customer. Table 7.2 shows that this percentage is significantly higher in Japan; i.e. the Japanese firms are more dependent upon a single large customer than the US companies. The Japanese plants reported an average of 42 percent of their sales going to their single largest customer as compared to 25 percent among the American plants. Likewise, the plants in our Japanese sample were more dependent upon particular suppliers than in the American sample. The mean percentage of a supplier's sales to the sampled plants was nearly 32 percent in Japan; no more than 10 percent in the US.

Table 7.2 also reveals certain industry differences in these measures of a plant's dependence on suppliers and buyers. Not surprisingly, the auto industry is significantly above average on both measures: plants in this industry are more likely to ship to large customers, and, correspondingly, their own sources of parts and raw materials are relatively highly concentrated. The other industry difference involves the case of printing, which is less dependent on sole-source suppliers than are other industries.

Technology

One expects there to be significant variation in production technology across a set of diverse manufacturing industries. Yet unless one adopts an extremely detailed industry classification, the diversity of products within an industry will encompass a significant diversity of technologies as well. Thus, we do not expect such a highly aggregated industry classification to account for a very high percentage of the plant-to-plant variation in technology.

The Woodward technology classification Our technology measures have seen frequent use in previous research. The first is based on the familiar classification employed by Joan Woodward (1965) in her influential study of British manufacturing firms. The managers of each plant were asked to rate their plants on five-point scales indicating the extent to which each of five basic production technologies were in use: custom production; small batch; large batch; mass production; and continuous process. The rating scales were such that the technology choices were not mutually exclusive; the same plant could report the use, in varying degrees, of multiple technologies. This was often the case among the plants studied: mass production assembly work would be coupled with a large-batch fabrication of parts; in food products, continuous processing would be combined with a large-batch or mass-production operation (Averitt, 1968).

Table 7.2 also presents results of regression analyses in which the plant managers' ratings of each technology are the dependent variables and country, industry, and plant size are the explanatory variables.[4] The contrasts in production technology among industries are in general those we would expect. The food and chemicals industries are significantly above the average in their use of continuous processing and below average in use of custom and small batch methods (though the deviation of chemical plants from the overall mean is not significant). The opposite pattern is found in the case of nonelectrical machinery: this industry makes greatest use of custom production; is average in the use of small-batch methods; and is least likely to employ large-batch, mass-production, and continuous-process technologies. The stereotype of automotive manufacturing as the quintessential mass-production industry is also confirmed by these data: it is the only industry to be significantly above the mean in reliance upon this technology.

The pattern of differences in the remaining three industries is less clear. Our electronics plants are not exceptional in their use of any of the five technologies. Prefabricated metals is an industry where one would expect to find "job-shops," and plants in this industry do make greater than average use of small-batch technologies. Finally, plants in the printing and publishing industry do not deviate from the overall mean on any of the five Woodward technologies, though the relatively small number of printing plants in our samples (especially in Japan) makes statistical significance harder to achieve. We do find that printing is second only to nonelectrical machinery in use of custom technology, but at the same time it ranks just as high on the large-batch and mass-production dimensions. This pattern makes sense, for large-volume production (e.g. of newspapers or books) is as much a part of this industry as is production (e.g. advertising) which is tailored to a customer's orders.

The associations of plant size with the five production technologies are surprisingly weak, although they are in the expected directions: continuous process, mass production, and large batch are all positive functions of size; while the correlations of size with small batch and custom production are negative. The zero-order correlations fall into a stronger pattern: custom $(-.146)$; small batch $(-.086)$; large batch $(.182)$; mass production $(.255)$; and continuous process $(.034)$. Thus, large scale is most characteristic of the middle range of the technology continuum (large batch and mass production), but there appears to be considerable variation within each industry.

Finally, much has been written in recent years on the distinctive features of Japanese manufacturing processes (Abegglen and Stalk, 1985; Hayes and

Wheelwright, 1984; Schonberger, 1982). We have noted that Japanese firms are perceived to combine greater efficiency as well as flexibility in their production processes than do American plants. Now-famous Japanese practices such as "just-in-time" inventory control and Toyota's *kanban* system produce low inventories at each stage of processing and achieve an extraordinarily fine-tuned orchestration of manufacturing processes. As Abegglen and Stalk (1985:93–104) observe, these innovations were aimed at introducing flexibility into Japanese manufacturing systems (which earlier tended to be highly focused on a narrow range of standard products), such that the short runs and small lot sizes required by greater product complexity could be achieved without incurring large changeover and setup costs. The hypothesis of greater flexibility of Japanese production processes was supported by Kagono *et al.*'s (1985) comparative study of 227 large US companies and 291 comparable Japanese corporations. Contrasting means of ratings on the five Woodward dimensions of production technology obtained from key informants in each company, they found significant differences on two: the Japanese corporations made more use of custom technology, whereas large batch production was more prevalent among the American firms. Furthermore, on an overall index of nonroutine production (continuous process = 1; custom = 5), the Japanese organizations scored significantly higher.

In our sample, on the other hand, Japanese plants are more likely than the American plants to make use of both small-batch *and* large-batch production systems. The greater use of small batch technology is compatible with the Kagono *et al.* (1985) finding regarding custom production, but the results of the two studies are obviously at odds with respect to large-batch systems. This divergence may be due to differences in the samples and units being compared: the unit studied in Kagono *et al.*'s research is the entire corporation and the sample consists wholly of very large companies. Their informants' assessments of technology type are thus highly aggregated across product lines and production facilities.

Workflow rigidity The index of "workflow rigidity" is a sophisticated measure of production technology devised by the Aston group of British organizational researchers (Pugh *et al.*, 1969). It is a composite of seven items which indicate the degree to which production processes are highly interdependent, specialized to particular products, and inflexible in various ways. The scale formed by summing these items has an alpha reliability of .63. A rigid workflow should be characteristic of "advanced technology" in the Woodward sense. That is, mass production and continuous process technologies should involve more rigid, specialized, and interdependent operations than small batch and custom technologies. In general, this is confirmed by our data. The workflow rigidity index correlates −.32 with custom technology, −.32 with small batch, .19 with large batch, .24 with mass production, and .19 with continuous process. Our Aston-based workflow rigidity measure, then, is related to the Woodward categories in the same manner as Kagono *et al.'s* index of technological nonroutineness.

Table 7.2 also presents the regressions of the workflow rigidity scale on the industry groups, plant size, and country. The key industry differences are that food processing is higher than average on this dimension of technology and machinery is lower than average. These results conform to our earlier finding of more continuous processing in the food products industry and relatively little custom or small-batch production; the opposite pattern obtaining in the case of machinery. Electronics is also somewhat below the overall plant mean on workflow rigidity, although the difference is only marginally significant. Moreover, plant size bears no relation to workflow rigidity.

The American plants appear to have more rigid workflows than the Japanese. This parallels Kagono *et al.'s* finding and supports the hypothesis that Japanese production processes are geared to more flexible production. Some of the items that comprise the workflow rigidity scale would appear to tap such Japanese production techniques as "just-in-time" scheduling, which aims to articulate processing stages and reduce pileups. One such item measures the extent to which buffer stocks accumulate between production stages. However, on this and one or two similar items, we do not find noteworthy differences between the Japanese and US plants.

Automation Our final measure of technology is the Amber and Amber (1962) automation scale, which scores machinery in the plant from minimally mechanized ("hand tools") to automated control involving feedback. As in the Aston studies (Pugh *et al.*, 1968), we obtained two scores for each plant on this scale: for the most automated equipment in use; and for the bulk of machinery. The correlation between the two items is .57, which is an acceptable reliability for a two-item summated index. The last column of table 7.2 presents the results of regressing this index on the set of predictor variables. As expected, larger plants tend to be more automated. Moreover, "job-shop" operations such as prefabricated metals production are below the mean, but the difference is only marginally significant. In contrast, plants in the printing and publishing industry are the only industry group markedly above the average in automation. The high automation of modern printing and publishing establishments is not surprising, since technology in this industry has advanced recently at a rapid rate, and even small local newspapers have invested heavily in new, computerized machinery. The introduction of this technology was prompted by the steady decline in industrial profit margins after World War II, due in part to the power of the craft unions in the industry. As a result of these technological innovations, many of the occupations in the industry became deskilled and the power of the craft unions was broken (Wallace and Kalleberg, 1982; Zimbalist, 1979).

Finally, we find no net overall level of automation difference between the

US and Japanese factories, though the composite automation scale conceals country differences in the component items. The bulk of the machinery in the American plants rates higher on the Amber and Amber scale than the bulk of machinery in the Japanese plants. Yet the scores of the Japanese plants average slightly higher than the American plants on the item measuring the most automated equipment in use. This pattern accords with intuition. Japanese plants are quick to take advantage of technological innovations, and much new and advanced machinery can be found on shop floors. But other operations are highly labor intensive and not very automated. Certainly there would seem to be limits to the degree to which Japanese firms can substitute machine for human labor while still providing guarantees of continuous employment to a large proportion of the workforce.

In general, then, our analysis thus far indicates that the market structures and production technologies of the plants in our sample vary with size, industry, and country in the manner anticipated. Net of industry and size, Japanese plants appear to differ from US factories in exhibiting stronger interdependencies with particular suppliers and customers and less rigid production systems. The primary force shaping production technology, however, proved to be the industry group in which the plant is classified. The observed pattern of technological differences among industries is a predictable one, as are the interrelationships among the three measures of technology we used. In addition to giving us some useful descriptive information on industrial and technological variation in our sample, then, this section has also served to validate our technology measures. This is important, for our central focus in the next section is the relative effects of technology and country on organizational structures, a question of considerable theoretical relevance to our research.

Determinants of organizational structures

An entire book could easily be devoted to the differences in Japanese and American organizational structures and management practices, and, indeed, numerous writings on these topics have appeared in recent years. Little of this material, however, reports the findings of systematic empirical research on Japanese and US organizations, being instead amalgamations of anecdotes, reviews of past writings, case studies, and qualitative observations. In this section, we present findings pertaining to the formal organizational structure of 106 American and Japanese manufacturing plants. While we attempt to replicate and extend past empirical studies of plant structure, our primary focus is on differences in structural properties and management systems between the two countries. Furthermore, as noted at the outset of this chapter, much of this analysis is motivated by our interest in identifying characteristics of organizational structures and employment practices of Japanese and US factories which help shape employee orientations to work.

To answer this question we need first to determine whether or not there are significant differences between the countries in the organization of manufacturing plants.

Effects of technology

In assessing the impact of production technology on the organizational structures of manufacturing plants, we modify our original Woodward measures, which consisted of ratings on five distinct technology types (custom, small batch, large batch, mass production, continuous process), by combining the custom and small-batch indicators into one unit-weighted scale and the large-batch and mass production indicators into another. The first two items correlate at .394, the second two at .472. This reduces the number of predictor variables we must deal with, and, though these correlations suggest low reliability, additional analyses using all the original five items suggest that little information is lost by creating composite scales. Moreover, the discussions by Woodward and subsequent students of these technology dimensions often conceptually combine them into custom-small batch, large batch-mass production, and continuous process.

Since the Woodward classification disaggregates the technology concept into separate indicators, it allows us to examine in a straightforward way both linear and nonlinear effects of technology. A linear effect on a measure of plant structure would be reflected in monotonically increasing regression slopes from custom/small batch to large batch/mass production to continuous process. A nonlinear function, such as the inverted U which Woodward (1965) and Blauner (1964) believed described the influence of technology on bureaucratic structuring, would be represented by negative or perhaps null slopes of custom/small batch and continuous process and a positive slope in the case of large batch/mass production. To get at nonlinearities involving the other two technology measures, we include quadratic terms for the workflow rigidity and automation scales. A regression equation of the form: $Y = a + bX + cX^2 + e$ fits a parabola (a curve with one bend) to the data points, and such nonlinear effects can be easily evaluated within a regression framework (see Stolzenberg, 1979). Where there is no evidence of a significant effect of the squared term, however, we present only the coefficient of the linear term.

We consider, then, five distinct measures of technology. An argument against this strategy is that, if all five measures are alternative indicators of the same underlying technology construct, we should not partial out their common variance. In fact, we presume a causal sequence orders the technology dimensions: automation and workflow rigidity may be construed as consequences of the Woodward dimensions which derive primarily from the homogeneity of raw materials and standardization of the product (Starbuck, 1965:503). We address this possibility, overlooked in past research, by presenting two coefficients for each Woodward technology category: a total effect obtained from an equation omitting workflow rigidity and automation, and the direct or net effect obtained when the latter are added to the regression.

There is finally the problem of assessing whether technological and other contextual antecedents of organizational structures exhibit the same relationships within each country. Our approach is to test, for each dependent variable, an overall hypothesis that the slopes differ by country.[5] If the null hypothesis is supported, we present a single equation which constrains slopes to be equal in the two samples but permits means (intercepts) to differ. This kind of model makes the task of detecting net country differences easier, since a difference in the means on the dependent variable will be constant over the entire range of the predictor variables. If, on the other hand, the test for heterogeneity of slopes proves positive, we present separate regressions for the Japanese and US samples. In the presence of such interaction, it becomes more difficult to say whether there exist Japan–US differences in structure, since the size and direction of a difference vary over the range of the regressors. However, we can make comparisons: (a) in the unadjusted means; and (b) at the overall means of the independent variables. Comparison (b) is equivalent to adjusting the intercepts of the regressions to the values of Y when the X's equal their overall (pooled) means. This has become a common choice as a point at which to evaluate population differences in an outcome variable given differences in slopes as well. Another difficulty in assessing the country-specific regressions is that we lose statistical power, as the number of observations in each equation is roughly half that of the total sample.

Other antecedents of structure

Production technology does not, of course, exhaust the array of forces bearing on the organization of manufacturing plants. We consider the following additional causal variables. First, we expect the larger organizations will show greater structural differentiation, formalization, and decentralization than smaller units; hence, we include as a regressor the employment size of the plant. Secondly, we include a dummy variable for whether the factory studied is an independent company ($=1$) as opposed to a subsidiary or branch plant ($=0$). Sometimes seen as a dimension of the dependence of the organization on agents in its environment, this is an important and mandatory distinction in a study of organizational structure, for many functions and structures not present in the local establishment may appear at some other location in the company (Pugh *et al.*, 1969). Branch establishments are more likely to appear centralized, for example, since certain decisions are made at higher corporate levels (Child, 1972; Lincoln *et al.*, 1978). We would further expect formalization to be high where the operations of a company are geographically dispersed.

Although there are obvious reasons to expect variables such as size, branch plant status, and technology to influence organizational structuring in their own right, we also view them as indicators of a more global phenomenon: location within the dual economy. As noted in the last chapter, dual economy theorists such as Averitt (1968) distinguish the unit and small-batch producers in the periphery sector from the high-volume, standardized operations of mass and process production in the core. Similarly, large employing establishments and units which are branch installations of regional and national corporations have been classified in the core, whereas small, single-site and locally owned companies are typed as periphery (Hodson, 1984). We expect to find the more elaborate structures typical of corporatist organization – taller hierarchies, narrower spans of control, more subunit differentiation, and more formalization – in center firms, due to the internal labor market and "divide and conquer" logic identified with this strategy of control. We also expect them to be characterized by more participatory decision-making through vehicles such as quality circles. Moreover, employee welfare services and social/ceremonial activities are, of course, key ingredients in the corporatist formula and thus should be more prevalent among large, branch plant, high-volume producers.

We also include a measure of the age of the plant – the number of years since its founding. The age of an organization reflects the condition of the physical facilities, the residues of history (for example, its pattern of industrial relations), and even the management theories and technologies of organization-building prevalent at the time of founding. We expect that, with age, organizations accumulate programs and subunits, delegate decision-making, and rely to a lesser extent on formal rules and procedures as mechanisms of control as custom and strong personal bonds grow in importance. Finally, we include as a predetermined variable whether (= 1) or not (= 0) the workforce of the plant is unionized. Clearly, unionization shapes organizational structure in important ways. Union-negotiated work rules, job classifications, and grievance procedures all figure significantly in the overall system of rules and procedures that define the plant bureaucracy (Baron and Bielby, 1984). The presence of unions may also lead to the creation of additional departments such as industrial relations and safety. Finally, unionization might be expected to decentralize decision-making by placing limits on management power and discretion or, conversely, concentrate it by causing managements to withdraw into an adversarial, closed-ranks posture. In general, we expect the impact of unionization on aspects of plant organization such as formalization and division of labor to be greater in the US than in Japan, for Japanese enterprise unions have been far less activist than US unions in demanding a role in job design and work rules within companies.

Measures of plant structure

Most of our indicators of plant structure have appeared in previous sample surveys of organizations. In particular, we have drawn from the battery of structural measures devised by the Aston group (Pugh *et al.*, 1968), probably the most elaborate and painstakingly constructed set of structural measures available for organizational research.[6] Moreover, their very wide use in a considerable number of countries gives us many points of comparison against which to evaluate our results (see Hickson and McMillan, 1981). However, as discussed below, we have modified certain of the original Aston measures to better adapt them to a comparison of Japanese and US firms, and we have added other measures not in the original Aston battery.

With the exception of our indicator of quality circle participation, all measures of organizational structure were obtained from our interviews with management personnel and documentary evidence, such as organization charts and rules manuals supplied by the firm. In many instances, we cross-validated informant reports with documentary evidence in measuring a structural variable. This gave us greater confidence in the validity and reliability of our data. We describe in detail our measures of organizational structure at the appropriate junctures in our discussion of results.

Results: Japan–US differences in plant structure

Table 7.3 shows that five F-tests for overall country differences in the regression slopes are significant at a minimum level of .10: the equations for numbers of departments and sections, the two Aston measures of formal and *de facto* centralization, and QC activity. It would appear, then, that the processes determining subunit differentiation and the distribution of decision-making are not equivalent in the US and Japan, and for these structural variables, we present separate regressions for each country (tables 7.5 and 7.6). For the remaining structural variables, we present, in table 7.4, additive models which permit intercepts (means) to differ between the countries, but constrain the slopes to be the same.

Structural differentiation   First we consider the plant's horizontal division of labor in terms of specialization of individuals' functional roles and differentiation of departments and sections. Using the basic format of the Aston functional specialization scale, we asked if each of 20 functions were assigned to individuals as full-time responsibilities. The measure is the proportion of the 20 functions so assigned. Tables 7.1 and 7.4 provide strong confirmation for the hypothesis of less functional specialization in the distribution of workroles among Japanese employees. Whereas $\frac{3}{4}$ of the functions listed are assigned to specialists in the US plants, less than $\frac{1}{3}$ are so assigned in the Japanese establishments.

Table 7.3 *F-tests for equality of country-specific regressions (N = 106)*

Dependent variable	F-value	Df
Specialization	.490	9,86
No. departments	2.61***	11,82
No. sections	3.72***	9,86
No. ranks	.898	9,86
CEO span	1.36	9,86
First-line span	.367	9,86
CEO ratio	.299	9,86
Management ratio	.530	9,86
Direct worker ratio	.821	9,86
Clerical ratio	1.54	11,82
Formalization	1.23	9,86
Formal centralization	4.13***	11,82
De facto centralization	1.82*	11,82
Proportion QC	1.99*	11,74
Welfare services	1.40	11,82

Notes: * $p < .10$
** $p < .05$
*** $p < .01$

Our version of the Aston measure appears to show less specialization in this sample of Japanese factories than appears in the samples studied by Azumi (see Azumi and McMillan, 1981) and Marsh and Mannari (1976). Part of the reason may be size: our plants average roughly half the size of those in Azumi's sample. The more important reason, however, may be that we took particular pains to ensure that only functions which were the full-time, *sole* responsibility of at least one individual were counted as specialties. Where employees performed other responsibilities as well, we coded the specialty as absent. Given inevitable ambiguity as to what constitutes a full-time specialist, there is, of course, some danger that the question will be interpreted differently by managers steeped in different traditions of organizing. Even so, an absence of specialists concentrating exclusively on narrow functional areas is widely perceived to be a distinctive feature of Japanese organizational structure, contrasting sharply with American methods of allocating responsibilities (Clark, 1979; Ouchi, 1981).

Drawing on previous, though mainly descriptive, accounts, we also hypothesized that a proliferation of subunits is another distinguishing feature of Japanese organization. At the department level, however, the adjusted intercepts in table 7.5 show the American plants averaging six units and the Japanese plants averaging 4.7. The Japanese plants have a larger number of

Table 7.4 Regression models of additive country effects (N = 106)[a]

Independent variables	Dependent variables								
	Special- ization	No. Ranks	CEO Span	First-line span	Manage- ment ratio	Production ratio	Clerical ratio	Formal- ization	Welfare services
US/Japan[d]	.455***	−.600***	−1.44*[b]	−.623	.007	.044	−.041***	−.020	−1.509***[b]
Independent	.074*	−.341	−.374	.280	.009	.053	−.024*	−.077**	−1.391***[b]
(ln) size	.104**	.458***	.834**	1.70***	−.021**	.026*	−.007	.063***	.572***[b]
Plant age	−.005	.006	.008	.024	.000	−.001	.000	−.002***[b]	−.006
Union	.049	−.321	−.798	.951	.003	.035	−.002	.096***[b]	−.044
Cust/small[c]	.014	.036	−.254*	−.794***	.001	−.006	−.002	.006	.012
	.010	.044	−.345**	−.697**	.002	−.003	−.003	.007	.017
Large batch/Mass[c]	−.003	−.019	−.065	−.021	.002	.005	−.003	−.013**[b]	−.089*
	−.003	−.023	−.007	−.044	.000	.003	−.001	−.012**[b]	−.068
Process[c]	−.004	.053	−.243	−.534	−.014*	−.003	−.004	.014*	.066
	−.002	.071	−.209	−.570*	−.014*	−.002	−.004	.013*	.109
Automation	.005	−.229	.102	−.134	−.011**[b]	−.041	−.038***[b]	.011**	.995**
Workflow rigidity	.164*	−2.67	3.15**	−3.32	−.018	−.292	.006	−.038	.336
Automation**2		.009				−.003*	.003***[b]		−.048**
Workflow rigidity**2		2.97*				.301	−.008	.082	
Intercept	−.515	4.43	3.01	11.5	.327	.412	.314	.373	6.762
Adj. R²	.495	.100	.084	.090	.069	.000	.102	.442	.448

Notes: * p < .10
** p < .05
*** p < .01

[a] Entries are metric regression coefficients
[b] Two-tailed test; otherwise one-tailed test
[c] Second row is reduced form or "total" effect; automation and workflow rigidity omitted
[d] Dummy variable coded "1" for US plant, "0" for Japanese plant

Table 7.5 *Country-specific regression models for subunit differentiation[a].*

Independent variables	No. departments		No. sections	
	US	Japan	US	Japan
Independent	1.06**	3.08**	1.89	6.36
(Ln) size	[1.06***	3.96**]	5.78***	15.1***
Plant age	−.011	−.065	.091**b	−.097
Union	1.01***	−1.23	−7.34**b	−5.18
Cust/small[c]	.105	.515	.229	.266
	−.013	.375	−.903	.272
Large batch/mass[c]	[−.179	.520**b]	−.895	.825*
	[−.106	.467**b]	−.595	.823
Process[c]	−.043	−.396	−1.06	−1.38
	−.016	−.412	−.471	−1.38
Automation	.212	−2.31	−.422	−.028
Workflow rigidity	12.6***	11.7	[30.1***	−.335]
Automation**2	−.012	.166		
Workflow rigidity**2	−9.27**	−11.8		
Adj. Mean	[6.03	4.66]	9.77	13.1
N	55	51	55	51
Adj. R²	.464	.563	.351	.593

Notes: * p < .10
** p < .05
*** p < p .01
[a] Entries are metric regression coefficients
[b] Two-tailed test; otherwise one-tailed test
[c] Second row is reduced form or "total" effect; automation and workflow rigidity omitted
[ ] Difference between estimates is significant beyond the .10 level by a two-tailed test

sections, although the difference (as measured by the adjusted intercepts) falls just short of significance at the .10 level. While obviously not strong, this pattern is consistent with the view that Japanese plants have taller, slimmer pyramidal forms than US organizations. We find firm evidence for that proposition in the numbers of authority levels in the two samples: the Japanese plants average more than $\frac{1}{2}$ a rank taller than their US counterparts; this is a difference smaller than that reported by Azumi and McMillan (1981) but a real and important one nonetheless (see tables 7.1, 7.4).

Our fourth hypothesis regarding structural differences between the two countries is that spans of control are smaller in Japanese plants, reflecting a tall, narrow pyramidal configuration, a heavy reliance on team production and decision-making, and dense supervisor–subordinate communications (Child, 1984; Dore, 1973:262; Woodward, 1965). We find no evidence for this prediction. The chief executive's span of control is, in fact, wider in the Japan sample by a net 1.44 subordinates (see table 7.4). How can we reconcile this finding with the earlier one that the number of departments one level below the chief executive is larger in the US plants? There are two reasons, both evident from a perusal of Japanese organization charts. First, top managers in Japanese firms are often surrounded by assistants and standing committees whose members are drawn from positions throughout the company. The second lies in the rigid Japanese system of standard ranks identifying the status level of organizational units and their managers (Clark, 1979). Departments (*bu*) occur at the first level of organization below the plant manager, followed by sections (*ka*), subsections (*kakari*), and teams (*han*). In both countries, we coded as departments all groups shown by the organization chart as one level below the manager of the organization studied, and sections as all units from the next level on down. However, it is not uncommon in Japanese organization to find some section heads (*kacho*) reporting directly to the factory chief executive, even though their status is clearly two levels down. This pattern sometimes appears on American organization charts as well, but with much less frequency.

The first-line supervisory spans appear slightly larger in Japan, though the difference is not statistically significant. This finding is inconsistent with the impressions held by past researchers, although there is little available large-sample evidence with which to compare it.

Further evidence on the configuration of Japanese and US plants may be gleaned from an examination of personnel components. We find no significant differences between the countries in the ratios of management and production personnel to total employment (see table 7.4). This would seem to refute, on the one side, claims that Japanese companies have leaner management hierarchies than US firms (Peters and Waterman, 1982; Pucik and Hatvany, 1983), and, on the other, notions that high vertical differentiation and *nenko* combine to place more Japanese employees in management positions. Thus, we have structural evidence that Japanese hierarchies are not simply "taller" than in US plants, but are more finely-graded in the sense that fewer people occupy each rung of the status ladder. This finding converges with the numerous indications in our analysis that job responsibilities and rewards are more equitably distributed across the levels of Japanese management pyramids.

Formalization   The ratio of clerical to total employment is the one personnel component on which there is a significant difference between the countries. The Japanese plants have a net 4 percent more clerical employees than the US plants, a difference which is not significant in the unadjusted means (table 7.1) but is highly so in the regression equation. This will come as no surprise to those who have toured Japanese companies and observed the large number of receptionists and other office staff who appear to be performing highly redundant duties. It is also consistent with what some scholars have perceived to be a Japanese penchant for record-keeping and paper work (Dore, 1973:243). Moreover, Japanese clerical work has remained labor-intensive because of the extremely cumbersome Japanese written language which still requires much transcription by hand. Recent technical developments in the computerized word processing of Japanese characters, however, have the (unsettling to Westerners) potential for vastly increasing Japanese office productivity.

Additional evidence for the hypothesis of greater formalization in Japanese organizations is provided by the country means on the Aston composite measure of this concept (see table 7.1). The Japanese average is higher, and the t-statistic for the difference in the means is significant at a p-value of less than .05. However, when controls are added for sample composition in size, technology, and the other organizational variables in our models (see table 7.4), the country difference in formalization disappears. Thus, we cannot conclude, on the basis of this indicator at least, that, Japanese manufacturing organizations tend to have more formalized procedures and communications than their US counterparts.

Centralization As we noted above, observations about contrasts in decision-making styles and structures figure pivotally in most accounts of Japanese *vis-à-vis* Western management. Moreover, Japanese decision-making practices are quite often claimed to be an important force in the harmony, integration, and consensus that seem to characterize Japanese organization and industrial relations (Clark, 1979; Yoshino, 1968).

The Aston centralization scale is a widely used measure of the level in the hierarchy that is assigned authority for a set of decisions commonly made by work organizations (Pugh *et al.*, 1968). Our variant of this measure consists of 37 decision items to which top management was asked to indicate: (a) the level in the organization with the formal authority to make the decision; and (b) the level at which, in practice, the decision was usually made. Each item was scored either 1 (= direct worker), 2 (= first-line supervisor), 3 (= middle manager), 4 (= department head), 5 (= plant manager), or 6 (= company official above the plant manager). We computed the total score as the mean of these 37 items.

Our distinction between the formal authority to make the decision and responsibility in actual practice is a modification of the original Aston scale which we believe conveys important additional information. This is a particularly important distinction to preserve in a comparative study of Japanese and US organizations, for, as we have discussed, there are good reasons to suppose that the two diverge to a considerable degree.

The hypothesized combination of formal centralization with *de facto* delegation is clearly revealed by the results for the two Aston-based centralization scales. As one might expect, in both countries the average authority level at which decisions are actually made is lower than the level of formal authority (compare the means on these two measures for each country in table 7.1). But the gap between formal and actual decision-making responsibility is far greater in Japan. The means on formal authority are 4.66 in the US and 4.99 in Japan. These indicate that authority for the 37 decisions averages somewhere between department head and plant manager in the American plants. In the Japanese plants, the mean authority level is almost exactly equal to the plant manager's rank; this would seem to be strong testimony for the proposition that relatively little formal delegation characterizes the authority hierarchies of Japanese organizations. With regard to *de facto* decision-making, the means are 4.36 in the US and 3.82 in Japan. Thus, the gap between formal and informal authority in the US plants is small: about one-third of an authority level. In the Japanese plants, *de facto* responsibility averages more than one full level below the rank possessing formal authority and this is notably lower than in the US organizations.

The adjusted intercepts in table 7.6 tell the same story. With controls added for technology, size and other variables, there are still highly significant (beyond the .001 level) country differences in both centralization measures that mirror those observed in table 7.1. As our hypothesis, drawn from Yoshino (1968), specified, the Japanese organizations delegate less formal authority than the American plants, but in practice they permit greater involvement in decisions by employees lower in the hierarchy.

Another aspect of the plant's authority structure is the presence and extensiveness of small-group programs such as quality circles (QC). Our analysis in chapter 4 showed that QC participation does make a significant difference in the level of cooperation and integration in the workplace perceived by Japanese and US employees. However, we and other observers have also speculated that, while circle activities foster in employees a sense of responsibility and participation, they have little overall impact on the power structure of the firm. We address the latter hypothesis now by considering the impact of QC activity on the concentration and dispersion of formal authority as well as decision-making in practice.

Our measure is the proportion of employees surveyed in the plant who reported that they are members of quality circles. This is a deviation from our measurement of other concepts in this chapter, which derived from documentary evidence and the reports of senior management informants. Employees' questionnaire responses would seem to be a better indicator of the extensiveness of this form of shop-floor decentralization of decision-making than the mere presence or absence of a program. However, it limits our sample to those plants from which we obtained questionnaire data: 52 in the US and 45 in Japan.

We have already noted that QC activity is far more prevalent in Japanese plants. Of the 3,735 employees in our sample, 76 percent reported that they were QC members; in the US, 27 percent of (4,567) employees participated

Table 7.6 Country-specific regression models of decision-making structure[a]

	Dependent variables							
	Formal centralization		De facto centralization		Proportion in QC		Ringi	
Independent variables	US	Japan	US	Japan	US	Japan	US	Japan
Independent	−.143	−.076	.028	.083	−.049	−.033	[−.172**b]	.036
(Ln)size	−.171***	−.091	−.208***	−.258***	.013	.018*b	−.039	.036
Plant age	.003**	.002	.000	.005	−.001	.174	.0002	.0004
Union	.290***	.022	.085	.387*	[−.040]	[.065***b]	.054	[−.136*b]
Cust/small[c]	[−.020]	[.058]**	[−.053]	.051	−.005	−.001	.013	.014
	[−.069]*	[.043]*	[−.077]*	.025	−.022**b	−.001	.006	.001
Large batch/mass[c]	.049*	−.018	.038	−.014	−.0006	.000	.027	−.010
	.012	−.014	[.057]	−.018	.001	−.001	.026	−.010
Process[c]	[−.077]**	[.056]	[−.123]**	[.070]	−.022	−.005	−.004	.007
	[−.052]	[.042]	[−.137]***	[.060]	−.022	−.006	.0003	.007
Automation	.009	.261	.006	−.141	.054	.015	−.007	−.020
Workflow rigidity	[3.76]**	[1.13]	5.02***	2.05*	[.945***b]	.054	.159	.105
Automation**2	−.005	−.016	−.001	.012	−.003*	−.000	−.004	
Workflow rigidity**2	−2.94***	−1.11	[−4.36***]	[−1.98]	[−.643*]	[−.032]	−.187	
Adj. Mean	[4.59]	[5.00]	[4.27]	3.81	[−.187]d	[.719]d	[.752]	.267
N	55	51	55	51	52	46	55	51
Adj. R²	.535	.039	.405	.019	.491	.492	.123	.000

Notes: *p < .10
** p < .05
*** p < .01

[a] Entries are metric regression coefficients
[b] Two-tailed test; otherwise one-tailed test
[c] Second row is reduced form or "total" effect; automation and workflow rigidity omitted
[d] Unadjusted intercept; otherwise adjusted to the overall means of the predetermined variables
[ ] Difference in estimates is significant at the .10 level by a two-tailed test

(see table 4.1). Judging from the comments of our informants, the US figure is growing rapidly, as most of the American programs were only recently in place, and many plants without QC were contemplating a program (Thomas and Shimada, 1983).

Our final dimension of organizational decision-making structure is the use of the *ringi* system in Japan. Our measure of the prevalence of *ringi* in the Japanese plants is simply a proportion of the 37 Aston decisions which top management reported were made in the *ringi* fashion. In the US sample, we asked the substitute question of whether the same decisions were made by a group as opposed to an individual. *Ringi* is more than simply group decision-making, however, and we do not view these as directly parallel indices.

Whereas quality circles are generally seen as mechanisms for engaging the decision-making participation of production workers, the *ringi* system is chiefly a management-level participatory structure. The presence of one does not imply the existence of the other, as their correlation of .031 suggests. Do both, however, contribute to overall decentralization? The answer should depend on whether the focus is centralization in the formal authority sense vs. *de facto* responsibility. *Ringi*, most observers believe, combines low formal with high actual delegation of decision-making (Clark, 1979). As we have seen, this combination is characteristic of Japanese decision-making in general, but it should be especially evident in organizations which practice *ringi*. To what extent quality circle programs contribute to real decentralization is a question which has generated some debate (Cole, 1980; Thomas and Shimada, 1983). There is considerable evidence that managers in both countries see their purpose as that of diffusing responsibility and increasing rank-and-file commitment without producing material changes in the authority structure of the firm.

To test these hypotheses, we regressed formal and *de facto* centralization on QC activity and RINGI with (log) size included as a control using the 52 US and 46 Japanese cases for which the QC data were available.[7] The coefficient estimates (standard errors in parentheses) for the formal authority models are:

US: Formal Centraliz. $= 4.718 \quad -.061 \text{SIZE} \quad +.214 \text{RINGI} \quad +.446 \text{QC} \quad R^2 = .021$
$(.044) \quad\quad\quad (.229) \quad\quad\quad (.387)$

Japan: Formal Centraliz. $= 4.407 \quad +.005 \text{SIZE} \quad -.169 \text{RINGI} \quad +.602 \text{QC} \quad R^2 = .027$
$(.065) \quad\quad\quad (.252) \quad\quad\quad (.868)$

The formal authority equations explain only a small amount of variance in both samples, and none of the coefficients is significant. Clearly, in neither country does QC have an impact on the official structure of authority in the organization. Furthermore, we find no evidence that the *ringi* system is associated with high formal centralization (or low delegation) in Japanese companies: neither the *ringi* index nor the corresponding "group decision-making" measure in the US sample is related to the dependent variable.

The regression estimates for *de facto* responsibility paint a quite different picture:

US: *De Facto* Centraliz.	$= 5.013$	$-.170^{***}$SIZE	$-.224$RINGI	$+1.557^{***}$QC $R^2 = .286$
		$(.054$	$(.282)$	$(.476)$
Japan: *De Facto* Centraliz.	$= 4.649$	$-.192^{***}$SIZE	-1.011^{***}RINGI	$+.488$QC $R^2 = .278$
		$(.083)$	$(.321)$	(1.108)

First, we find strong evidence that *ringi* in Japanese companies is associated with dispersion of actual decision-making to lower levels in the management hierarchy. This was our prediction, and the evidence thus bears out the belief that Japanese decision-making methods encourage lower level participation. There is no evidence, on the other hand, that "group decision-making" in the US organizations has a similar impact.

Secondly, these estimates, like those for formal centralization, run contrary to the hypothesis that QC activity disperses influence over decisions to lower levels in the plant. In the Japanese sample, the effect of QC is nonsignificant, and in the US data there is a strong positive association between circle membership and centralized decision-making. This finding sharpens the suspicion that quality circle programs are in large measure carefully controlled devices orchestrated by management to create the perception, but not necessarily the reality, of worker involvement and participation.[8] They would indeed seem to be effective in instilling in workers at least a perception of participation, as our individual-level analyses in chapter 4 showed that in both countries quality circle membership enhances the employee's organizational commitment.

A possible explanation for the findings regarding QC is that centralization, as measured by our Aston-type scales, reflects the delegation of authority and responsibility to managers rather than workers. Only the lowest level of the 6-point scale on which each of the 37 decisions is scored has to do with input by workers; the other five codes tap management control, from first-line supervisor on up. Decision-making, then, may be highly decentralized among managers and still allow for meager participation by workers. It is likely that quality circle programs operate to reduce the power and authority of first- and second-line supervisors, who traditionally make the shop-floor workflow decisions that become the province of circles.

Welfare services Our measure of employee services is an unweighted sum of nine binary items measuring the presence or absence of a set of training, service, recreational, ceremonial, and communications activities in the firm. These include: company support for enrollment in high school or college courses; in-house training programs; a company-sponsored employee newspaper; ceremonies for retirement or the launching of new products; company-sponsored sports, recreational, and social activities; a formal orientation program for new employees; an employee handbook; regular peptalks or meetings with all employees; and a program of regular calisthenics for employees. More of these programs are likely to exist in the Japanese firms, specifically: in-house training (by a small margin), formal ceremonies (present in all), sports and recreational activities, formal orientation programs for new employees, peptalks or gatherings at which management discusses goals and encourages striving to achieve them, and morning exercise sessions, which are nonexistent in the US plants. On the other hand, the American firms are more likely to encourage and support enrollment in high school and college coursework (by a large margin), and (by a small one) to provide employees with a company handbook. There is essentially no difference between the countries in the propensity of firms to publish a company newspaper. The indices produced by summing these items have a Cronbach's alpha reliability of .60 in the Japanese sample and .62 in the US sample. The difference in the means of this index reveals that the bundle of employee welfare services is larger in Japanese plants.

The impact of technology

Thus far we have not discussed the effects of technology, size, and the other "context" variables in our models. Yet the question of whether task-related contingencies shape structure through similar causal mechanisms in the US and Japan is a critical one for comparative organizational theory. We have good reason to suspect that the forces molding plant organization in Japan, a late-developer with a distinctive set of institutions and strong cultural traditions, might differ substantially from those impinging on organizational design decisions in the US.

Given the diversity of methods, samples, and (perhaps consequently) findings of past research on the technology-structure relationship, a baseline set of expectations is hard to come by. We first consider the regression equations in table 7.4 in which there is no significant evidence of country differences in slopes. Consistent with the findings of Woodward (1965) and the Aston researchers (Pugh *et al.*, 1969; Hickson, Pugh, and Pheysey, 1969), we find a small positive effect of workflow rigidity on functional specialization. Woodward (1965:51) reported that vertical differentiation rose linearly with technological advance, although Blauner (1964:149) argued that tall, finely graded hierarchies distinguished continuous process industry from the relatively flat pyramids of mass production factories. The Woodward technology measures are unrelated with the number of ranks, but the workflow rigidity index does reveal a significant nonlinear relation. Setting the partial derivative of the number of ranks with respect to workflow rigidity to zero, we find that the minimum of the function occurs at a workflow rigidity value of .450, approximately midway between the US and Japanese means on this scale (see table 7.1).[9] This pattern seems to conform to Blauner's hypothesis that, net of size and other factors, mass production plants have relatively flat hierarchies.

Woodward found chief executives' spans of control increasing linearly with technological advance, and we, too, find a positive linear effect of workflow rigidity. This appears to capture part of the total negative influence of unit small-batch processing, as that coefficient is attenuated when workflow rigidity and automation are added to the model.

A quite consistent finding of past research is that first-line supervisors' spans of control are narrower at the extremes of the technology continuum than in the center (Blau *et al.*, 1976; Child, 1984; Child and Mansfield, 1972:381; Woodward, 1965:60). This is assumed to reflect the higher skill levels of custom/small batch and continuous process workers, the organization of work in teams, and the lower level of machine control of work behavior (Child, 1984; Galbraith, 1977; Woodward, 1965). We, too, find that supervisors' spans are negatively associated with custom/small batch and continuous processing (see table 7.4). This pattern is consistent with the earlier finding of taller hierarchies at the extremes of the technology continuum.

Automation reduces the proportions of both managers and direct production workers in the plant. This suggests the common observation that percentages of non-line personnel (administrative, staff, and technical workers) are high in automated, process industry. The only such component we measured directly is the clerical ratio. This is unrelated to the Woodward process measure, but is strongly and nonlinearly linked to automation, the function bottoming at an automation value (6.33) roughly half a standard deviation below both sample means. Thus, over most of the range of the automation variable, its association with the clerical ratio is strongly positive.

Contrary to Woodward's findings, we observe formalization to be low in large batch/mass production. This seems to be mainly in contrast with process production, where we expect, and find, formalization to be high.

Technology theorists such as Blauner and Woodward have argued that firms with advanced technology have a propensity to invest in employee welfare services and thereby achieve high levels of workforce integration and commitment (Gallie, 1978:13). Such companies can afford to be generous because of the capital intensity of continuous-process industry, which results in a proportionately small percentage of labor costs. Moreover, the team spirit and wide-ranging responsibility expected of workers in these industrial settings demand extraordinary investments in training, social and recreational programs, and the other services (Blauner, 1964).

Our data provide mixed evidence for this hypothesis. Table 7.4 shows the direction of the associations between the Woodward classification and the services index to roughly support it, although, with one exception, these effects are not statistically significant: services rise with use of continuous process production methods, fall with large-batch/mass production, and are unrelated to the unit/small-batch indicator. The workflow rigidity coefficients likewise suggest an upwardly sloping curve relating plant services to production technology but, again, these are not significant. There is, on the other hand, a highly significant curvilinear relation between services and the automation index, but it appears to take a form *contrary* to the technology theorists' prediction that plant expenditures on welfare services accelerate toward the high end of the automation continuum; i.e. in the continuous process range. Our data show the level of services rising with automation up to a point which is roughly one standard deviation above the automation mean, then falling off. We are hard pressed to find an explanation for this pattern of investments in services declining at the very peak of the automation distribution. Recall, however, the evidence in table 7.2 that automation levels were highest in the printing industry. It may be that the decline in service investments that we find in very highly automated establishments reflects practices more or less peculiar to the printing industry in our sample and may not have a more general significance.

Technology: country-specific effects

Now we consider the effects of technology on subunit differentiation and centralization of decision-making, the two sets of structural variables whose antecedents appear to differ between the Japanese and US samples. In the models predicting proliferation of departments and sections (table 7.5), we find that large-batch/mass production technology has a positive effect in Japan but a nonsignificant and negative one in the US. We also find a nonlinear relation between workflow rigidity and departmental differentiation which is virtually identical in the two countries, though it fails to reach significance in Japan. In both samples, the best-fitting function is an inverted U, peaking at roughly half a standard deviation above the workflow rigidity means (US = .680, Japan = .496). This pattern is consistent with that shown by the Woodward measures in Japan: high departmental differentiation in the middle of the technology range. Overall, there is little evidence here of important contrasts between the Japanese and US samples in the processes determining the proliferation of departments.

In the US equation for number of sections, the workflow rigidity effect is positive, highly significant, and linear. Though slightly different in functional form, this pattern generally conforms to Blau *et al.'s* (1976) finding of a higher mean for process industry than in the unit and mass production types. In the Japanese sample, on the other hand, our measures of technology are generally unrelated to number of sections. This is the pattern we predicted at the outset: strong effects of technology on organizational structures in the US; weak or absent relationships in Japan.

By far the firmest evidence that operations technology plays a greater role in determining organization structures in the US than in Japan is found in table 7.6, where the dimensions of decision-making structure are the dependent variables. Considering just the Woodward technology indicators,

214 Culture, control, and commitment

we find striking support in the US data for her claim (Woodward, 1965:64) that: "a high degree of delegation both of authority and responsibilities for decision-making ... was characteristic of firms at the extremes." In the US, both scales – formal authority and *de facto* responsibility – are negatively influenced by custom/small-batch and continuous process and positive functions of large-batch/mass production. Yet this pattern is wholly absent in the Japanese sample, and there is even some indication of the opposite: more centralization in unit and process industries. This, we suspect, is the kind of finding that Hickson *et al.* (1979) might characterize as a "terrifying" societal effect: a strong, theoretically meaningful pattern in Western data coupled with wholly contrary evidence from an equally modern and industrial but Asian society (Brossard and Maurice, 1976).

What forestalls speculation on the need to start from scratch in building contingency theories of structure that fit the Japanese case is that the relation of workflow rigidity to centralization takes the same form in both countries, although it is much weaker in Japan. That form, moreover, is the inverted-U predicted by Woodward and Blauner and observed in the Woodward measures in our US model. The highest points in the functions relating the centralization measures to workflow rigidity in both samples are just above the means of workflow rigidity (for formal centralization, US: .64; Japan: .51; for *de facto*, US: .58, Japan: .52).

We thus have considerable support for the hypothesis that the impact of technology on organizational structure is larger among US organizations and in greater conformity with mainstream contingency theory. The hint of evidence from the Woodward measures that centralization may follow a pattern *opposite* to the US one (and that obtained in Woodward's original British survey) is intriguing and has been reported in research on other samples of Japanese manufacturing organizations (Marsh and Mannari, 1981:46). A speculative explanation for the only significant such effect in Japan – that of unit/small batch on formal centralization – is that this technology indexes a plant's location in the periphery of the dual economy, where personal control by owner/entrepreneurs is high (Averitt, 1968; Baron and Bielby, 1984; Edwards, 1979). It might be that such an effect is found only in Japan because its economy is more dualistic than that of the US, and, owing to Japan's late industrialization and the occupation-imposed reforms, more enterprises remain under founding families' direct control (Clark, 1979).

Further support for the conclusion that technology is not the critical contingency in Japan that it appears to be in the United States is conveyed by the regression results for QC. Our earlier analysis showed that quality circle activity in the US – a putative form of worker participation in management – was associated, not with overall delegation of authority and responsibility, but instead with centralization. That conclusion is underscored by the evidence in table 7.6 that QC activity in American plants is related to technology in a fashion similar to that displayed by centralization: low in unit and process operations; low at the extremes of workflow rigidity but high in the region surrounding the mean. As with centralization, similar effects of workflow rigidity can be observed in the Japanese data, but they are much weaker.

We also note that technology, as we have measured it, seems to be unrelated either to the application of *ringi* to decisions in Japanese companies or to the corresponding index of group decision-making in the US. Nevertheless, the correlations of the *ringi* scale in the Japanese sample with the more detailed Woodward measures are suggestive: custom (.288); small batch ($-.033$); large batch ($-.089$); mass production ($-.151$); and continuous process (.034). This pattern of correlations, while not strong, does conform to the Woodward/Blauner U-curve of greater participation in decision-making at the extremes than in the middle of the technology continuum.

Is there any support in our data for the highly speculative yet intriguing hypothesis of similarities between Japanese organization and the modes of organizing associated with advanced production technologies? While not wishing to push that idea too far, a case for this might be built with the present evidence. Our Japanese plants have taller hierarchies, as do organizations at the high end of the workflow rigidity scale. The Japanese plants have broader chief executive spans of control, and we find broader CEO spans where technologies are more automated and uniform. Japanese plants have higher clerical ratios, and we find strong evidence that clerical ratios are high in highly automated plants. Though the evidence is weak, the impression from our data that Japanese plants have fewer departments but more sections is also consistent with the general configuration of advanced technology plants: fewer departments at the highest levels of workflow rigidity, but (in the US only) more sections. Finally, the *de facto* (but not the formal) decentralization of Japanese plants is what we would expect – and find – in plants at the high end of the Woodward and workflow rigidity scales. This is spotty and circumstantial evidence to be sure, but it is consistent with the tantalizing proposition that Japanese organization is an emergent form which represents the future, not merely a carryover from the Japanese feudal past, and which, as Dore, Ouchi, and others have argued, can be seen with growing regularity in the structures and management styles of modern organizations in the West.

Other effects

The last set of results we review here concerns the influences of plant size, status, age, and unionization. Size is an important control in any study of structure and also serves as a proxy indicator for the sectoral position of a plant in the dual economy. The relationships between structure and size closely parallel the findings of other studies and are indeed consistent with the dual economy model: structural differentiation, formalization, decentralization and QC activity, plus a high level of employee services generally characterize large plants.

Whether the organization studied is an independent company or a branch plant has several interesting effects which make intuitive sense but constitute mixed support for the presumption that this variable indexes location in the economic core. Branch plants, at least in Japan, have fewer departments, probably because more functions are performed at higher corporate levels. They are also more formalized, perhaps because of the corporatist/dual economy mechanism we have discussed, but perhaps more simply because personal control gives way to bureaucracy as units of a company become geographically dispersed. Also consistent with the dual economy perspective is the finding that branch plants in the US at least are more likely to practice group decision-making, the intuitive reason, we suspect, being that in principal units owner/entrepreneurs are more likely to retain control. Finally, the very strong tendency for independent plants to provide fewer employee services is, of course, in line with dual economy/welfare corporatist predictions.

Older organizations are, as we predicted, less formalized, and, in the US only, more differentiated into sections. The only significant effect of age on decision-making structure is an unexpected positive association with formal centralization in the US sample.

Unionized plants are more formalized, no doubt because of union work rules and job classifications. In the US, they have more departments (e.g. industrial relations) but fewer sections. There is also evidence in both countries that unions encourage centralization, suggesting that adversarial industrial relations lead managements to retrench and concentrate control at higher levels:[10] formal centralization is higher in US union plants; *de facto* centralization is higher in unionized plants in Japan, and *ringi* is less likely to be practiced. On the other hand, QC is more prevalent in unionized Japanese plants. Thus, unionization in Japan appears to reduce the extent of participatory decision-making at the management level (*ringi*), but increases it at the shop-floor level. In the US, however, QC is less prevalent in US union shops. This is no surprise, given the skepticism with which American unions have generally greeted management-sponsored work reforms. Moreover, it is in line with our earlier findings that American QC is associated with centralized management decision-making.

Summary

This chapter has evaluated a number of hypotheses pertaining to the links between the "context" of a manufacturing organization (country and industry location, market organization, technology, size, unionization, age, independent status) and its internal structure. We have found at least partial support for several key speculations: Japanese organizational structures differ in certain particulars from US designs; the *processes* whereby task contingencies such as technology condition some organizational variables also differ; *and* Japanese organization may indeed be the wave of the future, if by that we mean it parallels designs associated with automated, process production and other enterprise forms at the frontiers of organization (Dore, 1973). On the first point, our survey evidence generally corroborates the impressions of other research: compared with American structures, Japanese manufacturing organizations have taller hierarchies, less functional specialization, less formal delegation of authority but more *de facto* participation in decisions at lower levels in the management hierarchy. These structures are consistent with the internal labor market processes (lifetime employment, seniority-based promotion) which characterize Japanese companies and the general emphasis on groups over individuals as the fundamental units of organization.

As for societal effects on the processes whereby task contingencies steer the choice of organizing modes, our key hypothesis was that operations technology was unlikely to have the impact on Japanese organization that it has on US structures. In fact, with respect to most structural variables, we did not find strong evidence that the influences of technology, size, and other variables differed between Japan and the US. To that extent, organizational scholars concerned for the generality of mainstream theory can rest assured. However, as for differentiation of subunits and the determination of authority and decision-making structures, our data supported the hypothesis that technology is a weaker explanatory variable in Japan. Yet, with some notable exceptions (e.g. the associations of the Woodward measures with centralization), the *form* of the technology effects proved broadly similar in the US and Japanese data.

In certain respects, our finding that production technology is not the determinant of structure in Japanese organization that it appears to be in the US is consistent with other general attempts to understand the contrasts between Japanese and US organizing styles and the historical paths that shaped them. Piore and Sabel (1984) have recently argued that the crisis in US manufacturing stems from industry in this country having grown too wedded to rigid production technologies, while other countries – Japan in particular – have developed systems of flexible specialization which tie product design, marketing strategy, and organizational form more loosely to the dictates of technology. A historical reason for this tendency may be the greater legacy in American job and organizational designs of the Scientific Management movement which pressed for maximal fit between the social organization of the factory and the rhythms and flows of its technical operations (Cole, 1979). Another may be the efforts by US unions to control work organization and labor allocation by making job boundaries conform to narrow technical tasks. These speculations go considerably beyond our evidence to be sure, but the data do unambiguously indicate that the technological imperative looms relatively large in the determination of American manufacturing organization, whereas other imperatives – perhaps, as some have argued, in order to provide employment, careers, and welfare and thus maintain legitimacy in a tight institutional environment – are more salient in Japan (Brossard and Maurice, 1976; Thurow, 1985).

This reasoning might also go some distance toward explaining our tentative finding that Japanese factory organization resembles the structuring of advanced technology plants. Recall Joan Woodward's (1965) view that in highly automated process industry, technology no longer determines factory social organization, for workers are separated from direct production tasks. Thus, the design of the organization becomes detached to some degree from the technology process and more attuned to the needs of the human workforce. The parallel between the structures of advanced production plants and Japanese organization is thus explained by the substitution in both cases of a "social" for a "technological" imperative. This in no way implies that production efficiency considerations exert a weak hold on the design of the Japanese workplace. The opposite is patently true. But there may be circumstances under which production efficiency and quality are better served by a flexible decoupling of the social organization of the factory from the organization of its technical workflow. We think it consistent with the drift of many accounts of Japanese work structures to suggest that some decoupling of this sort may indeed typify the organization of the Japanese factory.

8 Work organization and workforce commitment: a multi-level analysis

Introduction

Our plant-level analysis in the last chapter presented an overall picture of the structure of Japanese organizations which was, in general, consistent with the corporatist ideal type. Tall hierarchies, high formalization, concentration of formal authority coupled with decentralization of *de facto* decision-making, structures such as *ringi* and QC which invite participation and diffuse responsibility, and an extensive bundle of company-sponsored welfare services and social activities were more characteristic of Japanese than US factories. All, moreover, as we have argued, are cast within the corporatist paradigm as structures which serve to evoke employee commitment. Another such structure is the Japanese enterprise union which, unlike US industrial and craft unions, intimately links the fate of workers to the fortunes of the individual firm (Hanami, 1979).

Yet it is one thing to observe that Japanese companies display the organizational form which Dore called welfare corporatist and other theorists agree is commitment-maximizing, and quite another to demonstrate that the elements of that model have the anticipated effects on employees' work attitudes and behaviors. The latter is our objective here: to evaluate the influence of plant-level variables on workers' commitment to the company and satisfaction with the job.[1] In line with the model laid out in chapter 1 and the discussion of chapters 6 and 7, we consider two classes of organizational variables: (1) aspects of the plant's context or task environment, including size, age, unionization, and technology; and (2) the structural variables treated in the last chapter and in most organizational theory as consequent to these. We first focus on the reactions that workplace contextual variables elicit in employees, inquiring, in particular, as to the degree to which such influences are direct or mediated by our measures of management practice and organizational structure. We then interpret the mechanisms – the employee-level task characteristics, social bonds, and job rewards – through which context and structure jointly mold employee reactions.

Effects of plant context on commitment and satisfaction

We first direct our attention to the organizational context variables of size, corporate status, technology, and unionization. In the tradition of a long and broad stream of organizational research, our analysis in the last chapter demonstrated that these factors have significant influences on the organizational structures and employment systems of manufacturing plants. Such contextual factors should indirectly influence commitment and morale, since we have reason to believe that plant organization has a strong impact on employees' work attitudes and behaviors. We would not, however, expect the effects of "context" to be wholly mediated by organizational structures, for several reasons. First, we may have failed to identify or measure adequately all the patterns of organization that are shaped by variables such as size and technology, and that in turn create the work environment to which employees' respond. Secondly, some such "context" variables are apt to be experienced directly by employees, not indirectly through the organizational arrangements they engender. For example, the nature of the production technology and the sheer number of people working in the same plant undoubtedly have some immediate impact on how individuals experience the workplace.

Plant size

A persistent theme in theory and research on work alienation pertains to the role of large work organizations. Marx saw the concentration of labor in large factories as a critical step in the development of working-class consciousness and political organization, for it would expose the reality of common exploitation and facilitate the communication and cooperation on which organized class struggle depends. Subsequent theorists saw the mass factory creating the conditions for extreme collective behavior. In such an environment, according to Kerr and Siegel (1954), workers become an "isolated mass": cut off from contacts with owners and top management, they reinforce each others' alienation and give vent to frustration in outbursts of militancy (Lincoln, 1978; Shorter and Tilly, 1974). Blauner (1964) likewise saw the large size of the mass-production factory as a key reason why it constitutes an alienating work environment: when the individual worker feels like a tiny cog in a vast machine, s/he experiences meaninglessness, powerlessness, and isolation. A worker in a similar structural position performing similar tasks in a small establishment, on the other hand, rightly senses that his or her personal contribution has a greater impact on the total operation of the organization. Moreover, the increased likelihood of developing personal ties with a high proportion of one's coworkers reduces the anonymity of the job, and fosters good feeling toward coworkers and managers. A number of studies provide some documentation for the hypothesis that worker alienation and detachment increase with establishment size (Indik, 1963; Ingham, 1970).

On the other hand, large firms and plants are likely to provide higher wages, better benefits and services, more training and promotion opportunities, and other inducements which small organizations lack the resources to supply. Jacoby (1985) has documented the leadership role historically played by large US firms in installing personnel departments, job ladders, grievance procedures, and employee welfare systems. The large company also confers more status on its workforce through its visibility in the public eye and reputation in the community. These considerations are particularly apropos to Japan, where job security and quality appear to vary markedly between a large firm core sector and a small firm periphery, and employment in the largest corporations is a source of much prestige. As Vogel (1963:36) puts it: "the fact that the large organizations offer more benefits than smaller enterprises helps explain the enthusiasm which the salary man feels toward his organization and which he manifests by wearing a company badge, carrying a company brief case, and using a company emblem as a tie clasp."

Recent theories of modern workplace organization which identify commitment as a central mechanism of labor control likewise view the core firms in the dual economy as the first to implement a corporatist (or bureaucratic control) strategy and to dispense with older forms that are less effective in aligning worker behavior with management interests. In the Marxist framework of Edwards (1979) and Gordon *et al.* (1982), the theory of bureaucratic control as the most sophisticated and effective management system for dissolving worker attachments to class and union while substituting commitment to the firm is closely wedded to the notion of a dual economy. The prerequisites for launching a corporatist control strategy – the capacity to manipulate and therefore stabilize demand; the resources necessary to absorb the costs of welfare services, employment security, and professionalized personnel management – are available to large, well-capitalized firms in concentrated industries, but not to the small, dependent concerns that populate the competitive periphery. For this reason, Edwards (1979) argues that older forms of labor control – the paternalism of the owner–entrepreneur, the close scrutiny and arbitrary domination of a first-line supervisor – are still commonplace among periphery firms.

The evidence in table 8.1 is indeed consistent with the hypothesis that commitment and satisfaction are higher in larger establishments.[2] In the US sample, the positive effects of size on commitment and satisfaction become non-significant when the organization variables are controlled. This pattern suggests that large plants are organized in ways (i.e. corporatist) that elicit a degree of loyalty from workers that small establishments cannot. The size effects in the Japanese sample likewise decline across the three commitment equations, though not as much. We speculate that this larger direct component of the influence of size captures the greater status value to the Japanese of employment in a large company. However, the positive relationships between size and satisfaction in Japan are wholly accounted for by the intervening variables.

Table 8.1 Standardized regressions of organizational commitment and job satisfaction on organization variables[a]

Independent variables	Commitment (1) US	Commitment (1) Japan	Commitment (2) US	Commitment (2) Japan	Commitment (3) US	Commitment (3) Japan	Satisfaction (1) US	Satisfaction (1) Japan	Satisfaction (2) US	Satisfaction (2) Japan	Satisfaction (3) US	Satisfaction (3) Japan
Plant context												
(Ln) size	.091**	.101**	.046	.072*	−.017	.046+	.061*	.058*	.037	.033	−.023	.013
Union	(−.167**)	−.025	(−.166**)	−.043+	[−.075**]	−.035	(−.140**)	.005	(−.150**)	−.002	[−.052*]	.002
Independent	−.082**	−.109**	−.053*	−.073*	−.060+	−.048*	−.053**	−.033	−.030	−.002	−.046+	.021
Cust/small B	−.052*	−.049*	[−.022]	−.061**	−.024	−.038+	−.023	−.050*	(−.007)	(−.070**)	−.020	[−.053*]
Large B/Mass	.045+	.061**	.056*	.069**	[.033]	.048**	[.017]	.056**	[.036]	.076**	[.014]	.061**
Process	(.020)	.081**	.022	.064**	.055**	.080**	.039+	.060**	.042*	.036	.079**	.058**
Organization												
First-line span			.098**	.016	.080**	.023			.066**	−.012	.054**	.000
No ranks			−.048+	−.073**	−.009	−.058*			−.049+	−.049*	−.011	−.025
No subunits[b]			−.055**	−.031	−.026	−.008			[−.075**]	−.041	−.026	−.012
QC			.152**	.075**	.082**	.026			.114**	.044+	.039*	−.009
Ringi			−.011	.068**	−.009	.079**			−.034	.012	−.028	.029
Formal centralization			.063*	.054+	.024	−.008			.086**	.105**	.044*	.035
De facto centralization			−.072**	.015	−.037+	.027			−.077**	−.042	−.039+	−.023
Formalization			−.030	.019	−.004	−.008			.011	.068**	.028	.037
Welfare services			.096**	.105**	.080**	.115**			.066**	.041	.055*	.067*
Adj. Mean	2.148	2.031	2.179	2.075	2.259	2.314	1.550	.986	1.507	.985	1.596	1.080
Adj. R²	.164	.183	.177	.205	.395	.390	.124	.131	.124	.145	.425	.388

Notes: [a] Equations 1 and 2 control for employee background and position variables; equation 3 in addition controls for task, social bond, and job reward variables
[b] Due to a multicollinearity problem, these estimates were obtained from a model which excluded (ln) size
+ p < .05
* p < .01
** p < .001
[ ] Difference between estimates is significant at the .05 level
( ) Difference between estimates is significant at the .01 level

Independent company vs. branch plant

Like the presumption that alienating work environments are found in large establishments, it has often been claimed that the absentee-ownership and decoupling of control associated with multiplant corporations contribute to labor disaffection and conflict-ridden industrial relations (Lincoln, 1978). Where owners and top management are not physically present at the site but occupy an office in another community or even region, workers feel little kinship with their bosses or identification with the company. The employment relationship under such conditions becomes a kind of colonial oppression, further contributing, in Kerr and Siegel's (1954) terms, to the workforce taking on the qualities of an isolated mass.

As with plant size, dual economy theory makes an opposite prediction. The local, one-site, independent firm sits on the margins of an economy dominated by large, diversified, national corporations. It is the latter which command the resources which trickle down to workers in the form of high wages and benefits, greater job security, and higher status in the surrounding community. The importance of employment in a large core firm for one's general social standing in Japanese society is often stressed by students of Japanese industry, but its implications for the American social stratification system should not be discounted. We find in table 8.1 that commitment in both countries – and satisfaction in the US – is greater in multi-site concerns. This pattern runs sharply counter to theories portraying large corporations and absentee-ownership as fertile settings for labor alienation and unrest (e.g. Kerr and Siegel, 1954). Rather, it is squarely consistent with the dualist/corporatist claim that the most effective systems of labor control – those focused on commitment and loyalty as the keys to compliance – are associated with center firm status in the dual economy.

Technology

As we indicated in earlier chapters, production technology figures centrally in a number of theories anticipating the rise of a new workplace community. We first consider the Woodward measures of the extent to which the factory's operations use unit/small-batch, large-batch/mass production, and continuous process technologies. The hypothesis from Woodward, Blauner, and others is that work alienation should be low in unit/small-batch plants and continuous process, high in mass production, and that these tendencies should be mediated by the organizational structures and employment systems of the plant (Gallie, 1978). Again, the dual economy perspective offers an opposing prediction: core firms – characterized by large-batch/mass and process production – are more likely to have in place the organizational arrangements distinctive of corporatist control. Therefore, commitment to the company should be higher among firms producing large volumes of standardized goods by means of mechanized technologies, and lower in the presence of job-shop technologies.

Once again our data provide substantial support for the dual economy/corporatist control perspective as against work alienation theory: instead of the "inverted U" relation between work attitudes and technology predicted by the technological imperative theories, we find effects in table 8.1 of *both* mass production and continuous-process technology which vary in magnitude but are consistently positive. In each country unit/small-batch production is associated with lower employee commitment and satisfaction.

Thus, three different pieces of evidence have favored a dual economy, corporatist explanation of the determinants of industrial workers' attitudes in contrast with the predictions of traditional work alienation theory: organizational commitment and job satisfaction are higher in large, core plants operated by multisite corporations utilizing large-batch, mass production, and process technologies than in small, independent periphery companies using craft technologies to produce small batches to customers' orders.[3]

It is sometimes asserted that the extent of dualism in the Japanese economy is greater than in the US (Broadbridge, 1966; Caves and Uekusa, 1976). Large, core firms occupy highly favorable capital market positions in the sense of having easy access to low-cost financing from Japan's major "city" banks (Wallich and Wallich, 1976). The privileged structural locations of core firms are also reflected in their subcontracting relationships with small, dependent suppliers, wherein the latter are required to take the parent's redundant workers along with high-risk and low-skill production responsibilities (Koike, 1984). Moreover, the benefits of permanent employment, welfare services, and *nenko* are often claimed to be confined to a narrow stratum of regular employees in large firms. Finally, sociological and anthropological accounts of Japanese community life frequently underscore the considerable status value conferred on one's family by employment with a major Japanese firm (Vogel, 1963). On the other hand, there is little clear evidence that labor market outcomes and processes diverge sharply between large and small Japanese firms. Koike (1984) notes that wage differences by firm size are no greater in Japan than in European countries, a pattern apparent in our own analyses as well (Kalleberg and Lincoln, 1988). In addition, Cole (1979) reports no difference between his Yokohama and Detroit samples in the association of inter- and intra-firm job changing with size of firm.

The evidence in our data of greater dualism in the Japanese economy – as indexed by the larger associations of size, corporate status, and technology with organizational commitment and job satisfaction – is small but fairly consistent (table 8.1). Though exceptions exist, these coefficients provide some support for the view that the differentiation of a large, multisite corporate sector from a small, local firm sector has proceeded further in Japan than in the United States. Moreover, these effects also tend to be mediated to a lesser degree in the Japanese sample by the intervening organization and job variables added in equations 2 and 3 (see below), which we think reflects the greater prestige value which the Japanese attach to employment in the large firm sector. US employees, it would appear, are more committed to core firms primarily because of the better jobs, benefits, and management practices present in such firms.

Indirect effects of size, corporate status, and technology

To what extent are the influences of size, branch plant status, and production technology mediated by the organizational structures and job characteristics of plants and employees? We find in table 8.1 a clear tendency for the effects of size and independent firm status to decline monotonically in both countries from the first column (no controls for organization and job characteristics) to the second (organization added) to the third (organization and job variables added). This pattern indicates that size and unit status give rise to organizational structures and job properties which, in turn, engender commitment and satisfaction. And the organizational indicators in our models, along with size and status, lead to job properties which also raise commitment. This pattern is not evident in a consistent way in the effects of the Woodward/Blauner technology measures. Only the influence of unit/ small-batch production in the US shows strong evidence of being mediated by the organizational and job variables. Other technology effects display little consistent change as the intervening variables are added, and in one case – process technology in the US – the coefficients increase across the three equations. These results, unlike those of size and branch status, suggest that the technology indicators are relating to the organization and job attributes in a more complex fashion than a conception of the latter as mediating variables would suggest.

Indeed, closer scrutiny of our data indicates that the important employee-level job attributes of complexity, autonomy, and intrinsic rewards do not vary with production technology in a way that supports the mediating hypothesis. Although many job characteristics have strong positive effects on commitment and satisfaction (see table 4.5), they depend on technology in a manner that is highly supportive of the Blauner/Woodward technological imperative theory of work alienation and integration. Though there are exceptions, there is a tendency for respondents' levels of job complexity and autonomy (table 8.2) and intrinsic rewards (table 8.4) to increase with unit/ small-batch production, and decrease with large-batch/mass and continuous process operations. This suggests that the job-shop may indeed be less alienating – in the sense that jobs are less routine, require more training and skill, and give workers more control – than more standardized, mechanized and high-volume production systems.

If job and organizational differences cannot explain the tendency for

Table 8.2 Standardized regressions of task characteristics on organizational variables[a]

Independent variable	Job Complexity		Teamwork		Supervisor contact		Supervisor control		Autonomy	
	US	Japan	US	Japan	US	Japan	US	Japan	US	Japan
Plant context										
(Ln) size	(.014)	−.064[+]	[−.046]	.028	(−.050)	.033)	[−.048]	−.080[*]	.015	.013
Union	(−.101**)	.010	.008	−.004	[.066*]	.026]	[.048+]	−.019	(−.066*)	.074**)
Independent	(.115**)	.016)	(.016)	−.061[*]	.006	.026	.002	−.045[+]	.002	.028
Cust/small	.080**	.081**	−.017	.061[*]	.011	.001	−.020	.099**)	−.034	−.004
Large B/mass	.002	−.084**)	[.048+]	−.021]	−.031	.010	.018	.044*	−.052[+]	−.029
Process	−.030	.002	.010	.019	.043[+]	.054*	.018	.087**)	−.018	−.069**]
Organization										
First-line span	[.027]	−.034	−.009	.009	.031	.035	(.004)	.086**)	(.023)	−.059*)
No ranks	−.049*	−.036[+]	.024	.012	.014	.000	.041[+]	.037[+]	−.033	.011
No subunits	[−.100**]	−.046[+]	.021	−.010	(.078**)	−.024)	(.054*)	−.022	[−.059**]	.016]
Ringi	[−.023]	−.094**]	(.068**)	.009)	.007	.017	[−.048+]	−.001	[−.043+]	.010
Formal central	.075**	.024	[−.022]	−.050]	[−.046+]	.016]	[−.072**]	−.081**]	.012	.004
De facto central	−.011	−.075[*]	[.020]	.066[+]]	[.027]	−.040]	.041	.022	−.020	.040
Formalization	[−.045+]	.011	[−.072**]	−.013]	.008	−.003	[.035]	−.106**]	−.047[+]	−.014
Welfare services	(.101**)	.012)	.045[+]	.010	.030	.037	(.033)	.115**)	.005	−.025
Mean	[3.297]	3.079	(3.216)	3.801	(2.125)	3.204)	1.069	1.075	[3.591]	3.236]
Adj. Mean	(3.386)	2.835)	[3.231]	3.792]	(2.162)	3.098)	1.060	1.089	[3.643]	3.243]
Adj. R²	.221	.211	.120	.050	.023	.042	.136	.182	.150	.085

Notes: [a] Equations control for employee background and position variables

+ p < .05
* p < .01
** p < .001

[ ] Difference in slopes is significant at the .05 level
( ) Difference in slopes is significant at the .01 level

Table 8.3 Standardized regressions of social bond measures on organization variables[a]

| | Dependent variable | | | | | | | |
| | Socializing | | Friends | | Quality vertical ties | | Quality coworker ties | |
Independent variable	US	Japan	US	Japan	US	Japan	US	Japan
Plant context								
(Ln) size	(−.146**)	.026)	.107**	.099**	.070+	.068+	(.168**	.059+)
Union	−.019	.011	.038	.027	(−.142**)	−.035	[−.061*	−.029
Independent	[.016	−.058*]	−.038	.047+	(−.008	−.078**)	.000	−.011
Cust/small	.034	−.016	−.011	−.051+	(.034	−.053*)	[−.017	−.060*]
Large B/mass	[.086**	.034]	.003	.051*	.065*	.058**	(−.001	.055*)
Process	[.004	−.048+]	−.061**	−.042+	[−.063**	−.0100]	[−.036+	−.010]
Organization								
First-line span	.032	.003	.020	.003	.039+	.040	−.075**	−.050+
No ranks	−.009	−.016	.039	.024	−.048+	−.059*	−.022	−.000
No subunits	−.028	.013	−.054*	.035	[−.058**	−.024]	(−.082**	−.018)
Ringi	[−.004	−.044+]	.026	.040	[.045+	−.019]	.041	−.001
Formal central	.051+	.037	(−.063*	.042	.090**	.133**	(−.066*	.061+)
De facto central	−.033	−.016	.026	−.007	−.053	−.038	.010	−.002
Formalization	.021	.020	(−.113**	.041)	(−.048+	.041)	(−.071*	.070*)
Welfare services	(.056*)	−.010)	.015	.043	−.047+	−.026	[−.015	−.066+]
Mean	(.409)	1.604)	.923)	2.033)	2.483	2.612	[3.950	3.540
Adj. Mean	(.471)	1.525)	.975)	1.866)	[2.574	2.373]	[3.998	3.403]
Adj. R²	.127	.027	.079	.108	.077	.085	.034	.023

Notes: [a] Equations control for employee background and position variables

+ p < .05
* p < .01
** p < .001
[ ] Difference in estimates is significant at the .05 level
( ) Difference in estimates is significant at the .01 level

Table 8.4 *Standardized regressions of intrinsic rewards and promotion expectations on organization variables*[a]

	Dependent variable			
	Intrinsic rewards		Promotion expectations	
Independent variable	US	Japan	US	Japan
Plant context				
(Ln) size	−.023	.016	[.069+	−.001]
Union	(−.112**	−.002)	(−.151**	.013)
Independent	.037	−.006	−.060*	−.039+
Cust/small	[.038	−.031)	−.020	−.037
Large B/mass	[.044	−.022]	[−.006	.039+]
Process	[−.027	−.051*]	−.009	−.030
Organization				
First-line span	[.033	−.036]	(.098**	−.024)
No ranks	−.033	−.006	−.018	−.019
No subunits	(−.020	−.080**)	.016	−.016
Ringi	[−.046+	−.007]	−.030	−.029
Formal central	.080**	.091**	[.042+	.092**]
De facto central	[−.071**	−.029]	[−.049+	.006]
Formalization	−.036	.027	(−.056*	.062*)
Welfare	[.042+	−.013]	.009	.040
Mean	3.517	3.486	.264	.256
Adj. Mean	3.612	3.440	(.307	.222)
Adj. R²	.159	.113	.183	.208

Notes: [a] Equations control for employee background and position variables
+ p < .05
* p < .01
** p < .001
[ ] Difference between estimates is significant at the .05 level
( ) Difference between estimates is significant at the .01 level.

commitment to be low in unit/small-batch operations, what does explain it? The reasons may lie in a number of deficits associated with the secondary labor markets of the economic periphery that we have not measured adequately. Fringe benefits and career opportunities are only partially indexed, and job security and prestige are measured hardly at all. We suggest that the low levels of these and other rewards provided by peripheral firms offset the positive effects of the rewarding, complex, and autonomous jobs that, as Blauner and Woodward observed, prevail in custom and small-batch organizations.

Unionization

The organization of unions represents a striking institutional contrast between Japan and the United States with numerous implications for the structure of labor markets and industrial relations. As our analysis in the last chapter demonstrated, unionization has a variety of influences on organizational and job structures in manufacturing plants, and operates through these mechanisms to shape employees' reactions to work and company. Some such indirect effects on employee attitudes are in opposite directions in the US and Japan. We know from chapter 4, for example, that quality circle activity enhances worker motivation and loyalty for Japanese and US firms alike. Yet we showed in the last chapter that QC programs are *less* likely to appear in unionized American plants, whereas the reverse is true in Japan (the very small number of plants in our sample without QC programs, however, cautions us against making too much of these results.)

A legacy of the postwar occupation reforms, Japanese unions are organized on a per-enterprise basis, concentrated in the largest firms, and combined into weak federations at higher levels (Kawada, 1973; Shirai, 1983). They organize all regular (blue- and white-collar) employees, including first and second-line supervisors. Much debate has centered on the question of whether Japanese enterprise unions are bona fide independent labor organizations. Some see them as highly dependent upon and easily coopted by the company, avoiding strong confrontations to advance their members' interests, and, indeed, as yet another corporatist control device, functioning to align the fate of unionized workers much more with that of their own company than with unionists of similar occupation and industry employed by other firms (Burawoy, 1983; Cole, 1971; Dore, 1973). As Hanami characterizes the relationship between the Japanese union and the firm:

> there exists a climate of collusion ... between the employers and the union representing the majority of employees ... Basically the relationship is one of patronage and dependence, though the unions frequently put on an outward show of radical militancy in their utterances and behavior. [Moreover] the president of an enterprise union is in effect the company's senior executive in charge of labor relations (Hanami, 1979:56)

Company unions and other labor associations organized by and/or dependent on individual firms have not been absent in US economic history (Edwards, 1979: 105; Jacoby, 1985). The same large companies that experimented with welfare programs in the 1920s as a way of fending off industrial unionism saw in-house labor organizations as a means of settling grievances and allowing participation on the company's terms. This bundling of company unions with welfarism as a strategy of labor control on the part of large US corporations in the 1920s is notable for its apparent parallels with Japanese welfare corporatism today. Dependent as they may be on the fortunes and support of the company (Hanami, 1979:55), the history of the rise of Japanese enterprise unions belies a simple characterization of them as company unions in the US sense (Koshiro, 1983:210–11). Collective bargaining, which was suppressed by the military rulers in the war years, was encouraged by the Supreme Command of the Allied Powers as part of a general mandate to increase economic and political pluralism. Organizing at the enterprise level was initially favored, not just by managers, but by leftist union leaders whose revolutionary strategy saw such unions becoming "factory-soviets," to use Koshiro's term. Another factor prompting enterprise-based collective bargaining was unionists' demands for equality of treatment for all employees, which led to white-collar workers and lower managers being included in the union. Moreover, the strong internal labor market character of Japanese firms made enterprise unions a logical form of labor organization, as they made employment conditions highly specific to the individual firm. Finally, as the Cold War deepened, SCAP reversed its policy of supporting union growth, making it difficult for unionists to expand the scope of labor negotiations to the industry level.

Yet other observers have argued that, despite the constraints imposed by dependency on a single firm, Japanese unions bargain hard on wage and benefit issues, and have effectively coordinated their militancy in the annual Spring offensives which present selected groups of employers with a set of unified wage demands (Hanami, 1979). Hard evidence is scarce, but a careful empirical analysis of the effects of Japanese unions on productivity (Freeman, 1984; Muramatsu, 1984) yields strikingly similar estimates to those obtained with US data. Moreover, a study by Koshiro (1983) concludes that union militancy (as indicated by the Spring strike offensives) has been an important force behind rising aggregate wage levels in the Japanese economy. In an analysis based on the present data (Kalleberg and Lincoln, 1988), moreover, we find no evidence of higher wage levels in Japanese union plants, although such a union effect of this sort is clearly evident in US data (Freeman and Medoff, 1984).

What, however, about the impact of unionism on employee work attitudes such as commitment to the company and satisfaction with the job? A considerable stream of survey research has produced remarkably consistent findings on the association between union membership and reported job satisfaction in the US (see Freeman and Medoff, 1984: chapter 9). Unionists report *lower* satisfaction with most aspects of the job and workplace than do comparable employees in nonunion establishments. This pattern seems consistent with the traditional strategic thrust of industrial unionism in the US: to aggregate grievances, foster an adversarial industrial relations climate, and provide an alternative anchor for workers' loyalty and identity. Paradoxically, however, unionized workers are *more* likely to report an intention to stay with their present jobs than nonunion employees, and, in fact, the actual quit rate is *lower* in union shops than in the nonunion workforce (Freeman and Medoff, 1984:139). An interpretation that has gained considerable credence is that "true" levels of dissatisfaction are probably no higher among union members but the union politicizes the employment relation and encourages workers to inflate and publicize their grievances. In the nonunion workplace, by contrast, workers have no such vehicle for airing dissatisfactions and therefore act on them by simply terminating their relationship with the firm. This interpretation, which is grounded in Albert Hirschman's (1970) "exit-voice-loyalty" model, is supported by evidence that grievance rates are higher in union shops even when objective working conditions are no worse (Freeman and Medoff, 1984:139).

Given what has been said of Japanese enterprise unions, we would not anticipate finding effects of this sort on the work attitudes of Japanese unionists. The company-oriented character of Japanese collective bargaining strongly suggests that unionization of the workforce in Japan may not induce the alienation from and loss of commitment to the firm that one associates with Western unionism. Indeed, what might be termed a "strong corporatist" model of Japanese industrial relations would suggest that enterprise unions play an opposite role: to build support for and loyalty to the company among the members of the workforce. We know of little direct research on this question which has been conducted in Japan. Odaka's (1975) survey of manufacturing workers examined the relationship between commitment to the company and commitment to the union. Although his findings are not easily summarized in a sentence or two, he does not find the two allegiances readily converging into one. Still, a sizable fraction of his sample did express equivalent commitment to union and company. These workers, moreover, appeared to have the highest levels of work motivation in the survey.

Table 8.1 demonstrates that there are indeed striking contrasts between the countries in the impact of plant unionization on employees' work attitudes. In the satisfaction model in the US, for example, the negative impact of unionization is by far the largest organization-level effect. About $\frac{2}{3}$ of this gross effect is explained by the intervening organizational and job measures. Importantly, there is *no* evidence that unionism in Japan is related to worker discontent; it simply bears no relationship to work satisfaction.

On the other hand, there is some evidence in table 8.1 that Japanese unions, like US unions, divert commitment from the organization: in both countries employees in union plants are less committed than their counterparts in nonunion companies. However, the difference in the Japanese case is so small as to be almost negligible, in contrast to the US sample where again it is by far the largest organization-level predictor. While Japanese unions may provide an alternative anchor for workers' loyalties and frame of reference in their dealings with the firm (Odaka, 1975), then, unlike US unions, they do not build or capitalize on alienation from the company, nor do they pose a serious threat to the corporatist strategy of fostering organizational commitment. In any event, these results cannot be easily construed as support for the "strong corporatist" thesis that Japanese enterprise unions are instruments in an overall strategy of corporatist control (e.g. Burawoy, 1983), for there is no evidence of their functioning directly to strengthen the bond between the employee and the firm.[4]

Effects of organizational structures on commitment and satisfaction

We now consider what is perhaps our most direct evaluation of the corporatist organization hypothesis: the effects of plant-level organizational structures on the work attitudes of individual employees. Within this set of phenomena, we believe, lie the specific organizational arrangements identified in the various threads of theory which we have woven into the corporatist conceptual umbrella. As with plant size, status, and technology, we have noted that other theories have made very different predictions from corporatist theory concerning the employee reactions elicited by organizational arrangements. In reviewing the next set of results, then, we ask whether each finding supports the welfare corporatist prediction, or, if not, the predictions of bureaucratic alienation and/or cultural contingency theory.

Structural differentiation

First, consider the shape or configuration of the organization: hierarchical depth, division of labor, and span of control. As we argued in earlier chapters, these figure prominently in accounts of Japanese and other corporatist organizational forms. High vertical differentiation and high subunit density are perceived to dissolve solidarities based on class and occupation, to increase interaction across ranks, and to provide opportunities for upward mobility. Such tall hierarchies, proliferating subunits, and small spans of control are widely described as characteristically Japanese organizational structures. Yet our own data, reviewed in chapter 7, were mixed as to the veracity of claims that these patterns of organizing are peculiarly Japanese structures: we found strong evidence of taller hierarchies in Japanese plants, weak evidence of greater subunit differentiation, and no evidence of narrower supervisory spans of control.

Discounting for now the contradictory evidence regarding span of control, our finding of greater vertical and (to some extent) horizontal structural differentiation in the Japanese plants can be taken as support for the thesis that corporatist structures are particularly characteristic of Japanese firms. Welfare corporatist theorists, as we have portrayed them, argue that structural complexity in firms divides the workforce, creates individual (as opposed to collective) paths to opportunity and reward, and enmeshes workers in strong dependency bonds with managers. If proliferating subunits and status divisions can be shown to enhance the commitment of employees in *both* the US and Japan, we will have materially advanced the argument that the commitment gap between these countries derives from the wider implementation of welfare corporatist control systems in Japanese firms.

Marxist writers such as Edwards (1979) and Gordon (1972) contend that detailed job classifications and descriptions, in addition to proliferating departments and status levels, serve to individuate workers and foster attachment to the firm (see also Baron and Bielby, 1986). This argument, of course, also runs strongly counter to the well-established bureaucratic alienation logic that differentiated, standardized, and formalized work roles and positions precipitate boredom, job dissatisfaction, and antipathy toward the company. But here the notion of bureaucratic control also diverges from the description of Japanese work organization, since Japanese companies minimize job formalization, preferring the flexibility of diffuse job categories and frequent job rotation (Aoki, 1984). We are inclined to think that job fragmentation, while it no doubt individuates workers and serves to rationalize payment schemes, does not operate as effectively as certain alternatives to bring about commitment to the organization. The alternatives are the practices associated with Japanese organization: high job rotation and low job definition within quite distinct work groups. As Williamson and Ouchi (1981) imply, Japanese organization involves a combination of high enterprise-specific skills and values combined with low potential for monitoring individuals' contributions. This state of affairs creates a bilateral exchange between the organization and the employee which renders each dependent upon the other. Narrowly focused jobs divide workers from one another but they also divide them from the firm, producing ignorance of other functional areas and excessive absorption in one's own work role.

There is, however, scarcely a shred of evidence in table 8.1 that hierarchical depth and subunit density are associated with stronger employee attachments to the firm. Japanese plants may have taller hierarchies (table 7.1), but in both countries this structural property is negatively related, if at all, to either commitment or satisfaction. Nor do we find horizontal differentiation (number of sections and departments) giving rise to positive work attitudes. The negative effects of number of units in the Japanese sample are made more dramatic by our knowledge that size, now uncontrolled, drives commitment in an opposite direction.[5]

Moreover, tall hierarchies and subunit density exhibit the same pattern of null to negative associations with virtually all the job attribute variables we have posited as intervening links in the complex causal chain relating organizational properties to workforce commitment (tables 8.2–8.4). Greater structural differentiation (either vertical or horizontal) is related to: less job complexity; fewer supervisory contact (in the US); less worker (vs. supervisory) control; less autonomy (in the US); fewer friendships (in the US); poorer quality of supervisory and (in the US) coworker relations; and fewer intrinsic rewards (in Japan). Moreover, structural differentiation is also unrelated to teamwork, outside socializing, and promotion expectations.

These negative effects of structural complexity on organizational commitment and job satisfaction refute the Marxist "divide and conquer" hypothesis and other arguments associating complex bureaucratic forms with a corporatist strategy of control. They are fully consonant, on the other hand, with the bureaucratic alienation model which takes simple and fluid organizational structures to be conducive to high morale and cohesive work relations. Previous research has likewise established more support for a view of structural differentiation as a source of negative social psychological reactions than for the corporatist idea that it elicits commitment (Aiken and Hage, 1966; Oldham and Hackman, 1981; Rousseau, 1978; Worthy, 1950). Indeed, despite the persuasive arguments of corporatist theorists for the role of vertical and horizontal differentiation in separating workers from one another and heightening their dependence on the firm, we know of no quantitative empirical evidence for effects of this sort.

Though the evidence from both samples conforms more closely to the bureaucratic alienation model than to the corporatist view, it is interesting to note that the effects of structural differentiation on the job and social variables (tables 8.2–8.4) are, with few exceptions, considerably stronger in the US data. This pattern might be interpreted in terms of a cultural contingency model of how Japanese and US employees react to organizational structures. The most likely explanation of this sort invokes the assumption that greater individualism and need for self-determination characterize US employees while a group- and hierarchy-centeredness prevails among the Japanese. Of course, strong support for such a culturalist hypothesis of how individuals react to organizations would imply that hierarchy and subunit proliferation elicit positive responses to the organization from Japanese employees and negative ones from US workers. While we do not find that, it is apparent that structural differentiation does not have the same alienating and disintegrating influences on Japanese employees that it has on US employees, and culture may be a substantial part of the reason.

Span of control   Small spans of control are another indicator of structural differentiation in organizations, for, without an increase in employment size, the average span declines as hierarchies elongate and subunits proliferate. We found no evidence in the last chapter that supervisory spans of control differed between Japanese and US plants, yet the *effects* of span of control on employee work attitudes are much more in line with the expectations we derive from corporatist theory. Indeed, the impact of the average first-line span of control is one of the strongest contrasts between the countries evident in table 8.1. Small spans have been construed by writers as diverse as Blau (1968), Blauner (1964), and Woodward (1965) as indicative of team production and close cooperation between superiors and subordinates. The observation that Japanese organizations have small spans (e.g. Dore, 1973:250) seems consistent with the highly distinctive leadership style of

Japanese supervisors, who develop strong personal and paternalistic ties with their subordinates and function more as nurturant, socioemotional leaders than task-oriented bosses. This is the corporatist interpretation: tall hierarchies and narrow supervisory spans constitute organizational architecture designed to separate individual workers from their natural class or occupational affiliations and draw them further into the organization's net of control. The bureaucratic alienation interpretation, on the other hand, sees small spans as structural proxies for close supervision, placing a worker under the direct and heavy hand of management, implying a loss of autonomy and flexibility on the job (Child, 1984:156).

Of course, the span of control is a crude and indirect indicator of the structure of supervision, disguising much about the form and content of the supervisory relationship. Numerous studies, including our own analyses in earlier chapters, have made it clear that vertical ties in Japanese companies have a very different quality from superior-subordinate relations in the US. Such differences are again sharply manifested in the effects of span of control. Narrow spans clearly do not function to bind the American employee to the firm: both commitment and satisfaction rise as density of supervision declines (see table 8.1). The complete absence of this pattern in the Japanese data suggests that "close supervision" may mean something quite different there, even if it fails to support directly the hypothesis that small spans in Japanese companies represent a corporatist control structure designed to foster commitment. The differences we observe here with respect to span of control are strongly reminiscent of the chapter 4 finding that contact with supervisors produced negative employee reactions only in the US.

Centralization of decision-making

Another defining feature of corporatist organization is the existence of structures for eliciting participation in decision-making and broadening the scope of worker responsibility for the operations of the firm. Japanese decision-making is widely characterized as participatory and consensus-based, the *ringi* system and quality circles being only the best known of an array of devices used by Japanese firms to diffuse participation and responsibility. Yet, as our inquiry in the preceding chapter demonstrated, formal decision-making responsibility is highly centralized in Japanese organizations (Yoshino, 1968). We have argued that this pattern is consistent with the general corporatist strategy of control: participatory structures serve to integrate workers in the organization and commit them to organizational decisions. Yet they involve little real redistribution of formal authority from top to bottom of the management hierarchy. As before, we do not consider the influences on employee work orientations of all the measures of decision-making structure obtained in our survey; only those whose relations to organizational commitment and job satisfaction have clear rationales.

QC and Ringi Our analysis here of QC participation simply underscores the findings presented in chapter 4, where we treated QC membership as an indicator of an individual employee's position in working groups within the organization. Yet QC programs deserve special consideration, as they represent a management-sponsored mechanism for encouraging worker participation in decision-making, and as such have considerable prima-facie validity as an indicator of corporatist organizing. Furthermore, their pervasiveness in Japanese industry and relative novelty in the West fits to a "t" the corporatist paradigm which holds that Japanese industry is in the vanguard of world trends toward the implementation of workplace structures of commitment-centered control.

Recall that our measure of QC participation is a binary indicator of whether (= 1) the employee is a participant in a quality circle. Table 8.1 repeats our earlier finding that QC membership is linked to greater commitment in both samples, and, to a lesser degree, satisfaction.

QC is a shop-floor strategy of organizing participation by rank-and-file workers and supervisors in production decisions. *Ringi*, on the other hand, is a method of drawing widely on the input and backing of managers in arriving at and forging a consensus around decisions. Chapter 7's inquiry concluded that, while both are in some sense participatory decision-making structures, *ringi* appears to mean real delegation of authority to lower management levels, whereas QC is found in conjunction with centralized factory governance. From the standpoint of corporatist theory, this configuration is not surprising, for participatory structures at the production-worker level are understood to be control devices in the hands of management.

We have seen, moreover, that QC programs succeed in both the US and Japan in producing the desired result: commitment *is* higher among QC participants. Can the same be said of *ringi*? We encounter a methodological difficulty here. Though we acknowledge a potential comparability problem in US and Japanese QC programs, they at least have a common base and origin – W. E. Deming's theories of statistical quality control and various small group movements found in both Western and Japanese management tradition (Cole, 1979). *Ringi*, however, is uniquely Japanese and has no meaning to most American managers. Our solution, as described in the last chapter, was to substitute for the *ringi* measure (the proportion of 37 decisions made in the *ringi* fashion) in the US an index of group decision-making (the proportion of decisions made by groups as opposed to individuals).

There is no evidence in table 8.1 that group (*ringi*) decision-making, as operationalized by our Aston-based index, has any impact on the work attitudes of American manufacturing employees. By contrast, the Japanese measure of *ringi* decision-making behaves very much as predicted. It is positively linked to the employee's level of commitment to the organization; though it is unrelated to job satisfaction. Moreover, the effect of the *ringi* index in the Japanese sample is comparable to that of QC and is quite impressive when one considers that: (a) *ringi* is almost entirely a management-level decision-making process; and (b) our index is defined at the organization-level and is thus a constant for all employees in a plant. Thus, QC at the shop-floor level and *ringi* at the management level perform as advertised: more typical of Japanese than US organizations, they are structural mechanisms for drawing employees into decision-making, producing the anticipated payoff of enhanced commitment to the firm.

Formal and de facto *centralization*   One of the sharpest contrasts turned up by our investigation of organizational structures in Japanese and US plants was with respect to the Aston-based measures of formal and *de facto* centralization of decision-making: the Japanese plants exhibited markedly greater formal concentration of authority but more *de facto* participation by lower-ranking employees. This implies a larger gap between the formal and informal structures of power in the Japanese organizations, a result antici-pated from our previous discussions of the operation of *ringi* and other Japanese decision-making systems. The question now is whether this pattern of decision-making enhances workforce commitment. We have argued that such a combination of formal centralization and actual participation is compatible with the overall corporatist stategy of control, and as such should be distinguished from the institutional apparatus of industrial democracy. Our reasoning was that informal mechanisms allow employees to experience participation by sharing responsibility for decisions, without producing significant shifts in the governance of the firm.

One could, of course, reverse this reasoning and argue that formal structures of participation are symbolic gestures, and the real question is who, in practice, wields power. Students of European-style industrial democracy have suggested that the formal system of codetermination masks a good deal of apathy and disengagement on the part of rank-and-file employees (Burns, Karlsson, and Rus, 1979). Our hypothesis, however, is in line with Dore's (1973) characterization of European industrial democracy as democratic corporatism, whose origins lie with the political programs of left-wing parties, as distinct from the management-orchestrated welfare corporatism of Japan (Cole, 1985). The notion of wider implementation of corporatist control systems in Japanese companies is, of course, a cornerstone in the conceptual framework that guides us in this volume. We have seen that forms of participatory decision-making such as quality circles and *ringi* do deliver on the corporatist promise of heightened commitment. Can the same be said of the distinctive Japanese decision-making system which couples formal centralization of authority with informal delegation and participation?

Table 8.1 does indeed lend support to this hypothesis. The effect of formal centralization on commitment and satisfaction are positive and significant in both countries (column 2). On the other hand, centralization of *de facto* participation, tends to be *negatively* associated with work attitudes though the pattern is stronger, in the US.

When the intervening job variables are added to the model (equation 3), these coefficients attenuate to near-zero. Such a pattern implies that the effects on work attitudes of the two forms of centralization are largely mediated by the employee's position, job, and relations within the organization. Since these centralization dimensions figure so prominently in our assessment of structural differences in work organizations between the two countries, these results deserve careful scrutiny (see tables 8.2–8.4, which give the regression estimates for the set of intervening job/positional variables).

We know that the intrinsic rewards of the job are strongly predictive of organizational commitment and job satisfaction in both countries. In fact, the pattern of centralization effects on intrinsic rewards is almost identical to that observed in the case of satisfaction. Job complexity and autonomy are the other perceptual measures of what, in the organizational behavior and design literatures, are termed enriched and enlarged jobs, involving variety and challenge (Hackman and Oldham, 1980). Management campaigns for job redesign fall squarely in the mainstream of corporatist strategies of control, as such programs are explicitly aimed at raising the integration and commitment of a workforce (Burawoy, 1983). In general, we find the same pattern of centralization effects with respect to complexity – positive with respect to authority, negative with respect to participation. Formal centralization raises US employees' perceptions of their jobs' complexity while *de facto* centralization has no influence. In the Japanese sample, it is the other way around, with formal centralization unrelated, and participation negatively related, to complexity. However, the autonomy index bears no relation to either form of centralization. This is surprising, for we would suppose autonomy to be that individual-level job property most likely to respond to organization-level shifts in the distribution of decision-making authority and responsibility.

Moreover, as we scan tables 8.2–8.4, we find that many of the intervening job characteristics depend on formal and *de facto* centralization in the hypothesized fashion. Relations with supervisors, promotion expectations, and after-hours socializing all rise to some degree with formal, but fall with *de facto*, centralization. Interestingly, the three such variables which exhibit very different relations to the two centralization indices all concern the cohesiveness of coworker relations (teamwork, friends, and coworker ties). In the US data, for example, formal centralization is associated with fewer coworker friendships and a poorer perceived quality of work-group relations. A possible explanation for this might lie in the findings of chapter 4 that, in the US, the strength of horizontal coworker ties in the workplace were inversely related to the strength of vertical ties (i.e. with superiors). If the decision-making pattern of high formal/low *de facto* centralization works to integrate employees along the vertical dimension by diminishing the authority of supervisors and lower managers, perhaps it also engenders a loss of cohesion among workers themselves.

To summarize, decision-making centralization is linked to employee reactions and adjustment to the organization in complex and intriguing ways. Earlier we found strong evidence that centralization of formal authority was higher in Japanese than in US organizations but that *de facto* responsibility was more widely dispersed. Reasoning that this decision-making pattern is congruent with the corporatist model, we hypothesized that it would also be associated with greater commitment. This is what we found: work attitudes were generally more positive where formal delegation is low but actual participation is high. Moreover, this pattern was almost entirely mediated by the effects of centralization on those job attributes which play key roles in determining employees' work attitudes. Again and again, we found the same pattern of positive relations with formal centralization coupled with negative effects of the informal measure.[6] Taken as a whole, these findings are consistent with the prediction from welfare corporatist theory that organizational structures typical of Japanese firms will foster positive work orientations, not just in Japanese employees, but in American workers as well.

How can we make sense of these findings? We suspect the reason for the divergent effects of formal and *de facto* centralization is rooted in the two rather different meanings that *decentralization* of decision-making has in organizational theory. On the one hand, it refers to a process of delegating authority down the hierarchy to functionally specialized roles performed by individuals. This, it seems to us, is the meaning tapped by the usual form of the Aston centralization scale (Pugh *et al.*, 1968). On the other hand, decentralization refers to a much less-structured process of broad-based participation in which decisions emerge through the give-and-take of group discussion and consensus-building. This is the meaning intended by theorists of organic organization such as Burns and Stalker (1961), and it clearly captures the sense in which Japanese organizations are decentralized as well. When *authority* is decentralized, it tends to mean delegation of responsibility to lower management positions, implying a broadening of participation in decisions in the narrow sense that more persons are required to perform managerial tasks (Lincoln and Zeitz, 1980). Indeed, such *specialization* of the decision-making process implies greater formalization, compartmentalization, and fragmentation of decisions – processes which likely operate to diminish the expansive, fluid, and networking kind of participation associated with Japanese companies, if not organic organization more generally. It is the latter which most organizational theory suggests should produce dividends in greater motivation, integration, and commitment in a workforce. Our findings of positive effects of formal centralization coupled with negative effects of *de facto* centralization are thus to be expected. This structural configuration – typical of Japanese firms – stands for less monopolization of decisions by holders of formal, specialized offices, and a more participatory, "town meeting" kind of structure. Now it may well be that in a system of centralized authority, most real decision power is closely held at the highest levels of management (Craig, 1975). There is much opportunity for unfettered airing of opinions but in fact the decision has already been made. Yet that state of affairs, once again, is what the corporatist model predicts: participatory structures are central to the overall control strategy of the firm, and exist for the purpose of building enterprise community and organizational loyalty.

Jacoby's (1985) historical account of the rise of professional and bureaucratic personnel management in US manufacturing firms demonstrates how centralization of authority in one area of corporate operations has, over time, led to better industrial relations and a stronger bond between the worker and the firm. In the early decades of this century, the primary mechanism of labor management in the workplace was the "drive system," which gave foremen almost total discretion in hiring, firing, sanctioning, and allocating workers. The personnel movement in industry sought to wrest authority over employee matters from foremen and locate it in centralized functional departments run by white-collar professionals with college-level behavioral science training. Partly motivated by humanitarian concerns, those who championed professional personnel management also wished to reduce the high levels of turnover and absenteeism associated with the drive system, while increasing labor discipline and loyalty. The bureaucratization of personnel management – aimed at centralizing authority, standardizing and formalizing employee rights and obligations, and developing internal labor markets and welfare benefits – was clearly central to the process of building welfare corporatist organization in US manufacturing firms.

As Clark (1979) has argued of the facilitative, negotiating leadership style of Japanese middle and lower managers, centralization of formal authority in work organizations may paradoxically become a force for widespread decision-making participation. When supervisors have very limited official authority or discretion in their management of workers, they may have little choice but to win the consent and cooperation of workers in carrying out the mandates of their jobs. Thus, the strong personal ties which Japanese supervisors cultivate with their subordinates no doubt have some cultural basis in Japanese *oyabun-kobun* and other tradition-sanctioned client-patron relations (Vogel, 1963). Yet they are also embedded in a highly conducive structure which deprives first- and second-line leaders of the authority to expect direct compliance with supervisory commands.

Formalization

A legalistic structure of corporate rights and obligations, by conferring legitimacy on workplace authority relations and buffering subordinates from arbitrary power, solidifies the bond between the worker and the firm. We address only one of the implications of this proposition, that the codification of organizational goals, norms, and procedures in written form brings about an increase in commitment and morale. As we observed in chapter 6, this hypothesis, which we derive from the corporatist model of work organization, is at odds with theories in the bureaucratic alienation and human relations traditions. These hold that formal rules and procedures, which routinize and depersonalize employee actions and relations, alienate the individual from the organization (Aiken and Hage, 1966). Such mainstays of contingency theory as Burns and Stalker (1961) and Woodward (1965) do indeed regard formalization as a core feature of machine bureaucracy, with all the implications for work alienation associated with that structural form. On the other hand, at least two other classics of organizational sociology have been mindful of the ways workers' interests are served when formal rules constrain supervisory discretion. Alvin Gouldner's (1954) commentary on the functions of bureaucratic rules was perhaps the first to make this point explicitly. But Crozier's *Bureaucratic Phenomenon* (1964) interwove it with a fascinating cultural argument for the over-formalization of French bureaucracy. In Crozier's view, the French have a singular distaste for personal dependency relations in the workplace. Formal rules and procedures, along with narrowly defined official and departmental responsibilities, proliferate in French organizations to satisfy a French cultural need to maintain distance between ranks and limits on the discretionary use of management power (see also Sabel, 1982).

As we have previously noted, high formalization has been observed in Japanese firms by several scholars (Dore, 1973; Yoshino, 1968), though our own analysis produced evidence for this hypothesis which was marginal at best. We found the unadjusted mean of the 18-item Aston formalization scale to be significantly higher in the Japanese than in the American plants, but the difference disappeared when we imposed controls for technology, size, and other covariates. Whatever our findings regarding the effect of formalization on employee work attitudes, then, we are hardly in a position to argue that this structural variable accounts for much of the US-Japanese commitment gap.

Moreover, there is meager evidence in these data for the corporatist hypothesis that formalization, as measured here, produces positive orientations to the firm and the employment relationship. In neither sample does formalization bear any significant relation to commitment. In the Japanese sample, the formalization effect is positive and significant but only with respect to satisfaction, and this association fades to nonsignificance when the intervening variables are controlled.

How is plant formalization related to the job attributes we have measured at the employee level? There appears to be a rather substantial pattern of differences between the US and Japan. Though the magnitude of the effects is small, the US regressions in tables 8.2–8.4 show that job complexity, autonomy, intrinsic rewards and even promotion expectations are all negatively influenced by formalization. More striking are the adverse implications of formalization for strong social ties in the American workplace. Team-work, friendships, and the quality of supervisor and coworker relations diminish (steeply in the case of friendships) with increments in the proliferation of written rules and procedures. These results constitute striking confirmation of the bureaucratic alienation paradigm and an unequivocal repudiation of the corporatist position that formalization, with its implied conferral of citizenship in an internal state, breeds enterprise community.

These patterns in the US data are, on the other hand, altogether absent in Japan. Indeed, rarely have we encountered so much divergence between the countries in a set of empirical results reported in this volume. Intrinsic rewards, job complexity, autonomy, and supervisor contact are unrelated to formalization in Japan. It does, however, diminish supervisory control, a finding which is directly in line with the corporatist prediction that formal rules curtail the discretionary power of foremen (Jacoby, 1985). As for the social integration variables, we find no association of formalization with teamwork and outside socializing, but the quality of ties with coworkers is significantly higher in formalized plants; this is an outcome diametrically opposed to the US case. Finally, promotion chances appear to rise with formalization in the Japanese plants, which is roughly consistent with corporatist assumptions about the operation of firm internal labor markets. This overall pattern of formalization effects in the Japanese sample is much more consistent than is the US evidence with the predictions we would derive from corporatist theory.

When we disaggregate the formalization scale into its constituent items and examine their correlations with commitment and satisfaction, we find further support for the idea that formal rules and procedures lead to positive worker reactions in Japan but not the US (table 8.5). Of 14 items (four are constants), all but two correlate positively in the Japanese sample with each attitude variable, and eight are statistically significant. In the US sample, the direction of the relationship seems to depend much more on the area to which the formal rule or description pertains. For example, there is a surprisingly strong *negative* correlation between a plant's use of a formal employment contract and each attitude variable. We suspect the reason is that formal employment contracts are often given to temporary or seasonal workers, explicitly bounding the onset and termination of employment. It is the least common document present of the 18 comprising the scale, with only one-third of the sampled US plants reporting its presence. The only other positive correlations are with: safety and hygiene regulations; descriptions and rules for training and educational opportunities; and job descriptions or instructions. All of these can be construed to be in employees' interests, particularly safety, where the relationship with commitment is strongest. In contrast to the Japanese results, these items do not appear to be related to work attitudes so as to suggest that *formalization per se*, as opposed to rules protecting particular areas of employee interest, is a unitary phenomenon to which US workers respond in a consistent way.

The dramatic differences between the US and Japan in the influences of organizational formalization on work attitudes, job attributes, and workplace relations are more consistent with a cultural contingency interpretation than either the welfare corporatist or bureaucratic alienation models. Yet it is not easy to make sense of the differences in US and Japanese responses to formalization. From one perspective, we might have anticipated these differences to be in the opposite direction, since many of the rules and classifications found in American industrial organizations arose in response to unions' attempts to control job assignments and wage rates (Freeman and Medoff, 1984; Jacoby, 1985). Hence, formalization in US plants might be expected to produce favorable reactions in workers. Japanese enterprise unions, by contrast, have generally left such matters to the discretion of management (Cole, 1979; Dore, 1973; Ohmae, 1982). Beyond this, Crozier's (1964) theory of divergences in how cultures look upon vertical dependency relationships would certainly have us believe that the Japanese, who, by all accounts, prefer such relations, would react less favorably than Americans to formal barriers inhibiting the emergence of such ties (Lincoln *et al.*, 1981). We speculate that the bureaucratic alienation model of employee reactions to organizational structures is a better fit to US reality, whereas the corporatist model is in closer accord with the case of Japan. This fits the presumption that an individualistic market-orientation on the part of US employees causes them to chafe under the yoke of formal rules, even though some of those rules may have originated with workers' demands. To the extent that regimentation and conformity permeate Japanese culture – and there is some truth to this generalization even adjusting for stereotypes – formalization may evoke the set of employee responses anticipated in corporatist theory.

Welfare services

Our final organization-level explanatory variable is the number of employee welfare services organized and sponsored by the plant. Central both to accounts of Japanese companies and to more general discussions of corporatist organization is the heavy use of welfare benefits, social and recreational programs, symbols and rituals, and socialization and training (Abegglen, 1958; Rohlen, 1974). These function to broaden the scope of employees' participation, to integrate the workforce in expressive social relations, and to build and transmit a strong culture in the firm (Peters and Waterman, 1982). Indeed, the "paternalism" of Japanese companies in providing an extraordinarily broad range of services to their employees has long struck Western observers as one of the most exotic of numerous distinctively Japanese management practices.

As we discussed in chapter 7, our measure of services is an unweighted sum of nine binary items indicating the presence or absence of a set of training, recreational, ceremonial, and communication activities in the firm. Welfare corporatist theory plus the documentation provided by numerous students of Japanese work life led us strongly to expect that these activities are more prevalent in Japanese than US firms, and our analysis in the last chapter found that to be true. Moreover, we found that plant size, corporate status, and production technology were linked to welfare services in predictable ways.

Table 8.1 shows that in both samples the activities index is relatively strongly and positively related to commitment, with a weaker yet still statistically significant link to satisfaction. It appears, then, that company investments in organized employee services and activities do yield returns in loyalty and morale which are very similar in the US and Japan. This pattern, as in the case of quality circle activity, is in complete harmony with the core proposition around which our study revolves. The essence of the welfare corporatist hypothesis, as we have framed it on repeated occasions, is that Japanese companies have taken the lead in setting in place a bundle of organizational structures and employment practices which successfully elicit commitment and compliance from a manufacturing work-force. The effectiveness of these structures and practices is by no means confined to Japanese workers; they produce returns in worker loyalty to US firms as well. However, as US (and other Western) corporations, have yet, for numerous historical and cultural reasons, to push the welfare corporatist program as far, aggregate levels of US labor commitment lag behind Japan.

The similarity of the effects of plant welfare services on employee work attitudes in the two countries is really quite striking. We might well have anticipated the reactions of Japanese and US manufacturing employees to company welfarism to be conditioned by cultural differences in work values and expectations. The concept of the firm as an enterprise community or corporate family, providing broadly for the needs of its employees, has waxed and waned over the industrial histories of both countries, yet there is little question that it has seen broader and deeper institutionalization in Japan (Bennett and Ishino, 1963; Dore, 1973). Moreover, the conception of the employment contract as a limited engagement, market-based exchange in which the firm stays clear of workers' consumption and lifestyle concerns is *prima facie* more in tune with Anglo–American values of personal privacy and individualism than with the collectivity-centered culture of Japan. On the other hand, recall our finding in chapter 5 of considerable support among American employees for employers' engaging in paternalistic welfare practices. At that time we speculated that the decline of manufacturing employment in the US heartland – in particular the recession conditions prevailing in the midwest at the time of our survey – may have aroused workers' insecurities and rendered the prospect of a benevolent, paternal employer a good deal more attractive than in times past when manufacturing labor markets were tighter and workers more assertive and secure.

In general, the expanded regressions for commitment and satisfaction which include task, social bond, and job reward variables suggest that they do not mediate these relationships to any great degree: there is very little change in the effects of welfare services between equation (2), which excludes these controls, and equation (3) which adds them. The coefficient estimates in the US regressions do attenuate slightly between equations (2) and (3) for both dependent variables, indicating that a small part of the effect of services is indirect. But in the Japanese sample, the slope estimates of the services index actually increase slightly when the job and relational variables are included. This means that the levels of these variables – which we know to raise commitment – are driven *down* by rising welfare services in Japanese plants. Indeed, when we scan the rows of coefficients in tables 8.2, 8.3, and 8.4, we find no instance in which a job attribute is affected by welfare services in a way that would produce a subsequent positive change in commitment.

We expect plant welfare services to influence work attitudes such as commitment and satisfaction primarily through the mechanisms of stronger social bonds with workmates and superiors and perhaps a perception of the work role overall as more interesting and intrinsically rewarding. There is some spotty evidence of this in the US sample. Welfare services do boost after-hours socializing and a sense of teamwork, and they appear to produce a very substantial increase in the perceived complexity of the job. We observe none of these effects in the Japanese sample, and there are even small tendencies toward lower quality coworker ties in high-service plants. However, as we noted above, even in the US sample they account for no more than a very small proportion of the total contribution that services makes to commitment.

What are the mechanisms through which employee information and training programs, social and recreational activities, ceremonies, and other services breed commitment in these countries? Though we do not claim to have successfully identified and measured all the job, network, and reward variables that might be mediating the effects of service programs, the simplest answer is that the impact of services on employee work attitudes is essentially direct. That is, welfare activities raise commitment not so much because they induce a material change in the employee's job situation or in the quality of his/her relations with coworkers and supervisors, but because they are interpreted directly as a positive gesture by the firm. This interpretation is supported by our disaggregation of the services index into its constituent items (see table 8.5): nearly every one is positively correlated with commitment in both samples. This is a diverse set of services, and while some (e.g. training) may influence job complexity, others (e.g. sports) increase quality of social relations, and so, when aggregated into a single index, such effects wash out. However, as the acceptable reliability of the composite measure

Table 8.5 *Zero-order correlations of formalization and welfare services items with commitment and satisfaction*

	Commitment		Satisfaction	
	US	Japan	US	Japan
Formalization[a]				
Employment rules	—	—	—	—
Employment contract	−.192**	.029	−.137**	.043
Goals and policies	.038+	.007	.023	−.039
Limits of authority	.037+	.114**	−.022	.067**
Personnel evaluation	−.015	.064**	.035	.059*
Labor/management contract	−.017	.076**	−.052*	.059**
Job classification	.002	.104**	.020	.050*
Hiring and firing	.034	.035	−.023	.019
Congrats and condolences	−.031	—	−.014	—
Safety and hygiene records	.111**	.080**	.063*	.050*
Fringe benefits	−.045*	—	−.047*	—
Retirement plan	.025	—	−.025	—
Training programs	.063**	.114**	.043+	.055*
Employee services	.050*	.035	.019	−.011
Job descriptions	.067**	.090**	.036	.060**
Job rules and procedures	−.030	.086**	−.050*	.079**
Production schedule	−.083**	−.028	−.009	.017
Research program/reports	.023	−.034	.009	.013
Welfare services[b]				
Outside training	.143**	.110**	.080**	.055**
Inhouse training	.069**	.096**	.042+	.040+
Company journal	.034	.159**	.043+	.061*
Ceremonies	−.002	—	.027	—
Sports programs	.058*	.099**	.028	.090**
Orientation program	.047+	.062**	.023	.035
Employee handbook	.101**	.163**	.060*	.111*
Information/pep sessions	.057*	.060*	.013	.053*
Calisthenics program	—	.067**	—	.059*

Notes: [a] Each item refers to the presence (= 1) or absence (= 0) of formal documents specifying the rules, procedures, or descriptions of each type
[b] Each item refers to the presence (= 1) or absence (= 0) of each service or activity
+p < .05
*p < .01
**p < .001

(about .6), suggests a company investing in one such service is likely to provide another. Such consistency no doubt strengthens the signal of corporate benevolence to which employees respond.

Summary

In this chapter, we have linked the two levels of analysis on which our inquiry has been based: the individual employee and the employing organization or plant. We explored how employees' commitment to the company and job satisfaction were molded, directly and indirectly, by organizational structures and other characteristics of plants. In so doing, we brought together a number of the key theoretical themes of our study.

Our findings with respect to the organizational context variables of size, corporate status, and technology fit nicely within the general corporatist framework, supporting in particular the idea that commitment-maximizing organization is associated with occupancy of a core location within the dual economy. These findings run sharply counter to an older strain of workplace theory, holding that small, locally owned workshops and craft forms of production breed commitment and community in the workplace. While some might see our evidence that Japanese enterprise unions slightly diminish workforce commitment as contrary to the corporatist position, we see it as generally supportive. Our data make abundantly clear that US unions are labor organizations which pose a strong challenge to the corporatist aim of fostering company commitment. Japanese unions, on the other hand, if not instruments of this strategy, at least pose little hazard to it.

Much of our evidence as to the impact of organizational and employment structures on employee commitment was also supportive of the corporatist argument. Whether in Japan or the US, "Japanese-style" decision-making (QC, *ringi*, formal centralization coupled with informal decentralization) and welfare services were found to enhance commitment and (to a lesser degree) satisfaction. On the other hand, the picture with respect to structural differentiation – believed by Marxists and other theorists to build commitment to the firm through "dividing and conquering" the workforce – was more in line with the bureaucratic alienation model. Finally, our evidence on the impact of formal rules and procedures on work attitudes was more in line with a cultural contingency explanation: while generally conforming to the predictions of corporatist theory in Japan, in the US it tended to support the bureaucratic alienation view.

9 The future of welfare corporatism in Japan and the US: conclusion

Our work in this volume has been motivated by a basically simple, yet important idea: that the presumed commitment and motivation advantage enjoyed by Japanese manufacturers over US firms and workers springs from the distinctive set of management practices, organizational structures, and employment systems that characterize the Japanese workplace. While conspicuous in Japan, however, those management styles and organizational arrangements produce similar dividends in workforce commitment whether they are implemented in Japanese or US factory settings. Not surprisingly, then, elements of welfare corporatism – an emergent control system well tailored to the organization-oriented nature of modern production regimes – have been proliferating in Western firms, though the evolution and implementation of this organizational form in the US still lags considerably behind its diffusion in Japan.

The welfare corporatist hypothesis, as we have adapted it from Ronald Dore's classic work, is a new and ironic twist on the old theme of convergence between Japanese and Western styles of work organization. It holds that the Japanese employment system has become the beacon of economic rationality and modernity, and it is the industrial countries of the West who are now faced with the necessity of sloughing off the shackles of tradition and other sunk costs in older, market-based modes of organizing. A unique synthesis of bureaucracy and paternalism, as Hill (1981:53) characterized it, welfare corporatism comprises: permanent employment guarantees that reduce turnover and increase the worker's investment in the firm; organizational structures such as tall job hierarchies and proliferating work units which break up occupational and class loyalties while encouraging the formation of organization-wide cohesive bonds; programs for relieving the fragmentation and monotony of jobs and tasks through rotation and enlargement that increase the intrinsic rewards of working and build identification with the organization as a whole; mechanisms for fostering employee participation in decision-making without the formal guarantees or high-level access that might threaten management control; a legal structure of formalized rights and obligations that confer corporate citizenship on employees and avert reliance on alienating personal forms of supervisory domination; and the

248

trappings of strong organizational culture – ritual, ceremony, symbolism, and the like – along with a potpourri of tangible welfare benefits including family subsidies, educational programs, housing, and health benefits.

Our hypothesis was that these arrangements, taken as a whole, represent a new organizational form; one possessing the qualities of an organization-wide enterprise community. Its ultimate objective is the maximization of workforce commitment. The capacity of our survey research design to locate Japanese and US factories along these dimensions of welfare corporatism was, of course, inevitably imperfect. We did not measure some of these attributes at all; we tapped others only glancingly. Even so, we believe our research design and measurement procedures suffice to provide a meaningful, if partial, test of the proposition that the US/Japan commitment gap is due to differences between these two countries in the diffusion and implementation of the corporatist form of work organization.

Of course, a genuine question can be raised as to whether our survey data have conclusively established that organizational commitment – as a social psychological state of deep identification with and dependence on an employing organization – is more pervasive in the Japanese than in the US manufacturing workforce. We concluded in chapter 3 that it is, although in the course of our inquiry we have become much more sensitive to the severe problems of interpretation that afflict cross-cultural comparisons of individuals' work attitudes.

If indeed Japanese employees are more committed to their organizations than employees in US manufacturing plants, the hypothesis that the Japanese commitment edge can be attributed to the wider implementation of a commitment-maximizing organizational form is only one of several potential explanations for it. A long-standing alternative is the simple culturalist claim that commitment to work and company reflects a Japanese cultural trait. The case for this interpretation rests on numerous observations that deep devotion to and identification with duty, superiors, and the corporate group pervade Japanese culture and tradition. At bottom, the culturalist explanation is probably impossible to test. In one sense, it merely asserts that work life and organizational commitment run deeper in Japan because the Japanese are just "that way." Put with more sophistication, this view holds that a larger component of the role model to which Japanese (males) are socialized from birth to aspire involves aspects of commitment to company and work life. To the extent that the culturalist explanation for the commitment gap is the foremost alternative to the welfare corporatist one, failure to find empirical support for the latter amounts to confirmation for the former. If differences in management practice and organizational form *cannot* explain the commitment gap, then the culturalist view, while not directly tested, remains a viable competing alternative hypothesis.

Even so, we devoted some effort to directly measuring differences in value orientations between our samples of Japanese and US factory employees and to evaluating the roles of demographic background, job position, social bonds, and other variables in molding those differences. We also examined the impact of employees' values on commitment and job satisfaction. This analysis yielded a variety of interesting and interpretable, though often subtle, patterns. But there was very little evidence that work values and expectations (as measured in our survey) sufficed to account for the variations we observed in employees' work attitudes.

If culture in general and work values in specific do not appear to make substantial direct or additive contributions to explaining Japanese/US differences in employee work attitudes, it may be that they moderate or condition the effects of job attributes, organizational designs, and management practices. This is a pervasive theme in the job design research of industrial psychologists, although it is not one that has produced a substantial body of confirming evidence. Nevertheless, it takes on compelling significance in this cross-national study: in the face of claims that the adoption of Japanese management methods will lead US firms out of the wilderness of stagnant productivity, poor quality control, and industrial unrest, numerous critics have hastened to point out that the effectiveness of Japanese-style work organization may well be confined to employees who have internalized Japanese work values and expectations. From this perspective, Japanese management *does* make a difference – worker motivation does not stem from culture alone – but its potential for motivating individualistic US workers is nil.

Our research turned up negligible evidence that measures of work values "moderated" or conditioned employees' responses to job attributes such as complexity, autonomy, and supervisory control. Moreover, though we uncovered a number of significant differences in the *magnitudes* of coefficients, our fully specified regression models for organizational commitment and job satisfaction were strikingly similar between the US and Japan in the overall *patterns* whereby employees' work attitudes were linked to our measures of individual, job, and organizational variables.

We did, on the other hand, find a number of specific differences between the countries in the processes determining social integration, job rewards, and the perceived complexity and autonomy associated with the work role. Some of these reflect differences in factory and work group organization that we have discussed elsewhere (e.g. chapter 7). In other cases, such as our measure of *ringi*/group decision-making, country differences are probably due to measurement incongruities between the Japanese and US surveys. In any event, they did not appear to fall into a clean and consistent pattern so as to suggest, for example, that Japanese values (of groupism, diligence, etc.) produce systematic shifts in the reactions of workers to facets of workplace organization.

This essential similarity in the antecedents of work attitudes among Japanese and US manufacturing employees provides preliminary support for the welfare corporatist hypothesis of a universally applicable commitment-maximizing organizational form. Moreover, it suggests that, while the role of culture is not trivial, it is primarily: (a) indirect through the role it presently plays and the residues it has historically left in the concrete organization of Japanese firms; and (b) additive in the sense that it contributes to attitude and behavioral differences between Japanese and US workers but does not markedly condition the ways employees respond to their jobs or other facets of their employment.

These parallels in the reactions of Japanese and US workers to dimensions of work and company life imply that where a hypothesis derived from corporatist theory fails, it fails in both countries; where it succeeds, it likewise succeeds in both. We found no evidence in either country, for example, for the arguments advanced most strongly by Marxists but also by writers such as Blauner, Woodward, and Dore that tall, finely graded hierarchies and high subunit density "divide and conquer" the workforce so as to shift commitments and loyalties to the firm as a whole. However, we did find evidence that structural (particularly vertical) differentiation of this sort tends to be greater in Japanese plants. Likewise, while tenure with an employer was, as expected, higher in our Japanese sample and is thus consistent with the presumption of greater internal labor-market development in that country, tenure in the workplace did not give rise to more favorable employee attitudes toward the firm. An employee's age, though, was strongly and positively related to his or her levels of commitment and satisfaction.

The effects of decision-making arrangements and welfare services provided perhaps the greatest support for the corporatist hypothesis. We found, as is commonly thought to be the case, that quality circle programs were much more prevalent in Japanese than US industry, but that QC in both countries significantly raised employee teamwork, social integration, and commitment. Relative to US plants, Japanese organizations are also less inclined to delegate formal authority but more likely to encourage informal participation in decisions. What we had not anticipated was the broad evidence that, *in both countries* this particular decision-making pattern of high formal and low *de facto* centralization would be associated with greater commitment and satisfaction. Finally, the evidence in our Japanese sample that the *ringi* method of decision-making enhanced commitment was quite consistent with corporatist theory, even though we found no comparable association with the group decision index in the US survey. The absence of an effect of this measure is not surprising, for it is a weak indicator and certainly is not directly analogous to the *ringi* measure utilized in our Japan survey.

Finally, our results for employee welfare services were in near-perfect conformity with the corporatist hypothesis. Though our composite index by no means exhausts the full array of services which at least some plants in these countries make available to their employees, it testifies that the Japanese plants in our sample offered more services and programs than did those in Indiana. But whether the services were provided in the US or Japan, the effect was the same: a substantial increment in employees' commitment to their firms and satisfaction with their jobs.

Other evidence fits the welfare corporatist perspective on Japan/US differences in work organization and employee work attitudes less neatly but is nonetheless intriguing. Plant unionization means quite different things in the US and Japanese economies, and, indeed, some theorists in the corporatist tradition have predicted that it has opposite implications for employee reactions to the firm; specifically, that Japanese enterprise unions are a cooptive control structure that increases employee dependence. What we found was not quite this but close: commitment and satisfaction are far lower in US union plants as we predicted and others have observed; unionization does not elicit these outcomes in Japan, though neither does it seem to work proactively to align workers' interests and identifications with the goals and practices of the firm.

We have noted that dual economy theory is closely linked to the model of welfare corporatist organization as an emergent form of labor control centered on the mechanism of commitment. Corporatist forms of organization such as internal labor markets, elaborate organizational structures, formal rules, participatory mechanisms, and welfare services are characteristic of the core sector, which comprises large plants and firms, multisite national corporations, and mass and process production technologies. Although our data provided only slight support for it, the frequent claim that Japan's economy is more dualistic than that of the US is one more building block in the corporatist argument that the West is following pathways already trod by Japan. Consistent with the dual economy argument, we found that commitment and satisfaction in both countries were higher in large, branch plants using mass production and process technologies. This contradicts some longstanding streams of theory on work alienation, which predict that large factory size, absentee-ownership, and standardized mass (versus craft and small-batch) production are forms of work organization that encourage the spread of work alienation in the manufacturing labor force.

In chapters 4 and 5, we considered the micro-level intervening processes at the employee, job, and work group levels through which organization-level structures and management practices shape the responses of individuals. Much prior research and the predictions of the corporatist model led us to anticipate, for example, that both horizontal (among coworkers) and vertical (across ranks) social integration and cohesion would be greater in the Japanese workforce. This would reflect both the collectivist values and tight-knit networks which culturalists attribute to Japanese society *and* the operation of corporatist control structures such as quality circles, finely graded status hierarchies and paternalistic welfare services. Part of our expectation was strongly confirmed: friendships, informal socializing, and other indications of warm social relations both within and across ranks were far more pervasive in Japan. On the other hand, the evidence that these arose from implementation of corporatist employment practices was mixed. While QC activity and the Japanese pattern of centralized authority combined with decentralized participation seemed to encourage strong social bonds, other organizational structures – such as welfare services, vertical and horizontal differentiation, and formalization – played either negative or negligible roles in this regard.

We also predicted that Japanese job design practice stressing low fragmentation and formalization combined with high rotation would enhance perceived levels of complexity and control, but this proved not to be the case. Japanese employees scored *lower* on our indicators of job complexity and autonomy than did the American respondents, a pattern that may not simply be a peculiarity of our sampling or measurement procedures, since it has been found by others as well (see Naoi and Schooler, 1985). This was one of several junctures in our study where we may have unearthed facets of the "dark side" of Japanese welfare corporatism, at least as seen by workers – the heavy discipline, the high speed of production, and the low levels of flexibility that *individuals*, as contrasted, perhaps, with work groups, experience.

A central hypothesis that we have sought to test is that systems of welfare corporatism rely heavily upon elaborate, highly differentiated organizational structures to divide and individuate the workforce, then re-integrate it around company goals. As we noted above, our plant-level measures of vertical and horizontal (subunit) differentiation did not support this prediction: these structural variables were not positively related either to commitment or job satisfaction, nor to the intervening variables of job complexity, job rewards, and social bonds. Indeed, the bulk of the evidence was consistent with the opposite proposition, one that has its own lengthy tradition in organizational theory: that complex, formal structures in work organizations evoke alienation and detachment on the part of employees.

Yet when we considered the impact of hierarchy, not as a global structural property, but as an individual-level attribute, we found numerous indications that Japanese status hierarchies *are* designed in ways which serve to minimize cleavages and maximize consensus across ranks. Our study corroborated the impressions of past observers that Japanese administrative hierarchies are more differentiated yet less unequal than is typical of management hierarchies in the US. We also found that the differences among managers, supervisors, and workers were consistently more pronounced in our US sample with respect to nearly every employee-level outcome we examined – attitudes, rewards, task complexity and control, integration, and so on. This, of course, is a somewhat different issue from the macro-level one of whether vertical differentiation engenders a higher average level of commitment to the firm. Taller hierarchies with more intervening levels may, on the one hand, produce the communication and control pathologies anticipated in bureaucratic alienation theory while at the same time reduce the distances in outlook and orientation between managers and workers.

As in any large-scale empirical study, then, our findings are complex and lend themselves to few pat interpretations. Nevertheless, they have yielded a portrait of the Japanese workforce as more committed to the company while simultaneously less content with the job which much organization behavior theory would regard as evocative of high motivation. Moreover, our findings of Japan-US differences in the decision-making structures and welfare programs of firms *and* in the responses of employees to these structures provide strong evidence that at least part of any commitment advantage enjoyed by the Japanese manufacturing economy derives from wider implementation of certain elements of welfare corporatist control.

The future of Japanese commitment and welfare corporatism

It is almost pro forma to conclude studies of Japanese work organization and work attitudes with a caveat to the effect that such patterns are undergoing rapid change and forecasts to the future are hazardous. Some of this uncertainty is well-founded. Work life and employment practice are fairly volatile phenomena – not only in Japan but in any industrial society – and they tend to be buffeted by changing social and economic conditions, exogenous shocks such as war and diplomacy, rising standard-of-living expectations of the population, and numerous other long- and short-term trends. Other forecasts, however, particularly those made by writers on these topics ten to twenty years ago, should be viewed with caution, for they represent the knee-jerk predictions of old-style convergence theorists still clinging to the antique notion that rational and American management practice will be forever one and the same. Japanese exceptionalism cannot last, this argument held, for only by assimilating the economic and administrative codes and value systems of the West can Japan hope to sustain its drive to world class economic standing. Not surprisingly, proponents of the view that Japanese values and organizational arrangements are anachronisms and inertial drags on Japan's future economic progress have been notably silent in recent years. Yet at one time these admonitions were taken quite seriously by the Japanese themselves, who fretted over the possibility that such "traditional" practices as *ringi, nenko,* and permanent employment would thwart Japan's historical ambition of catching up to the West (Yoshino, 1968)

Now that the Japanese economy is the premier producer of high quality manufactured goods and Japanese banks and trading companies have become the largest and most powerful in the world, no one is saying that the use of unconventional (read nonwestern) management practices will get in the way of Japan's competitiveness. But there are clearly forces at work producing changes in work organization and work attitudes in Japan and in the US alike.

Consider first the case of work values and attitudes. An endlessly repeated assertion among the Japanese is that the commitment and dedication to work and company which so rapidly advanced the nation from postwar devastation to the front ranks of economic powers are not shared by the young. Though no doubt overstated in the usual hyperbole that characterizes older generation wailing about the shortcomings of "today's youth," there are good reasons to believe this is so. The generation that emerged from the rubble of Japan's wartime defeat had precious little going for it apart from a determination to survive and rebuild. Expectations for the personal rewards of economic effort – leisure and affluence – were minimal. Japanese political and industrial leaders have long capitalized on the scarcity mentality of the Japanese populace, evoking the spectres of foreign competition and Japan's frail natural resource base, to drive the workforce to higher levels of sacrifice and dedication. In the 1980s, when Japan's enormous wealth and economic prowess are secrets to no one, large numbers of younger people, born under conditions and expectations of scarcity, are embracing the rewards and values that societal affluence brings. Our own data consistently revealed evidence of steeper age gradients in work values and attitudes in Japan, suggesting greater age-based divergence of outlook than in the US.

Even so, there are numerous indications that commitment to a company continues to be impressively high among the Japanese. The usual indicators of behavioral commitment (low strike activity, absenteeism, and turnover; high average hours worked) reveal little evidence of major negative shifts accompanying Japan's phenomenal surge in wealth (see, e.g. Keizai Koho Center, 1987). Foreign companies operating in Japan still face substantial barriers to successful recruitment of experienced employees because of the strong ties that bind such workers to domestic firms.

On the other hand, a case can be made that work and company commitment have been rising in the United States. In manufacturing, this trend reflects in no small measure the severely weakened and hence dependent position of labor vis-à-vis management. Declines in manufacturing jobs, which have accelerated under the merger-and-acquisition waves brought on by Reagan-era deregulation, have left industrial unions with little bargaining power and have led to strong competition among workers for the jobs that remain. Another force operating in the same direction is the internationalization of production, wherein US manufacturing is outsourced to foreign cheap-labor sites or eliminated altogether, such that the US firm becomes, in *Business Week's* (1986a) terms, a "hollow corporation," promoting and distributing goods produced exclusively by foreign contractors. The power and security enjoyed by American labor in the 1950s and 1960s, and its concomitant affluence and security, stemmed from strong unions, weak foreign competition, and tacit collusion with large US corporations to pass on negotiated hikes in labor costs to consumers in the form of higher prices. Today, as the decline of manufacturing employment and the rise in foreign competition leave in their wake a severely wounded labor movement, companies across the country have mounted a sharp offensive to force concessions from unions and even drive them from the workplace. The net result of these trends has been a more dependent and docile labor force, having lower expectations for job security and benefits, and inclined to close ranks with management in defending the firm against the onslaught of foreign competition.

Now a docile, nonunion labor force that is heavily dependent upon the good graces of its corporate employers is an end product which seems very much consistent with the ambitions of the welfare corporatist organizational form. Yet when external circumstances are encouraging these developments, companies lose the incentive to work for them by providing employees with positive inducements. Job ladders, employment guarantees and welfare services were seized upon by Japanese and US companies alike as means of imposing discipline on a mobile and unruly workforce in a time when manufacturing jobs were in abundance. There are signs that welfare corporatism is endangered in both countries: first, by the competitive pressures on companies to cut labor costs and eliminate bureaucracy (which *Business Week*, 1986b, thinks may spell "the end of corporate loyalty"); and secondly, by the perception that high unemployment and weak unions have reduced the need for corporatist strategies of controlling and motivating employees.

A recent economic trend which a number of observers feel is impeding the progress of US firms toward further deployment of welfare corporatist arrangements is the "externalization of employment" (Pfeffer and Baron, 1987). This refers to the rapidly expanding practice on the part of US companies of hiring temporary and part-time labor to perform jobs once held by regular, full-time, career-ladder employees. This retreat from the internalized bureaucratic employment relation to a set of ongoing transactions with the open labor market harkens back to an earlier era in economic organization when factory labor was not continuously employed but rather subcontracted from the outside (Williamson, 1985). Indeed, accompanying the rise in demand for part-time and limited-tenure workers is, not surprisingly, a surge in the supply of temporary-help agencies, offering trained employees for a lower and more flexible wage and benefit bill.

Like Pfeffer and Baron, the *Wall Street Journal* sees the rise of temporary employment signalling the demise of welfare corporatist employment in America:

> For longer than most Americans can remember, a good job with a big company has meant lifelong economic security and much more. It has provided a place to meet and gossip, people to love or to hate, ball-point pens and expense-account lunches, bowling leagues and United Way drives, Christmas parties and hats emblazoned with corporate logos, cheerleading with catch-phrases ('the Hewlett-Packard Way') and a metaphorical 'family' usually headed by kindly but authoritarian father figures. In recent years it has even provided a corporate 'culture.' But

imagine a company town a decade hence: To 1980's sensibilities, many of Mega Corp.'s employees seem unusually sobersided. One reason is that their jobs are only as secure as their next quarterly performance review ... Once-mighty Mega Corp. has shrunk to a third of its peak size in the late 1970s. A great deal of its engineering, data processing and advertising are done by a satellite system of smaller concerns nearby ... A two-tier work force is taking shape: 'Inside' employees still enjoy benefits, perquisites, and a degree of job security. New 'outside' workers have an uncertain tenure. (Bennett, 1987)

From the perspective of our work in this book, the cost to the company of dismantling the apparatus of welfare corporatist organization and switching to short-term market contracts for a substantial percentage of its labor requirements should be severe in terms of loss of commitment to the firm and its goals. Do top corporate managers believe that the decline of unions, rising slack in the labor market, and xenophobia with respect to foreign competition will provide the discipline and motivation that welfare corporatism buys with internal labor markets, bureaucratic control, and "paternalism?" Some managers do not appear to think so. To quote the *Wall Street Journal* (April 18, 1987) again:

That arm's-length relationship (between the company and its temporary workers), however, can be a drawback. 'They don't tend to be dedicated to the corporate ideal,' says Hewlett-Packard's Mr. Prather. 'They're here to make money, not to fulfill the corporate vision.' As a result, he says, free-lancers won't 'put in the extra-mile' or get involved in touchy situations.

This manager's observations suggest that there are limits to the extent to which companies are willing to substitute temporary people for regular career-track employees. As another *Wall Street Journal* writer put it (Melloan, 1987):

some corporations aren't sure they like temps. That very lack of identification with the corporation and its aims and the absence of loyalty to the corporation and fellow workers is seen as a business handicap.

Most of the jobs that are subcontracted will continue to be those traditionally held by relatively low-skilled, highly substitutable employees. Aside from the question of motivation and commitment, companies' incentives to realize long-term returns on investments made in enterprise-specific skills and knowledge will likely ensure that a high proportion of employees in the key production as well as management positions will continue to participate in the internal labor markets, strong cultures, welfare systems, and bureaucratic structures that together comprise welfare corporatist work organization.

From the point of view of our comparative study of Japanese and US work institutions, what is intriguing about the trend in the US toward greater and more formal segmentation of the workforce – into a core stratum of regular employees holding permanent jobs and a peripheral group of adjunct workers in temporary jobs – is that this has long been Japanese practice. A substantial percentage of the workforce in that country consists of temporary workers (largely women and post-retirement employees) whose low wages and benefits and lack of job security reflect their exclusion from the permanent employment system and the other trappings of Japanese welfare corporatism.

Thus, we contend that the current US trend toward segmentation between permanent and temporary employees *in the same firm* presents no fundamental challenge to the prediction of a drift toward welfare corporatism in US companies. Indeed, to the extent that the Japanese employment system constitutes the archetype of welfare corporatist organization, the externalization of a portion of the firm's workforce is one more compelling piece of evidence for corporatist theory. We suspect that in the years to come, we will see still further shifts in US patterns of work organization and employment, which, accelerated by the rising chorus of concerns about American competitiveness, will impel US industry further toward the model of Japan.

Notes

1 Work organization, culture, and work attitudes: theoretical issues

1. The concept of "corporatism," of course, has a distinct meaning in (especially European) political theory. Though definitions vary widely, most writers use the term to refer to an industrial relations system by which the interventionist state tries to bind workers to it and its policies by using leaders of centralized labor organizations to control their members in the state's interests. There are some parallels between our use of the term to refer to intra-organizational relationships and its use to denote more macroscopic, societal structures. In each case labor derives its rights from others: employees from owners; and labor from the state. Moreover, both are bargained relationships which require a normative consensus in order to be effective. Nevertheless, there are important differences; in particular, the role of the state is very different in mediating intra- as opposed to interorganizational relations. While welfare corporatism is an apt term to describe commitment-maximizing work organizations, then, we need to bear in mind its specialized meaning in Dore's writing as well as our own.

2. However, there are numerous indications of subgroup rivalry in Japanese organizations, particularly among the *habatsu*, or cliques formed around school ties and common cohort membership (Yoshino, 1968).

3. Yet another view of the relationship between cultural norms and individual sentiments is that, when the two are aligned, the former accentuate the latter. Dore (1973:214–15) states it well in the following insightful passage from *British Factory-Japanese Factory*:

"[English Electric workers] too have some feeling for the firm... But still they feel themselves less totally and definitively English Electric men than their counterparts would feel themselves Hitachi men because personal experience is translated into sentiment and attachments only by refraction through the norms of the work community – the *shared* norms of their fellow-workers. It is overstating the case to say that one feels only what one is supposed to feel, but it is safe to say that one is more easily disposed to feel what one is supposed to feel – the more so the more oversocialized and conformist the society is. And in English Electric the relevant norms faithfully reflect the organizational assumptions underlying them – the limited commitment, the basic market orientation ... It is not just that the Japanese system enhances enterprise consciousness; it also – the other side of the coin – does less to develop individualism. Man-imbedded-in-organization has no

259

great need to make personal moral choices; the organization's norms set guidelines; the organization's sanctions keep him to the path of virtue. It is the man between organizations, the man of limited commitment, who has the greater responsibility of choosing."

2 Research design, data collection, and the samples

1. In the US, representatives of three plants approached us and asked to be included in our study; we added them to our sample. There were no volunteers in the Japanese sample, though a few plants were included because members of our Japanese research team had personal contacts with them.
2. For example, lists were sometimes out of date with respect to information on local plants; some had gone out of business; and some plants housed administrative and distributive outlets as opposed to production and manufacturing.
3. In two cases in the US, we distributed questionnaires to employees in two plants of the same firm. Since we did not conduct separate interviews with managers in these plants, however, we combine them in our analysis and regard them as single organizations. In another case, we were able to distribute questionnaires to employees of three plants of a single firm; we regard these as distinct organizations because we also interviewed key informants in each of these plants. In Japan, we did not study more than one plant per firm, though in several cases we collected data from affiliated companies (for example, a "parent" company and one of its "child" subcontractors).
4. A number of our questionnaire items, for example, are derived from instruments devised by Koya Azumi (see, e.g. Azumi and McMillan, 1976).

3 Commitment and job satisfaction in the US and Japan

1. The response categories for the work commitment items in table 3.1 are the same as those used in the questionnaire: an "agree" response denotes low commitment. We reflect these categories when combining these items in the scale of work commitment used in subsequent chapters.
2. There is a problem in interpreting the results for the question, "my work is only a small part of who I am," since the item translates in Japan as "work is a small part of my life." The concept of "who I am" is difficult to render in Japanese.
3. Surprisingly, we find no significant difference between Japanese males and females on the item comparing work and family. However, only 16 percent of the Japanese sample is female, a high percentage of whom are young and unmarried.
4. In order to simplify the presentation of the percentage distributions in table 3.1, we have collapsed more detailed response codes (e.g. strongly agree, agree, undecided, disagree, strongly disagree) into a simpler three-category classification.
5. In the regression analyses reported in later chapters, we have collapsed codes 5 and 6 (at the agree end) and 2 and 3 (at the disagree end). We also conducted analyses collapsing the extreme two codes at each end of the scale. A detailed examination of the distributions of cases for each coding scheme suggested that the former coding was most sensible. However, our results are similar regardless

of which of these alternative modes of coding the Japanese attitude items is used, or whether a third approach is adopted where all three agree and three disagree items are collapsed to produce a three-point scale (see table 3.1). Moreover, comparisons between the countries based on the three-point scale are almost totally indistinguishable from comparisons based on the five-point scale in which the middle codes are collapsed. The five-point coding collapsing the extremes deviates a bit more, but not enough to alter our substantive conclusions. These similarities among coding schemes are not surprising, since all the alternatives preserve the ordinal ordering of the categories.

6. To simplify the presentation in table 3.1, we have collapsed more detailed response categories into three-way classifications: positive, undecided, and negative. To maximize comparability on the direct indicator, we collapsed into the middle categories the "weaker" degree of satisfaction and dissatisfaction. Thus, for the American questionnaire, "somewhat satisfied" and "somewhat dissatisfied" are combined as "undecided"; and in the case of the Japanese questionnaire, "undecided," "slightly agree," and "slightly disagree" were combined, as were "completely agree" and "agree" on the positive side, and "completely disagree" and "disagree" on the negative. In both countries, workers who did not express rather strong positions on the question of job satisfaction were included in the middle category.

7. In multiple-group comparisons, it is common to relax the assumption of constant measurement structure across populations in the case of measurement error variances and covariances (see Miller *et al.*, 1981).

8. The likelihood-ratio Chi-Square statistic was 449 with 59 degrees of freedom. By prevailing standards (see, e.g. Sobel and Bohrnstedt, 1985), this indicates poor fit, but our very large sample size would appear to be the reason. The LISREL goodness-of-fit index, which is unaffected by sample size and has an upper bound of 1.0, is .99 for the fit of the model to each data set. Relaxing the equality constraints on the loadings (lambdas) lowers the Chi-Square value to 299 with 51 degrees of freedom, but the increments in the GFI are minimal (US: .991; Japan: .994).

9. As these models are estimated on the pooled sample of 8,302 observations, we devised a new measurement model whose loadings were the same but whose measurement error dispersion matrices differed from the sample-specific models. Chi-Square = 425 with df = 34 and GFI = .99.

10. Given the general sensitivity of the kinds of nonrecursive models presented in table 3.3 to shifts in specification and our unwillingness to take too seriously the identifying assumptions needed to estimate them, we drop the specification of reciprocal causation between commitment and satisfaction in our analyses in subsequent chapters.

4 Job attributes and work attitudes: an employee-level analysis

1. Unless otherwise noted, all regression models were estimated with Ordinary Least Squares (OLS). Because of the arbitrary metrics of many of our variables, plus our interest in the relative influence of predictors within the same equation, much of our analysis (chapter 7 is an exception) reports *standardized* regression coefficients

only. These, however, are well known to present problems in cross-population comparisons, as their magnitude depends on sample variances as well as on the unstandardized slopes (Hanushek and Jackson, 1977). Our inferences about Japan/US contrasts in effects, however, are based, not directly on the standardized coefficients, but on the difference-in-slope tests presented in our tables of regression results.

The regression models were estimated from pairwise data-present covariance matrices. Degrees of freedom were downwardly adjusted to the mean number of observations present for all variables: 4,418 in the US; 3,516 in Japan.

2. We considered the possibility that the means on the supervisory control item were masking subtle differences between the US and Japanese distributions. Specifically, from the assumption that teamwork and group dynamics typify the Japanese workplace, we would predict that more Japanese would select the middle category of this item, which implies joint decision-making between the worker and the manager. This, however, proved not to be the case: 56 percent of the Japanese vs. 60 percent of the Americans selected the middle category.

3. We factor analyzed the three autonomy items along with the four job complexity items. This produced two factors, providing initial evidence for construct validity in tapping two distinct concepts.

4. As Cole (1979:99) has suggested, there are severe problems of comparability in reaching a common definition of "job" in the US and Japan. Job categories tend to be less sharply and formally defined in Japanese work settings, even when the tasks involved may be the same.

5. We analyze the structure of earnings inequality more extensively in Kalleberg and Lincoln (1988). There we examine the processes of earnings determination separately for male managers, male workers, and female workers in each country. Moreover, our multilevel analysis in that paper examines the role of both organizational and individual variables in generating earnings inequality within each of these groups.

6. As promotion expectation is a dichotomous dependent variable in these regressions, ordinary least-squares is not an optimal estimation technique. It seems justified here, however, by the fact that the equations for promotion are part of a larger causal system which is estimated with OLS. To switch to a different estimation technique (e.g. probit or logit analysis) for this one set of estimates would complicate our interpretation of results. Moreover, the distribution on the promotion variable in each country is not so skewed that OLS estimates are likely to be severely biased (see, e.g. Knoke, 1975).

7. Evidence that these four measures of social integration (quality of relations with supervisors; quality of relations with coworkers; off-the-job socializing; and number of close friends) tap distinct concepts was provided by the results of an oblique factor analysis of all of the social integration questions, which revealed that the items measuring these concepts formed separate factors. Moreover, the social integration items loaded on factors that were distinct from those representing task characteristics and job rewards when all of these variables were factor analyzed together. These results provide initial evidence for the convergent as well as divergent validity of these measures of social integration.

8. The proportion of the total effect of a variable that is mediated, or indirect, is

calculated by subtracting its direct effect (table 4.5, column 3) from its total effect (table 4.5, column 1 or 2), and dividing by the total effect. In this case, the total effect on satisfaction of being in a line production department in Japan (relative to "other" departments) is $-.114$, while the direct effect is $-.058$. Therefore, the indirect effect of being in a direct production department is: $-.114 - [-.058] = -.056$, and the proportion of the total effect that is mediated by all the job characteristics and work values is: $-.056/-.114 = 49$ percent. We can also compute the indirect effects on a work attitude of any independent variable in table 4.5 via any specific intervening variable. To do this, we simply multiply the effect of the independent variable on the intervening variable (see tables 4.2 – 4.4) by the direct effect of the intervening variable on the work attitudes (see table 4.5). For example, the indirect effect via autonomy on satisfaction of being in a line department in Japan is: $-.071 \times .071 = -.005$. Thus, $-.005/-.114 = 4.4$ percent of the reason why Japanese employees in production departments are less satisfied with their jobs than those in office departments is because they have lower levels of autonomy.

9. The equations whose coefficients are presented in table 4.5 included measures of employees' backgrounds as well as the plant-level variables that we discuss in chapters 6–8. This is consistent with our focus in chapter 4 on microscopic determinants of work attitudes that operate *within* organizations.

5 Work values and employee background effects

1. Evidence for the construct validity of the three-item work commitment scale is provided by the results of both oblique and orthogonal factor analyses, which in both samples showed that the three commitment to work items formed a separate factor from the organizational commitment and job satisfaction items.
2. A number of the managers in our Indianapolis study mentioned that in the past they had typically filled skilled craftsmen positions through internal training and promotion. In recent years, however, rising unemployment among skilled manufacturing workers had made it less costly to pass over present employees and to hire directly from the outside.

6 Technology, society, and organization

1. This chapter draws in part on material that appeared in Lincoln and McBride (1987) and Lincoln, Hanada, and McBride (1986).
2. Although our focus is on control structures in modern capitalist enterprises, there are some remarkable parallels between welfare corporatism as a control system in capitalist firms and the employment systems of state-owned enterprises in the Soviet Union and the People's Republic of China (see, for example Walder, 1986). In these countries, employment in a state firm is a lifetime and broadly inclusive commitment in which the worker is highly dependent on the firm for basic services.

7 *Organizational structures in Japan and the US: a plant-level analysis*

1. This chapter is in part based on material that appeared previously in Lincoln, Hanada, and McBride (1986).
2. These results, based on a pooled sample of US and Japanese plants, assume parallel regression slopes in each country. Although we do not explicitly test that hypothesis here (as we do later for the case of organizational variables – see table 7.3), we found no marked differences between the country-specific regressions.
3. A logarithmic transformation of size is commonly used in regression analyses of organizational data, since the absolute values are quite skewed in most samples, a property that tends to produce nonlinear relationships. The logarithmic transformation reduces the skew and linearizes the functional form of the relation (for discussions, see, e.g. Blau and Schoenherr, 1971; Stolzenberg, 1978).
4. These regression models hardly provide definitive causal explanations for each plant-level dependent variable. The causal role of plant size with respect to technology is particularly problematic. Economists view size of the production unit as an expression of economies of scale which vary as a function, not a cause, of product type and technology (Bain, 1959). On the other hand, the volume of production and scale of operations constrain the range of technologies that might be used to produce the same material. Our inclusion of size as an explanatory factor in our equations is warranted because of its pervasive association with many apects of plant structure and functioning, and because some of the variables we examine are expressed in forms which make them definitionally dependent upon size (e.g. the number of subunits).
5. The formula for the F-test for heterogeneity of slope is:

$$F(k_2-k_1, N-k_2) = \frac{ESS_1-ESS_2/k_2-k_1}{ESS_2/N-k_2}$$

where: ESS_1 is the error sum of squares from a regression model in which intercepts differ by country but slopes are constrained to be the same. ESS_2 is the error sum of squares from an unconstrained model; i.e. both intercepts and slopes may vary. k_1 and k_2 are the number of parameters estimated in the constrained and unconstrained models, respectively. And N is the number of observations. See, e.g. Hanushek and Jackson (1977:126).
6. The Aston scales have been criticized for their heavy reliance on the perceptions of top management, and we acknowledge this to be a limitation of our research. The usual defense is that the items in most such scales (functional specialization, formalization, centralization) call for fairly objective statements of fact, rather than opinion or preference. At many of our interviews, moreover, managers in addition to the plant manager were present. In these cases, the answers at least reflect a consensus among knowledgeable informants. In addition, we took pains to impress upon our informants the need to avoid guesswork and to consult others or documentary sources if they were unsure about an answer.
7. We also entered QC and *ringi* in the full equations for formal and *de facto* centralization. The coefficients we obtained were not appreciably different from those presented here, although there were some symptoms of the presence of multicollinearity.
8. This reasoning raises the possibility that the causal ordering between centraliza-

tion and QC should be reversed: that plants under high-level management control are more likely to take the initiative to experiment with participatory programs like QC. A powerful chief executive could impose such a program by fiat and, responding to corporate personnel and labor relations policy, might be more inclined to do so than operating managers farther down the line.

9. Given the equation, $Y = a + bX + cX^2 + e$, the derivative of Y with respect to X is: $b + 2cX$. Setting this to zero permits a solution for the value of X that corresponds to the maximum or minimum of the function (Stolzenberg, 1979). Such an exercise provides useful information on the exact nature of a nonlinear relation.

10. Again there is the possibility that the causation runs the other way: centralized plants are more likely to be unionized. We think this an unlikely explanation for the patterns in our data, since, in the great majority of cases, formal collective bargaining in these companies had been well established for years prior to our measurement of centralization.

8 Work organization, and workforce commitment: a multi-level analysis

1. Portions of this chapter are based on material previously reported in Lincoln and Kalleberg (1985).
2. The statistical analysis of this chapter retains the individual employee as unit of observation to which measures of organization-level variables are assigned. A consequence of this method is that the standardized regression coefficients we report combine information on the explanatory power of organizational differences and the importance of specific organizational measures in explaining those differences. This means that measures of organizational variables may account for a very high percentage of the variance that lies between organizations, but if the between-organization component is a small percentage of the total variation, the standardized effects will appear to be small.

    In our data, the percentage of the total variance in the factor score composite for commitment which lies between plants is 9 percent in the US and $9\frac{1}{2}$ percent in the Japanese sample. For satisfaction, the figures are $5\frac{1}{2}$ percent and $7\frac{1}{2}$ percent, respectively. These are not trivial percentages. Taking into account the multitude of forces producing variation among individual employees *within* plants, not to mention the complex causal chains that filter the effects of organization variables such as centralization or size, these are in fact substantial percentages, which signal that organizational-level causes are of real significance in understanding employee-level outcomes.

    Beyond the question of the proportion of variance in work attitudes that falls between plants, there is also the issue of the extent to which our measures account for it. Plant differences might constitute a sizable percentage of the total variation in commitment, but this will not advance our knowledge if the organizational variables we have measured cannot explain the between-plant component. Comparing the R^2s from the full equations in table 8.1 with R^2s from equations in which plant means on the dependent variables are substituted for the entire set of plant measures yields the following differences: commitment, US, .025, Japan, −.003; satisfaction, US, .011; Japan, .013. The R^2s from the regressions including the plant-specific means indicate the proportion of total variation which lies between plants. This, moreover, is the upper bound on the amount of variation which plant-level variables can explain. Thus, the plant variance unexplained by our measures ranges from a low of zero (the $-.003$ is calculation error; measures of plant characteristics cannot account for more variance than the plant differences themselves) to a high of 28 percent (.025/.09). These small to nonexistent residual plant effects buttress our claims to successful measurement and model specification.

A case could be made for an aggregate analysis, in which group means, adjusted for the effects of composition on individual-level covariates, are taken as the dependent variables (Lincoln and Zeitz, 1980). If the research question is the extent to which organizational variables explain the differences among employees in different plants, we may have little interest in the variation among employees within plants. For example, suppose our interest ultimately lay with the implications of workforce commitment for variations in plant productivity, quality, and other performance outcomes. Since these are defined at the level of the plant, only plant differences in commitment can contribute to explaining them.

Although a systematic aggregate-level analysis is too great a digression from our main concerns, we get a rather different picture of the relative impact of individual and plant-level causes by standardizing the metric slope estimates of the plant variables on the pooled, within-country, plant-level variances. The effect is to increase the coefficients on the organizational measures by a factor of 3.7 in the satisfaction equation and by 3.0 in the commitment equation. For example, using the plant-level standard deviations of the commitment and satisfaction factor scores to standardize the slopes of the plant variables in the full Japanese commitment equation (table 8.1) raises the coefficient for welfare services from .115 to .345, for *ringi* from .079 to .237 and number of ranks from $-.058$ to $-.174$. To avoid confusion, the coefficients reported in this chapter are based, as in the usual multilevel model, on the individual-level standard deviations. However, judgments as to the absolute or relative importance of predictors based on these coefficients should be made with extreme caution, as the latter paint an unduly conservative picture of the impact of organizational variables.

3. Hodson and Sullivan (1985) also address the hypothesis that workforce commitment is higher in core sector firms. Their reasoning is wholly congenial with our understanding of corporatist theory: large, visible, national corporations use their material and reputational resources to create a work environment and enterprise community which instills pride in membership and identification with the firm. However, in contrast to our findings, their analysis of 4,493 private sector employees in Wisconsin suggests that job satisfaction and commitment are *higher* in locally owned plants than in Fortune 500 corporations and other multi-site firms. This apparent inconsistency may be explained by the fact that their measures do not tap directly the concept of commitment to a company. Rather, job commitment in their data refers to: (a) the expectation that the employee will remain in the job ten years hence; and (b) the worker's satisfaction with how s/he perceives others perceiving his or her job.

4. With cross-sectional data, it is, of course, not easy to sort out the direction of causality between workforce commitment or alienation and the presence or absence of a union. To the best of our knowledge, however, none of the plants in

either of our samples had recently been organized. In the majority of cases, the union contracts stretched far back in time. We thus find it unlikely that negative associations between unionism and employee commitment and satisfaction at the time of the survey could reflect a process of unions forming where worker disenchantment is high. Far more probable is our assumption that unions mobilize worker sentiment against the company and present major obstacles to management efforts to foster loyalty and dedication to the firm.

5. We encountered clear symptoms of multicollinearity upon entering the number of units in the equations in table 8.1 for Japan, due chiefly to a .66 correlation with plant size. The coefficients presented for this variable were therefore obtained from a parallel model from which size was excluded.

6. We also disaggregated the centralization indices and examined the correlations of their 37 specific items with employee commitment. We found the same pattern of positive correlations with the formal authority items and negative correlations with the *de facto* centralization items in both countries. In the US, for example, only six of the formal authority items displayed significant negative correlations as compared with 14 of the *de facto* items. On the other hand, 11 of the authority items exhibited the predicted positive correlations while only three of the *de facto* items had significant positive correlations. In Japan the pattern was even stronger. Only two of the authority items correlated negatively with commitment, while 17 of the *de facto* items were significant and negative. On the other hand, 20 of the formal authority items were positively correlated, compared to five of the *de facto* items.

References

Abegglen, James C. 1958. *The Japanese Factory: Aspects of its Social Organization.* Glencoe, Illinois: The Free Press

Abegglen, James C. and George Stalk, Jr. 1985. *Kaisha, The Japanese Corporation.* New York: Basic Books

Aiken, Michael T. and Jerald Hage. 1966. "Organizational alienation: a comparative analysis." *American Sociological Review,* 31:497–507

Allston, Jon P. 1986. *The American Samurai: Blending American and Japanese Managerial Practices.* New York: DeGruyter

Amber, George S. and Paul A. Amber. 1962. *Anatomy of Automation.* Englewood Cliffs, NJ: Prentice-Hall

Angle, Harold L. and James L. Perry. 1981. "Organizational commitment and organizational effectiveness: an empirical assessment." *Administrative Science Quarterly,* 26:1–14

1983. "Organizational commitment: individual and organizational influences." *Work and Occupations,* 10:123–46

Aoki, Masahiko. 1984. "Aspects of the Japanese firm." Pp. 3–43 in Masahiko Aoki (ed.), *The Economic Analysis of the Japanese Firm.* Amsterdam: North-Holland

Aranya, N. and D. Jacobson. 1975. "An empirical study of theories of organizational and occupational commitment." *Journal of Social Psychology,* 97:15–22

Armer, J. Michael and Allen Schnaiberg. 1972. "Measuring individual modernity: a near myth." *American Sociological Review,* 37:301–16

Averitt, Robert T. 1968. *The Dual Economy: The Dynamics of American Industry Structure.* New York: Norton

Azumi, Koya and Charles J. McMillan. 1975. "Culture and organization structure: a comparison of Japanese and British organizations." *Studies of Management and Organization,* 35:201–18

1976. "Worker sentiment in the Japanese factory: its organizational determinants." Pp. 215–29 in Lewis Austin (ed.), *Japan: The Paradox of Progress.* New Haven: Yale University Press

1981. "Management strategy and organization structure: a Japanese comparative study." Pp. 155–72 in David J. Hickson and Charles McMillan (eds.), *Organization and Nation: The Aston Programme IV.* Aldershot, Hampshire: Gower

Azumi, Koya, David Hickson, Dezso Horvath, and Charles McMillan. 1981. "Bureaucratic structures in cross-national perspective: a study of British, Japanese, and Swedish firms." Pp. 537–63 in G. Dlugos and K. Weiermair (eds.), *Management Under Differing Value Systems.* New York: Walter de Gruyter

1984. "Structural uniformity and cultural diversity in organizations: a comparative study of factories in Britain, Japan, and Sweden." Pp. 101–20 in K. Sato and Y. Hoshino (eds.), *The Anatomy of Japanese Business*. Armonk, NY: M. E. Sharpe

Bain, Joe S. 1959. *Industrial Organization*. New York: John Wiley

Baron, James N. and William T. Bielby. 1984. "The organization of work in a segmented economy." *American Sociological Review* 49 (August):454–73

1986. "The proliferation of job titles in organizations." *Administrative Science Quarterly*, 31:561–86

Bartholomew, James. 1981. "The impact of modernization on Japan". Pp. 325–32 in Bradley M. Richardson and Taizo Ueda (eds.), *Business and Society in Japan*. New York: Praeger

Bell, Daniel. 1973. *The Coming of Post-Industrial Society*. New York: Basic Books

Bennett, Amanda. 1987. "Growing small: as big firms continue to trim their staffs, two-tier setup emerges." *Wall Street Journal*, May 4

Bennett, John W. and Iwao Ishino. 1963. *Paternalism in the Japanese Economy*. Minneapolis: University of Minnesota Press

Berg, Ivar, Marcia Freedman, and Michael Freeman. 1978. *Managers and Work Reform: A Limited Engagement*. New York: Free Press

Beynon, H. and R. M. Blackburn. 1972. *Perceptions of Work: Variations Within a Factory*. Cambridge: Cambridge University Press

Blau, Peter M. 1968. "The hierarchy of authority in organizations." *American Journal of Sociology*, 73:453–67

Blau, Peter M. and Otis Dudley Duncan. 1967. *The American Occupational Structure*. New York: Wiley

Blau, Peter M. and Richard A. Schoenherr. 1971. *The Structure of Organizations*, New York: Basic Books

Blau, Peter M. and W. Richard Scott. 1962. *Formal Organizations*. San Francisco: Chandler

Blau, Peter M., Cecila M. Falbe, William McKinley, and Phelps K. Tracy. 1976. "Technology and organization in manufacturing." *Administrative Science Quarterly*, 21:20–40

Blauner, Robert. 1960. "Work satisfaction and industrial trends in modern society." Pp. 339–60 in Walter Galenson and Seymour Martin Lipset (eds.), *Labor and Trade Unionism*. New York: John Wiley

1964. *Alienation and Freedom*. Chicago: University of Chicago Press

Blood, M. R. and Charles L. Hulin. 1967. "Alienation, environmental characteristics, and worker responses." *Journal of Applied Psychology*, 51:284–90.

Braverman, Harry. 1974. *Labor and Monopoly Capital: The Degradation of Work in the Twentieth Century*. New York: Monthly Review Press

Broadbridge, Seymour. 1966. *Industrial Dualism in Japan: A Problem of Economic Growth and Structural Change*. Chicago: Aldine

Brody, David. 1980. *Workers in Industrial America*. New York and Oxford: Oxford University Press

Brossard, Michael and Marc Maurice. 1976. "Is there a universal model of organization structure?" *International studies of management and organization*, 6:11–45

Brown, Michael E. 1969. "Identification and some conditions of organizational involvement." *Administrative Science Quarterly*, 14:346–55

Buchanan, Bruce II. 1974. "Building organizational commitment: the socialization of managers in work organizations." *Administrative Science Quarterly*, 19:533–46

Burawoy, Michael. 1979. *Manufacturing Consent: Changes in the Labor Process under Monopoly Capitalism*. University of Chicago Press

1983. "Between the labor process and the state: factory regimes under advanced capitalism." *American Sociological Review*, 48:587–605.

Burns, Tom and G. M. Stalker. 1961. *The Management of Innovation*. London: Tavistock

Burns, Tom R., Lars Erik Karlsson, and Veljko Rus. 1979. *Work and Power: The Liberation of Work and the Control of Political Power*. London: Sage

Business Week. 1986a. "The end of corporate loyalty." August 4:42–9

1986b. "The hollow corporation." March 3:56–85

Carroll, Glenn R. and Yangchung Paul Huo. 1986. "Organizational task and institutional environments in ecological perspective: findings from the local newspaper industry." *American Journal of Sociology*, 91:838–73

Caves, Richard and Masu Uekusa. 1976. *Industrial Organization in Japan*. Washington, DC: The Brookings Institution

Child, John. 1972. "Organization structure and strategies of control: a replication of the Aston study." *Administrative Science Quarterly*, 17:163–76

1981. "Culture, contingency, and capitalism in the cross-national study of organizations." Pp. 303–56 in L. L. Cummings and B. M. Staw (eds.), *Research in Organizational Behavior*, volume 3. Greenwich, CT: JAI Press

1984. *Organization*. London: Harper and Row

Child, John and Alfred Kieser. 1979. "Organization and managerial roles in British and West German companies: an examination of the culture-free thesis." Pp. 251–71 in Cornelius J. Lammers and David J. Hickson (eds.), *Organizations Alike and Unlike*. London: Routledge and Kegan Paul

Child, John and Roger Mansfield. 1972. "Technology, size, and organization structure." *Sociology*, 6:369–93

Chinoy, Eli. 1955. *Automobile Workers and the American Dream*. Boston: Beacon Press

Clark, Rodney. 1979. *The Japanese Company*. New Haven: Yale University Press

Clark, Peter M. and James Q. Wilson. 1961. "Incentive systems: a theory of organizations." *Administrative Science Quarterly*, 6:129–66

Clawson, Daniel. 1980. *Bureaucracy and the Labor Process*. New York: Monthly Review Press

Cole, Robert E. 1971. *Japanese Blue Collar: The Changing Tradition*. Berkeley: University of California Press

1972. "Functional alternatives and economic developments: an empirical example of permanent employment in Japan." *American Sociological Review*. 38:424–38

1979. *Work, Mobility, and Participation*. Berkeley: University of California Press

1980. "Learning from the Japanese: prospects and pitfalls." *Management Review*, Fall:22–42

1985. "The macropolitics of organizational change: a comparative analysis of the spread of small group activities." *Administrative Science Quarterly*, 30:560–85

Cole, Robert E. and Ken'ichi Tominaga. 1976. "Japan's changing occupational structure and its significance." Pp. 53–96 in Hugh Patrick (ed.), *Japanese Industrialization and Its Social Consequences*. Berkeley: University of California Press

Cook, Alice H. and Hiroko Hayashi. 1980. *Working Women in Japan*. Ithaca, New York: New York State School of Industrial and Labor Relations

Craig, Albert M. 1975. "Functional and dysfunctional aspects of government bureaucracy." Pp. 3–32 in Ezra F. Vogel (ed.), *Modern Japanese Organization and Decision-Making*. Berkeley: University of California Press

Cronbach, Lee J. 1951. "Coefficient alpha and the internal structure of tests." *Psychometrika* 16:297–334

Crozier, Michel. 1964. *The Bureaucratic Phenomenon*. University of Chicago Press

Daito, Eisuke. 1984. "Seniority wages and labour management: Japanese employers' wage policy." Pp. 119–30 in Shigeyoshi Tokunaga and Joachim Bergmann (eds.), *Industrial Relations in Transition*. University of Tokyo Press

Deal, Terrence and Alan Kennedy. 1982. *Corporate Cultures*. Reading, MA: Addison-Wesley

DiMaggio, Paul J. and Walter W. Powell. 1983. "The iron cage revisited: institutional isomorphism and collective rationality in organizational fields." *American Sociological Review* 48:147–60

Doeringer, Peter B. and Michael J. Piore. 1971. *Internal Labor Markets and Manpower Analysis*. Lexington, MA: D. C. Heath

Dore, Ronald. 1973. *British Factory–Japanese Factory: The Origins of Diversity in Industrial Relations*. Berkeley: University of California Press

    1983. "Introduction." Pp. ix–xl in S. Kamata, *Japan in the Passing Lane*. New York: Pantheon

Dubin, Robert. 1956. "Industrial workers' worlds: a study of the central life interests of industrial workers." *Social Problems* 3:131–42

Dubin, Robert, Joseph E. Champoux, and Lyman W. Porter. 1975. "Central life interests and organizational commitment of blue-collar and clerical workers." *Administrative Science Quarterly*, 20:411–21

Durkheim, Emile. 1933. *The Division of Labor in Society*. New York: Free Press

Edwards, Richard. 1979. *Contested Terrain*. New York: Basic Books

Edwards, Richard, David M. Gordon and Michael Reich (eds.). 1975. *Labor Market Segmentation*. Lexington, MA: D. C. Heath

Elder, Joseph. 1976. "Comparative cross-national methodology." *Annual Review of Sociology* 2:209–30

Etzioni, Amitai. 1961 *A Comparative Analysis of Complex Organizations*. New York: Free Press

Foreign Press Center. 1980. *Facts and Figures of Japan*. Tokyo: Foreign Press Center

Form, William H. 1979. "Comparative industrial sociology and the convergence hypothesis." *Annual Review of Sociology* 5:1–25

    1980. "Resolving ideological issues on the division of labor." Pp. 140–55 in Hubert M. Blalock (ed.), *Sociological Theory and Research: A Critical Appraisal*. New York: Free Press

Fox, Alan. 1974. *Beyond Contract: Work, Power and Trust Relations*. London: Faber and Faber

Freeman, Richard B. 1984. "De-mystifying the Japanese labor markets." Pp. 103–24 in Masahiko Aoki (ed.), *The Economic analysis of the Japanese Firm*. Amsterdam: North-Holland

Freeman, Richard B. and James L. Medoff. 1984. *What Do Unions Do?* New York: Basic Books

Friedman, Andrew. 1977. *Industry and Labour*. London: Macmillan

Fullan, Michael. 1970. "Industrial technology and worker integration in the organization." *American Sociological Review*, 35:1028–39

Galbraith, Jay. 1977. *Organization Design*. Reading, MA: Addison-Wesley

Galenson, Walter. 1976. "The Japanese labor market." Pp. 587–672 in Hugh Patrick and Henry Rosovsky (eds.), *Asia's New Giant: How the Japanese Economy Works*. Washington: Brookings Institution

Gallie, Duncan. 1978. *In Search of the New Working Class: Automation and Social Integration Within the Capitalist Enterprise*. New York and London: Cambridge University Press

Gerlach, Michael. 1986. "Business alliances and the strategy of the Japanese firm." *California Management Review*, 30:126–42

  1989. *Alliances and the Social Organization of Japanese Business*. Berkeley: University of California Press

Goffman, Erving. 1961. *Asylums*. Garden City, NY: Doubleday

Goldthorpe, John H., David Lockwood, F. Bechhofer, and J. Platt. 1968. *The Affluent Worker: Industrial Attitudes and Behavior*. London: Cambridge University Press

Gordon, David M. 1972. *Theories of Poverty and Underemployment*. Lexington, MA: D. C. Heath

Gordon, David, Richard Edwards, and Michael Reich. 1982. *Segmented Work, Divided Workers*. Cambridge, MA: Harvard University Press

Gouldner, Alvin. 1954. *Patterns of Industrial Bureaucracy*. New York: Free Press

Granick, David. 1972. *Managerial Comparisons of Four Developed Countries*. Cambridge MA: MIT Press

Hackman, J. Richard and E. E. Lawler III. 1971. "Employee reactions to job characteristics." *Journal of Applied Psychology Monograph*. 55:259–86

Hackman, J. Richard and Greg R. Oldham. 1980. *Work Redesign*. Reading, MA: Addison-Wesley

Haire, Mason, Edwin E. Ghiselli, and Lyman W. Porter. 1966. *Managerial Thinking: An International Analysis*. New York: McGraw-Hill

Halaby, Charles N. 1986. "Worker attachment and workplace authority." *American Sociological Review*. 51:634–49

Hanada, Mitsuyo. 1984. *Twelve Questions Regarding Japanese-style Management*. Tokyo: SANNO School of Business Administration

Hanami, Tadashi. 1979. *Labor Relations in Japan Today*. Tokyo: Kodansha International Ltd

Hannan, Michael T. and John Freeman. 1977. "The population ecology of organizations." *American Journal of Sociology*, 82:929–64

Hanushek, Erik A. and John E. Jackson. 1977. *Statistical Methods for Social Scientists*. New York: Academic Press

Hashimoto, Masanori and John Raisian. 1985. "Employment tenure and earnings profiles in Japan and the United States." *American Economic Review*, 75:721–35

Hatvany, N. and C. Vladimir Pucik. 1981. "Japanese management practices and productivity." *Organizational Dynamics*, 9:5–21

Hayes, Robert H. and William J. Abernathy. 1980. "Managing our way to economic decline." *Harvard Business Review*, July–August:67–77

Hayes, Robert H. and Steven C. Wheelwright. 1984. *Restoring Our Competitive Edge–Competing Through Manufacturing*. New York: John Wiley

Herzberg, Frederick, Bernard Mausner, and B. Snyderman. 1959. *The Motivation to Work*. New York: John Wiley and Sons

Hickson, David and Charles McMillan (eds.). 1981. *Organization and Nation: The*

Aston Programme IV. Aldershot, Hampshire: Gower

Hickson, David J., C. R. Hinings, C. J. McMillan, and J. P Schwitter. 1974. "The culture-free context of organization structure: a tri-national comparison." *Sociology*, 8:59–80

Hickson, David J., Charles J. McMillan, Koya Azumi, and Dezso Horvath. 1979. "Grounds for comparative organization theory: quicksands or hardcore?" Pp. 25–41 in Cornelius J. Lammers and David J. Hickson (eds.), *Organizations Alike and Unlike*. London: Routledge and Kegan Paul

Hickson, David J., Derek S. Pugh, Diana Pheysey. 1969. "Operations technology and organization structure: an empirical reappraisal." *Administrative Science Quarterly*, 14:378–97

Hill, Stephen. 1981. *Competition and Control at Work*. Cambridge, MA: MIT Press

Hirschman, Albert O. 1970. *Exit, Voice, and Loyalty*. Cambridge, MA: Harvard University Press

Hodson, Randy. 1984. "Companies, industries, and the measurement of economic segmentation." *American Sociological Review*, 49:335–48

1983. *Workers' Earnings and Corporate Economic Structure*. New York: Academic Press

Hodson, Randy and Robert L. Kaufman. 1982. "Economic dualism: a critical review." *American Sociological Review*, 43:534–41

Hodson, Randy and Teresa A. Sullivan. 1985. "Totem or tyrant?: monopoly, regional, and local sector effects on worker commitment." *Social Forces*, 63:716–31

Hofstede, Geert. 1980. *Culture's Consequences: International Differences in Work-Related Values*. Beverley Hills: Sage

Holden, Karen C. 1983. "Changing employment patterns of women." Pp. 34–46 in David W. Plath (ed.), *Works and Lifecourse in Japan*. Albany: State University of New York Press

Horvath, Deszo, Charles J. McMillan, Koya Azumi, and David J. Hickson. 1981. "The cultural context of organizational control: an international comparison." Pp. 173–86 in David J. Hickson and Charles J. McMillan (eds.), *Organization and Nation: The Aston Programme IV*. Aldershot, Hampshire: Gower

House, James S. 1977. "The three faces of social psychology." *Sociometry* 40:161–77

Hrebiniak, Lawrence G. and Joseph Alutto. 1972. "Personal and role-related factors in the development of organizational commitment." *Administrative Science Quarterly*, 17:555–72

Hsu, Cheng-Kuang, Robert M. Marsh, and Hiroshi Mannari. 1983. "An examination of the determinants of organizational structure." *American Journal of Sociology*, 88:975–96

Hull, Frank M., Nathalie S. Friedman, and Theresa F. Rogers. 1982. "The effect of technology on alienation from work: testing Blauner's inverted U-curve hypothesis for 110 industrial organizations and 245 retrained printers." *Work and Occupations*, 9:31–57

Indik, Bernard P. 1963. "Some effects of organization size on member attitudes and behaviors." *Human Relations*, 16:369–84

Ingham, Geoffrey K. 1970. *Size of Industrial Organization and Worker Behavior*. Cambridge: Cambridge University Press

Inkeles, Alex. 1960. "Industrial man: the relation of status to experience, perception, and value. *American Journal of Sociology*, 66:1–31

Itami, Hiroyuki. 1985. "The firm and the market in Japan." Pp. 69–81 in Lester Thurow (ed.), *The Management Challenge: Japanese Views*. Cambridge MA: MIT Press

Jacoby, Sanford M. 1985. *Employment Bureaucracy: Managers, Unions, and the Transformation of Work in American Industry, 1900–1945*. New York: Columbia University Press

James, Lawrence R. and Allan P. Jones. 1976. "Organizational structure: a review of structural dimensions and their conceptual relationships with individual attitudes and behavior." *Organizational Behavior and Human Performance*, 16:74–113

Johnson, Chalmers. 1982. *MITI and the Japanese Miracle–The Growth of Industrial Policy, 1925–1975*. Stanford University Press

Junkerman, John. 1983. "We are driven: life in the fast lane at Datsun." *Mother Jones* (August):21–3, 38–9

Kagono, Tadao, Ikujiro Nonaka, Kiyonori Sakakibara, and Akihiro Okumura; in collaboration with Shiori Sakamoto and Johny K. Johansson. 1985. *Strategic vs. Evolutionary Management: A U.S.–Japan Comparison*. Amsterdam: North-Holland

Kalleberg, Arne L. 1974. "A causal approach to the measurement of job satisfaction." *Social Science Research*, 3:299–322

   1977. "Work values and job rewards: a theory of job satisfaction." *American Sociological Review*, 42:124–43

Kalleberg, Arne L. and Ivar Berg. 1987. *Work and Industry: Structures, Markets And Processes*. New York: Plenum Press

Kalleberg, Arne L. and James R. Lincoln. 1988. "The structure of earnings inequality in the U.S. and Japan." Special issue of *American Journal of Sociology* on "Organizations and Institutions," edited by Sherwin Rosen and Christopher Winship, 94:S121–S153

Kalleberg, Arne L. and Karyn A. Loscocco. 1983. "Aging, values and rewards: explaining age differences in job satisfaction." *American Sociological Review*, 48:78–90

Kamata, Satoshi. 1983. *Japan in the Passing Lane*. New York: Pantheon

Kanter, Rosabeth M. 1968. "Commitment and social organization: a study of commitment mechanisms in Utopian communities." *American Sociological Review*, 33:499–517

   1977. *Men and Women of the Corporation*. New York: Basic Books

   1984. "Variations in managerial career structures in high-technology firms: the impact of organizational characteristics on internal labor market patterns." Pp. 109–32 in Paul Osterman (ed.), *Internal Labor Markets*. Cambridge, MA: MIT Press

Kawada, H. 1973. "Workers and their organizations." Pp. 217–68 in Bernard Karsh and Solomon B. Levine, *Workers and Employers in Japan*. Tokyo: University of Tokyo Press

Keizai Koho Center. 1983. *Japan 1983: An International Comparison*. Tokyo: Japan Institute for Social and Economic Affairs

   1987. *Japan 1987: An International Comparison*. Tokyo: Japan Institute for Social and Economic Affairs

Kelley, L. and C. Reeser. 1973. "The persistence of culture as a determinant of differentiated attitudes on the part of American managers of Japanese ancestry." *Academy of Management Journal*, 16:67–76

Kerr, Clark, John T. Dunlop, Frederick Harbison, and Charles A. Myers. 1960. *Industrialism and Industrial Man.* Cambridge, MA: Harvard University Press

Kerr, Clark and Abraham Siegel. 1954. "The inter-industry propensity to strike – an international comparison." Pp. 189–212 in Arthur Kornhauser, Robert Dubin, and Arthur Ross (eds.), *Industrial Conflict.* New York: McGraw-Hill

Khandwalla, Pradip. 1974. "Mass output orientation of operations, technology, and organizational Structures." *Administrative Science Quarterly*, 19:74–97

Knoke, David, 1975. "A comparison of dummy variable regression and log-linear models." *Sociological Methods and Research*, 3:416–35

Kochan, Thomas A. and Peter Cappelli. 1984. "White-collar internal labor markets." Pp. 133–62 in Paul Osterman (ed.), *Internal Labor Markets.* Cambridge, MA: MIT Press

Kohn, Melvin L. 1971. "Bureaucratic man: a portrait and an interpretation." *American Sociological Review*, 36:461–74

Kohn, Melvin L. and Carmi Schooler. 1973. "Occupational experience and psychological functioning: an assessment of reciprocal effects." *American Sociological Review*, 38:97–118

1983. *Work and Personality: an Inquiry into the Impact of Social Stratification.* Norwood, NJ: Ablex Publishing Corporation

Koike, Kazuo. 1978. "Japan's industrial relations: characteristics and problems." *Japanese Economic Studies*, 7:42–90

1983. "Internal labor markets: workers in large firms." Pp. 29–62 in Taishiro Shirai (ed.), *Contemporary Industrial Relations in Japan.* Madison: University of Wisconsin Press

1984. "Skill formation systems in the U.S. and Japan: A Comparative Study." Pp. 47–76 in Masahiko Aoki (ed.), *The Economic Analysis of the Japanese Firm.* Amsterdam: North-Holland

Koshiro, Kazutoshi. 1983. "The quality of life in Japanese factories." Pp. 63–88 in Taishiro Shirai (ed.), *Contemporary Industrial Relations in Japan.* Madison: University of Wisconsin Press

Lammers, Cornelius J. and David J. Hickson. 1979. *Organizations Alike and Unlike.* London: Routledge and Kegan Paul

Lawrence, Paul R. and Jay W. Lorsch. 1967. *Organization and Environment: Managing Differentiation and Integration.* Boston: Graduate School of Business Administration, Harvard University

Lazear, Edward P. 1979. "Why is there mandatory retirement? *Journal of Political Economy*, 87:1261–84

Leung, James, 1986. "Young Japanese executives becoming reluctant to park savings in the bank." *Wall Street Journal*, December 1

Lincoln, James R. 1978. "Community structure and industrial conflict: an analysis of strike activity in SMSAs." *American Sociological Review*, 43 (April):199–220

Lincoln, James R., Mitsuyo Hanada, and Jon Olson. 1981. "Cultural orientations and individual reactions to organizations: a study of employees of Japanese-owned firms." *Administrative Science Quarterly*, 26:93–115

Lincoln, James R., Mitsuyo Hanada, and Kerry McBride. 1986. "Organizational structures in Japanese and U.S. manufacturing." *Administrative Science Quarterly*, 31:338–64

Lincoln, James R. and Arne L. Kalleberg. 1985. "Work organization and workforce commitment: a study of plants and employees in the U.S. and Japan." *American Sociological Review*, 50:738–60

Lincoln, James R. and Kerry McBride. 1987. "Japanese industrial organization in comparative perspective." *Annual Review of Sociology*, 13:289–312

Lincoln, James R., Jon Olson, and Mitsuyo Hanada. 1978. "Cultural effects on organizational structure: the case of Japanese firms in the United States." *American Sociological Review*, 43:829–47

Lincoln, James R. and Gerald Zeitz. 1980. "Organizational properties from aggregate data: separating individual and structural effects." *American Sociological Review*, 45:391–408

Lipset, Seymour Martin, Martin Trow, and James S. Coleman. 1956. *Union Democracy*. New York: Free Press

Littler, Craig. 1982. *The Development of the Labor Process in Capitalist Societies*. London: Heinemann

Loscocco, Karyn A. 1985. "The Meaning of Work: An Examination of the Determinants of Work Commitment and Work Orientaton Among Manufacturing Employees." Unpublished Ph.D. Dissertation, Indiana University

Maguire, Mary Ann and Richard Tanner Pascale. 1978. "Communication, decision-making, and implementation among managers in Japanese and American managed companies in the United States." *Sociology and Social Research*, 63:1–23

Mallet, Sergio, 1975. *The New Working Class*. Nottingham: Spokesman Books

March, James G. and Herbert A. Simon. 1958. *Organizations*. New York: Wiley

Marsh, Robert M. and Hiroshi Mannari. 1976. *Modernization and the Japanese Factory*. Princeton: Princeton University Press

Marsh, Robert and Hiroshi Mannari. 1980. "Technological implicaton theory: a Japanese test." *Organization Studies*, 1/2:161–83

1981. "Technology and size as determinants of the organizational structure of Japanese factories." *Administrative Science Quartrly*, 26:33–57

Marx, Karl. 1964. *Economic and Philosophic Manuscripts of 1844*, edited by Dirk J. Struik. New York: International Publishers

1967. *Capital*, volume 1 (1867). New York: Modern Library, 1906; New York: New World Paperbacks

Maslow, Abraham. 1954. *Motivation and Personality*. New York: Harper and Row

Maurice, Marc, Arndt Sorge, and Malcolm Warner. 1980. "Societal difference in organizing manufacturing units: a comparison of France, West Germany, and Great Britain." *Organization Studies* 1:59–86

Mayhew, Bruce H., Robert L. Levinger, J. Miller McOherson, and Thomas F. James. 1972. "System size and structural differentiation in formal organizations." *American Sociological Review*, 37:629–33

McMillan, Charles., D. J. Hickson, C. R. Hinings, and R. E. Schneck. 1973. "The structure of work organizations across societies." *Academy of Management Journal*, 16:555–69

Melloan, George. 1987. "Temps now take a turn at executive jobs." *Wall Street Journal*, May 19

Merton, Robert K. 1968. *Social Theory and Social Structure*. New York: Free Press

Meyer, John W. and Brian Rowan. 1977. "Institutionalized organizations: formal structure as myth and ceremony." *American Journal of Sociology*, 83:340–63

Meyer, John W. and W. Richard Scott. 1983. *Organizational Environments: Ritual and*

Rationality. Beverley Hills: Sage Publications, Inc.

Miller, Joanne, Kazimierz M. Slomczynski, and Ronald J. Schoenberg. 1981. "Assessing comparability of measurement in cross-national research: authoritarian-conservatism in different sociocultural settings." *Social Psychology Quarterly*, 4:178–91

Mincer, Jacob and Yoshio Higuchi. 1987. "Wage structures and labor turnover in the U.S. and in Japan." Working Paper No. 2306. Cambridge, MA: National Bureau of Economic Research

Mowday, Richard T., Lyman W. Porter, and Richard M. Steers. 1982. *Employee-Organization Linkages: The Psychology of Commitment, Absenteeism, and Turnover*. New York: Academic Press

Mowday, Richard T., Richard M. Steers, and Lyman W. Porter. 1979. "The measurement of organizational commitment." *Journal of Vocational Behavior*, 14:224–47

Muramatsu, Kuramitsu. 1984. "The effect of trade unions on productivity in Japanese manufacturing industries." Pp. 103–24 in Masahiko Aoki (ed.), *The Economic Analysis of the Japanese Firm*. Amsterdam: North-Holland 1984

Nakane, Chie. 1970. *Japanese Society*. Berkeley: University of California Press

Norsworthy, J. R. and Malmquist, David H. 1983. "Input measurement and productivity growth in Japanese and U.S. manufacturing." *American Economic Review*, 73:947–67

Naoi, Atsushi and Carmi Schooler. 1985. "Occupational conditions and psychological functioning in Japan." *American Journal of Sociology*, 90:729–51

Odaka, Kunio. 1975. *Toward Industrial Democracy: Management and Workers in Modern Japan*. Cambridge, MA: Harvard University Press

1982. "The Japanese style of workers' self-management: from the voluntary to the autonomous group." Pp. 135–48 in Velnko Rus, Akihiro Ishikawa, and Thomas Woodhouse (eds.), *Employment and Participation*. Tokyo: Chuo University Press

Office of the Prime Minister, Japan. 1973. Sekai seinen ishiki choosa hookokusho (Report of the World Youth Attitude Survey). Tokyo: Youth Policy Office

1984. "Attitude survey of the world youth." Tokyo: Youth Policy Office

Ohmae, Kenichi. 1982. "Japan: from stereotypes to specifics." *McKinsey Quarterly*, Spring: 2–32

Oldham, Greg R. and J. Richard Hackman. 1981. "Relationships between organizational structure and employee reactions: comparing alternative frameworks." *Administrative Science Quarterly*, 26:66–83

Ono, Tsuneo. 1980. "Postwar changes in the Japanese wage system." Pp. 145–76 in Shunsaku Nishikawa (ed.), *The Labor Market in Japan*. Tokyo: University of Tokyo Press

O'Reilly, Charles, III and Jennifer Chatman. 1986. "Organizational commitment and psychological attachment: the effects of compliance, identification, and internalization on prosocial behavior." *Journal of Applied Psychology* 71:492–9

Osako, Masako. 1977. "Technology and social structure in a Japanese automobile factory." *Sociology of Work and Occupations*, 4:397–426

Ouchi, William G. 1980. "Markets, hierarchies, and clans." *Administrative Science Quarterly*, 25:129–41

1981. *Theory Z: How American Business Can Meet the Japanese Challenge*. Reading, MA: Addison-Wesley

Ouchi, William G. and J. B. Johnson. 1978. "Types of organizational control and their relationship to emotional well-being." *Administrative Science Quarterly*,

23:293–317

Pascale, Richard Tanner. 1978a. "Communication and decision-making across cultures: Japanese and American comparisons." *Administrative Science Quarterly*, 23:91–110

1978b. "Zen and the art of management." *Harvard Business Review*, 56:153–62

Pascale, Richard T. and Mary Ann Maguire. 1980. "Comparison of selected work factors in Japan and the United States." *Human Relations*, 33:433–55

Perrow, Charles. 1979. *Complex Organizations: A Critical Essay*. Glenview, IL: Scott, Foresman (second edition)

Peter, Thomas J. and Robert H. Waterman, Jr. 1982. *In Search of Excellence: Lessons from America's Best-Run Companies*. New York: Harper and Row

Pfeffer, Jeffrey and James N. Baron. 1987. "Taking the workers back out: recent trends in the structuring of employment." Pp. in Barry M. Staw and L. L. Cummings (eds.), *Research in Organizational Behavior*, volume 10. Greenwich, CT:JAI Press

Phillips, Lynn W. 1981. "Assessing measurement error in key informant reports: a methodological note on organizational analysis in marketing." *Journal of Marketing Research*. 18:395–415

Piore, Michael J. and Charles F. Sabel. 1984. *The Second Industrial Divide: Possibilities for Prosperity*. New York: Basic Books

Porter, Lyman W. and Edward E. Lawler III. 1965. "Properties of organization structure in relation to job attitudes and job behavior." *Psychological Bulletin*, 64:23–51

Porter, Lyman W., Richard M. Steers, Richard T. Mowday, and Paul V. Boulian. 1974. "Organizational commitment, job satisfaction and turnover among psychiatric technicians." *Journal of Applied Psychology*, 59:603–9

Przeworski, Adam and Henry Teune. 1970. *The Logic of Comparative Social Inquiry*. New York: John Wiley

Pucik, V. 1984. "White collar human resource management: a comparison of the U.S. and Japanese automobile industries." *Columbia Journal of World Business* (Fall):87–94

Pucik, V. and N. Hatvany. 1983. "Management practices in Japan and their impact on business strategy." *Advances in Strategic Management* 1:1103–31

Pugh, D.S., D. J. Hickson, C. R. Hinings, and C. Turner. 1968. "Dimensions of organization structure." *Administrative Science Quarterly*, 13:65–91

1969. "The context of organization structures." *Administrative Science Quarterly*, 14:91–114

Quinn, Robert P. 1977. *Effectiveness in Work Roles: Employee Responses to Work Environments*. Ann Arbor: Institute for Social Research, University of Michigan

Quinn, R. P., K. Staines, and M. R. McCullough. 1974. *Job Satisfaction: Is There a Trend?* Washington, DC: US Department of Labor

Riley, Matilda White. 1973. "Aging and cohort succession: interpretations and misinterpretations." *Public Opinion Quarterly*, 32:35–49

Rohlen, Thomas P. 1974. *For Harmony and Strength*. Berkeley: University of California Press

Rousseau, Denise M. 1978. "Characteristics of departments, positions, and individuals: contexts for attitudes and behavior." *Administrative Science Quarterly* 23:521–40

Roy, Donald. 1952. "Quota restriction and goldbricking in a machine shop." *American*

Journal of Sociology, 57:427–42

Sabel, Charles F. 1982. *Work and Politics: The Division of Labor in Industry*. New York: Cambridge University Press

Salancik, Gerald R. 1977. "Commitment and the control of organizational behavior and belief." Pp. 1–54 in Barry M. Staw and Gerald R. Salancik (eds.), *New Directions in Organizational Behavior*. Chicago: St. Clair Press

Salancik, Gerald R. and Jeffrey Pfeffer. 1977. "An examination of need-satisfaction models of job attitudes." *Administrative Science Quarterly*, 22:427–56

Sasaki, N. 1981. *Management and Industrial Structure in Japan*. New York: Pergamon Press

Schonberger, Richard J. 1982. *Japanese Manufacturing Techniques*. New York: Free Press

Scott, W. Richard. 1987. *Organizations: Rational, Natural and Open Systems*. Englewood Cliffs, NJ: Prentice-Hall (second edition)

Seeman, Melvin. 1959. "On the meaning of alienation." *American Sociological Review*, 24:783–91

Sengoku, Tamotsu. 1985. *Willing Workers: The Work Ethics in Japan, England, and the United States*, Westport, CT: Quorum Books

Sheldon, Mary E. 1971. "Investments and involvements as mechanisms producing commitment to the organization." *Administrative Science Quarterly*, 16: 143–50

Shepard, Jon M. 1971. *Automation and Alienation*. Cambridge, MA: MIT Press

Shimada, Haruo. 1983. *Japanese Industrial Relations – A New Model?* Pp. 3–27 in Taishiro Shirai (ed.), *Contemporary Industrial Relations in Japan*. Madison: University of Wisconsin Press

Shirai, Taishiro (ed.). 1983. *Contemporary Industrial Relations in Japan*. Madison: University of Wisconsin Press

Shorter, Edward L. and Charles Tilly. 1974. *Strikes in France, 1830 to 1968*. Cambridge and New York: Cambridge University Press

Snyder, David. 1975. "Institutional setting and industrial conflict: comparative analyses of France, Italy and the United States." *American Sociological Review*, 40:259–78

Sobel, Michael E. and George W. Bohrnstedt. 1985. "Use of null models in evaluating the fit of covariance structure models." Pp. 152–78 in Nancy B. Tuma (ed.), *Sociological Methodology, 1985*. San Francisco: Jossey-Bass

Starbuck, William H. 1965. "Organizational growth and development." Pp. 451–533 in James G. March (ed.), *Handbook of Organizations*. Chicago: Rand McNally

Staw, Barry M., Nancy E. Bell, and John A. Clausen. 1986. "The dispositional approach to job attitudes: a lifetime longitudinal test." *Administrative Science Quarterly*, 31:56–77

Steers, Richard M. 1977. "Antecedents and outcomes of organizational commitment." *Administrative Science Quarterly*, 22:46–56

Stinchcombe, Arthur L. 1965. "Social structure and organizations." Pp. 142–93 in James G. March (ed.), *Handbook of Organizations*. Chicago: Rand McNally

Stolzenberg, Ross M. 1978. "Bringing the boss back in." *American Sociological Review*, 43:813–28

1980. "The measurement and decomposition of causal effects in nonlinear and nonadditive models." Pp. 459–88 in Karl F. Schuessler (ed.), *Sociological Methodology*. San Francisco: Jossey-Bass

Straus, Murray. 1969. "Phenomenal identity and conceptual equivalence in cross-national research." *Journal of Marriage and the Family.* 31:233–41

Suleiman, B. N. 1974. *Politics, Power, and Bureaucracy in France.* Princeton: Princeton University Press

Takezawa, Shin-ichi. 1976 "The quality of working life: trends in Japan." *Labour and Society,* 1:29–48

Takezawa, Shin-ichi and Arthur M. Whitehill. 1981. *Work Ways: Japan and America.* Tokyo: Japan Institute of Labor

Talacchi, Sergio. 1960. "Organization size, individual attitudes and behavior: an empirical study." *Administrative Science Quarterly,* 5:398–420

Tannenbaum, Arnold S., Bogdan Kavcic, Menachem Rosner, Mino Vianello, and Georg Wieser. 1974 *Hierarchy in Organizations: An International Comparison.* San Francisco: Jossey-Bass

Terkel, Studs. 1972. *Working.* New York: Avon

Thomas, Robert J. and Haruo Shimada. 1983. "Work organization and quality control practice in the U.S. and Japanese auto industries." Paper presented to the American Sociological Association, Detroit

Thurow, Lester C. (ed.). 1985. *The Management Challenge: Japanese Views.* Cambridge, MA: MIT Press

Tokunaga, S. 1983. "Marxist interpretation of Japanese industrial relations, with special reference to large private enterprises." Pp. 313–29 in Taishiro Shirai (ed.), *Contemporary Industrial Relations in Japan.* Madison: University of Wisconsin Press.

Touraine, Alain. 1955. *L'evolution de travail ouvrier aux usines Renault.* Paris: Centre National de la Recherche Scientifique

Tracy, Phelps K. and Koya Azumi. 1976. "Determinants of administrative control: a test of a theory with Japanese factories." *American Sociological Review* 41:80–94

Turner, Arthur N. and Paul R. R. Lawrence. 1965. *Industrial Jobs and the Worker.* Boston: Harvard Business School

Uchida, Hiroshi. 1985. "Nemawashi: The Structure of Informal Power in the Sogo Shosha." Unpublished paper, Harvard University

Umemura, Mataji. 1980. "The seniority-merit wage system in Japan." Pp. 177–87 in S. Nishikawa (ed.), *The Labor Market in Japan: Selected Readings.* Tokyo: University of Tokyo Press

United States Department of Health, Education and Welfare. 1972. *Work in America.* Cambridge, MA: MIT Press

Villemez, Wayne and William Bridges. 1986. "Informal hiring and income in the labor market." *American Sociological Review,* 51:574–82

Vogel, Ezra F. 1963. *Japan's New Middle Class.* Berkeley: University of California Press
    1975. *Modern Japanese Organization and Decision-Making.* Berkeley: University of California Press
    1979. *Japan as Number One: Lessons for America.* New York: Harper Colophon

Vroom, Victor H. 1964. *Work and Motivation.* New York: John Wiley and Sons

Walder, Andrew G. 1986. *Communist Neo-Traditionalism: Work and Authority in Chinese Industry.* New York: Columbia University Press

Walker, Charles R. and Robert H. Guest. 1952. *The Man on the Assembly Line.* Cambridge, MA: Harvard University Press

Wallace, Michael and Arne L. Kalleberg. 1982. "Industrial transformation and the decline of craft: the decomposition of skill in the printing industry, 1931–1978." *American Sociological Review*, 47:307–24

Wallich, Henry C. and Mabel I. Wallich. 1976. "Banking and finace." Pp. 249–316 in Hugh Patrick and Henry Rosovsky (eds.), *Asia's New Giant: How the Japanese Economy Works*. Washington, DC: The Brookings Institution

Weber, Max. 1947. *The Theory of Social and Economic Organization*. Translated by A. M. Henderson and Talcott Parsons. New York: Free Press

Wharton, R., F. Hull, and K. Azumi. 1986. "Market share, organization, and productivity in Japanese factories." Presented at Annual Meetings of the Academy of Management, Chicago

Whitehill, Arthur M. and Shin-ichi Takezawa. 1968. *The Other Worker: A Comparative Study of Industrial Relations in the U.S. and Japan*. Honolulu: East-West Center Press

Williamson, Oliver E. 1975. *Markets and Hierarchies*. New York: Free Press

1985. *The Economic Institutions of Capitalism*. New York: Free Press

Williamson, Oliver E. and William G. Ouchi. 1981. "The markets and hierarchies and visible hand perspectives." Pp. 347–70 in Andrew H. Van de Ven and William F. Joyce (eds.), *Perspectives on Organization Design and Behavior*. New York: John Wiley

Woodward, Joan. 1965. *Industrial Organization: Theory and Practice*. London: Oxford University Press

Woronoff, Jon. 1981. *Japan's Wasted Workers*. Tokyo: Lotus Press

Worthy, James C. 1950. "Organizational structure and employee morale." *American Sociological Review*, 18:169–79

Wright, James D. and Richard F. Hamilton. 1978. "Work satisfaction and age: some evidence for the 'job change' hypothesis." *Social Forces*, 56:1140–58

Yoshino, Michael Y. 1968. *Japan's Managerial System: Tradition and Innovation*. Cambridge, MA: MIT Press

Zimbalist, Andrew (ed.). 1979. *Case Studies on the Labor Process*. New York: Monthly Review Press

Zwerman, William L. 1970. *New Perspectives on Organizational Theory*. Westport, CT: Greenwood Press

Name Index

Subject Index